JUST PLAIN
Charlie

∙∙

The Last Roundup

CHARLIE KRAVETSKY

ISBN: 978-1-63385-521-2

Published by
Word Association Publishers
205 Fifth Avenue
Tarentum, Pennsylvania 15084

www.wordassociation.com
1.800.827.7903

CONTENTS

Prologue

Charlie, why don't you write a book? You've got all these stories about how interesting a life you have had, in so many different businesses and other involvements.

I said, "Who would read it?" She said, "I would."

This was a scenario repeated in the recent past, and, having reached a point where I no longer could physically stand the rigors, and risks, of being out in difficult terrain, thought it would be fun, and interesting to reduce to written form the hundreds of noteworthy experiences my life has produced, by design or chance.

Having neither training nor experience in writing, it is admitted that more of a down to earth, Mark Twain-style presentation should dominate the writings, with professional structure only as needed or appropriate.

This forthcoming, all encompassing, disclaimer should, I hope, set the stage for a long term read, the reader comfortable in clearly understanding the intent of this telling of the life story as it actually happened in real life, of an ordinary person, but extraordinary in his relentless pursuit of a better life than the one he originated in, is to show an example of what is required to succeed and to progress in life when no outside source is ever there to purposely help.

No story was manufactured, written just to make up another story.

These stories are not sitcoms, purposely written by professionals to entertain. Many start slowly, end slowly, are non-entertaining; just plain, ordinary life experiences as I battled my way through 88 years. Only rarely has it been easy, and it is called Life. Some, I hope, will give cause for your reflection of the message found therein.

Reaching into the archives of mind, identifying, then retrieving so many memories; restructuring them into writable stories has been enormously delightful, and yet soberingly reflective.

It is my sincere hope you, dear reader, upon completion of the reading of this book, will pause, reflect, and say to yourself– WOW!

—Charlie

Warmup to Introductory of Just Plain Charlie— The Last Roundup

Hello: My name is Charlie Kravetsky, and I am Just Plain Charlie. I've been here on this fair Earth for some eighty-eight years, am in good health, live in the same backwoods I was born and raised in. I live alone with my beautiful Black and Tan German Shepherd, Thor, in the same beautiful, stone encased home I built for my wonderful, now departed wife of fifty-nine years, Dolores, sixty years ago.

I am blessed with four beautiful, personable, hard-working children still providing valuable services to the local community every day.

Cynthia, the first born, as Borough Manager in the town where she lives.

John, the second, managing the Lifestat Ambulance Service, serving multiple communities with emergency and other services, along with various services to local medical facilities; Steve, the third, a budding entrepreneur in his own right, offering industrial appliances in the aggregate arena and technical services to local machine shops, and James; the fourth, a longtime, widely known expert in primarily transmission repair services, along with innovative tooling for the auto service/ repair Industry.

Great neighbors surround me always ready with a smile, wave or hello when passing or meeting.

Ingrained chronic love Of God, Family, People, Dogs, Animals, and Planet Earth provides me with a life of relative serenity I trust will endure until I begin the first chapter of my next Great Adventure.

In God we Trust; The Story Begins.

My Father's Story,
Setting the Stage

My father, Alex, playing a major role in the preamble to the story to be told, requires some background to be embodied herein to set the stage for the main chronicle featuring me, Charlie, and so: My father's story as told here, observed, and listened to by me during those formative years, apparently caused a subconscious resistance in me to acceptance of destitution and lack, as a way of life, instilling in me the desire to create prosperity not only for myself, but for everyone I touched in one form or another as illustrated in the telling of my forthcoming story.

Alex was born in Ukraine in 1885 in a typical village/farm setting, raised in unremarkable circumstances until the age of twenty, when the atmosphere surrounding him changed dramatically.

Notable civil unrest was escalating in Ukraine, and military conscription of eligible males was beginning. That possibility had little to no appeal to him, so the decision was made to absent himself from the area, to escape that probability by emigrating to America, the great land of peace and opportunity.

In discovering that doorway to freedom had already been closed by the local authorities, it behooved him to find a way to circumvent that impediment.

In sync with the times, he simply searched for, and soon found a sympathetic emigration official, and with the princely sum of two, yes two, dollars convinced him to sign all the forms necessary to be permitted to leave Ukraine.

He thus came to America, where he worked in various menial jobs for a short time, accumulating adequate funds to return to the Ukraine to participate in a prearranged marriage for him, and Martha, by their parents, and then returning to America immediately, leaving his new wife, Martha, My mother-to-be some thirty years later, as an indentured servant, not necessarily by decree, but by inferred consent, in having agreed to move into her now in-law's home, who, according to my mother's telling of the story, made her life into pure misery for the next twenty-two years.

She remained in that position for the entire twenty-two years, until Father booked passage for her to join him in America, which is where and when the history of their involvement in the coal mines of Appalachia begins, and my arrival and life experiences originate.

Welcome to the Story of; Just Plain Charlie— The Last Roundup

Are you ready for a breath of fresh air, something out of the norm? Numerous videos, and various presentations, exist out there featuring great people and momentous events. Nice.

This series Is just a bit different.

These upcoming stories center on the lifetime of an ordinary, little-known individual, me, Just Plain Charlie, detailing many of my real-life experiences in that remarkable journey.

My being someone relentlessly driven by my inborn entrepreneurial spirit in reckless pursuit of ever greater economic and commercial achievement, encompassing some eight decades, plus, to the present time.

And my showing a pathway similar to those blazed by countless other early dreamers and doers in the painstaking process of development in small and great industrial and commercial enterprises worldwide.

This biography denotes life as it transpired within the immigrant communities of the coal fields of Western Pennsylvania, and also across the vast area now known as Appalachia, just before and during the Great Depression of '29 to the onset, generally, of World War II, and beyond, well into the Twenty Second Century.

Some detail is included to illustrate actual physical conditions in these mines, which ranged from workable to inhumane, according to my personal experience, and as told by others who were there at the time. The treatment of miners is related as told by former victims.

Mining as referred to here is all classified as hand loading, (self descriptive) the predecessor to mechanical mining. Loading 16 tons is no small feat, as the song implies.

And so, begins the recital of my real life personal, professional, and business oriented stories, narrated by Me as best remembered by me in and having lived in and around the experience. That part of my life story experienced by me before the age of reason is set from my recollection of it as told to me by others present at that time.

Stories are all isolated, told with only partial semblance of chronological order. No attempt has been made to place or to relate them in precise group sequence, regardless of topic, dating or event.

Human interest stories are randomly sprinkled into business and professional ones. Stories vary widely in subject, theme, and content due to widely varying sources. Some are informative and factual, some mildly dramatic, some a little amusing or even entertaining, some a bit melancholy or downright sad, and others a bit dull or even boring at times, since they are simply illustrating real life events as they occurred, absent of any extraordinary drama.

Please, read the story slowly, deliberately, become one with it, become a part of it. The actual event may have transpired in minutes, hours, days or longer, so enjoy the happening of it as if you were me, the central figure, in so many different involvements.

Please overlook places where incorrect or improper terminology is used, understanding it's an experience reduced to words painting a picture for the reader to reproduce imaginatively, and experience it too. Don't hurry through a story, there's another one just a page away.

It is possible you may even find yourself identifying with certain stories or their components during the recital.

The intention here is to create an enjoyable, upbeat, light-hearted atmosphere for individuals while listening to or reading this presentation; then, hopefully, they will be looking forward to the next episode. Come on, come along for the ride, it could be interesting, it could be fun.

No names will be included in the telling of sensitive stories. There is no intentional harm intended to anyone.

Disclaimer – Unhappy Stories

When God created man, and of course woman, there is no doubt whatsoever that we were all made uniquely different, there being no need to expound on that at all, except to recognize that we think differently, look different, act, and react differently and simply put, we are different, and do not always agree with each other.

For purposes in the telling of my life history, I am focusing solely on relationships within any family, parent to parent, parents to children, children to children and are all included in the within outlined disclaimer.

Please understand, anyone who has lived with or grown up around both family and animals of any, or many kinds, there will be unhappy, unpleasant events or experiences one may, or must, be involved in, inadvertently or intentionally, and certainly I have been there on more occasions than I care to recall and record.

Therefore, there will be no stories of any subject that are wholly unhappy or unreservedly unpleasant, recited in this chronicle. NO harm to anyone or anything is ever intended herein.

Introductory Part 2

And, so, it begins.

In the middle of winter, with a major snowstorm being ushered through by a howling wind, at a small farm in the backwoods of Western Pennsylvania. An Arctic front had moved in, and it was bitterly cold.

The Setting:

Date: January 13, 1935.
A three-room hovel.

Onsite at the house, there were already eight people living in the house.

There was Father, Mother, brother, four sisters, and an elderly friend.

The only heat source for the house was a woodfired, potbellied stove.

The only light in the entire house was a small kerosene table lamp.

There was no running water inside the house.

The small stove could provide only minimal hot water from a pot on top.

There was no electricity in the house.

There was no telephone.

There was no indoor plumbing of any kind.

There was no travelable access way to the home site from a public road.

There was no midwife available.

There was no doctor present.

There WAS a newborn baby boy.

They named me Wassel, Ukrainian for Charlie.

I was, am, living proof there is a God.

How else could I have survived, those were desperately bleak times, with Mother as the only source of nourishment for me.

Economic Runup

In the economic runup prior to the great depression, the Roaring 20's, burgeoning expansion in the Iron and Steel Industry created demand for enormous amounts of coal.

The central point of industrial activity, Pittsburgh, was in close proximity to unlimited reserves of high-grade coal, in great part, the appropriately named Pittsburgh Seam.

In response to this great demand there came a widespread surge in the opening of coal mines, both large and small.

Larger mine complexes would install entire villages, towns, with as many housing units, single and double family, as were necessary to provide, at minimal rental and utility cost, nearby accommodations for the hundreds, or more, miners and their families, needed to extract the bituminous coal and bring it to a ravenous steel making facility.

There was always a company owned store, offering most of the domestic needs of a family, in those days, of food, clothing, shoes, and so forth.

Miners were expected, required, to patronize the company store, where credit was readily available, since repayment was deducted from a miner's earnings. A miner could, theoretically, owe his soul to the company store when only limited work was available.

Towns were usually named after the primary developer, or a related female.

Buying the Farm

In the relatively prosperous period ahead of the '29 market crash, my Father, a long time Ukrainian immigrant, was fully employed as a miner then living with his family in a company house in the town of Patton, near Slickville, Pennsylvania.

Coupled with the low cost of housing and typical immigrant frugality, he was able to accumulate funds sufficient to purchase a small farm, a noteworthy four miles from the mine, in a remote location.

In total absence of good judgement, and dismissing misgivings of his pregnant wife, in the depth of a hard winter, he abandoned the relative comfort of the company house, and the ready presence of other people, and moved the family to the distant farm.

Father's Personality

Mother arrived here from Ukraine belatedly, after her marriage to Father, who then returned to America immediately to leaving her in the care of his parents, her new in-laws, until her emigration to America to join him in 1927.

It is unknown what sort of life she had in her original home, but can be assumed it was what could be considered as normal in child - parent relations.

She spoke of a dominant, non - abusive father, and a quiet, obedient mother.

Her Mother-in-Law and Father-In-Law were hostile and demanding, giving her little quarters.

Her life of 22 years, trapped in her in-law's home, was anything but pleasant, according to her own reluctant admission in those rare occasions when she would respond to our questioning about it.

One of the admissions she did make was that she was relegated to sleep with the cows in such barn as they had over the entire time of her stay, since all of the house was already occupied by her in-law's family. If there's a bright side to it, it would be that it was warmer in the barn in the winter than it was in the house.

Her unobtrusive, deeply religious personality, unfailing in her duties to God, family, animals, and vast garden plantings, created an unpremeditated contrast wherein her quiet, loving kindness always clashed so visibly with Fathers' Dr. Jekyll-Hyde personality.

I, last born, weakest and least able to defend myself, was a constant target - when he was in his Dr. Hyde mode from the alcohol - of demeaning, denigrating verbal, only verbal, abuse imaginable, details which are not important to the telling of this story.

He died peacefully at age 78.

Father Works in Patton

Moving the family away from the mine caused several significant issues to emerge. First was the lack of electricity at the home site, compounded by the overwhelming distance from the Patton Mine where he was employed.

Having moved to the recently purchased farm to achieve a certain level of perceived independence, my Father now faced the task of commuting to the mine.

Onslaught of the Depression

The onslaught of the great depression quickly changed everything. Demand for coal evaporated, eliminating countless jobs in the coalfields, along with the hopes and dreams of thousands of poverty-stricken immigrants, including my family, now isolated on a small farm in wretched conditions.

Entrenched by circumstance within the coal mining community meant that my father, limited in skills to mining, was part of the lengthy list of men anxiously waiting for the opportunity to return to work in the mine.

Having neither a vehicle nor the ability to drive a vehicle, apparently were not seriously considered enough, when deciding to move away from the place of employment.

On those days when my father was offered work, he would rise at 3 o'clock in the morning, consume a breakfast of several hard-boiled eggs along with some coffee, then set out on foot to walk the four miles across fields, woods, and roads to the mine, rain or shine, to catch the mantrip, (ride) into the mine and his "place" (workplace).

Once there he would engage in such safety related needs that may be present , then load coal, (shovel coal) into empty mine cars having been placed there previously by others , until noon, lunch, when he would indulge himself in a lunch of, typically, two slices of dry homemade bread, and two slices of homemade cottage cheese, washed down with water he carried In the bottom half of his lunch bucket. Then more shoveling till quitting time, exiting on the mantrip, and then walk the 4 miles back home.

Relief from this arduous process was found when the onset of World War II created once again a huge demand for coal, and another mine opened near to my home, employing Father there, within easy walking distance of one mile.

Father retired when the big war ended, living some eight years thereafter, his income derived solely from a U.M.W. pension of one hundred fifty dollars a month, and a minimum Social Security payment of sixty dollars per month.

Clock Problem

The critical issue was clock accuracy, not having electric denied the use of electric clocks or radio for ready confirmation of the correct time.

Having just one mechanical, spring driven clock, the probability of inaccurate time was continually present.

Mother was always in charge of early morning activity. If Mother forgot to wind the clock before retiring, and it stopped during the night, all hell would break loose when it was discovered in the morning. The prospect of losing a day's income in this time of great need was emotionally very explosive.

Not knowing the real time, then being late, or absent, set the stage for severe consequences immediately, for instance, missing the mandatory management directed mantrip, (ride) into his workplace.

Missing the mantrip would give him the choice of walking to his place, (work site) several miles into the mine, or to go back home, generating no product for the company, or income for himself. Needless to say, management was quite intolerant of this, and the threat of dismissal was ever present.

Management policy was quite simple, if work was available, you went to work, rain, snow, sick or whatever, you went to work, or you quickly learned you no longer had a job, and if you lived in a company owned house, eviction and physical placement of you, your family, and any possessions out onto the nearest street was swiftly executed by coal company police, a truly nasty group. Someone was always waiting to replace you, your job, and occupancy of your quarters.

Human Dynamics - Mules

My Life Story revolving in great part in and around the coal industry provides a peek into its role as a vital part of the Industrial Revolution, the trials and tribulations of the people who were instrumental in the physical execution necessary in the production and delivery of a commodity highly instrumental in the development of the Iron and Steel Industry, the backbone of the Industrial Revolution.

This Life Story parallels the life stories of the people in hundreds of mining communities in the vast area now known as Appalachia.

From its early onset utilizing human dynamics as the sole means of production, and ordinary mules as the primary means of transport of heavy loads in mine cars carrying supplies, such as posts, timber, rail and so on used in mining, into the mine, and also shifting cars filled with coal from a workplace to a rail load out making up a train to market, then shifting empty cars back into the workplaces.

High Risk Mining

Some, not all, mine owners considered immigrant and itinerant workers to be, at best, expendable. Conditions in mining sites, (places) ranged from workable, (dry, sound) to inhumane, (flooded, water raining down, roof unstable, unsafe). Mining of coal underground in that era was the most dangerous widespread occupation in existence. Disabling injuries and death were commonplace in the coalfields everywhere.

Widows of miners killed, and miners disabled by injury, unable to work, living in company housing were indulged for just a brief time by management before eviction, forcibly at times, by the coal police, and set out on the street to fend for themselves.

Danger was everywhere, inside the mine or outside around the rail system.

Miners desperate for income, were risk takers to the extreme, and all too often, would pay a dear price in doing so.

Enforcement of safety regulations, such as they were, was for the most part, nonexistent. Safety was solely the miners' responsibility. Risk-taking miners, to increase their tonnage, would often engage in extremely dangerous practices.

Typically, a miner would find his "place" ready for load out of the coal in the morning, but also exposed roof (overhead area) above the loose coal. Roof material was usually a conglomerate of unconsolidated, very heavy loose mineral, much of it ready to fall at will. This usually required extensive support by the miner setting posts, or takedown and removal of the rock, taking much time, and being severely hard work, especially in the Pittsburgh Seam, which is commonly about eight feet in thickness.

Rock falls were the principal cause of injuries, and even death in many cases. High risk miners would often in engage in the common practice of "pillaring", done, generally, as follows:

All supports would be removed from around a standing pillar left unmined previously for roof support, (a stump), then additional mining of the stump would be started, inducing overhead strata (roof) to begin downward movement, slowly crushing the remaining coal out of the stump, eliminating the need to cut, drill or blast to loosen the coal for its harvesting.

As the process continued, the overhead strata's move continued down, very slowly initially, with ever increasingly loud cracking and popping, as solid rock began shearing far overhead, with small pieces beginning to drop along the edges of support, while the miners are frantically shoveling the free-falling coal into a nearby car.

Assigned mules stayed with them all day, each serving a defined section, remaining inside at all times. Many of them, who had been born and raised inside the mine had never seen, nor would ever see, daylight.

They would spend their entire life inside the mine. They had developed a sixth sense, and knew when danger was present, or a collapse (roof fall) was imminent. If so, they would become very anxious and begin braying loudly, a signal miners knew not to ignore, immediately leaving the scene with the mules, to a safe area.

Welfare Programs

Additional subsistence was provided in having subscribed to a government sponsored welfare program then known as relief, where basic staples, such as flour, rice, beans, cornmeal, but no meat, were delivered to many homes, including ours.

Lamentably, most items were packaged in sacks, which, coupled with primitive storage and handling facilities, could and did, promote the proliferation of certain undesirables, bugs, worms, etc. which occasionally accompanied the products into the home.

Prior to cooking and consumption of these handouts, it was the fate, role, generally, of women and girls to sift and screen out as many of these unwanted, unwelcome visitors as possible.

Mother, with past experience gained in the old country, had no qualms about the process. The girls, my four sisters, hated it with absolute passion, but, being well versed in the consequences of inadequate execution of the task, reluctantly cooperated. Brother always had more important, more urgent duties to attend to, mostly imaginative, such as they were. I, fortunately, was way too young, and not knowing the difference between a bug and a grain was dubbed as worthless for the job by the girls anyhow.

Apparently, true hunger, a powerful motivator, along with thorough cooking was adequate to override emotional resistance to consumption, and so, survival ensued.

The cow and chickens continued to play a significant role in our survival during this time.

Sacks

Sacks being the primary packaging vessel, were a valuable by product to us, and society overall, in as much as they were made of a material suitable for secondary reuse. Flour, and so on, sacks appeared everywhere, as women converted them into dresses, shirts, sheets, and many other uses. The Heavens may well have smiled when viewing the appearance of the four sisters in their First Communion dresses made out of flour sacks.

Early on, as the practice spread, certain providers actually began using material in the sacks with colorful patterns on them to make it easier for women to use.

Selling Eggs in Saltsburg

In the late 30's the Depression still maintained its terrible grip, with little sign of let up anytime soon. People, searching for any means of generating money, discovered selling consumables to sympathetic town dwellers was one option available.

With the chicken hatch complete, the arrival of spring and warmer temperatures, the production of eggs would escalate to the point of excess and, with the ever-expanding demands of a growing family, the need for money was paramount. Mother would fill two baskets with eggs, fresh from the nests. Having nowhere to safely leave me, she would prepare me for a long trek, admonish me to stay close, and off we would go, baskets in hand, facing an arduous 3 miles of travel on foot.

The initial part of the journey was around or through farmed fields and woods, following a trail formed by cows commuting from their barn to a remote pasture, then onto a major public road, Route 380, reaching, finally, the small town of Saltsburg.

Oh, wonder of wonders. To a small, totally ignorant backwoods farm boy first seeing the vast expanse of moving water, the Kiskiminetas River, to be crossed by a bridge of, in my fearful mind, questionable integrity, then having safely navigated the crossing, the appearance of endless houses and buildings all congregated close together was, to me, awe inspiring. To top it all off, the sound of a whistle, then the rumble, of an oncoming freight train which, at that time traveled directly through the town, blocking all vehicle and foot traffic in or out of town, then seeing for the first time in real form that, which had, until now, only been imagined from just the distant sounds heard at my home.

The approach, then the passing of this monstrous entity within mere feet, the chuff chuff of the engine working, pulling its heavy load of freight toward its ultimate destination, was spellbinding to a little boy.

The train passed, dust settling, noise diminishing, now safe to cross the tracks, we continued on into town, visiting previously known customers, all readily accepting the eggs, paying the then pricey sum of fifty cents per dozen.

It was indeed a happy trip home for Mother, with a purse containing some money, but not necessarily for me, already dog-tired and hungry, with a very, very long way yet to go, on foot, one little step after another little step.

Childhood Memories—Bucky

Shuffling through my main desk drawer, hunting for something, I paused to focus on a gift from some organization soliciting money for some worthy cause, a brand-new penny still in its enclosure.

The action propelled me back in time to when I was four or five, I do not remember which. I was being raised in a family atmosphere that was nearly completely void of any physical demonstration of endearment, parent to child and certainly not between the children.

Simply put, that is just the way that it was, apparently a carryover from the Old Country, us being first generation offspring.

As a child, do not remember ever being picked up or carried and held.

It just did not happen. One day, a family friend, Bucky, came there, why I do not remember, and of course, I gravitated to him, he being a very personable individual, always smiling and laughing.

I recall him reaching down, grasping me in his huge, strong hands, lifting me high over his head, thrilling me as never before, holding me up for a time, then carrying me for some distance back to the house before carefully setting me down.

I am very much aware this action is insignificant to many, but to me, it was memorable beyond belief at the time, and over a lifetime, and lingers still.

Later, in that same visit, he was invited to visit our water source, a beautiful spring house constructed by some unknown, truly gifted Mason, long before our appearance in the area.

I clearly recall having crawled down the stone steps leading into the structure but was facing a real problem in getting back out, no one having noticed my dilemma.

Except Bucky, who, once again, reached down, picked me up, and safely carried me back upside, then setting me down on the ground before handing me a bright, shiny penny, a never-before event in my life.

One I will never forget.

Once again, an insignificant event in the eyes of many, but truly memorable to me.

About sixty years later I, a Professional Land Surveyor, was called to perform a survey for him.

Sadly, he did not remember me, not having ever seen me in the ensuing interlude, but I will never forget him.

Be safe, my friend, in God's great hands, and may you be uplifted by Him, as I was uplifted by you – when it meant so much to me.

Muitz Educating Me

I was four, as I recall. One summer day, with nothing really interesting to do, I wandered into an open shed we had there, and happened to spot our big mutt, a Shepherd mix dog, Muitz, lying there, sound asleep, dead to the world.

There being little of anything, including common sense, in a four-year-old's skull, I apparently thought it would be entertaining, fun, to sneak up on him, lean close and holler boo! So, I did.

Well, it startled him no end, and he must not have shared the feeling of levity in my action, so he jumped up, knocked me down, placed his open mouth completely enclosing my head, bit down only gently, if you can believe, and let me go, chastised, fearful, running to the house.

I do not remember there being any broken skin or blood, but I do remember maintaining a healthy respect and distance from him from that day on.

Avonmore Story

I was five when it was determined that, in anticipation of my forthcoming admission into the school system as a first grader, along with the looming arrival of Winter, it was time to equip me with my first real pair of shoes, having functioned until now, with misfit hand me downs, or simply going barefoot much of the time.

The nearest source for such being in the small town of Avonmore, some two- and one-half miles distant.

As the hour was growing short, my father, only sporadically employed as a coal miner, had a day available to follow through on purchasing the shoes.

And so, on a sultry, threatening early Autumn day, contrary to Mother's misgivings, Father and I set out, having no vehicle, on foot to visit the shoe store. Even with the excitement of the pending experience motivating me, it required many little steps and several hours to cover the distance, tiring me no end.

The purchase procedure was magical, with all the new people paying attention to me, the building and its smells, and of course, the shoes to be displayed and treasured. Leaving the store in high spirits, eager to return home to show off my prize, we started in that direction.

However, between the shoe store and home there happened to be a bar, saloon as it was referred to then, and in view of Father's fondness, his addiction, to experiencing extended altered levels of consciousness, he intended to visit there prior to our heading home For some unknown reason, I was not welcome in there, and was left standing out on a street corner, which one I do not know, and firmly ordered to wait there.

And wait I did, time passed, no Father, anxiety began building, more time passed, anxiety was joined by fear, and still no rescuer. I apparently determined I had been abandoned, so I decided to go searching for my father. Threatening skies turned dark and a light rain began to fall.

Having been at the Saloon only once briefly, I had no idea where its location was. I vividly recall walking up and down Westmoreland Avenue, terrified, crying uncontrollably. A passing middle-aged woman, pushing a baby carrier, stopped me and asked why I was crying, but made no effort to help me find my father, or to find shelter from the rain. I vaguely remember going to the guardhouse at the nearby Iron Foundry and asking the guard there if he knew where my father could be, or where he was. He simply shrugged and went back into the guardhouse. I left him and continued walking aimlessly. After what seemed like an eternity, my father appeared out of nowhere and collected me. We then started for home, with ever darkening skies assembling ominously overhead.

I do not remember much of the torturous trip back home, being told later that I had passed out, not having had anything to eat or drink all of that day. I was told I had to be carried much of the way and slept for days after that ordeal.

To this day, there are times that whenever I travel across Westmoreland Avenue, I still see and hear that shivering, crying little boy.

Pre-School Problems

Raised by illiterate, recently immigrated parents incapable of fluently verbalizing, much less teaching the English Language to me, I learned only menial Ukrainian, and practically no English prior to entrance of the school system as a first grader.

She, and Father, having no formal education of any type whatsoever, created a distinct void in the family setting, in as much as we children were rapidly gaining the ability to speak, read and write the English language now predominant in our lives. We, by necessity, were forced to communicate with them in our increasingly limited Ukrainian tongue. They became ever more confused and unable to understand any verbal exchanges among us children when in their presence.

Due to some quirk in the rules relative to birth date in the school system, formal schooling began early for me, at age 5, irrespective of a glaring communication deficiency. The tutoring of English after school by four language proficient older sisters, daily, soon resolved the language and other barriers.

Climbing the Mountain

Mandated schooling being the law, and residence in the remote backwoods being the reality, there was no choice but to choose the most palatable course of travel from home to a waiting school bus at a pick-up point.

That being a path, initially presenting itself in both appearance and makeup not unlike Mount Everest itself, to a five-year-old at a loss as to what is the real reason he is involved here in this.

In agreement or not, the five other family members have already begun the climb, rain, shine, sleet, or snow notwithstanding, breaking trail if necessary for the five-year-old boy, ultimately merging at the school bus's open door, waiting to transport them to an institution of higher learning, the school.

The path itself was comprised of a variety of physical conditions, ranging from the steep ascent initially, gradually softening up through a field, deep in blowing snow at times, to a wooded area where roaming cattle had carved a path in their travels, to another cultivated area where the path changed course annually, as farming dictated, then the descent through an operational orchard, where delicious fruit was often confiscated by a hungry boy, then the final vertical descent to the bus stop.

This is where brother Andy, declaring his preference to pack education into his skull at a slower pace than prescribed, would hide behind a corn shock so as to not be seen by the bus driver, and miss a day of schooling. I 'm sure the driver cared.

The return trip at the end of the day after drop off, repeated the travel way of the early part of the day, reexperiencing whatever weather conditions presented, good, bad, or other.

This all ended when all but me had graduated, and I, having a '37 Chevy pickup, drove to school every day.

Occasionally, I retrace my steps that were taken, or given, in that path, and a certain melancholy creeps in, when I begin to hear the singing we did as we, carefree, happily traipsed along when going to that bus.

Oh, it was so very long ago, so very long ago.

Entering First Grade

I am tested in remembering the details of that first day of school, but find a muted sort of excitement here now, 8 + decades later, in re-experiencing, even mentally, that major milestone of my life.

Emergence from a tiny circle of daily activities involving minimal people, to entry into an unimaginably vast real world, to say the least, was beyond my ability to comprehend as a five-year-old.

Leaving the predictably secure world I had and entering into the exact opposite of that, as yet unequipped to cope with it, but perhaps, sensing I was on the verge of discovering the pathway to greater understanding.

Aren't we, those of us who are willing to admit it, still, years and years later, just a little excited at the approach of the first day of school, even though we know we will not be a part of it.

Never having been in one, then actually getting into, and riding in a bus across miles of unfamiliar terrain, then being led by Big Brother into that huge building, to me, already teeming with little people, in such numbers as I had never seen, obviously students in other grades.

I was taken into a room at the extreme end of the building, designated as the first-grade room, and dumped there, with the stern instruction to listen and obey the teacher, she having been pointed out to me.

I, and the other equally confused first graders assembled there, were soon calmed by a soft-spoken adult, then assigned seating in alphabetical order, then given our first peek into the incredibly vast world of knowledge, details of which escape me at this point in my life.

Beginning here, in grade school, then high school, exposure to and subsequent absorption of knowledge, in general, apparently built a solid base from which I was able to successfully challenge the business world, starting from basically nothing and nowhere, to ultimately reaching desired levels of achievement as are articulated herein elsewhere.

I never attended any college, due to both lack of funds, and lack of interest, preferring to circulate in hands-on occupations, as a "gentleman farmer" initially, then numerous others, as addressed in greater detail elsewhere.

Teacher's Pet - Teachers

As a child starting in first grade, I must have been what is referred to as cute, attractive to older women, but it never followed through to younger women, girls, for some unknown reason.

It being common knowledge that cute, good-looking, is nearly always favored in the world of harsh reality, much of the time unfairly, in the selection of life partners, adoption of children or animals, employees and even politicians, to name a few.

I, an admitted compassionate fool, cannot go into any animal shelter, being unable to emotionally cope with seeing the long term unadopted animals imprisoned there, most being in the less than attractive category.

I must have subconsciously promoted this, as my first-grade teacher, Violet, took me under her wing, seating me up close to her desk, making sure I understood classroom subjects being taught, even placing me on her lap during playtime breaks, teaching me socially proper manners and so on.

She apparently recognized I was a near total illiterate, hungry for learning, a wide-open empty vessel of humanity, she did everything in her ability to quietly promote my advance into progressive learning.

I loved her then, and still, in memory, which I will keep, forever.

Then came Second Grade, Miss M.

She, too, took me under her wing, close seating, special attention, straight A's on my report card.

Now Third Grade, Miss M.

Pretty much the same pattern, special attention as the class year progressed, upon her realization I was somewhat intelligent, eager to learn everything and anything, I became the class champion in spelling, never losing a spelling bee, and was advanced in mathematics.

Teachers love an interested learner; it justifies their existence when visible results surface.

Fourth Grade, Miss F.

She, being the one I unsuccessfully attempted to bribe favoritism from, by gifting her a generous dose of Mother's homemade cheese, that found a discordant note upon her family's unsympathetic rejection of the cheese at a group dinner.

That story is found elsewhere and did not affect the positive relationship I maintained with her.

She was a good teacher, and friend. She still gave me straight A's on my report card.

Fifth Grade, Miss M.

An administrative switch moved her from the third grade to the fifth grade, and a continuation of a teacher's pet relationship, I, adding to the friendship, dusting erasers, and washing the blackboard daily for her.

She just happened to pick my name for the class Christmas gift exchange, gave me a kaleidoscope for my gift, a rare plaything, envied by the rest of the class.

She also being the teacher who refused to punish me for having whacked the bully with my shoe. That event also appears elsewhere in this series of stories.

Sixth Grade, the end of multiple classes by homeroom teachers. Miss W.

She was the most attracted to me of all, flagrantly showering me at times, to the point of embarrassment, with small gifts, holiday cards, candy and so on, including straight A's on my report cards.

Humorously memorable, though, was the time I apparently responded improperly in a classroom debate, and she, holding a book in her hand, in response to my apparent indiscretion, round housed me full in the face with the book, firmly ordering me to be seated, and to remain silent.

She also kindly obliged me in scoring the county test, explained elsewhere, so I would know the results of the test immediately.

I always have, and always will consider her as being among the finest of friends and teachers.

Seventh Grade Changed Everything.

Multiple teachers, additional classes, shop, gym, health, library to name some of them, a different teacher for each class.

No more teacher's pet, we're now beyond that, no longer children, approaching adulthood.

However, my homeroom teacher Mrs. B.

Living on a farm, as did I, still engendered a certain kinship, along with my ongoing search for knowledge, endeared me to her, resulting in extra assistance in my pursuit.

The library class introduced me to Mrs. F.

Who, in another story, will be the one that I air mailed a bucket of water to, in retaliation for a vicious verbal attack on one of my sisters several years prior.

The gym and health class introduced me to Mr. H.

Who immediately didn't like me due to my less than star level athletic capabilities, I having carried a reputation with me of intellect more so than athletics.

For the record, I didn't like him either, in his self-appointed importance and arrogance.

I never earned a single letter, even though in defiance, I tried out for basketball and baseball, but not making either team.

After three winning seasons, with our class of '52, being the primary players in all three sports, football, basketball, and baseball, he jumped ship and moved on to greener pastures, so to speak.

Eighth Grade homeroom, and math class were interesting. The teacher, Miss S. was a pleasant, straight-laced spinster, well into her 60's, who drove her impeccably maintained '39 Chevy coupe, top speed 30 mph, to school daily, parking in exactly the same spot every day.

I quickly became her favorite, I being highly proficient in math, gobbling up the study books rapidly, proceeding out into advanced workbooks with her approval and guidance.

Straight A's, of course.

Then there was Mr. Mc, a really fine history and geography teacher, who unfortunately was very mild mannered, too mild mannered for his own good, being only about 5 feet tall and weighing about 100 pounds, and of course being the subject of much uncalled-for ridicule, bordering beyond disgusting, bringing him to tears occasionally.

Someone actually coined the unkind statement; he has a suit for every day of the year, he's got it on now.

He retired from teaching early, extending no thanks or regrets to us.

In typing class, Mrs. M. was as good as it gets. I credit her for guiding me in developing my future ability to type, at about 130 words per minute.

When I was in signal school in the military a few years later, I amused everyone with my being able to type 10 letters ahead of the electronic typewriters we used there.

I would finish the sheet of five letter groups of coded messages, then wait for the typewriter to catch up to me from its memory bank.

Ninth Grade was Mr. P.

Homeroom and a science teacher.

A former military officer, punctual and precise, so he imagined.

There is more of him in another story, skipping study hall, elsewhere.

Sophomore class we returned to Mrs. B.

Having been my seventh-grade homeroom. She taught us English literature and had a study hall. I, still on very friendly terms with her, was occasionally counseled toward the future, in academic subjects, of course.

Then, in my junior year, I dropped the proverbial bomb, to anyone who may have been concerned.

Few, if any after Mrs. B, were.

The sophomore teacher, she being a special friend expecting me to go on to higher learning, via the academic course, was the only one who cared at all.

Two of my sisters, Anna and Mary, both having been their class valedictorian, had set the stage of expectation for me to emulate them, to perpetuate the reputation of the Kravetsky Family as intellectually gifted.

Personally, I had little to no interest in beating my brains out for some vague, remote title yielding little to nothing measurable in the world of reality.

I was already in pursuit of commercial achievement, eventual elevated net worth, leaving accolades for scholastic achievement to those who desired and earned it.

In my sophomore year, I switched to the vocational agricultural course of study.

Homeroom teacher Mr. S. welcomed someone truly interested in agriculture and all that went with it, to become a part of it.

The rest of that story also appears elsewhere.

Finally, study hall eighth Miss R., who also appears elsewhere in this story telling series, as the observer of the mini play put on, featuring Charlie and Stush at the beach.

God bless their memories, all.

Onset of WWll, Upgrade

Relief from that hopeless environment, in general, came upon the onset of World War Two, and the mechanization of the mining industry. Mining machines replaced muscle and bone, and electrically powered locomotives (motors) replaced the mules, who, in some cases, saw their first daylight ever, and were put out to pasture, where by the grace of sympathetic superintendents, more likely their wives, they lived out their lives in relative luxury as self-propelled ornaments in nearby fields, and quoting a famous speech, free at last, free at last, thank God, free at last.

Welfare Exit

At this point in history, the mind set of most people on relief, welfare, was that it was a stigma to be removed as soon as humanly possible, to exit a class of society considered to be totally unacceptable unless unavoidable circumstances predicated such.

Father, a dedicated coal miner, with a strong belief in self-sustenance, immediately returned to work at a large local coal mine, one reminiscent of the inferences and conclusions drawn in the song, 16 tons, written featuring a miner and to some degree the hardships of employment in pre-mechanized coal mines ruled by despotic taskmasters.

Risky Business

It was somewhere in the thirties, that an influx of entrepreneurship must have struck Father, when he and a friend decided to compete with our more famous friends in Chicago, and elsewhere in the remote hills and dales in making and marketing a little shine.

Where the knowledge as to the correct equipment and then the correct procedure originated, forever remains a mystery, because they were ignorant coal miners, not moonshiners, completely out of their element.

At any rate, from what I overheard long ago, a crude setup was in place, inside a fenced enclosure, next to a cow and horse barn, pretty well out of sight.

Progress was being made, as a sizeable amount of raw whiskey, such as it was, was already in a wooden cask, and more coming.

So were the Revenuers, as they were known everywhere.

In their conversations, there was an uneasiness mentioned, as it was well known retailers of sugar were being watched, and purchasers of unusual quantities were being identified.

Families usually bought sugar in five-pound bags, not multiple 25 pound sacks.

There was further discussion, after the fact that Revenue Agents had come during the night, and posted themselves in view of the cooking site, observing the activity.

Then, when proof was positive, they came in and identified themselves, ending the party.

To their credit, there were no arrests, just a dumping of what finished product was there, along with the destruction of the mechanism involved.

And, of course, a stern warning.

The wooden barrels were around for years, used for making legal grape wine.

The wine was very tasty in its early stages to an 8-year-old boy. I know because I got very drunk, and quite sick drinking it, one hot summer day. I never drank anything like that again.

Curds and Whey

I was probably in second, or at most third grade, and in one form or another, Olde English Poems would be read to us in class.

I, generally hungry, as were others, was drawn to the poem: Little Miss Muffet, sat on her tuffet, eating her Curds and Whey.

As I wondered just what she was eating, imagined it was quite palatable, and wished I could have some, too, every time it was read to the class.

Finally, I asked a neighbor's wife what it was, and she explained it to me.

Whey is the cloudy, yellowish liquid that is left after processing raw milk for making cheese, and curds are the coagulated parts of the milk, also a part of the cheesemaking process.

I decided I was not that hungry after all, anymore.

Kitchen Stove

One of the most terribly memorable, and most frightening experiences I witnessed as a child, was the evening I had refilled the kitchen stove with an armload of freshly made kindling, then forgot, failed to close the air intake of the stove.

It was Winter, very cold, high winds blowing, and very quickly, the dry wood was burning fiercely, sending flames up the ancient chimney, turning the old brick red orange, setting the boards next to it on fire, flames now beginning to form on the kitchen side.

Thankfully, that's when Mother smelled the smoke, and screamed, grabbed the ever-present bucket of water and doused the flames out, the fire just having reached the ceiling. We carried our water from our spring those days, as we did not have electricity yet, so it was providential that there was a full bucket available.

That was 75 or 80 years ago, and I still resist recalling that memory, as the nightmares following that experience took years to finally dismiss.

We were, essentially, still an immigrant family with no relatives to turn to, and the thought of two illiterate parents with six little kids suddenly homeless in that location in the backwoods without communication of any kind in the night was, is, too extreme even now, for me.

I keep bringing up Guardian Angels. don't I?

DeForno's Orange

I only remember, with lingering regret, not when it occurred, but what it was that did occur.

Being in the depth of winter, father was unable to maintain some vital needs at home, bread I believe was one of them.

Since I would already be at school, in the proximity of a store selling bread, I was delegated to go there, in the time between arrival in the bus, and starting bell, which was sufficient time, to buy a loaf.

I am somewhat still ashamed, these many decades later, I can see me standing in the store, typically hungry, I was always hungry, looking at the vast assortment of good things to eat, oranges being the closest to me in a big bin, enticing.

The store owner, clerking by herself that morning, had gone to retrieve the loaf of bread, leaving me alone for a few moments.

Bypassing better judgement, I reached into the bin and took an orange, quickly putting it in my jacket pocket, covering it with my hand, the owner's return being imminent.

She, returning, somehow appeared to know I had taken something, but did not speak or react, just gave me a long, penetrating stare, then turned away, handing me the loaf of bread, refusing payment for it (it cost $0.15 a loaf at that time).

I have never related that event to family, or anyone else, until now. I know, it does not really matter.

I do not know if my substantial contributions to food banks over the past many years are payment of that debt, or not.

Someday, I may find out.

Stella Chocolate Milk

It was in second grade, the big war is raging over there, shortages of nearly everything over here.

As part of a nutritional program, dried apricots were distributed free of charge to underprivileged students, which of course I qualified as one.

Along with the dried fruit, but not free of charge, small cartons of chocolate milk were offered at the cost of a nickel, five cents.

Never having tasted chocolate milk, but never having a nickel, I could only observe longingly as others purchased and consumed them.

Well, great day, I don't remember who gave it to me, but I had the nickel, and it was the day of chocolate milk distribution.

The great moment came, and I eagerly exchanged my nickel for the carton of chocolate milk.

Opening it, preparing to take a sip, who do I see standing right beside me?

It was my sister Stella.

She, knowing I had had a nickel, designated for the purchase of a carton of chocolate milk, followed the sales team to my homeroom where I was to make the long-awaited transaction.

I, knowing she also had never tasted chocolate milk either, offered my carton to her, which was gladly taken, she drinking half of it without stopping, then returning it to me.

Her friend with her, Velma, refused to share, and I finished it off, savoring every drop.

It never happened again, but I still see that moment in my mind's eye, which I will never forget.

Andy—Coon Hunting

I was about 10 or 11 when my brother Andy became involved with several others in hunting raccoons. As I know it, that is done exclusively at night, with one or more specially trained dogs, and powerful lights.

In retrospect, I now believe that in order to be a dedicated coon hunter, one must be of questionable sanity, being willing to subject himself, or herself to many natural hazards, like rough terrain, multiflora rose, slippery hidden logs, and so on and on, all in exchange for the miniscule value of some poor little raccoon's body cover, if it's not too full of holes from the shotgun blast that brings it down out of some high tree.

That all being confirmed, I, too, did some coon hunting, but only to the extent I was a tagalong, just there to shine the light, while the hunter did the shooting.

Just for you Who never knew its fine points:

It can be done a number of ways, which I won't explore more than the two we employed, by choice or circumstance.

The choice was in letting the dogs hunt, following them in a generally predetermined direction, they baying when having picked up a coon's trail yelping when the coon has climbed a tree, or letting the dogs hunt, then going to where they're yelping, having treed the coon.

My good, yeah, fortune was that one of our fellow hunters was a narcoleptic, someone who sleeps readily anytime, anywhere, for extended periods. There were occasions where he would fall asleep; and we would sit and wait for hours at times, freezing, angry, disgusted. We avoided his participation when we could, gracefully.

Andy – Retrospect 2

The time when we were coming home from school, walking through the patch of woods enclosing the path, when the sound of a coon hound baying from across the nearby valley caused us to stop and listen.

Andy an avid coon hunter at that time, became reverently silent, then listened raptly for a few emotionally charged repetitions of the howl, obviously affected, and solemnly uttered "that's' moosic to muh ears".

Andy, being socially reclusive, ever carefully guarding his actual upbringing, and certain habits and Interests, like coon hunting and trapping, from his workplace peers, and the public in general, was very sensitive to having been heard making that statement.

I, unkindly, occasionally would mimic his words at the most inopportune times.

He finally quit both hunting and trapping.

Pet Racoon

The area we lived in was ideal for hunting raccoons.

Our house, surrounded by hundreds of acres of farmed fields and woodland, orchards and gardens, with two small year-round flowing streams traversing thousands of feet through them, provided raccoons with ample nutrition for sustenance and procreation.

My brother, Andy, having gone hunting one night, taking a break from the pursuit of the dogs, sat down beside a hollow tree, dozing off within a short time.

Something, a movement, a whimper awakened him from his nap, attracted his attention, then coming fully awake, quickly.

A baby racoon, apparently motherless, had crawled out of the hollow tree and climbed into a coat pocket, whimpering as it settled into the warmth of his coat, it being a cold night.

Now he is facing a dilemma. Now what?

Even he, a seasoned hunter, evokes compassion for the innocent, helpless little creature, unable to consider ending its life then and there, ending his problem.

Terminating the hunt, calling in the dogs and heading for home was the temporary decision, biding time for more constructive thought regarding the, as of now, adopted baby racoon.

A baby racoon, already indicating advanced hunger and desperate need for something to eat, or drink, as the case may have been.

Reaching home, he takes care of the dogs then faces the new problem; you've got something's life in your hands.

He awakened Mother, explaining the situation, and asking for advice and help.

She filled a small dish with milk, warmed it a bit, found a small syringe and placed a few drops of milk into the baby's mouth. It responded favorably. More milk and a piece of lunchmeat, and the baby was asleep, they placing it into a cardboard box.

The next day he decided to keep the little girl, and built a cozy little box for her, placing it into our corn crib, which was quite secure.

Mom usually fed her; she would eat anything. Stella and I would visit her daily, bringing her tidbits, attempting to make a pet of her.

Somehow, it never worked. Try as we would, her wildness never softened, she would snarl and snap at my fingers unfailingly when I tried to touch her.

This went on for years, she imprisoned in her cage, we not realizing she should have been offered her freedom upon reaching adulthood, long ago.

Finally, while I was away in Korea, and brother Andy was away at work, Mother took it upon herself to open the cage door and leave it open, going about her daily affairs.

When she returned for evening feeding, she was gone.

Never to return.

I still feel the pain and guilt of imprisoning that innocent, sweet little creature for such a long time.

Maybe she'll be at the Rainbow Bridge.

I hope so, so I can make amends.

We had never even given her a name.

Andy—Retrospect 1

There being just a shade over 7 years age difference between my brother Andy and I, set the ongoing stage in difference of attitude and opinion regarding many of our life topics, to mention a few.

I was looked upon as a nuisance, occasionally needing to be baby sat, just a pain in the ***.

As the age of reason developed in me, I was often the outspoken critic, relentlessly making fun of some of his antics, like;

Refusing to wear a wristwatch on his wrist, preferring to keep it in a pocket.

Carrying a bagged lunch in his suit coat pocket to avoid being seen carrying it.

Discussing or admitting he lived on a small farm in the backwoods when among his peers at his place of employment.

Compass – Survey

From a very early age, I had this thing for compasses. Why, I do not know, maybe was an explorer in another lifetime.

I remember seeing the offer on a Cereal box, way back when, that for ten cents and the box top, I would get this proven compass that I could sail around the world with and be guided safely home.

My dime, and top go out, and I anxiously wait, and wait, and wait.

Finally, way later, the compass arrives. Oh, what a bust.

Not having the slightest idea as to how you work with it, stuck on one finger like a sore thumb, I was laughed at by my brother, and my peers.

Being about the size of an aspirin, barely readable, it soon went the way of the dodo bird, extinction.

Was this the forerunner of a 63-year career?

Then, I got interested in Morse Code, the first method of long distance communication, becoming somewhat knowledgeable enough to get the merit badge in scouting.

Next was scoring high in the aptitude tests given in Military Basic Training, sending me to Camp Gordon Signal Corps schooling.

Learning Morse Code there, quickly running up to 30 words per minute, the maximum necessary, by hand key.

Learning teletype transmission to the level required for placement with the ROK Army communications in Korea.

Then, the real Start in the Seanor Mine as a Surveyor Helper, graduating to Mine Surveyor at the Jamison Mine.

Finally , the acquisition of a professional Surveyor's License in 1967, fame and fortune assured.

The rest is History, recorded in Memory, and told in these many Life Stories.

Oh, what a ride It has been, and it ain't over yet! World War 2 I was five when the big war to end all wars was underway in Europe, six when it was announced Roosevelt had declared war on Germany and the axis powers.

l, we, were understandably uneasy, quietly fearing when it was just over there, openly terrified upon the Roosevelt declaration, believing the hostilities, the bombing was soon to be arriving here.

Not yet having a radio, word-of-mouth was our only source for ongoing information.

In school, we received weekly updates of a sort, mostly propaganda of questionable accuracy, keeping us somewhat calmed, and comforted.

At home, we were counseled to keep our window blinds pulled down at night, subdue any conversation involving the war, since loose lips, sink ships, was part of our instruction to be aware of, and we believed all of their spiel, both the true and the false.

Everything was rationed, gasoline, tires, and cars. Food of many kinds, particularly imported food, like meat, sugar, coffee and so on.

Trading food stamps was common among everyone.

Mondays were designated as war bond day.

Every kid was expected to buy at least a dime stamp, filling a book towards a $25 bond, requiring $18.75 to fill it up.

Needless to say, neither me nor my brother or sisters ever bought a stamp.

Cheering would actually erupt in class, if on some rare occasion some ultra-rich parent would send the entire $18.75 in with a child, buying the whole bond.

We would have air raid practice, where all the students assembled in the hall for 10 or 15 minutes, mostly silent, waiting for the bombs to drop.

It was less fearful at home, we being so isolated, frightened only when air raid sirens would be screaming, in practice.

Seeing the Goldstar flags appear was hard to know.

Getting a radio halfway through the war didn't really help, just hearing more propaganda.

Great relief was in hearing the pronouncement of surrender by the enemy, half a day of school off, in celebration.

God Bless America.

School Show - No Dime

There were those occasions in grade school and even at times including junior high when some program or other was being offered, requiring a dime to attend.

I am aware this is mentioned elsewhere, inasmuch as there were always kids that didn't have a dime, for only God knows what reason, and would be left in their homeroom to sit out the duration of the program, I always being among those.

What is most dismaying to me now, in retrospect, decades later, is of those times when a presentation was about to get underway, and in order to free up as many teachers as possible so they could attend, is that they would delegate just one homeroom for all of us deplorables (current terminology, not then) herding multiple grades into the one room, which, to put it mildly, was both depressing and embarrassing as hell. I really don't know if there was any or much long term negative effect out of this or not.

Shame on them.

I'm probably the only one to remember it.

Anyhow.

Growing Up - Bumblebee

Growing up, I was very curious just about anything and everything.

This one day, at age 8 or nine, I guess, I saw a big bumblebee go into the back rest of an old abandoned buggy off to one side of the barnyard.

Wondering where she had disappeared into with her load of pollen, I know it was a she, since only the females work in the bee domain, unlike humans in our world. I went over to the buggy to get a closer look.

I found it all right, the nest was inside the seat, but as one might suspect, the guard bee found me.

I took off running, and so did she, after me.

Less than 100 feet away, she nailed me right on the back of my neck, a clear message to leave them alone.

No, I did not retaliate, I was the invader.

To this day, I have not only a healthy respect for these ultra-beneficial creatures, but a certain love of them as fellow travelers on this planet.

Father Shooting at Owl

Someone, I don't remember who, came running into the house one day, alarmed at some creature's presence in a small tree out behind the house.

Father, slightly inebriated at the time, quickly rising to meet the adversity, grabbed a 12 gauge shotgun and some shells, and headed towards the Invader.

It was just a barn owl perched, resting in the tree, looking for something to eat, presumably.

Father, determined to either expel or dispatch the creature, not knowing it was harmless, loaded the shotgun with a pumpkin ball shell, aimed and blasted away, the recoil knocking him to the ground in his somewhat unstable condition.

The scene was repeated six times, we were told, when he finally gave up, with a very sore shoulder needing medical attention – but not getting it.

The owl must have known he was in the safest place to be – where Father was aiming. It flew away, untouched.

Horse Spooked

With the onset of the great war, employment soared, and father was earning a more comfortable level of household income.

Never having had any viable means of transportation, other than on foot, a one-horse buggy was procured sometime in the early 40s, making life much easier, especially when acquiring and delivering domestic essentials, food, clothing, wine.

A gallon of wine weighing about 10 pounds, was not very easy to hand carry for the 3 miles distance from the state store to home.

The buggy solved that problem nicely, there being a compartment with a lid, safely enclosing not only the foodstuff, but also the jug of wine.

In the acquisition of both, groceries and wine, a stop into a local bar was always part of the program.

The usual time for this was Saturday afternoon, sometimes stretching into the evening, into the night, into the dark.

This one Saturday, the normal pattern was playing out, and as it transpired, it was well into dark when the horse, who had patiently suffered waiting around, harnessed all day, was finally signaled to head for home.

It's common for horses to memorize the pathway home, from often visited points, so it was of no real concern that the horse was being relied upon to take him home, he being in no condition to drive after the extended visit in the bar.

The return trip was uneventful until, for some reason, the horse suddenly stopped, refusing to move.

It being quite dark, Father, alerted by the stopping, saw that a fairly large limb had broken off a tree, landing on the roadway, not realizing there was a second limb attached.

Assuming they could easily run over the blockage he vigorously slapped the horse's butt and shouted out the giddy up order, panicking the horse. It being very dark, the horse took off, wildly careening along the crude trail through the woods that made up the road, and within a short distance had upset the buggy into a ditch, spilling all of the contents of the enclosed box onto the ground, and, unforgivably, smashing the jug of wine.

It was a welcome, peaceful, quiet, stress-free weekend for us. End of story.

Father's Hideaway 1

Father was a relatively mild-mannered individual, reclusive and detached from all potentially interactive social occasions, preferring to remain aloof and distant most of the time.

There being just three rooms in our house for eight people, his solution for elimination of at least one from the crowding, was to build himself a shanty, about 100 feet from the house, a crude 10' x 10' wooden box like structure with a door.

And a window, no heat, no electricity, no plumbing, just a place to sleep, and oh yes, a place to drink, privately.

It was architecturally barren, devoid, no one cared.

It had no foundation, no insulation, no ventilation other than the free flow of air through the knot holes and spaces between the boards making up the sides, that being cured to some extent after the first winter, with rolled asphalt siding nailed on.

Flat roof, with no gutters, and there was space for a full-sized bed, a stand, and a dog that slept in there with him much of the time.

This shanty provided the place for Solace, away from six obnoxious children, a place to ponder reality, and life. Sure it did.

Having a lock on the door.

It was forbidden territory, off limits, to me. It was a place for him to hide, no more, no less.

Its departure followed closely after his.

Homemade Cheese, Fourth Grade

One day, when I was in fourth grade, our homeroom teacher Mrs. F. Was discussing homemade cheese. How many countries considered it as a primary staple in their foodstuff, and how much was consumed here in comparison.

She brought out how many different animals were the base source of the cheese, cows, goats, sheep and camels to name a few. She asked if anyone in the class was familiar with homemade cheese, and if their family had any of the animals used to produce it.

Bingo! I scored big. I was the only farm-related student in the class, and my hand shot straight up.

She asked what type of animal we had, and did we make cheese from their milk. I proudly stated that we had two cows, both milkers, and that making cheese was routinely done to use the excess milk, and to provide a principal provision for my father, who liked the cheese.

So she asked if a sample was available for not only her and her family to try, but even to give each student a taste.

I excitedly raced home to share the great news with Mother, and she readily agreed to provide a more than generous portion in a large bowl.

I carefully guarded my prize in the delivery of the cheese the next day, proudly presenting the dish to Mrs. F.

While turning away to go to my seat, I noticed she had opened the cover at one corner of the dish just a little, unobtrusively sniffed it, then quickly re-covered the open corner.

I, assuming she would immediately personally sample it, and then distribute enough to each student for their reaction for class discussion, but she did not, she said that she preferred to take it home to consume it at a family gathering that evening.

Also, there were not enough spoons available just then, and she would get more for the class the next day.

I was disappointed but resolved to accept the wait, patiently.

The next day when class began, I noticed an empty dish in the teacher's hand, the one I had given her the day before.

She approached me right away, handing me the empty dish.

I said, did you like the cheese?

She, with a straight face, looking into my eyes, was overwhelming in her praise, how delicious it was, and how her family simply adored it. I, an innocent simple kid, said would you like me to bring you some more?

Her response was electrifying. I know the sound of my voice in asking the question had not yet reached the outer perimeter of the room, when she hypersonically blurted out a succession of no no no no's, turned and went back to her desk.

Years later, well into the age of understanding and reason, we here at home re-examined that response.

The obvious conclusion: Lady, you answered way too quickly, way too quickly.

The truth: The cheese I brought her was the real McCoy, the product made and aged by my mother.

The problem was that that particular batch had been set back, forgotten for several years, aging in less than a perfect, prescribed atmosphere for proper aging, thereby reaching a status so acidic it could, according to our tasting after her trial, repulse any living creature, or liquefy cast iron.

Testing it on the dogs, they sniffed and ran.

We gave the remainder which was being stored in a hardwood keg, a proper burial.

Food was never mentioned again in fourth grade.

Flag At School

I'm not sure, or care, what grade I was in, when the call came, so to speak, for someone to raise the flag in the morning, and lower it at day's end.

l, a budding patriot, volunteered, along with my best friend, Jim to take care of it.

Every day, rain or shine, warm or cold, we would get the flag out of the music room, carefully connect it to the chain that raised it up the pole, then pull it up, anchoring it for the day.

A repeat of those actions, in reverse order, was done just before ending bell every day.

I remember the feeling of pride in having brought it down at day's end, carefully folding it in the prescribed manner, in a series of triangles, if I remember correctly, never allowing it to touch the ground, then returning it to its secure space in the music room.

I clearly recall that feeling of inner pride being present in those years I was a Boy Scout, and certainly when I was in the US Army.

God Bless America Again, a beautiful song sung by Bobby Bare, you should listen to it.

Carry Bread to Cafeteria

Early in the sixth-grade year, the teacher Mrs. W stopped me one morning, and mentioned there was a need for help in the pickup and delivery of bread to the cafeteria.

The situation was that the store in town, where the cafeteria got its bread, was unable to deliver the high-volume at the exact time it was needed.

The offer was to trade the pickup and delivery, daily, just before lunch, for a free lunch which cost at the time was twelve cents.

My best friend Jim E agreed to help me so I accepted the offer, continuing that entire year, rain or shine, pickup delivery of a big box of bread to the cafeteria just before lunch, every day.

I do not count that as an early career move.

Nearly Drowning

As a young person, I developed an inordinate love of swimming. It reached the point of ridiculous: in walking, I would pretend I was swimming, practicing the action as I went along.

In the process of actually learning to swim, we had a number of water holes we visited, Wolford Run nearby, abandoned surface mining pits, deep mine impoundments, but without professional guidance it was a very slow process.

I believe I was ten when I was visiting a new swimming hole at Beaver Run, just below what is now the Beaver Run Dam.

This being my first visit there, I was totally unfamiliar with the configuration of the hole, staying away from the obvious deep part where others were diving in from a high bank.

Having progressed somewhat in my ability, I, standing at the edge of the hole, scanned the distance across the creek to the opposite bank, confidant I could easily swim across. I dove in, but apparently panicked and froze in fear as I contacted the water and sank, losing all confidence, out of control.

I vividly remember sinking, fighting, coming up once, sinking, coming up again, feeling hopeless, desperate for air, starting to sink again.

Suddenly, a strong hand was pulling me up, taking me back to the shore, air now free flowing, setting me on the ground.

Opening my eyes, I saw it vas Ed ___ an occasional acquaintance from school, who had observed the whole event.

His question, and then mine, was why I hadn't simply waded across the creek at that point, the water being less than four feet deep there, well below my standing height of 5 feet+. I finally learned to swim at Scout Camp a couple of years later.

Was he my Guardian Angel?

Someone was.

Threshing – Lunch

I was 10 years old, and a great day was coming soon, threshing, incorrectly referred to as thrashing, day when I was very young, and was a high point of the year for me.

Harvesting in those days was a far different story than today.

Then, when our grain was ripe, we hired a contractor who brought his binder, a machine which cut and made sheaves out of the grain, like those you see in picturesque scenes of harvested grain fields, which we would gather and build into small clusters. These clusters were left outside, supposedly to dry the grain, before taking them to the barn to further dry until threshing day.

In anticipation of the thresher arriving, preparations were always done to handle the grain, and also for the high point of the day, the after threshing dinner, the farm, and neighboring women would prepare for the men.

The dinner, one for the proverbial ages, one everyone looked forward to.

The big day began when a huge, to me, steel wheeled tractor, pulling this monstrous machine came slowly down the roadway, maneuvered into position at the barn doors, leveled up by digging high wheels into the ground and, finally rev up the tractor's engine, engaging the long belt that drove the thresher's internal apparatus, separating the grain from the stalk as it was fed into the thresher, then blowing the remains, the straw, into an ever growing pile, which, to our delight, became our playground for the next number of weeks or months, never mind the chaff clinging to us for weeks.

Typically, after the threshing was completed, the men engaged in the process would all go to the kitchen, where a huge, delicious meal had been prepared for them.

After an appropriate time with dinner, it was often the case where a second farm was visited for a repeat of the threshing procedure there, into evening if necessary.

So it was very important the men were fueled for the second part of the day's work.

The part of this story that I personally am still emotionally pained by, silly as that may be, is that the last time we here, on our farm, ever went through the threshing day experience, the usual expected dinner was a total disaster, sending a group of politely resentful farmers away to the next threshing event hungry, facing a hard afternoon's work, with no sustenance.

Sadly the gossips had a field day handed them.

Here is what actually happened.

Our mother, emigrated from the Ukraine, never really having learned American cooking and meal preparation, besides not having adequate dishes, silverware, or even space for a large number of diners, along with inadequate food preparation facilities, in just having a coal stove, and so on, just couldn't be expected to provide such a meal for a considerable number of people.

Facing this, I and sister Stella, age 11 1/2, took on the responsibility for providing the dinner.

Being woefully untrained, near completely ignorant of foodstuff required, in addition to simply not having either the food on hand or the ability or funds to acquire such, we made do with whatever we had, which was scant at best.

I only remember bits and pieces of the fare we had prepared and set out, and will not enumerate such in pure embarrassment, but what I will say is that just a few of the men came in, looked, shook their heads, mumbled no thanks and politely left. Not many even approached, while Stella and I stood and watched, dejected, until they were all gone.

The picture of them heading up the road is seared into my psyche, is as clear now as it was then, of them leaving.

The bright side of this story is that, at least, our hogs got a good meal out of all of this, certainly meeting their standards.

Growing Up - Plantar Fascia

Being an active, energetic kid, I was somewhat prone to minor accidents, carelessness and stupidity being a common factor in most cases.

Summer, of course, was when we prepared the hay for winter consumption by our horse and cows.

We, firmly entrenched well below what today's description of poor would be, the poverty line, the only means of processing the grass, hay, was by hand.

First, cutting the grass was with a scythe, back breaking work, then turning it over for better drying was with a crude, heavy, homemade rake, and after several turnings, rake it into a winrow with the homemade rake, then load it into a wagon with a three-pronged fork for transport to the barn.

That day, the hay was in a winrow, ready for loading, when I, every playful, thought that using the fork as a pole in vaulting over the winrow would be fun.

So I ran toward the winrow, fork in hand, jammed the fork into the ground expecting to be propelled over the top.

As luck would have it though, the fork hit a flat stone that tore it out of my hands and it went flying up into the air, with one of the tines coming down precisely into one of my heels, into the plantar fascia.

I went down hard, in intense pain.

Being alone at the site at the time, unable to get up, I crawled all the way to the house on my hands and knees.

I spent the rest of that summer hobbling around healing, not of much use to anyone, including myself.

No medical treatment was available or attempted, I had to trust only time to heal me, and after what seemed like forever, it did.

Did I say stupidity, somewhere?

Charlie - Puppy Love
Sixth Grade

I clearly recall it being in the sixth grade, when the fifth and sixth grade teachers were doing some kind of a teaching experiment, combining the two grades into one classroom to expedite the program.

For some reason, the chairs were pushed together in double rows for this class, probably necessary to correctly carry out the terms required by the program.

My good fortune was that the cutest girl in the fifth grade, Anna M. was, by alphabetical order dictate, placed right next to me, with our arms naturally touching much of the time, as the teachers droned on.

This went on for several weeks, one day a week.

Just enough time to fall in love.

So, on the final day of this experiment, I was chatting with Anna, and I told her she was my favorite, that I liked her.

In response, she coyly leaned over toward me and said I like you, too, right after Jack, Jim, Bill, and Sam.

My heart skyrocketed for just that one brief, electrifying second, and then plummeted, forever.

However, once in a very great while;

I think of her still.

Which remembers better, your heart or your head?

I never saw her again.

My First Puppy

When I was 10, I really really wanted a puppy of my own. Growing up with dogs, usually two nondescript mongrels that were not pets, just conveniences of a sort, kept as a presence to warn us of and drive away intruders of whatever kind, mostly hungry raccoons, groundhogs and possibly a fox looking for a chicken that happened to get left outside the pen overnight.

They spent more of their time, being untied and free to roam, out cruising in the unlimited woods surrounding our house hunting rabbits and rodents, than they did around home on duty, so they were only rarely craving human attention, other than being fed.

They occasionally, stupidly, ran into a skunk, that quickly reminded them why they shouldn't mess with a skunk.

I must have verbalized this intense desire for a puppy frequently enough to have gained the attention of big brother, and as it happened, he went to the local annual fire departments' carnival that summer. While there, circulating he stopped at one stand where, hoping for a prize, you throw a light baseball at a heavily weighted doll, trying to knock it over and down.

It's well known it borders on the impossible to accomplish that, and after several tries he had not.

Anyhow, what he did see was a beautiful little tan and white puppy, a part Cocker Spaniel, eight weeks old. He asked the guy there at the stand if she was for sale, which he said yes, for the price of five dollars, which, in 1945, was a lot of money.

Brother had been working weekends for a local contractor in the white washing business (applying a white lime mixture to stone walls of barn foundations). He did have that much money with him, which he then used to buy the puppy. He brought her home and proudly presented her to me, to my absolute joy and delight, never having had any type of notable gift prior to that tremendous moment.

That Titanic gift ranks as one of the most thoughtful, permanently memorable events in my entire life and will never be forgotten.

I named my adorable puppy Sandi, and spending time with her was pure joy over the years. Sadly, I, growing up and becoming ever more involved in activities away from home in business and other time-consuming ventures, did not allow time or ability to give her the attention she needed and wanted, so she gradually turned wild in the company of the other two free-roaming dogs, and slowly became one of them, more so than being my pet.

By pure life circumstance, we pretty much abandoned each other when I entered into the military in 1955.

She died of old age while I was gone.

God Bless You, my dear, dear puppy.

County Test

At the end of my sixth-grade year, being the official send off from grade school into junior high school designate, a presumably major uptick in the hierarchy of humanity. An all-inclusive test was routinely administered by the county of residence.

This told the world, and yourself, if the first six years of school attendance was fruitful, a serious measurable advance, or a waste of time, for the most part, in my view.

The great test, revered by some, feared by others in anticipation of the truth being shown.

I was one of those revering it, eager to know not only if I had learned anything, but how much I had retained.

The fact that I had started six years earlier, illiterate, language deficient, socially inept, near total ignorance of so many facets of life.

I had become an insatiable reader and thinker.

The great day came, the next to the last day of school as a grade school student. I breezed through the test, all 600 questions.

Finishing quickly, actually first, the teacher had ample time to check the answers. Excitedly I asked how I had fared.

I was very disappointed when she said I had only answered 596 of the questions correctly.

I had expected to hear – all 600.

My reward?

Nothing, absolutely nothing. Silence.

I am still waiting for my letter of commendation, plaque and blue ribbon.

Should I give up hope? It has only been 76 years.

Pittsburgh Field Trip

It was in the sixth grade, springtime, I remember it well.

The great day was here, we're boarding a bus, heading for Pittsburgh on a class field trip.

By vote, we had voted ourselves the title, the sixth-grade bone crushers.

Silly, but we thought it was appropriate.

I had never been any further away from home than Slickville, 7 miles distant, and the prospect of becoming a world traveler was exciting indeed.

Away we went, each side of the bus counting cows, the miles flying by.

The cow count was diminishing rapidly as we approached big town; the number of houses, however, increasing rapidly till it was mostly houses. No cows at all.

Soon, the buildings became more numerous, taller, and wondrous.

First stop, the Carnegie Museum. Dinosaur skeletons and Indian artifacts, Civil War stuff. Then on to the Highland Park Zoo, with all the exotic big cats, desert dwellers, and more.

Then magically, lunch at Isaly's, the most famous ice cream store of all. Pittsburgh's finest restaurant, so we believed. Oh, yeah.

After Isaly's, the Buell Planetarium, for a fabulous sky show, the big and little dippers, the Milky Way, North Star, and of course the Aurora Borealis, the fabulous northern lights.

A truly memorable outing for us country bumpkins.

Dolly and I retraced that journey 50 years later, but it just wasn't the same. Isaly's had not really changed much.

There is a submarine that can be toured now, and a number of new, taller buildings.

And the Parkway.

Bob - Ape

I was still in high school when a radio newscast alerted the public that a fully grown ape had escaped from a local zoo. It cautioned that it could be dangerous, and to remain clear of it, if it was in your proximity.

Shortly after the broadcast, a rumor began circulating at school, that it had been seen entering a wooded area locally, the rumor reaching a fever pitch within a few days.

I dismissed the rumor in general, having better things to do. Like throwing rotten tomatoes and corn onto cars on Route 380, from our favorite perch, high above the roadway.

Bob and I decided to do some Halloweening in the same time frame, and, of all the silly things I could think of, two of my sisters, Ann and Stella, asked if they could go with us, looking for some fun for a change.

Bob and I readily agreed, and we all met at our spot above the highway.

Things went routinely, until one motorist, not particularly happy with having been pelted with several rotten tomatoes onto his fine, new car, screeched to a halt, bailed out and headed for where the projectiles came from.

Observing this, we quickly abandoned the site, running as fast as we could go to the edge of the field we were in, and into the vast woods bordering the field.

We felt quite safe there, since it was very dark, and it appeared that the angry motorist have given up the chase.

Irregardless, we remained very quiet, just in case. Tension was running high because of two girls with us, when we heard a loud SNORT, SNORT directly behind us.

Everything went even more silent momentarily, when suddenly Bob blurted out – APE!

Instant panic! We all forgot about any fear we may have had of an angry motorist and sprang out of the woods, running back toward Bob's house, which was close to our throwing spot.

Halfway, we came to our senses, realizing that deer snort loudly when alarmed.

My two sisters swore off Halloweening forever, then and there.

Gas Wells as a Kid

There were a number of gas wells drilled in close proximity to our house in those years I was 10 to 12.

The guys who worked doing the drilling were always nice to a kid interested in what they were doing, and how it was done.

I watched as the derrick was built, 40 or 50 feet high, with two big pulleys on top to be able to raise and lower the drill steel and water bailer.

There was always a big, gas fired forge for reshaping the drill bits to the correct size.

I spent hours just watching from a bench inside the rig, no shields, no safety precautions, just stay out of the way when things are happening.

Two men with heavy sledges pounding rhythmically on the red-hot drill bit produced a clonk, clonk sound I can easily re-produce and relive. Somewhat haunting, but pleasant.

Changing the bits was downright fascinating. A big engine driving a long belt that created the force to pull the drill steel and bit from the hole would roar to life, pulling them up, up and up, ultimately as much as 4,000 feet at the conclusion of drilling, by a big, really big, rope.

The rumble and the shaking of the whole rig when lowering them back down. Then the bailing process, much easier overall, lifting a much lighter load.

It was more than fun, to me. It was part of my real-life ed-ucation in the real world, useful in some future time and place.

Then, one day, they're gone, just some pipes sticking up out of the ground, and the faint smell of natural gas.

Never to be the same again, it's all mechanized now.

I'II bet there won't be a single person who will remember that they, too, watched this process happen.

I really hope there is.

Loved to Run

Growing up, somehow, I was gifted with a level of energy I will never be able to understand or explain. I loved to run, plain, simple running for no good reason.

After lunch at school, in that time period between finishing eating and the starting bell, many times, weather permitting, I would go out onto the dirt ballfield, and run. Round and round the field. Other kids looked at me like I was nuts. At home, with just mowed hay fields available, I would still run, one end of the field to the other, continuing till tiredness or even exhaustion overcame me.

I have often observed animals, dogs, and deer do this. Why?

Where, oh where, has this energy gone?

Growing Up - Building a Dam

Growing up, I spent a lot of time in and around a beautiful little creek that was nearby, Wolford Run, named after a pioneer family that had settled here early on, so I was told. To say it was little could be a bit of a misnomer, since it would require an Olympic broad jumper to span it and stay dry. I considered it to be just right. Gentle flow most of the time, a powerful force in flood time. A place to play, ice skate in the winter, or deep wading in the summer.

Sadly, it had been and remains highly polluted by early deep mining of the Pittsburgh seam of coal, but on the bright side the recovery has already begun. Slowly, marine life is building. It may take hundreds and hundreds of years, but nature has unlimited time, and eventually it will be completely healed, once again a life-giving entity to all who engage in it.

My brother and l, along with two neighboring boys, Bob and Richard had this silly thing about dams. We were bound and determined to build a dam across Wolford Run.

The creek really was not deep enough anywhere to swim in it, but we thought we could deepen one natural pool by building a dam just below it.

So, we worked, day after day, using feed sacks, filling them with soft material out of the creek bed, carefully placing the sacks in a pattern similar to a brick wall across the stream opening. It worked; the pool was getting deeper. Soon a smaller person could swim a few strokes before bottoming out. Enthusiasm was elevating, we felt sure that soon we will all be able to swim in the pool.

Silly boys, not thinking that nature may have other less glamorous events in the offing. Rain, rain, rain, lots of rain. It happens every year. All that extra water has to go somewhere, the creek rises and rises, filling up to its banks, then spilling out over.

Real dams are carefully engineered for their ability to safely hold back the water that is behind it.

This dam wasn't engineered at all, and when the floodwaters came, the dam simply washed away, all that hard work for nothing.

Oh well, life lesson number _____.

Wait till next year, but next year never came, we grew up. The two older boys discovered other interests - - - girls. I had a business to start or a career to find.

Bullying Me

In fifth grade when the weather wasn't suitable for outdoor activity, we were confined inside our homerooms just studying or socializing in that 15- or 20-minute wait between finishing eating lunch and class to resume.

I, being slight of build and not physically strong, became the target of the clique boys, the object of their derision, and it soon became physical, bullying me, wrestling me to the floor and so on. I became the laughingstock of the class.

I fought back as best I could, but I was just not tough enough to effectively respond. Day after day, the same scenario. I refused to tell on them.

Finally, one day, weary of the whole ongoing activity, I waited for their ringleader to come in and start their fun.

Lunch hour was underway, eating had finished, and here he comes into the room, heading straight for me.

I faced him and said, "You better not start, I'm warning you just this once."

He laughed loudly and said, and then what, while moving toward me threateningly.

As he got close, I reached down, took off my already un-buckled work-style shoe, stood up and smashed his face with the heavy shoe, hard.

He turned and retreated before I could get another shot at him, bursting into tears, holding a badly bleeding nose as he headed for the first-aid room.

To his credit, he let out the story that he had tripped and fallen, causing his injury.

I am sure the truth was revealed to the teacher, but I was never reprimanded.

The bullying ended on that day.

There comes a time.

Jim, Our Horse

Growing up, we were a true one-horse farm, and that horse's name was Jim, and quite a character. Big, black, smart, very likeable.

He shared a rather large pasture with two cows, with a good spring for lots of water, so he had plenty of places to hide, if we needed him anytime.

He must have been able to think, because on days when he would be needed to work, plowing, harrowing, hauling manure or whatever, he would be hard to find, even harder to catch.

The only way we could catch him was to grab him first thing in the morning when feeding him his breakfast.

For some reason, he would only tolerate me riding him when we had to cultivate the corn every year.

We did not have a saddle, and he was wise in discouraging us from riding, just for fun.

Mounting him was tough without a saddle, he was very tall, and when I was able to get on his back, he would head for an apple tree close by with several low hanging branches and try to scrape me off. It didn't work, because I ducked down, hanging on.

Oldest sister, Kay, tried, got on his back somehow, so he bit her, leaving a lifelong scar on her leg, a real beauty. She gave up horseback riding for good.

Brother Andy said he could ride him, I said, let's see you try. Andy got on him, no saddle, of course, Kicked his heels Into Jim's ribs, startling him, and he took off running, hard, made a quick, hard right, dumping Andy onto the ground, and kept on going, never looking back.

Andy warned me not to call him Tex again, and he only limped around for a week or so from the eviction.

Our next-door neighbor, Mazie, had nice garden, and was so proud of the two rows of early sweet corn, already a foot high in mid-May, showing them off to everyone.

Jim thought they were special, too, as he jumped the fence one night, went to visit her garden, and ate every one of the beautiful corn stalks, every single one. She was a true Angel, never complained about it.

Finally, a tractor took over all of his duties, with never a problem finding it when it was needed.

It was a truly sad day, as I stood silently, and watched him being led up the driveway, no longer of any use to anyone. How well do I remember it.

God bless you, Jim.

Dream Horse

I was thirteen, a voracious reader, and had read, somewhere, the secret to getting anything you want is to identify it, focus on it relentlessly, imagine having it, and act as If you already have it, and you will.

At that time, I was in love with Elizabeth Taylor, the famous movie starlet, after watching the movie, National Velvet, and was equally enamored with having a racehorse just like hers, unlike the work horses I grew up with, real clunks.

So, I determined, since I have the secret to manifestation, that I will apply It faithfully, and my dream horse will materialize, for sure.

I had set the date of arrival of the horse as January 13, my birthday. I followed the prescribed process for months, day and night, never forgetting.

The great day finally came, my Birthday, the 13th. I got up early, dressed, left the house without any breakfast, and raced to the horse barn.

What a shock, there was no horse in the stall I had prepared for him. I was heartbroken, disappointed beyond words, how could this be, I had followed all the rules. Or did I? Somewhere, something fell short.

Thankfully, I recovered quickly as youth is want to do.

However, never giving up on the truth of that early reading, I studied the truth, and its application without pause, and eventually gained the knowledge to make it happen.

In order to succeed, double your rate of failure, never, never QUIT.

Hunting Deer – Part 1

It was a given that I would be a deer hunter, born and raised in the woods, deer all around.

Hunting deer was a dominant activity around us, and provided many nutritious meals, at minimal cost, for those willing to suffer through the whole process.

My first hunting began at or about age 12, barely able or big enough to carry the single shot 12-gauge shotgun delegated to me.

With several pumpkin ball shells in my pocket, I tromped about 1/2 mile into the woods to a huge oak tree, my so-called blind.

I climbed up about 20 feet to a big limb, straddled it, sitting quietly, watching for a suitable buck deer.

I sat and sat, soreness creeping in from sitting on the hard limb, unable to shift position because of the round shape.

I wondered how could I shoot anyway, locked into one direction only, sitting, unable to stand up.

It being December, it was cold, getting colder. I did not have a coat able to keep me warm in these temperatures, nor shoes, gloves or hat.

Further, I was getting hungry, having had just a bowl of flake cereal for breakfast.

And it had started to snow, the flakes landing on bare skin, melting, compounding the growing aggravation. I kept trying to convince myself I was having fun, I was part of something big, the first day of legal deer hunting of the year.

To make it worse, all I even saw was chipmunks, cherk, cherk, cherking to each other, irritating me to no end.

I wouldn't call it coming to my senses, because obviously, there was a demonstrated lack of sense just in being in this untenable position, but more like being driven to decide; to get down out of that miserable spot in the tree and go defrost my body and get something to eat.

The next year, and the next year and so on, pretty much duplicating that first stage setting year, varied some, with no edible harvested in any of them.

I had curtailed my hunting, due to both loss of interest, and a developed fear that was, plainly put, what if I got one? Knowing full well the steps needing to be taken after making the kill, all repulsive and disgusting to me. Also, I had a huge workload developing, in other interests.

Nonetheless, my three boys had joined the local sportsmen's club, had been trained, and qualified, in the rules and regulations of hunting, and were demanding we go deer hunting, there being plenty of deer around.

I readily agreed they could go, and due to rules, I had to accompany the younger ones on the hunt.

I was so dedicated to the hunt that I didn't even take a gun, assuring that one of my fears would not become a reality, at least by my hand.

No longer interested in the freeze, defrost, thaw sequence I tolerated growing up, I stipulated that, as long as the house chimney was in view, we would go further into the woods, halting when it was no longer in sight.

Each successive year thereafter, I shortened the distance from the house that I would accept. First year was top of the chimney, second year the gutters on the house, third year top of the foundation, fourth year the kitchen door – from the inside!

They were now old enough to be on their own.

The youngest, Jim, discovered Giant Eagle grocery chain already had plenty of good meat available, minus all the fuss and mess, ready to cook, besides – he had a transmission to repair for a client, the remuneration for the service enabled him to buy a lot of steak.

I am not sure he even cleaned the gun before putting it into its permanent resting place.

Second son, Steve, actually went on, becoming an accomplished hunter, and excellent long-distance shooter, hunting locally and later gravitating out into the far West, lining his sports room with numerous rack mounts, creating a real lineup for, as he puts it, the eventual yard sale his daughter will be having.

Daughter Cindy went deer hunting just once.

A male friend had convinced her it would be great fun, a memorable experience.

It was memorable all right.

The great day arrives! Early, very early, I load her into my pickup and away we go.

She, already miserable with a fresh cold, arrives at the crack of dawn at the prearranged hunting spot with the others, bundled up in layers and layers of warm clothes, warm boots, warm parka, ready to confront the tundra, the Arctic Circle itself. Her father's heavy high-powered rifle firmly clutched in hand, dreading the moment she may have to fire it, ready to go!

8 inches of fresh snow had fallen overnight, wind was picking up sharply, the temperature already at dangerous depths, dropping, enthusiasm diminishing rapidly.

I believe she was a full 200 yards away from the vehicle when she discovered she was already half frozen, exhausted from wading through the deep snow, increasingly miserable from the cold, and wondering, what in heaven's name am I doing out here? It flashed in her mind – I'm having fun!

Apparently, having had her fill of this kind of fun already, she came back to the truck, permanently uninspired, and said let's go home, abandoning deer hunting then and there, forever.

Never to return again.

Finally, the first son, John, against what little better judgment I still possessed, convinced me to take him hunting up in Potter County, where the trophy buck were plentiful.

John ultimately became a great salesman later in life. He could sell Eskimos front row tickets to the next Aurora Borealis sky show at the North Pole.

Anyhow, it was just a short jaunt, according to him. It was, leave early, very early one morning, drive a mere 130 miles in the dark to Potter County, arriving by daybreak.

I had secretly planned a short hunt, of about 2 miles start to finish, not far at all, for most avid hunters, a couple hours, at most, tramping slowly through the woods, watching, and listening carefully, for the arrival of the big one, the trophy to be.

The area was all on state game lands, open to all.

Knowing the general area fairly well from previous trips there, I was confident my plan could be executed easily, without any undue issue.

The plan was, essentially, I marked a spot along the main road we use to travel there, with several feet of bright orange surveyor's ribbon, where I planned to emerge from the woods, that being the designated endpoint of the hunt.

Watching my odometer carefully, I then traveled south a short distance on the main road to an existing dirt road, noting the mileage, then I turned left, east, onto that road for about 2 miles, then turning north, running parallel to the main road, going the same distance north, the exact reverse of my previously southerly move on the main road, and looked for a spot to park.

Reiterating the plan for the hunt, it was quite simple.

Mark the endpoint along the main road, go south a short-measured distance, turn left, go about 2 miles, turn left again, travel north the same distance as had been traveled south initially, to a point, then presumably in a direct line west, for the 2 miles or so back to the marked end point.

Then walk the four or so miles back to the vehicle, an easy hike in cool weather for two strong men.

So, we're parked, ready to hunt. Look out, big deer, here we come! We climbed up to a steep bank off the road for about 30 feet, then set off, heading west towards the marked ending point.

For whatever it's worth let's understand; I was a somewhat experienced land surveyor, confident, maybe overconfident that my instinctive inner abilities would easily guide me to our destination, so I did not feel a compass would be necessary, and off we went.

It had started to snow, and was ever more gloomy, ominous.

Away we went, with less than exuberant enthusiasm, time passing quickly.

We tramped and we tramped, even picking up our pace as we went, lunch time now behind us, and still no endpoint marker, no main road sounds. How long should it take to walk two miles?

On and on we went, no longer watching carefully for the non-existent trophy buck, just looking for the marked ending spot, then the now long hike back to the vehicle.

Finally, we heard the sound of a passing vehicle, soon, hopefully, we would be at the end of this miserable hunt. Relief, it's getting late, the snow is still falling lightly, getting darker by the minute.

Arriving at the top of a road bank, and looking down, what did we see?

Our own parked vehicle! Praise the Lord!

What we had actually done, was to walk a huge circle without realizing it, and had returned, precisely, to our parked vehicle.

That was my last deer hunt, ever!

Being lost in the woods, in the snow, on a winter night was not my idea of having fun. Plus, having to live with the decision, in fun of course, by those knowing me, was not necessarily a happy outlook.

I don't remember cleaning my gun, either.

Have I ever mentioned Guardian Angels?

Anywhere?

Inveterate Dreamer

From an early age —was the inveterate dream endlessly aspiring development of some new venture, or becoming a competitor to an existing establishment.

At or about the age of 13, inspired by, and adopting a slightly revised version of the cliché written by Henry Wadsworth Longfellow; great heights reached, and great heights kept, are not attained by sudden flight, but men, while their companions slept, toiled onward, upward, through the night. —fearlessly charged into that arena, ultimately embarking into at least 40 different undertakings, some of which were successful and remain operational, some successful and intentionally concluded in one form or another, and others terminated in due time by, or for, various pertinent reasons.

Being naturally aggressive and progressive, by age 13 I was already a somewhat capable vehicle and equipment operator, and I was already driving our 37 Chevy pickup all around, including local towns up to 20 miles distant.

Summer Work

Summer work at a neighbor's farm operating a mid-sized tractor, a Farmall H, pulling a grain combine, doing custom combining for nearby farmers, traveling as necessary on any public road. Local police were few and far between those days, and state police were rarely seen.

Traffic was sparse. Along with the combine I often operated a single row corn picker. Those two machines were extremely dangerous, with multiple unguarded moving belts, chains, and pulleys, which, combined with stupidity and carelessness, would readily contribute to missing fingers, hands, and even arms.

That career ended early on after a blow up caused by my having harvested a sizable area of a farmer's field with an inexperienced helper whose job is to make sure the combined grain ends up in an empty sack he puts onto a chute, then change out the filled sack for a new one. Well, he didn't realize that a cleanout door had inadvertently fallen open, allowing a considerable amount of grain to pour out onto the ground in a long streak instead of going into a sack.

Needless to say, neither the Farmer, nor my employer were totally happy about the event. So much for another career, but fortunately I already had a budding new career in mind, much less dangerous, and much more promising.

Work Cheap

Having been born and raised in abject poverty in the height of the '29 Depression, I had no parental assistance in the pursuit of success, whatever that was. One really weird practice I did learn, by default, was that I was unworthy, that my time and effort should be given away, and the value of that was minimal. In scanning back through the years, I recall mostly refusing payment for many of the services I rendered, or accepted token pay only.

An example of this involved my farmer neighbor, Jim. In my thirteenth year, I often worked on his farm weekends, and also much of the summer making hay, riding on his combine sacking grain, and so on. I was not paid at all during the summer, but school time was looming, and it was time to square up.

Typically, I refused to set a value, so he did. He gave me the princely sum of two, yes two, dollars. Worse, I accepted it without any complaint. There are numerous other examples I could relate, but it would take hours and reams of paper. It may well reside in the Ukrainian DNA, as I have heard other Ukrainians say they can't understand their penchant to give away everything.

Fortunately, this belief was dispelled in great part through the passing of time, but it still showed up in cases of Human hardship when I was not paid for my work, and yet, in 60+ years, I have never sued anyone, or placed a lien against anyone's property.

I have said it many times: Often, it appears that I 'm losing, but somehow, I keep winning.

Growing Up - Bob and Smokey

One Sunday morning Bob, Ken and I met for another day of adventure. So we set off for a visit to a recently opened surface mining operation not far from home. Ken had recently observed his uncle removing stumps from a lot he was clearing for a future house, by blasting with ordinary dynamite, and had been shown how to trigger a blast in the usual manner, using an electrical blasting cap Inserted into a stick of dynamite and set off with a common size D flashlight battery.

So, we get to the strip mine, that Sunday morning, finding no one present on site, we look for and find the magazine, the dynamite storage box, which we promptly broke into, and took a number of blasting caps and sticks of dynamite, and went our merry way to a common playground where we often played ball.

It may be of some humorous interest to know the ball field was located on a sparsely traveled state highway, with the catcher, home plate, pitcher and second base all located on the center of the roadway, first base was as far into a bordering wooded area as possible, third base was in a homeowner's lawn. It worked for years, till we all grew up.

At the playground, we went to a nearby home; the owner, who just happened to be an experienced coal miner, recognized what was sticking out of our pockets: live dynamite and caps in the same pocket of Ken's coat! He couldn't get us out of there fast enough, making up a story that they were just leaving for a visit somewhere, and that we should leave – post haste!

We left and headed for an isolated area deep in a nearby valley to play with the explosives.

We would break an 8-inch stick in half, insert a cap into a punched hole, place the set into a low spot in a small creek nearby, hide behind a log lying on the ground, and trigger the blast.

It was fun. There were no local police at that time. State Police were 25 miles away, and weren't called for mere noises, so we had free run. We played for quite some time, till we ran out of toys.

The only ones who really recognized what was going on and informed our parents the next day were several coal miners in the small town of Tinsmill, three air miles away. Our parents just shrugged it off, boys will be boys.

There were no consequences whatsoever. We were regarded as somewhat like Tom Sawyer and Huckelberry Finn by our peers, once they learned what actually had been done.

So much for what could have caused juvenile correction center number one for three boys.

Maple Syrup Rock Growing Up

It was early autumn, a pleasant sunny Sunday, when Bob, Smokey and I set off on foot for what was known as maple syrup rock, some four air miles and six miles by roads from home, for a day of fun in the woods. No one in their right mind would do this, but we did, easily qualified.

Maple syrup rock is a huge rock protruding out of the side of a somewhat steep slope, providing a sizable open area of suitable height and width to allow various activities to go on underneath it there, sheltered from the elements.

It is located in an area dominated by sugar maple trees, its namesake allegedly having had maple syrup processed there decades ago.

We hiked the 4-mile route shortcutting in part through dark woods in daylight, and with typical youthful energy, tramped around exploring, fishing up and down a small creek there for hours.

We even tried cooking several small fish over an open campfire, total of about an ounce each. That amounted to the total of lunch and dinner and to say it was barely edible, is not really the truth.

Such as dinner was, being distracted, we were not really paying attention to the sun's inevitable descent, and daylight beginning to fade, ever so slowly.

Finally coming to our senses, we acknowledged that it was past time we should head home, a long way off.

With rapidly diminishing daylight it was clear we could not use the shortcut through the heavily timbered woods, we now faced a 6-mile hike by roads to get back home, mostly in total darkness.

Hunger and thirst soon reared their ugly being, becoming an issue, as we had eaten only breakfast, no lunch and the joke of a dinner that yielded no measurable nutritional value. Vigorous activity all day had drained us of just about all of our energy reserve.

And so, energy severely lacking, hunger pangs building, thirst an ever-demanding factor, and growing. Off we go, now silent, dreading the immediate future.

The first mile was practically all downhill, some very steep, so not much energy was expended, except retarding gravity's downhill push to a limited extent.

The second mile was mostly uphill, the rest alternated up, then down, endlessly, or so it appeared.

Extreme hunger, thirst and tiredness with near total absence of energy remaining, sheer will only was forcing the feet to move forward, the body screaming for me to stop, yet that is not an option. Still have miles to go, push on.

When we finally arrived at Smokey's home, some two miles yet to go for me and Bob, we paused just long enough to ask his father if he would drive us home. He flat out said no…end of discussion. Our respect for him dimmed at that point, sadly.

Incidentally, for reasons unknown, he died not much longer afterward, at age 47. God bless his soul.

And on we trudged, step after excruciating step, and as a self-proclaimed philosopher, me, has often said since, "nothing lasts forever." And it didn't, we finally made it home, just a bit wiser, so you may think.

As you age you will learn, you're never smart enough.

The next time I visited maple syrup rock was 63 years later, when, as a professional land surveyor, I surveyed a tract for a client that included the big rock within it.

It had never changed.

Did anyone expect it to?

Here, Why

Sometimes when I am in a reflective mood, I wonder:

What is life all about. Who put me here, and equally important, why?

Do we own anything, or is it all borrowed, to be returned, sooner or later.

Growing Up - Posts on the Road

When Halloween time came, Bob and I would go out on warm evenings to do what boys did those days, at least, more questionably innovative boys.

Many years later, I still shudder when I recall two of the most dangerous, incredibly stupid things we did.

It was a long a well-traveled state highway Route 380, there happened to be a pile of posts a local farmer was preparing for a coal mine. These posts were 4 feet long, 6 to 8 inches in diameter, and are routinely used as roof support underground.

Coincidentally, the pile was located on a curve in the road, limiting site distance for oncoming vehicles.

Well, what we did was to take five of these posts, wait till there was no traffic, then string them across the entire width of the paving. We thought it was funny to hear the screech of the tires as the frantic driver was trying to stop without hitting them.

There being only limited traffic those days after dark, and only by the grace of God did some poor soul not smash into that barrier, inflicting very serious harm to occupants or vehicles. The driver would stop, throw the posts aside, and drive on. We would then reload what I now view as the potential deathtrap and wait for the next unsuspecting motorist to come along. Since it was hard work reloading the barrier, it was not repeated, and the posts cleared away.

The other dangerous so-called trick we did was to go to an area where a farmer had built shocks out of field corn, done to dry the ears of corn before husking and taking them to a crib for storage prior to sale.

These shocks were commonly about 2 to 3 feet in diameter, 8 to 9 feet in height, weighing in at about a hundred pounds.

We would drag five or six of these shocks to the nearby road, build a corn shock wall across it, hide, and wait. The wall being much more visible gave the motorist more time to see it, then stop, so it was nowhere near the fun, ending that deadly game sooner.

Once again by the Grace of God alone, no one was ever injured. Cold weather came, and the awful game ended.

No one is more aware than I of the mindless, senseless motivator compelling two generally decent young boys to expose an innocent traveling public to this wholly unacceptable behavior.

Somewhere in these stories is a reference to my being close to a career in juvenile detention center, which either of these actions could easily have made that nightmare come true, and well deserved.

Growing Up - Cornstalk on Car

In the Halloweening season, Bob and I would occasionally station ourselves in what was an old fruit orchard, along with a large garden Bob's parents maintained there, providing us with plenty of ammunition to throw at passing cars. We had the clear advantage, the spot was at the top of a highway cut of Route 380, some 40 feet straight up to our throwing point.

We had become a bit bored with throwing just rotten tomatoes and cabbage, and looked for a more exciting cannonball, so to speak.

We found it in the form of a large corn stalk, cut off about 18 inches above the root ball corn commonly has. Pulling it out of the ground, earth clinging to the roots, weighing about 3 pounds made a perfect projectile.

So, I waited for the next vehicle, and being well practiced at the timing necessary, I threw it in the most perfect arch, slamming down directly on the vehicles hood with a loud Bam!

We thought it was really funny, but the vehicle operator didn't. He slammed on the brakes, parked quickly, and being obviously very athletic, started a run up the steep bank, with fire in his eyes, I believe.

The decision for us was easy. Get out of Dodge as fast as you can or face the consequences. We both being quite fleet of foot put considerable distance between a very angry man and ourselves, with no pause being planned anytime soon by us.

Seeing our rapidly disappearing forms apparently discouraged him, and he was probably tired by the steep climb, so the chase was over, or so we thought.

Being blessed with at least a little bit of common sense, and a little self-serving wariness, we began the return to our original place, but circumventing the direct route, going in a wide circle instead.

Sure enough, there he was, club in hand, waiting to see if we would come back. He was to our West, we quietly and quickly headed East, done with Halloweening for the night, going home the long way around.

I don't know how much damage was done to his car, but that was the last time we ever went out Halloweening again.

Andy Carving

I Like to go for walks in our beautiful woods, a fairly large area, well over a hundred acres. I often retrace where our cows used to travel to and from their barn to grazing areas, silently reminiscing ancient events, calves born in some remote part, floods, fixing old, barbed wire fences, tree to tree. Activities of so many years ago.

Spotting an old Beech tree, smooth gray bark, straight, fully round, I drifted over to it.

There, plainly visible, not really marred by the passing of time, was the inscription. I photographed it.

"Andy K 3-20-41"

That sent me back in my own history, I was probably with him at the time of the carving, just 6 years old, 81 years ago. The big war was raging, somewhere, far away.

What did the future hold, for us, who could know.

It's in these stories.

Camping Out Bob

Bob, having been born and raised to the age of 10 or so in the big city, had never been camping.

So, one day we agreed to do so, in a patch of woods fairly close to my home.

I instructed him what to bring, a bit of food for supper, a flashlight, blanket, and pillow, pretty much summing it up.

I would provide a large sack to carry his and my gear to the campsite. We left everything on the porch of my home, and went to do some target shooting.

So, returning, we headed for the campsite, which was located up on the hill above the house. Bob had grabbed the sack containing our stuff, and away we went, up the fairly steep hill.

Stopping several times in the climb, Bob would always say, boy, this sack sure is heavy. It's like it's full of rocks. Keep on going, we finally made it to the designated camping spot.

Preparing to set up the tent, we unloaded the sack, and when reaching the bottom, guess what we found.

Yes, rocks.

Brother Andy, ever the practical joker, had filled the bottom of the sack with rocks while we were away target shooting.

We laughed about Bob's comment, "it feels like this sack is full of rocks" for years.

It was. Boys will be boys.

Camping Out Smokey

I did a lot of camping growing up, most of the time alone, but not always.

One day, Smokey and I decided to go camping. We went that same evening to a small hemlock cluster not far away, a beautiful setting, near a small stream, and all. It was a clear day, warm in the evening, and the freedom of youth was all a glorious part of it.

We go through the usual motions, fish a little, climb a tree, make up a fire pit, cook supper (heat up a can of baked beans), put up a tent, (a piece of old canvas.)

Supper over, we simply throw the un-eaten remains into the fire pit, and go about other business before turning in.

There's time to talk about our future dreams, girls, and so on, sleep finally taking over.

Sometime during the night we're awakened by the sound outside at the fire pit, now cold, being kicked apart. Raccoons were common in our area, and being full-time scavengers, we were unconcerned as to them searching out a little food, so we went back to sleep.

Awakening and rising in the morning, we had quite a surprise waiting.

Not only was the fire pit torn apart, but there was also a gift waiting. A pile of bear dung just a few feet away!

That ended any more camping there for us.

A few years later the beautiful hemlock grove was cut for timber.

Relax. In 100 years or so it will have recovered, and maybe a couple of young boys will camp there again.

There may even be a bear visit them in the night.

Lawn Care

My initial entrance into the business world was by way of a simple verbal agreement with several nearby homeowners to provide periodic lawn and grounds care, mostly mowing, trimming, and storm cleanup.

The process was simple enough; walk a mile or two to the site, retrieve the push (you provide the push) mower and go. Watch where you're going kid no skips. Powered mowers were not yet commonplace, dependable, or affordable.

In spring and early summer when the grass was thick, you earned that dollar or two. Late summer and early autumn when the grass was sparse, it was a breeze. Mowing season was about over, see you in the spring.

Unless you found something better.

Crabby wives gave me my first lessons in human resource management. I being the primary resource, they the managers.

The first career attempt ended upon my entrance into activities where higher levels of operative skills, along with higher levels of compensation prevailed.

Farming

The class of '52 yearbook indicates I had high hopes of being a "gentleman farmer".

As it was, that career was already underway prior to graduation, utilizing equipment available at the home farm, in effect a small tractor, a Farmall Super A (16 hp), a single 12-inch plow, a 6 foot harrow, a steel wheeled wagon and a small grain drill. That was it. Other equipment as necessary would be either borrowed or hired.

The home farm, two rented farms, one from a neighbor, and one from an evil, mentally deranged individual which I was not aware or warned of, provided the land in which to plant 10 or so acres of wheat and oats each, and 26 acres of corn, mostly on the mentally ill person's farm.

Inexperienced as I was, I did understand the farming process, but did not realize the total amount of time required, not only with the physical land, but the assembly of everything else involved in the installation of, and then the final disposition of the product.

The other major failing was in not adequately researching actual out-of-pocket cost this great dream would exact immediately, and ongoing.

The preparation of the land to be planted required, in those times, separate functions; plowing, harrowing, sometimes disking (leveling the furrows), and drilling (planting), which, with such limited capacity in the equipment I had, involved many more machine hours I had failed to anticipate, oftentimes working far into the night.

One field, being one full mile in length, took one hour to make a cycle, over and back. At the end of a ten-hour day, I had a strip about twenty feet wide plowed, with one hundred feet of width yet to do, not really much of a visual impact.

The dream, thoroughly calculated on paper by me, the dreamer, to eventually husband hundreds, even thousands of acres, as current farmers actually do, did not quite fit immediate reality – proving how much time is required, especially with small equipment, to accomplish even the minimal target I had set for myself.

God, Guardian Angels, or both must have stepped in one day when the grain drill disconnected itself from the tractor while going up a small grade and rolled backwards several yards, picking up speed. It hit a high spot and stopped suddenly, flipped the tongue completely over and slammed violently to the ground, narrowly missing my father, who was riding on it to make sure it was dropping seed and fertilizer correctly while drilling.

There is a God!

The end result from the wheat crop I planted was my very first real lawsuit (at age 17) when the evil landowner brazenly stole the entire crop right out of the field, then lied to me when I questioned him about the missing wheat.

I subsequently contacted a kindly older attorney (there still are, believe it or not, such good people around) who, seeing an ignorant 17-year-old being taken advantage of, handled the entire case involvement clear through a court judgement in my favor, even delivering a check to me as a settlement for $225.00.

His fee for the whole thing; $25.00.

There is a God!

I realized a net zero or a break even from the planting of the oats and corn, as what didn't get moldy was given away at or near cost to salvage whatever could be, as quickly as possible.

My entire work force – consisting of myself, an elderly (age 72) father and equally elderly mother picked the entire 26 acres of corn by hand, not having access to, or financial ability to hire help, over an 18 consecutive day's span of clear skies.

So much for an agricultural career and being a gentleman farmer.

I've got to find a job!

Friends

Born and raised on a remote farm in the backwoods, I had few friends growing up, and I don't remember much of anything up to the age of four, when some recall surfaced clearly.

My brother vas seven years older, and of course, had his own Interests, not particularly keen on having a full time tag a long pain in the a**.

Four sisters, all older with the same outlook, except Stella, the youngest, who was the closest to being a friend, but natural aging gradually ended that.

A kid my age moved in next door, in fourth grade, and became my best friend for about eight years, but a gradual parting caused a separation, and he left for military service, and now, after over 25 years, there was little, or nothing left.

There was another at the same time, but he, being a bit older than me, soon discovered girls, and was also soon gone.

Fifty years later when he died, I didn't even attend the funeral, never having been in contact even once in the interim.

In grade school, I had just one friend, and that was not until the sixth grade.

He abandoned me on the first day of seventh grade, bluntly. I had another, briefly, in seventh grade, but all he talked about was trapping foxes, a subject which I hated, so I avoided him, and he found other more interesting friends.

I was just a farm kid, not interesting at all.

There was a void until our junior year, when I had changed curricula to Vocational Agriculture, and became friends with a fellow Ukrainian kid. That ended shortly after graduation, when he was killed in a motor vehicle smashup into a pole.

At the end of graduation year, 1952, I found my last best friend of all, Dolly, my wife afterwards, of 59 years, after 5 great warmup years dating.

Then, a brief time was spent with an old acquaintance hunting work out of state; that ended when he joined the Army.

Two years in the U. S. Army, I had a number of understandably temporary friends, none of which endured beyond one or two letters before disappearing forever.

Working at a coal mine, I became friendly with a great guy, Leo, that became my golfing buddy, and other collaborative activities for several years.

I abandoned him when my entrepreneurial beckoning became such that I turned away from friendship in pursuit of them, bound and determined to achieve success levels far above employee subservience.

And I did, but there was a price to be paid. No friends.

There was one, a fellow Ukrainian I met in the coal mine where I was employed when I was the Surveyor.

I met him that day when he was a roof bolter, working alone in an extremely dangerous mine entry.

I was finished with my work for the day and was waiting for a ride outside of the mine, just loafing.

When I saw him in there, I decided to go in to stand guard for him in case something went wrong that he was in risk of. After that, we were friends for life, with him and his great family to this day, after he died of old age.

A good friend I had for some forty or so years and I parted company when a business involvement caused considerable loss to me, financially and emotionally.

I still wish well for him and his great family. We had a good, long-term association, highly beneficial to both.

The following is part of a letter I wrote to my now dear friend in California, a former high school classmate also mentioned elsewhere in the last roundup series.

Dear Joan:

Thank you for the ongoing updates, as you have become an important part of my life, as we went our way toward our ultimate rendezvous with eternity.

In one of my earliest letters when I was reminiscing about our final year in high school, which, in retrospect, was a truly dreamy time, I made the statement that most of the people we were parting from were not really our friends.

You, possessing superior intellect, and emotionally elevated, experienced as did I, a certain inner hunger for some level of connection with our past, which was not then shared with most of our closest comrades, so life went on.

I, like most, still have a small number of acquaintances, all with their own interests and involvements.

Living far apart out here in the wilderness, I have great neighbors, but we do not socialize much with each other, each with our own lives to lead.

A great family can be considered as friends, but they, too, have their own worlds to conquer and cope with, and I am more than happy to stay back and cheer them on, helping if necessary.

And that leaves me alone, with Thor, my wonderful German Shepherd buddy. I am content with this life. He was God's gift to me, one of many, and I am totally grateful.

My Bike and More

About age 11, I desperately wanted a bicycle, and having accumulated six dollars from my lawn mowing services, I let it be known in school that I was in the market for one.

A student several years older than I, had won a two wheeled bike at a raffle, and thereby apparently having no intrinsic value in it, abusing it to the point of minimal worth.

So, he had heard of my desire, and approached me with an offer, it's yours for $10.

I stated simply, I only have six dollars, and he said that'll do it, he knowing what I was buying, but I did not.

The next day he delivered it to the school, I accept it, and on the way home, about 3 miles, the front axle came apart, so I had to nurse the bike home, pushing it about half the distance. I'm off to a great start.

The next day was Saturday, and I, borrowing a dollar from father, replaced the axle, walking 8 miles to and from the hardware store where I purchased it.

Within a few days, the drive chain broke. Another 8-mile hike for chain links. A short while later, the sprocket stripped, then a tire blew out.

I was trading my mowing efforts for parts for the bicycle, but there was a bright side.

I was becoming a half decent mechanic, but with practically no modern tools, it was a real experience.

Then it was fenders falling off, and a new rear brake, so I had just about rebuilt the thing.

My first, but certainly not my last education in the old adage, Caveat Emptor, let the buyer beware.

Oh, what wisdom resides in there, but we just don't adhere to it much of the time.

I finally had rebuilt the bike and could trust it to go long distances.

Going to Scout meetings, Bob, Smokey, and I would saddle up, one on the seat, one on the center tank, and one on the rear carrier, and off we would go, of course with no front headlight or taillight.

Down over one long, steep, winding hill on our dirt road, about a mile, another mile of roller coaster road, and a final half mile steep hill into town on a state highway.

Then a mile of street to the meeting place.

We went to different places, movies, hiking, swimming and so on.

Somehow, we always made it, coming in daylight, going home in the dark.

There was minimal traffic then, though.

Aging, getting older, we reverted back to walking and hitchhiking.

Finally, Bob got his own bike, Smokey being a bit older than us, got a '32 Ford Runabout.

Speaking of the Runabout.

The day he bought it, he proudly picked up Bob and me, saying, boy, this thing really runs, it's really hot. Let's go for a ride, I'll show you.

So, we proceeded, planning to drive about a seven-mile circle back to home, there being a long, very steep hill to climb along the route.

As we approach the bottom of Mercer Hill, as it's known, at a moderate 30 to 40 mph, he blurts out, okay, watch this, as he floors it, and away we go, picking up speed rapidly, almost to the bottom of the hill when there is a loud bang. Looking back, a long streak of black oil is behind us on the road.

We now slowing very quickly, coasting to a stop, pulling off to the side of the road. Dead in the water.

Demonstration over, a connecting rod had come out through the side of the engine block.

We're now back to bicycling or walking.

That ended when Bob's parents bought him a beautiful '36 Ford from a widowed friend.

That ended when an inexperienced driver, him, unfortunately challenged an old law of physics, which is:

No two objects may occupy the same space at the same time.

The '36 Ford was junked, too damaged to repair.

Bop then joined the Air Force, a big win for the Air Force, and remained there for 25 years or so.

I still had my '37 Chevy truck, raggedy or not, it was a dependable ride.

Till I got my brother's '51 Chevy when he was drafted. Smokey found a girl and lived happily ever after, rarely seeing each other thereafter.

Boy Scouts

The year I turned 12, a close friend, Kay, had joined the Avonmore troop of the Boy Scouts of America. He spoke so highly of the group and the activities they were involved in, that I became very desirous of becoming one of them.

No qualifying virtues were required, as I recall, and soon I was officially a Boy Scout, a tenderfoot, the raw recruit.

I was issued an official Boy Scout manual, which I practically memorized, all 200 to 300 pages.

Quickly learning how to tie a few knots in a rope, cut away from your body when whittling, among some other noteworthy training, I soon became a second class scout, now starting to rise in the ranks.

There being time elapse stipulations in the rise, I studied and practiced requirements for the next rank eagerly and faithfully, being more than ready for such testing immediately upon expiration of the time period. Soon I was a first-class scout, setting my sights on the next one, star scout.

The time lapse for that was a bit longer, but applying the same approach, I was well prepared for that test, passing it easily. In the minimum time required, I had gone from tenderfoot to star, not bad.

I loved the whole process; I was a part of something big. Okay, life scout was the next rank on the horizon, considerably tougher.

As I recall I went through all the prerequisites, except lifesaving, having no facilities to train or to test in, so that was delayed, otherwise focusing on what, unknowingly, would become a closely related parallel to my future primary career, land surveying, mapping, compasses, and geodetics.

Time marched on, and I passed the allowable age limit for Boy Scouting, 15, so I never rose to life Scout, or to that most revered rank, Eagle Scout, but not without some regrets.

Stating that I loved scouting is an understatement of no small stature.

First and foremost was the wonderfully kind, knowledgeable scoutmaster, Joe A. and his sons, Joe and Paul, great guys who became friends for life.

He gave meaning to the subject, helped in promotion of my interests, cheerfully participated in activities, and took us to various scouting programs.

One of my fondest dreams and hopes was to be able to attend the annual scout camp, a full week at an organized facility for Boy Scout training and education, along with association with numerous neighboring scout troops.

I will never forget, my oldest sister Catherine, just graduated from high school and recently employed at some menial minimum wage job, granting me the great sum of $13 for the fee to attend the camp that year. It was my dream come true.

It was indeed a magical trip traveling to camp Bucoco, in Butler County, Pennsylvania.

Arriving there in late evening, ominous skies overhead, we disembarked the truck, running between those proverbial raindrops to our designated teepee, settled in just as the serious rain came.

I, having no sleeping bag or any of the usual camping gear, spread my burlap sacks on the flat spring bed as a mattress, not sleeping all that well, but sleeping well enough, often camping out, I always slept on the ground.

My patrol guide, having noticed that I had no mattress, found me a straw tick as one, making sleeping much better afterward.

Rain ending by morning, we assembled early, to begin the week, receiving an agenda outline, which was very exciting to me. Just after a military-style reveille we were served breakfast, the first time I had ever experienced such a thing.

It was somewhat embarrassing though, seeing I was the only one with no scout uniform clothing, but that was nothing new to me.

The next day, we were given the assignment to go out into the woods, find some survival food, and to bring it back to the tent for evaluation.

I, growing up in the woods, often hungry, astonished the evaluators with the high number of foods I found and displayed, teaberry, sassafras root, Indian pipe, berries, and dandelion, to name a few.

I remain grateful to this day for having learned how to swim there, able to swim long distances with ease, safely.

Evening sessions were great, campfire stories and all.

There were numerous other training and recreational experiences that I thoroughly enjoyed sharing with all the other scouts.

A truly memorable week in my magical life.

As with so much in life, time moved on, and so did I.

Butch Riding in Super A

It was spring plowing time, so brother Andy hooked up the plow to the Farmall tractor.

And off they would go, to continue plowing the rented field I had started the day before.

The very field that in the future would have the house I live in located on it.

Tagging along with Andy is Butch, father's dog, a combination breed pup, small to mid-sized, about 50 pounds, pleasant demeanor, exploring the terrain, minding his own business, enjoying the outing.

So, Andy arriving at the east end of the field, drops the plow into the ground, and heads west, it being 1500 feet to the other end.

At the west end of the field the owner, Paul W is working, clearing some small brush, accompanied by his dog, a big, mean boxer laying near him, casually watching.

As Andy is proceeding west, Butch gets ahead of the tractor by about 50 yards or so, when the boxer spots him, and in turn he spots the boxer, who is now charging at him, full speed ahead.

Butch, survival now the top priority, turns and races flat out toward the tractor, which is still moving towards him.

The boxer is closing fast on Butch, and just as he reaches him, Butch reaches the tractor, making one desperate leap, landing up on Andy's lap, safely settling there, and on the floor space of the tractor where the operator's feet reside.

The boxer, now frustrated, gives up on the chase and returns to his sentry position near his owner.

Brother comes to the west end of the field, turns the tractor around, heads east, back to his starting point, Butch riding along, staying on his lap for about 100 yards, that appearing to be a safe distance out of the boxer's sight, then jumps off the tractor and resumes his normal sniffing around.

Following the tractor to the east and, surprisingly, continues to follow back towards the west, in the next round.

They continue on traveling west till once more, they are within 100 yards or less, when the boxer sees them, and is once again charging.

Butch sees the boxer coming, signals Andy that he wants back onto the tractor, and jumps on, settles into a comfortable position between Andy's feet, seated on the tractor's floor, and waits, the boxer arriving a few seconds later.

The boxer, frustrated, now circling, as Butch, nose up in the air, arrogantly rides past, out of reach, heading back east.

Less than 100 yards away, though, Butch again signals he wants off, repeating this same cycle several times before Paul and the boxer leave.

Butch lived about 12 years, much of that in father's shanty.

Puppy Love - Dottie J

Eighth grade. One beautiful, bitterly cold winter Saturday morning, Bob, Smokey, and I met, and headed for the Kiskiminetas river at Edmon, PA, 4 miles away, to go ice skating, the river having frozen over in the past few weeks.

An established spot, the ice known to be at least a foot thick, we were comfortable being there.

Especially since there were already three or four girls there, all in our age group.

Uninvited and unintroduced, we joined in with them, participating in their games, whatever they were. Thoroughly enjoying ourselves in such enchanting company, especially Dottie, who seemed to be staying close to me.

It was one of the most enjoyable days, ever, and I was in love again, this time with Dottie.

The following Monday, back in school, I had another conversation with a classmate, Eloise, another Edmon citizen, asking her for some details regarding Dottie.

I learned Dottie was attending another school but would be coming to Bell Township in the following autumn, into our ninth grade, our freshman year.

I asked her if she would pass a note from me to Dottie, they living close to each other, and she agreed to become our mail correspondent, taking my note.

Shortly after, Eloise delivered a note in return from Dottie, and so began an ongoing exchange of notes for the remainder of our eighth-grade year.

No contact of any kind was made during the ensuing summer, why I do not know.

The first day of school, ninth grade, I am there, Dottie's there, but no move was made by either of us, none. No contact at all, why not, I don't know, not even a hello, as I reached back in my mind.

We were in the same class for the next four years, with only a distant friendship association, no more.

At graduation, there were no parting gestures of any kind, by either of us.

Fast forward 50 years, to our class reunion.

I am there, with my wife. Dottie's there, with her husband.

Neither acknowledgement nor interaction of any kind was made at the reunion.

Several weeks later, I received a short, to the point, letter from Dottie.

It said, dear Chuck, I've always wondered, why did we not ever follow up on our first meeting, all those wonderful notes we passed to each other, how I looked forward to meeting you at the beginning of the ninth-grade year. Were we just too young?

I responded, dear Dottie, my firm belief is that yes, we were not only too young, but too immature and shy to know what the correct approach should have been.

For that to have persisted over our entire time in high school is something I have no sensible answer for.

I continued on; I would like to know how life has treated you throughout all these years.

There was no response to my letter.

I have been told her life's experience was somewhat difficult and could have been better.

She died not long afterward.

God bless and keep her, always.

Paul W -- Farmall BN

Our next-door neighbor, Paul W. farmed his entire life with a team of horses, as did all other local farmers, up to the time when gasoline engine powered tractors began taking over the horse's part.

Their many advantages, you only feed the tractor when it Is running, they never need to rest or sleep, accept an unlimited workload, so it was inevitable it was only a matter of time till the horse was returned to its original primary domain, transportation of people in peace, and war.

Paul bought a small tractor, a Farmall BN, capable of handling the various functions in small time farming.

After several weeks of operating it, as needed, he was immensely proud of his choice, openly bragging how well it performed.

One day, he was plowing in a field close by to where a group of us were playing softball, not paying any attention to him.

He, taking a break, stopped near us, soon had all of us standing around, discussing the virtues of the tractor.

He brought up Its versatility and maneuverability, how it could turn on a dime, a common laudatory statement, and said, watch, show you how well it makes a full turnaround.

As was the case, the field bordered the township road, and had a 4 or 5-foot drop-off from the field surface to the road surface in that area.

He got onto the BN, powered it up, put it in gear, and away it went, he steering hard to the right, full turn, the tractor not responding to the right, the field edge getting close, fast.

The BN, having twin front wheels, was unable to resist the hard forward thrust, was unable to make the turn, just sliding forward in a straight line, going over the edge of the field, down the drop off, landing on its side, partly on the road partly still on the field when it stopped, rear wheels off the ground, up in the air.

He thrown off the tractor onto the road, was not injured, but thoroughly embarrassed, jumped up and said: don't nobody laugh, I'm warning you, and left to go get the horses to pull it upright.

We didn't laugh much, then, but we have ever since.

The Steps

We attended both Grade and High School in the little town Of Salina, a nice school in a nice town, reminiscent of the words in an old song, I love those dear hearts and gentle people, etc.

There was, still is, another small town built by a coal magnate to house miners/ for his coal mine nearby, and an onsite feed mill, powered by dam across Wolford Run.

Measured in a straight line, the distance between the two is just about 2,000 feet, but there's an issue. There Is a 100-foot-deep chasm between them, carved out by Wolford Run over the eons. Sheer cliff on one side, steep slope on the other, 600 or so feet wide.

The school being in Salina, with many kids living in Tinsmill needing schooling, created an obvious problem.

They solved it by building a stairway, all the way across, 300 feet sloping down over the cliff, 200 feet across the level bottom with a foot bridge across Wolford Run, then 300 feet sloping up the steep slope into town.

It was well built, heavy wooden steps that were strong and wide, pipe siderails the whole way.

Some kids hated It, some loved it. Some Of the boys became expert at sliding down the pipes, girls didn't even try. I wonder why.

On a nice Spring or Autumn day, it was fun, a bit adventurous, it was over a thousand steps.

On a snow-covered day, it was downright dangerous, many an injury from slippery, snow-covered boards.

The steps were abandoned in the late 50's when busing was instituted, ending that last link to the past.

I used them a number of times, mostly when skipping school and seeking adventure, and it was a shortcut from school to home.

4 Leaf Clover

It was the summer of 1951, Mother had a potato garden high on the hill above our house, she, still anchored in survival mode from her childhood, and formative years, when having an ample supply of potatoes was critical, year-round.

I was of little to no help, as she was the expert, I only in the way, as she tended to them day in, day out.

I would go to the patch and just be company, as it was a bit isolated, well away from the house.

One day, I noticed a 4-leaf clover growing in a clump of red top, so I marked it with a stake to protect it.

Returning fairly often to the garden to be with her, I watched the plant grow, new stems from 4 leaves I first found, to 5 leaves, then to additional stems with 6, then 7, then 8 and finally to 9, a real life 9 leaf clover, all growing from one clump.

Time had passed through to September, when, as nature dictates, they started dying off, one by one, till, finally, the ninth one was gone, too.

Even now, years and years later, 71 to be exact, I still experience just a bit of melancholy when I rerun that one in a lifetime real life movie through my mind: my mother diligently tending to the winters' food supply, the activity, and of course, watching a simple 4 leaf clover expand out to a nine leaf clover, all in one place.

Was that a record of some sort, I'll never know.

Regardless, it's a nice memory.

Snowstorm – 1950

November 21, 1950 was the so-called Big Snow of Appalachia, and was it ever, was 15 years old, and remember it well.

It was dark and gloomy, started sifting snow ever so lightly, then more seriously, then a steady, relentless dropping, starting to pile up.

Interesting, at first, growing concern as it continued, uneasiness, fear creeping in as it passed levels of 12, 14, 18 inches.

Restless sleep, awakening early, viewing the white cap growing on all of the buildings, including the house, all poorly constructed.

Ominous creaking as the snow load increased, the need to begin pulling or pushing the snow off the roofs to prevent their collapse onto animals, or on people.

The fear of your cows and horse being trapped under a caved in roof, the wide front porch collapsing, trapping us inside.

Snow removal is a must, but ill equipped to do so, still snowing or not. Finally, it stops.

Go measure it with a yardstick, find it's 32 inches deep. Wow!

Walking through it is very hard, must get to the barns to tend to the animals.

We're a mile away from an open road, our vehicle buried in snow, unable to move.

Friends living along main roads deliver groceries to a drop point, a mile from home. Carry the goods home, struggling through the deep snow.

School temporarily closed, but soon we had to walk through the deep stuff to get to the bus, not quite a mile.

Two weeks later, a big bulldozer finally breaks trail from the State Road to the house, helping some, but not that much.

Thankfully, a warm spell, and it quickly melted away.

I remember it like it was yesterday, it was really hard going.

There is a God.

The Salina Bridge

I was a junior in High School, part of a group horsing around, talking, when a friendly argument broke out between a hot-headed kid, and a confirmed daredevil, an idiot.

The argument escalated into a bet that the daredevil, nicknamed Popeye, couldn't ride his bicycle across the top beam of the first arch in the steel superstructure of the bridge between the town of Salina, and the Village of Edmon.

So, away we went, down to the bridge, after school, Popeye riding his bike.

A couple of guys helped get him and his bike up the out sloping beam, then, he was on his own.

The beam is 20 inches wide, and he rode It to the end of the first arch where he could get off, a distance of about 160 feet, while we all held our breath, watching.

He was about 50 or 60 feet off the ground, probable death if he wavered and fell.

It's not something I can say am proud to have witnessed.

He was killed several years later, challenging a dangerous, improperly designed highway curve, in a car.

Have you ever heard of Evil Knievel, the same mind set, apparently.

I think of that every time I cross over that bridge, which Is to be replaced, soon.

Foot note: Popeye claimed if you could ride the painted center line of a State Road, you could ride the 20-inch beam on the bridge.

No, thanks.

Growing Up - Smokey Visit

One Sunday morning, I decided to go and visit my friend, Smokey, who lived about 2 miles distant, not exactly a hop, skip and jump, on foot.

Arriving there, at his home, I found no one there at all.

We rode the same bus to school, so the next day when he boarded the bus and sat down beside me, I immediately bounced him regarding my visit, saying, hey I walked all the way to your house yesterday.

His response, very casually, Was I home?

Life, Victory/Defeat

As a teenager, and into my twenties and thirties, I was a decent pool shot, having some natural ability, along with doing a lot of shooting through the years.

In the Military, stationed in Korea with no fireworks going on, I had a really light work schedule, one 24-hour day on, and nine days off, so I have plenty of time to stay sharp, shooting every day for hours at a time in the Rec Room available to us.

There were days when guys would come in to play eight ball, chalk up their cue sticks, then get to watch me break, run the table, and sit back down to wait for the next opportunity.

Having a good pool table here at home was beneficial, but family, career and other business development soon superseded the expenditure of precious time over play, so the interest and skills soon disappeared.

During the months I spent in Georgia, we threw horseshoes quite a lot, and I got to be a fair, just a fair, thrower.

Nevertheless, I got to thinking I was pretty good because I readily dispatched the other nobodies I played against, so when I heard our Platoon Sergeant was an old, good, thrower, I decided to challenge him to a game. He would smile, and usually say, No, I don't want to embarrass you, and maybe lose a friend, while you are here.

This was the case a number of times, till the time came when I was soon graduating, and told him that, so he finally agreed to play the next Sunday.

Well, Sunday after Church and lunch arrive, and we line up and start. I threw first, one ringer and one point.

He throws, two ringers.

I throw, no ringer, one point.

He throws, two ringers.

Need I go on? He almost skunked me in the first game. He did skunk me, 21 to 0 in the second game, or whatever score skunked is. There was no third game, I conceded defeat, congratulated him not only for his uncanny ability, but his integrity, initially, not embarrassing me right off.

A real man.

There are natural performers in every sport, he was the Roberto Clemente equivalent in Horseshoe Pitch.

Andy Wild Cherries

It was about mid-September, a nice, warm late summer day when my brother, Andy and I connected up our old steel wheeled wagon to the super a tractor and, I am driving, and set out to go to the far southerly corner of our farm, to gather some firewood we had previously cut and stacked.

It was quite warm, and I being shirtless daily all summer, was again bareback.

As we traveled, the track I took just happened to pass under a big wild cherry tree, and it was loaded with ripe wild cherries, which are about the size of a very small marble, and just right for throwing.

As we passed under the tree, he grabbed a sizable branch with numerous ripe cherries on it. He was standing in front of the wagon, doing an effective, moving balancing act, standing upright as we traveled over the uneven terrain, just five or six feet away from me.

Now, having an armload of ammunition, he began throwing the cherries at me, bouncing one after the other off my bare back, and it soon became quite irritating.

So, I turned around facing him, still moving, and said, calmly, stop it. I resumed facing forward, continuing to move at about 5 miles an hour, which in the tractor-wagon world was quite fast, in those days.

Then ponk! A few seconds later, ponk! Another cherry off my bare back. The game continued on as we traveled.

Still moving, I hollered back – stop it, dammit, stop it! Now I am becoming much more irritated. He was laughing, having fun at my expense.

Ponk! Another cherry, this time off the back of my head, not hurting, just aggravating.

This time, I kept moving, but turned fully around and screamed – stop it or else!

He shouted back; or else what?

Moving at 5 miles an hour, I slammed on the brakes, he, totally unexpecting that, did a beautiful nosedive out of the wagon, hitting hard on the ground, just missing the wagon tongue. I had come to a dead stop. He, writhing in pain on the ground, me jumping off the tractor anticipating what was yet to come.

That's when he erupted, and all hell broke loose.

I, anticipating his certain fury, had already bailed off the tractor and, being a very capable distance runner, had quite a bit of space between us by the time he got up and started after me, screaming mayhem in his voice. It was really no contest.

I walked back to the house where, safety in numbers, mother, father, and sisters all present prevented any serious follow up.

He was not seriously injured, mostly just his pride, and drove the tractor and wagon back home, and quietly licked his wounds, physical and egotistical.

Later, after peace was restored, I congratulated him and awarded him a perfect 10 score on his Olympic-worthy dive and promised him a gold medal.

I regret to say, it restarted the war.

Didn't I say we all have a Guardian Angel?

Jim Two Acres of Corn

I believe I was 12, helping a neighboring farmer, Jim, who also worked full-time in a steel mill. He was smart and progressive, saw in me the early inklings of an entrepreneur, said one day, I'm going to help you make a little extra money.

He had a nice little meadow of 2 acres, that he offered me to farm, at no cost, and I accepted.

Using my parent's equipment, the Farmall A, and other necessary equipment, I prepared the field for corn, which he planted for me, again at no cost.

I cultivated and hoed it as necessary, and watched it grow, which thanks to God, there was ample sun and rain that summer, so it resulted in a crop of epic proportion.

I husked at it all by hand, he buying it by the measured bushel basket, me delivering it directly to his crib.

If I recall correctly, I netted close to $500 for my efforts, a colossal sum for a 12-year-old, and a taste of a business world.

Imagining Greatness

As a kid growing up, admittedly silly now from a senior viewpoint, I indulged in all kinds of imaginary involvements, from wondering how I would be Respected if I were King, to gaining world fame in athletic achievement, being a glamorous Hollywood star and so on .

Early on, I thought it might be great if I were a native American as a teen, enjoying a life communing with nature, until I realized how cold a tent would be in the winter and, specifically, how uncomfortable a bed of pine limbs on the ground would be, and that I would have to kill what I would eat.

Then, I thought I'd like a life in the far north, living among the wolves, for whom I have the greatest admiration, panning for gold.

The lifestyle became unacceptable during a stretch of subzero days that I had to spend out in, and the prospect of months of the same was quite convincing and discouraging.

Stay in Pennsylvania, silly, average temperature about 40⊠ F.

I spent a lot of my idle time throwing a ball against the side of the barn, imagining I'm a great baseball pitcher, striking out most of the batters I would ever face, setting unbreakable win-loss records.

Having no money for the real equipment, or facility to play in, I would knock out the bottom of a worn-out canner, mount the remainder on a tree, as a basketball hoop, get a one gallon antifreeze can for a makeshift basketball and there also I would set never to be broken scoring records.

The unhappy truth was that I was never good enough at any of the sports to qualify for even the lowest level of high school participation.

Which, in retrospect, I view as a blessing in disguise, since I've enjoyed a lengthy lifetime completely free of injuries carried over from those arenas.

I was good at ping-pong; being a local champion for years, until my youngest son Jim dethroned me.

Time and life soon replaced all these childhood dreams.

Besides, I had a fortune to make.

Fox Andy Hit

One night, my brother Andy, coming home from work, hit a red fox when he was almost home. Stopping to see if the fox was moving, he saw it was, so he picked it up, and put it into the trunk.

Arriving, he transferred it into the corn crib, it's being secure, in having screen around it, making it scavenger proof.

We fed it daily, watching it recover, slowly, ever so slowly, never eating in anyone's presence, but apparently eating, because the food was always gone in the morning.

Observing it, close up or distant, there was never any movement whatsoever by the fox.

Day after day, the same, recovering, eating, but possibly suffering debilitating injuries invisible externally so we kept on.

After about two months of this same process, we were getting weary of the whole deal, no movement, and no hope whatsoever.

So, we agreed to try something, anything. We put it into a large cardboard box and took it up to the top of a hill, in a hayfield on the farm.

Once there, we opened the top of the box, and no movement – for about 10 seconds!

Suddenly, it exploded, springing up out of the box, and bolted. We're sure it set new world records in the hundred-yard dash, and probably the 400 yard sprint, until it was completely out of sight.

It never looked back, never said thanks.

Andy Selling Falling Aircraft Insurance

We were always thinking of some way to make money, single shot, or career, and quite often were ridiculed for our stupid suggestions.

One day, Andy announced he had found a way he was going to make a lot of money, possibly extending out into a career, in view of the probable expansion of the airline industry.

I, future entrepreneur in the making, eagerly awaited this notable revelation, and when the great moment came, burst out laughing.

Andy proudly announced he going into the Insurance Industry, he was going to sell falling aircraft insurance to homeowners. He said that since more and more airplanes are in the sky, it was a sure thing.

We couldn't stop laughing. What are the odds? This is not a war zone, so, what are the odds of an airplane falling on your house?

I never let him off that one, never.

Note: About 70 or so years later, an airplane did fall onto a house about two air miles from our house.

Andy Sets House on Fire

One evening Andy announced we were going coon hunting. So, he dressed accordingly, helmet and head light, a carbide gas utilizing light used commonly in coal mines, the source of light being an adjustable open flame mounted on a miners' cap, leaving hands free for any other necessary activity.

He lit the flame, adjusted it to some moderate level, and went to the living room where the dog food was kept, to get some feed for the usual pre hunt feeding.

He reached down into the bag several times, filling the bowls, and left, heading for the dogs to feed them.

Shortly after he left, my sister Mary, went into the living room, why I do not know, and suddenly screamed "Fire, Help". What she had discovered was that Andy, with the open flame light, had accidentally set the living room curtains on fire when he reached down for the dog feed.

The flames were already licking against the ceiling when Andy, still close by, heard her screams, came running back, yanked the burning curtains down and stomped the fire out .

I still shudder when I think of the awful future for us if she hadn't gone in there when she did.

Carbon Monoxide

I believe it was in January, when I was about 14, when I found a note for me from my brother Andy, who had gone to work early, riding with a neighbor that day. The note simply said, start the truck around noon today, and run it for a little while.

Not having an open driveway passable for a motor vehicle due to a recent heavy snowfall, with no means to plow it open the '37 Chevy truck was being parked 1/2 mile away from the house, on the public road.

It being very cold, temperature falling that day, the concern was that the truck would not start on the next day if a day was missed its running.

No problem, I thought, I had done it many times before.

Checking the thermometer on my way outside, I mentally recorded that it was 10° below zero, very, very, cold, even for me, accustomed to being outside much of the time in other activities.

I was able to start the Farmall A tractor, and I drove it up through the snow-covered road to the parked truck.

Thankfully, the truck started without much cranking, and I just set the throttle to a reasonable engine rotation speed, turned the heater on, and sat in the cab.

The truck, being quite aged, had already had all its fenders replaced due to rusting, the cab had been patched with sheet metal at the corners, and the floorboards were badly rotted, there having been no serious repairs made there at all, allowing a nearly free flow of air into the cab from below.

After sitting in the warm, running truck for about 15 to 20 minutes, I began to notice I was getting sleepy. Thinking I had sufficiently warmed it, and that I had fulfilled my assignment, I decided to go home.

And I was still very sleepy.

I shut the truck off, and got back onto the tractor, which had no cab, and was wide open to the elements.

Yet, moving in the open air, at 10° below zero, I was still continuing to fall asleep.

Snapping to, I finally realized I had been seriously exposed to carbon monoxide.

How much longer in that cab and I would have become a statistic?

Are there actually Guardian Angels out there?

Anyone?

Charlie - Call of the Wild

There remains within me, some unexplainable appeal to return to the deep mine world, almost akin to the call of the wild within me to join the wolves.

Sandi – Chasing the Ball

Sandi, my first puppy growing up, loved, was addicted to, chasing tennis ball. She would bring me a ball anytime, drop it at my feet, feign running away, return and signal throw it, human; throw it now, over, and over.

There were those times, though, when she would need to defecate, you know, and would move to a spot, stop and assume the correct position, squatting, ready for nature to proceed.

That's when the tennis ball I already had, hidden out of her sight till now, I would quickly throw right past her.

She, prepared for one thing, addicted to the other, would instantly respond to the addiction, and quickly terminate whatever natural function was occurring referred to that as "snapped one off", taking off immediately after the ball.

Catching up to it, she'd grab it, stop, then return to her former spot, stop, reposition, and finish what had been interrupted, holding the ball in her mouth the whole time, bringing it back to me afterwards for another throw.

I miss her still.

Girls in Outhouse

I am aware the telling of this story will be a bit distasteful to some, disgusting to others, but since it happened more times than I care to admit, and being so funny to Andy and I on those occasions, I feel it should be told.

As with so many aspects of life, and enmeshed in poverty, we having no plumbing in the house at all, had the typical, flimsy, poorly constructed, naturally well-ventilated outhouse, located in fairly close proximity to the main house.

In the early years, in summer, when there was no school, no work, minimal occupying interests, we would all be generally around and about the close area near the house, seeing any activity that might present itself.

With four sisters, openly unsympathetic to many of the antics of their dear brothers, especially towards them, who understandably used the outhouse when necessary, but were not adequately diligent in being on guard when in there.

So, on occasion when we would see one or more of the girls go into the outhouse, we would pick up a baseball sized stone, usually readily available, wait until they were well settled in, and then heave the stone sharply against the outhouse door.

The usual result was that there would be a horrendous bang, the door latch usually smashed open, and then a verbal explosion of epic proportion from the unlucky girls in there, screaming at us, which I am somewhat ashamed to admit, that I still find quite amusing in recalling it, he and I being the only ones to find the humor in it.

It wasn't the event being so funny, it was the predictable reaction.

Knowing they weren't capable of retaliation in kind, made it even funnier for us.

Boys will be boys.

Fixing the latch was no big deal. We had plenty of practice.

Andy - Hiding my Bike

My brother, Andy, loved playing tricks on me, seven years his junior, he being the favored son, considered important in the Ukrainian world, I, bringing up the tail end, less than.

I loved riding my bike every chance I got, now fully operational, my having rebuilt it completely. I had space for riding close to the house, where I would park it at the ready, where it was convenient.

This one Saturday, I did my early riding, parked it, and went down to a small creek not far distant to work on a small dam I was constructing.

While I was gone, Andy once again took my bike and hid it, then left for parts unknown.

Returning for lunch, I wanted to ride a little, so I went to my bike's usual resting place.

Once again, no bike. I know he hid it, but where this time? I hunted and hunted, anger and frustration growing by the minute. No bike, no brother to scream at.

Okay, I thought, two can play this game.

So, I untied one of his prized Coon hounds, put a leash on him and took him down to where I was building the dam, well out of sight of his usual box, some distance away.

I tied him to a tree and went back to the house and waited.

Andy, upon returning home, couldn't help but notice his dog was gone, immediately, accosting me, where is my dog?

This time, I'm the one doing the laughing as he approached me.

He screeched at me, where the hell is my dog, I know you put him somewhere.

I screeched back, I don't know, where's my bike.

Now it's no longer a laughing matter, he says, get my dog and you'll get your bike.

I said you first, not trusting him, or it's no deal.

He pointed to the barn and said, in the granary, covered up with straw.

I pointed towards the dam and said, tied to a tree, I needed a watchdog while I worked.

He didn't think that was funny and didn't laugh at my joke, or ever hide my bike again.

Maple Sugar Camp

We were Boy Scouts, and the troop had a campout scheduled at a wooded site called Maple Sugar Camp across the river from Avonmore, on top of what is known as Hicks' Hill, named after a coal baron from the past.

Me, Bob, and Smokey, collectively employing no common sense on an evening indisputably promising heavy rain, set out early, and walked the three miles to Avonmore, then proceeded to the camp site, accessed only from the River side by climbing up the severely steep slope some 300 feet almost straight up, or so it seemed.

Getting up there, we found we were alone; everyone else had the good sense to stay home.

Then the Heavens opened up, and kept their promise of rain, heavy rain.

We're now in the very dark, pouring rain, up on some God forsaken ridge, the path back down a muddy mess, a long, slippery dangerous way down.

We have no alternative, move out, head toward town lights, stumbling, sliding, down to the bottom, to where it is safe.

At that time, there was an abandoned Railroad Station there, inactive.

All three of us are a muddy, soaked mess, a disconnected downspout spewing roof water down, and it being quite warm that night, we took turns standing under it to rinse the mud off ourselves.

Then we headed for town, on the way home, only three miserable miles to go, already dead tired from the activities.

Once into town, got the bright idea that I told Bob and Smokey, let's go into the movie, dry off, then call your Dad to come and get us, since the Campout was cancelled.

That's exactly what came to be, the truth now having been told, as if it mattered to anyone but us.

We paid a dear price for stupidity, didn't we?

Combine at Palko's

I was riding combine for my farmer friend, just having finished one field, traveling toward another, stopping at the barn for lunch.

Lunch over, we saddle up, start out towards the next field, when he, driving the tractor, a Farmall H, realized he'd forgotten something at the barn, so he stopped, and as it was on a fairly steep grade up, setting and locking the brakes, but not stopping the engine, and dismounted, going to the barn, me on the combine just waiting.

Well, he hadn't gone far, maybe halfway to the barn, when for no known reason, the brakes let loose, the whole unit moving backward, ominously, toward the barn, several hundred feet away.

I shouted, Jim, we're moving. Jim whipped around, running back toward the tractor, thankfully timing it exactly right, jumped onto the tractor, corrected a developing jackknife, successfully directing the combine and missing a big tree, then jam on the brakes, stopping just short of the barn.

Then we continued on to the other field, where we worked till dark.

Bull Running Loose

Preparing to combine grain at the Palko farm one morning, the sound of pounding hooves alerted us to the fact their huge breeding bull had escaped from his pen, running free, coming toward where we were at work.

The bull, big, probably 1500 pounds, mean, socially unconcerned, apparently had mayhem in mind, and was approaching us with a menacing look in his eyes.

I climbed up onto the combine, safely out of reach, he homing in on Stanley Palko the owner.

Stanley, knowing he couldn't stop and redirect the bull back to his enclosure on foot, jumped on a fairly big tractor, starting it and confronting the bull with it.

Hesitant, but undeterred he circled around the tractor, viewing the operator instead.

The contest went on, Stanley unsuccessful in herding the bull, the bull unsuccessful at reaching Stanley, a standoff.

The bull had to be re-penned, we just couldn't leave him running loose, so now what?

Well out of the clear blue, here comes their collie dog, running toward the fray.

He, having been kept in the house to prevent his following the tractor and combine till they were gone, was turned loose by Stanley's mother at the house.

The collie immediately took over, aware of the danger presented by the bull, nudging the bull towards his enclosure; circling, barking, threatening, the bull reluctantly responding, moving toward his pen.

Finally, he was in, the gate closed and locked, we on our way, the collie settling down with his reward, a big meaty bone, after being assured that he was a good boy, job well done.

Andy - Threshing Walkers

It was late summer, threshing time locally for small grains, oats and wheat.

As was the usual custom, farmers hired a contractor who owned a threshing machine to come to their farm to separate the grain from the stalk, setting up at the barn, or in some cases, storage sites of the grain to be taken care of, sometimes well out in a distant field.

That day, it was happening next door to my home about a mile away, so I was conscripted to help the threshing, being big enough to throw sheaves into the thresher.

I was assigned a spot inside the barn, and the process began. It was a big barn and being well away from the intake point of the thresher, it required double handling of the sheaves, throwing them as far as I could, to another participant, who would then throw it into the machine, an extremely dusty process.

To compound the dust, where I was spotted had a prior years unthreshed crop, naturally deteriorated, creating an indescribable cloud of fine, abrasive dust.

The dust hanging in the air was overwhelming both to vision and respiratory functions, horribly.

There was no provision whatsoever for dust filtering or eye shielding in those days, so the misery went on, and on, and on, hour after miserable hour until just before dark.

By then I was extremely ill, barely able to come down out of the barn's second level, where I had been all afternoon.

Seeing my brother Andy, I asked him to drive me home, as I was in a desperate condition.

He said no, you can walk, it's only a mile, and besides, I want to stay and visit with the family.

So, I painfully stumbled and staggered my way, first up a long steep hill, and then it was all downhill.

I made my way to within about a quarter of the way before I collapsed, falling along the private part of our roadway.

I was sound asleep when my brother, coming home after the visit, found and awakened me, telling me to get into the pickup truck, and get on home.

Now awake and furious, I told him to go to hell, and I staggered on home.

Thankfully, 12 hours of sleep recovered me with no lasting issues.

High School Spinning Circles

When I was 15, I regularly drove to school in my '37 Chevy pickup, gasoline was only $0.24 a gallon, insurance $22 for six months, a driver's license was required, but absent. No one asked, and no one cared.

An interesting fact about my '37 Chevy, was that the gasoline tank was located directly under the driver/passenger seat, and in order to get gas, refill the tank, the passenger, if any, had to get out of the vehicle, rain or shine, lift up the half seat on that side, and there it was, the gas cap, the hole where you pumped in the gas. You didn't need a gas gauge at all, you could see right into the tank.

I still cringe when I remember that, how extremely dangerous it was.

You wonder what idiot designed that system and what greater idiot approved it.

Anyhow, on nice, dry days after lunch, I would get half a dozen or so of my classmates, also idiots, and drive up to the all dirt ball field, which was situated in full view of the east side of the school, and proceed to spin wild circles around the field, round and round, dust flying everywhere, entertaining not only ourselves, but onlookers in the classrooms on that side.

When school resumed after lunch, we were always there right on time, good little boys.

No repercussions were ever instituted, and I'm not sure why not, even now.

Boys will be, or were, boys.

High School Wet Paper Towels

In high school, I was most closely associated with several other free-spirited thinkers who all cooperated in doing what we called silly, funny things that were not necessarily in agreement with the teachers and administration of the school.

Lunch was one hour, 12 to 1 PM, and there was always ample time left after doing lunch for entertaining ourselves, especially on rainy or snowy days.

We had observed early on that the principal would always eat in the school cafeteria, which was located in the basement, and that in engaging in conversation with fellow diners, teachers, he would be delayed until almost to the end of the lunch hour.

So, we knew when he'd be leaving, exiting up the stairwell at pretty much the same time. Just ahead of that time, we would load up a bunch of paper towels, soak them, and take up watch on the third-floor stairway, visibility being clear to the basement stairs.

A co-conspirator located at the top of the basement stairs would give us a signal when the principal was just starting up the steps, and we would say, bombs away, and drop all of our wet paper towels in his direction, and then, not waiting around to see the results, but putting distance between our drop point and us.

No witness ever squealed on us, and we were never held accountable.

Boys will be boys.

High School Puppy Love

Bell Township had a well-respected home economics class, which, in my senior year had a teacher who simply captivated me.

She was, oh so cute, and the memories of her in that beautiful yellow dress haunt me still, was sooo nice, and she seemed either somewhat attracted to me, or at least amused by me, as I would routinely skip eighth period Study hall to go to the home-ec classroom, make sure she saw me outside the door, and wait till she came out, then spend as much of the days' remaining time visiting with her as possible.

I was in love with her, but in vain, and I knew it. My being 16 then 17 in my senior year, and her being at least 22 created a situation that was a bit untenable, and the relationship was limited to that, and ended upon my graduation.

I never saw her again until, at least 50 years later, when l, as a professional land surveyor, received a call for a property survey, from yes, her.

I responded to the request immediately, my curiosity really aroused, and met her the next day.

My eagerly anticipated rendezvous with her after all those years was somewhat disappointing, inasmuch as she had no recollection whatsoever as to who I was, and to make it worse, had grown a beard and a mustache.

So much for puppy love memories.

High School
Watering the Library

The high school library was administered by a somewhat surly, less than likable teacher, prone to insulting lower-level students for any reason, appearing to enjoy their pain. Eighth-period study hall, she would usually have 30 to 40 students in there since it was the library.

Wishing to brighten her day, we skipped out of the study hall we were assigned to by telling the teacher there a barely partial truth, and away we went to the janitor's closet nearby, it being on the third floor, the same as the library was.

From the janitor's closet, we took a large bucket, filled it mostly full of water, quietly going down the hall to the library with it.

Once there, one guy, on the count of three, quickly opened the door wide. l, with the bucket in hand, heaved the contents into the room, directly at her, in her chair.

He slammed the door shut, and down the stairs we went, not stopping till we were safely outside, innocently picking up trash around the building, engaging in a community service endeavor.

The perfect picture of innocence.

Again, there was no repercussion whatsoever from the administration.

Word circulated later from the students in there that the laughter didn't end till dismissal.

High School Skip Study Hall

In passing through junior high school, years seven through nine were a breeze, gaining for me a reputation of sorts, as a brainiac, with the full expectation of the academically oriented teachers that I would follow the academic course of study on into the final tier of classes 10 11 and 12.

Having acquired, by some, possibly misdirected subconscious prompting to become a gentleman farmer, I had no interest in English literature, foreign languages, I already had one, higher level trig, or calculus, or science since farmers don't use any of them, and as a sophomore I opted to join the vocational group, viewed as the lesser of the two. Just get them through here, into the mills and mines was the general attitude.

The irony is that in fact, they all ultimately played a major role in my professional life, survey, engineering, and all that comes with them, considering I studied none of them.

As it happened, as seniors, we, were reviewing our classroom assignments, discovering that on every Friday, third period, halfway through the morning we had a study hall in Mr. P's room, a nice but tough science teacher, one I knew sometimes ignored certain details, a bit lackadaisical.

So, I said to my two closest confidants, look, let's skip third period Study Hall from day one. That way we won't be on his roster, and he'll never know we are missing. They agreed, and we hid out.

Week after week, Friday after Friday we skipped, sometimes hiding in the furnace room with a cooperative janitor, or out for a ride in the country; I drove my brother's '51 Chevy sedan to school every day, in the school shop or even a washroom.

Finally, it was a February morning, I said, hey guys, maybe we've played the game long enough. Let's get caught and see what happens. They all agreed.

So, we drifted by the principal's office, and of course, we were seen.

He, quickly coming out and inquiring what we were doing, and why we were not in a class somewhere.

I told him where we belonged but did not tell him how long we had been absent from that study hall.

He then triumphantly marched us up to Mr. P's room, and announced to him, I have your skallywags here.

Mr. P. said, incredulously, what skallywags? I've never had them here , are you sure?

Yep, I said.

The kids in the room thought it was hilarious, but the teacher and principal did not, as they were publicly embarrassed at such a thing happening right under their noses.

We, of course, were instant heroes, at least for a couple of days.

Our punishment was that we were put on the roster, and thereafter faithfully attended that study hall until graduation.

Like good little boys.

And here I am, 72 years later, still laughing.

Vocational Ag Class

When I opted to join the vocational agriculture course of study group as a sophomore, I found the perfect atmosphere in which to promote, and portend a life-long tendency to seek and find, the humor in just about anything and everything, much of the time providing myself, and others, with entertainment, but also at times, inviting pain and embarrassment into my own life.

However, it being a subconscious compulsion, I have never attempted to either stifle or discourage what in my view, is a positive attribute, rescuing me from many seriously negative experiences, emotionally, of one form or another through my 8+ decades of involvement in so many different aspects of life, some wildly successful, some dismal failures.

There were 10 of us in the Ag class, with a reasonably personable teacher, and the freedom from the stress demanded by the intellectually challenging academic class study, which I had been targeted for by family, and well-meaning teachers, so we had an opportunity to do silly or even questionable things.

Even though it was never openly expressed, I always sensed an undeserved awe of us, when a class combined us 10 with the other three classes, academic, commercial, and home economics.

I guess we were viewed as the bad boys, the ones who were outlaws of conventional rules and regulations.

Which, in great part, we were.

At a future time in life, Dolly, my wife-to-be, admitted that she had had a reserved fear of me at that time, and when we appeared on the scene she would exit the scene as quickly as possible.

She could not explain to me why. She couldn't know I would ultimately become her life companion, her Guardian Angel.

High School Charles Atlas

Some of our teachers could tolerate a joke, some would not. One who would, Miss R——who couldn't help but laugh at our antics, and did, at whatever we did or even said. She was okay, in our view.

It always seemed that late day class was the most amicable time in delivering the results we wanted, when everyone was ready for some entertaining humor, to fill out the day, including ourselves.

We, always looking for the humor in anything and everything, two of us decided to put on a silly little play for the class, just for the fun of it, not intending it to be funny, just humorous.

This was to be a reenactment of a comic strip advertisement for a catalog physical fitness course, then known as the Charles Atlas muscle building course. That was sold well back in the 40s, and it featured a bully kicking sand onto a very skinny guy in front of his girlfriend.

Fortunately, or unfortunately, I'll never know, we fulfilled the key ingredients of the show, which was our physical structure.

I, at 6'1", weighing in at 120 pounds, fit the scene perfectly, tall, and skinny.

Stush, at 6'2", weighing around 200 pounds and muscular, was the ideal size to be the bully.

Stush would be sure to enter and be seated in the classroom ahead of me by a few minutes, while the teacher is patiently taking and recording the head count.

I would come in last after everyone was seated and start crossing over in front of the class toward my seat, when Stush would jump up and shout loudly, hey, Charlie, your ribs are showing, in an antagonizing manner.

I would react angrily and kick the corner chair hard, proclaiming firmly, that's it! Gosh darn it! I'm tired of having sand kicked in my face! Tired of being laughed at and being called a sissy. I'm going to sign up for the Charles Fatless Muscle Building Course!

I would then go quiet and sit down, restoring order. Not intended to be funny, just amusing.

High School—Farm Show

In my Senior year, I was a member of the PEA, Future Farmers of America, and as such was quite Interested in learning as much as possible about real agriculture, its progress in equipment, methods, crop genetics, and so on.

There being an annual farm show in the State Capitol is a big deal. Its all there on display, with knowledgeable people ready to answer your questions, along with contacts for future inquiry. It went on for a full week, 16 hours a day.

So, I, desiring to attend, and possibly benefit from an extended visit, requested permission from the Principal to be excused from school for 3 days to attend the show.

Not surprisingly, he said no, I will not allow you 3 day's absence for such a questionable excursion.

Undeterred, I, and my 3 confidants, Stush, Herk, and Shasha all agreed to go anyway. That day, I having a vehicle, loaded everyone and away we went, Harrisburg bound, 200 miles away.

The fact was, the educational value of the journey could be summed up, and rated at or about zero, as the entertainment value was much higher, having met some girls there, fellow future farmers of America. Yeah, Sure.

Time marched on, and the inevitable return has to occur. So, we returned four days later, presented our homemade plea for forgiveness: Please excuse Charles for his absence due to his a "constructive career learning" class in Harrisburg, PA, signed by my Father. Yeah, I'm my own Grampa.

The Principal couldn't help but to be amused at what he read, calling it quite innovative, then telling us all we were duly suspended, and demanded our presence at an already arranged school board meeting that evening to look over our case.

Here's where this gets a bit sticky.

Those days, being a very small School district, having less than 400 students, only 3 members made up a quorum for a school board meeting.

Well, it just happened all 3 were close personal friends and neighbors of mine, living in close proximity to my home, having grown up with them.

So, I visited each one of them during that day, presenting my case, and surreptitiously pleading for mercy, which was promised somewhat indirectly, discreetly.

7:00 pm and we, the School Board, Principal, and teachers are all assembled. The meeting starts with a presentation by the Principal, giving the facts, just the facts.

I was up next, pleading our case: how important the attendance at the show was, how much we learned, hopefully benefitting Society in some future time; and worst, or best of all, how we had been promised by our Vocational Ag teacher he would intercede, guaranteeing approval of our absence for the 3 days – which he, in fact, had said.

The meeting remained somewhat civil, and a decision was rendered then and there.

No suspension, get back to school, be good little boys, study hard. We did, we were, thereafter, for a while.

Boys will be boys.

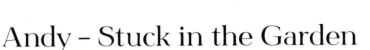

Andy – Stuck in the Garden

The time he was plowing the garden with our Farmall Super A, where the one side of the garden bordered on a steep drop off of about 50 feet into a small creek, and you had to be careful in that area.

He was plowing and stopped, coming over to where I was working and said "I'm stuck, go see if you can get it out."

Here, he had gotten too close to the edge, and one wheel of the tractor had slid down, dangerously close to going into the ravine, and that's where it had stopped.

I, being quite capable, even at age 14, of driving tractors, climbed on, revved it up full throttle, locked the high side brake, let the clutch go, out it popped. I jumped off Without saying a word; and left.

I never did let him live it down. I could be a jerk, too.

Andy – Wagon Pushing

Another time during the harvesting of our wheat crop, the combine had completed its work, and the filled sacks of wheat were piled up, ready for pickup and transport to the granary.

So, we loaded the heavy sacks into the wagon, overloading it, in fact, since the tractor was not really very big and heavy, weighing far less than the combined weight of the wagon and the grain we had piled into it; the path to the barn was quite steep, and I remember cautioning him to be alert to the possibility of the wagon pushing him when he'd lose control entirely, very likely directing him over the edge of a deep chasm at the edge of the field above a creek bed.

He poo-pood my warning, saying he knew what he was doing, and away he Went, starting down the steep grade.

In less than 50 feet of travel, gravity took over with vengeance, pushing him; sliding with ever increasing speed toward the chasm, already totally out of control.

Maybe it's redundant, that I keep mentioning Guardian Angels, but......

For some unexplainable reason, now sliding wildly out of control, he, fearful of trying to bail out, I standing transfixed watching the deadly event happening, the tractor is guided into a soft right, uphill, turnout, completely contrary to the dictates of gravity, up the grade of the field, finally the tractor reaching a level position, and then stopping where he shut off the tractor, set the brakes, got off and said, "It's yours."

He never hauled a load of anything again. I was 15, he was 22.

Andy – Military

November 8, 1951, my brother Andy, was formally drafted into the U. S. Army, boarding a bus in New Kensington, PA.; the first step in his abbreviated military career. The bullets were flying in Korea at the time, so it was not a pleasant outlook for anyone.

I, just 16, a senior in high school, was still too young for the draft. Having ferried him to the pickup point in his almost new '51 Chevy; made the amicable, but less than tearful goodbyes, I now faced the prospect of taking full control of the car, putting me into a somewhat enviable position at school, being the only one in such a situation. Father had never driven, and had neither interest nor control over the vehicle, so I was free to run.

After the aptitude tests were tabulated, Andy was shipped to some base in Hawaii for basic training, and then retained there for advanced Infantry level training, a truly unenviable position.

Now that was a bit disconcerting because the bullets and bombs were really flying in Korea, with the entrance of the Chinese army into the fray, ominously advancing south, the U.S. and ROK Army in full retreat. Making it even worse, he wrote that it rained every day in Hawaii, and it was miserable.

I keep mentioning Guardian Angels, but consider:

In his civilian life just prior to induction, Andy had a brief stint at the construction company he was working for as a timekeeper, giving him the opportunity to be considered for an opening in, of all places, Fort Knox, Kentucky, that being not only back Stateside, as it was close to home, as a purchasing agent and supply Sergeant, a truly cushy permanent assignment.

From that day on, it was fun and frolic for the remainder of his Army involvement, taking full advantage of all the social amenities it had to offer.

He admitted he seriously had considered a six year re-up, but coming to his senses, he knew it most Iikely would not end well, and came home.

In a positive note, the experience he gained there was instrumental in his acquiring a high-level job as a purchasing agent within a progressive construction company, which he made a lifelong career of.

Parting Compliment

It is my firm belief, that when someone is leaving you forever, or if you are leaving someone forever, the greatest compliment you can give them, or the greatest compliment they can give you are the four simple words :

I will miss you.

Don Ankeny

I first met Don in the late sixties, when a farmer friend told me a coal stripper had moved some equipment onto his farm, to mine the remaining coal left from prior stripping during WWII.

That part of the seam is known as the crop coal, as it is what is first seen. The economic value, such as it was, unsaleable due to its heat potential was very low.

He was a beginner, with just one open-type D8 bulldozer, brutally cold in the winter, wet in the rain, along with a small mechanical shovel.

I had just left a good job at the Jamison Coal Company, and was looking for technical work in the coal industry.

Don was very friendly, soft spoken, congenial then, and over the years I knew him as a client and a friend.

I went on to other interests, and did not meet again for several years, when it was becoming known I was able to prepare Mining Permits, and he was successfully expanding his scope of operations.

Through the years, he became a major client, and a major operator, reaching UMW Status for 50+ employees. His production level ranked him very high, among the top producers, top income generators. A long way from the day I first saw him, so long ago.

One day my phone rang, and it was Don, requesting me to meet him the next day at his shop. It being well known I always have a German Shepherd with me, He asked if I would be sure to bring him along. I assured him he would be there with me.

Arriving there, we met, and he said, come on, let's go for a ride, bring the dog, believe it was Bori, my second Shepherd, a friendly pup.

I believe, now, he was taking me on a sentimental journey, revisiting past mining sites, and future new sites that he had purchased recently. We toured a couple of beautiful farms he had purchased, for future playthings in retirement. He was typically soft spoken, almost melancholy in our conversation as we drove along.

Finally, beginning the return trip back to his shop, he said, Charlie, I'm in serious trouble. He went on, I have just gone through an Internal Revenue Service trial, and they've ruled that I owe them almost three million dollars, or they'll take everything I own.

Also, he went on, I got a certified letter from the United Mine Workers Union demanding two and a half million dollars for unpaid assessments. He went on, I told them both if you can find it you can have it. There was a faraway look in his eyes, and he hugged Bori, my German Shepherd, when we parted.

I thanked him for the tour and the visit, and left, wondering. I drove home slowly, a developing sadness as I traveled.

The next day, I was told. Don was found by an early-arriving employee, in his shop, never to mine coal again.

I will never forget him, may he be in peace, forever.

Does anyone know what or who caused this sad ending of a truly fine, fine man?

Maybe.

Water Pipe

The Beaver Run Dam was about complete when I was 18 in 1953, and the pipes to convey the water to be impounded to their future customers were being installed.

The pipe taking water to the North, to the Apollo area, was underway, and as curious teenagers, I and a couple of guys saw the exposed pipe and stopped to take a closer look. I 'm not sure, but believe it was a 36-inch diameter, big enough to crawl in, with effort.

There was a tee there in the line with a cover over it, so we took the cover off and went into the pipe.

Once we were in it, we discovered you could produce an echo, a rebound of your voice, and the further we were apart, the more words you could echo back to you. So, we moved apart, I went North, they went South, testing the rebound as we went.

I have no idea how far apart we were, but we had reached at least 3, maybe 4 words when we agreed it was far enough, already a long crawl to the exit.

Sore knees by the time I emerged, but well worth the experience.

Now, no one using Beaver Run water now could possibly know, or care, that long, long ago, there were three silly kids inside that pipe, where the water running right now.

Boys will be boys, won't they?

Wittiest

Over the course of the twelve years of schooling, the grand total of what I consider noteworthy achievements is in the eyes of the world; none, but in my eyes it stands at exactly one, the only one I felt I was entitled to.

I discount being the best speller in the class because that class ended in the third grade.

Not being overly scholarly in any subject but math, which ended in my sophomore year, not athletic at all, the athletes all carried high school injuries of one kind or another into adulthood, but I did not; I was a good typist, but many of the girls were better, I tried out for chorus and was quickly disqualified and booted, tried out for band on the big horn, the great big one, whatever that was, and dismissed when I couldn't make it toot, the school newspaper suggested I raise rabbits instead of writing or publishing, which is probably still apparent, and as a reporter, my reports were too bland, uninteresting. I had few, if any friends, never had a girlfriend, and even though my openly stated dream in the Future Farmers of America program was to be a farmer, already had done considerable actual farming prior to, and up to our graduation, but then, a perceived slight by me to my Ag teacher, Wenroy, caused him to give the best Farmer award to a classmate who had planted a strawberry patch the year before.

I'm not now, nor ever was a successful farmer but I bless anyone who has the courage to be one.

The only talent I had, then, and was recognized for it was when I was voted the wittiest in the class.

My only win in school, it's in the class of '52 yearbook.

Disposition Children, Radio

This story is a rundown of some of the activity leading to the final disposition of the children, opening them to their own lives, and their own fortunes.

During world war two, a truly dismal time, having no electricity in the house, and an ongoing potent clock/ time issue, father purchased a battery radio, from Sears and Roebuck, and a battery for it that was at least a foot square, weighing in at 25 pounds or so, a real behemoth compared to today's batteries.

Those batteries' life expectancy was at best, brief, and would conk out at the most inconvenient time if it was used more than sporadically, which to our father, was get the news, weather, and time, then shut it off! Now! Or else!

Replacing those batteries was a real pain.

First, they were very costly, and there being only limited funds available in general, it was never a purchase made in anticipation of the inevitable future need, but only when the present one died or was fading to the point it could barely be heard.

When ordering a battery via catalog sales, payment had to accompany the order. There was no such thing as a checking account.

So, a trip had to be made to the post office, on foot, to get a money order and a one-cent stamp.

Then the endless wait began. There being a shortage of everything during the war, it could take weeks until it finally came, and once again, to be able to hear the radio comfortably.

That's when the fun would begin.

During the week, with school homework demanding attention, then early bedtime, it was not much of an issue. But over the weekend it was.

We kids, craving any kind of entertainment, began listening to station WWVA in Wheeling, West Virginia – country music, on the sly.

Well, Father really wasn't concerned at all about our emotional desires, dismissing them with the ongoing edict: shut it off, you'll kill the battery!

Weekends also were when Father would be mostly occupied in his private quarters, his 10' x 10' shanty located 100 feet or so from the house, with the usual jug of Port wine present, normally unconcerned with much else.

We would watch for Father to emerge from his shanty, so when he was absent we would listen to the radio.

The game went on, afternoons and evenings, when the jamboree would have a variety of performers, many of whom we really like coming on; we would listen, volume turned way down low.

This bridged the gap between emptiness and fulfillment, in great part, at least temporarily.

We had little else. It created memories that lasted a lifetime.

At times we were careless, occupied in our actions, and Father would catch us in the act. All hell would break loose, with us scurrying about to escape the wrath, but never being physically abused.

Ultimately, due in part to experiences similar to this, and among other unhappy times, sister Catherine, being a favorite of a widowed, daughterless neighbor, took up living with her, in great part, until graduation when she was employed and moved away.

Sister Ann became a recluse, devoting her home time to study, struggling with only having a kerosene lamp to study by, and yet having achieved, as yet an unbroken record - to the best of my knowledge – of the only student to ever have had straight A's over her entire school attendance time of one through twelve grades. Upon graduating she went to work in Pittsburgh. She was offered a scholarship at Geneva College of $50.00.

Sister Mary was belligerent, and continued, as did I, to surreptitiously listen to the radio until the year 1947 when electricity was finally brought in and installed in our remotely located house. Upon her graduation she departed to big town for work.

Sister Stella simply eliminated the desire to listen to the radio altogether under such trying circumstances, among other issues, and occupied her spare time endlessly reading books from the school library.

I, being the last of the proverbial Mohicans, so to speak, was left alone with my parents and brother Andy, a relatively peaceful interlude, until his induction into the U.S. Army in 1951.

Just one of the sisters, Mary, ever married, forming their own family, successfully and happily.

Did the others' experiences in growing up create a subconscious determination to avoid a duplication of their current and past life's trials and tribulations?

We'll never really know.

Alcoa Carpenter Apprentice

At the end of the agriculture planting/harvesting season of 1952, I abandoned my dream of being a big time farmer and went looking for work. I managed to convince the aluminum company of America to employ me even though I was only 17, and a new horizon, or so I thought, had opened up for me.

I worked as a laborer initially, loading trucks and building shipping boxes in the box shop, as it was called. But, that connection exposed me to a carpenter apprenticeship aptitude test being offered, so I applied to take it and then did so.

After the test, having been informed that I had had a perfect score, I was fairly confident going in for my post-test interview that I would soon be on my way to a career in carpentry, in which I had considerable experience from my home repair services, and did like the work.

Oh, surprise, surprise, the interview lasted less than two minutes, when I was abruptly informed I was disqualified due to a company rule that, in order for me to apprentice there, my father must also be an Alcoa employee, which was certainly not the case. Could they have informed me of this rule when applying for the test?

However, I was still employed there, but soon afterward the war in Korea ended and the demand for the aluminum company products stopped and the layoff came.

The beautiful red '53 Chevy convertible I had bought and financed, anticipating long-term employment with such a large company, was no longer affordable, so I had to kiss the convertible and the carpenter career goodbye, both at about the same time.

Fort Wayne Job Search

With no jobs available locally, a friend, Joe, and I were invited by Joe's brother and wife to come to Fort Wayne, Indiana, to seek work, where there was, purportedly, ample opportunity.

The hard fact, in those days, that being eligible to be drafted into the military, draft bait, we were referred to, pretty much disqualified you from landing almost any type of mid-level job.

We pounded the streets day after day, with the same refrain; would love to hire you but, your draft status negates that possibility.

Finally, we were hired by a big-time meat processor, whose name I do not recall, unloading refrigerated trucks, trucks we were certain had the capacity of a Chinese container, full of beef sides weighing anywhere up to a ton, or so it seemed, by hand, carrying the sides about 200 feet into a room-sized freezer with its temperature set similar to the Arctic Circle in January, or so it appeared.

We worked from midnight to 6 am, with no breaks, no lunch, no future, minimum wage.

After a very short tenure, then retreat, defeated, back to Pennsylvania.

It being some 330 miles to home, Joe drove for a while and then said, how about you drive the rest of the way, I being the more experienced driver at age 19, having driven since I was 13.

I continually keep returning to Guardian Angels, but was mine – ours – at work in his request for me to drive? We'll see.

It was just getting dark on a clear, late autumn Sunday, and I'm travelling along a straight, not flat, but rolling highway. I don't remember the route, at a legal 70 mph in his 1952 Chevy. Looking directly ahead, I notice cab overhead clearance lights of a big truck approaching me – just clearance lights.

It immediately flashed in my mind that he, being in a dip in the road, would soon emerge into full view, and no issue. Well, he emerged alright. He was passing a string of cars, coming straight at me at a very high rate of speed, almost to me.

At that precise moment a wide spot suddenly appeared on my right side, and instinctively I swerved hard right at 70 mph into that tiny spot, the truck roaring by me, then being out of space, I swerved hard left, getting back onto the road, unscathed, breathing a huge sigh of relief, the truck disappearing into the gloom.

Didn't I mention something about Guardian Angels somewhere?

Fabricating

Entering into early adulthood, I became interested in steel fabrication, having befriended the owners of a local fabricating shop by visiting there occasionally, offering them free help in trade for training in the business, especially welding, which is the heart and soul of fabrication. Since they built warehouse type rolling ladders exclusively, there was no potential conflict of interest.

It was a good relationship, and gave me access to equipment I didn't have and certainly couldn't afford, plus their - three of them - expertise was praiseworthy and benevolent.

Never mind a heated, well lighted shop to work in.

Combining time I spent, often late into the night, in my own shop, and theirs in regular time, I designed and built several semi-automatic electrically powered machines used in the re-sharpening of tool bits, cutters, used in coal mining equipment.

I explored patenting, and learned it was such an expensive, time-consuming process that I opted to run the risk of marketing without a patent. Furthermore, I was told that, in fact, a patent would not provide much protection anyhow.

So, I marketed both of the machines without patent protection. One was used as intended in sharpening tool bits; the other, I was told later, was purchased by pirates who soon reverse-engineered the device and improved it, and so much for my invention.

I spoke with a lawyer about the possibility of suing them but there were several problems. The first was trying to find them; second, it's a terrible expense to sue anyone, especially for something like this where they can prove they improved it and changed it, so you're pretty much out of luck at that point, and that ended the thought of lawsuits.

I never heard from either one of the buyers again.

There were other inventions and products that I actually produced and sold to the coal industry, one in particular that lasted about 20 years.

That was a cable hanger, a device addressing the problem of suspending trailing cables of mining machinery so as to prevent other mobile equipment from running over and damaging the cables. These cables are very costly, very heavy, and extremely dangerous if an injury to one causes a short-circuit and the cable catches fire, which creates deadly, toxic smoke that is totally disabling almost immediately if you breathe any of it.

I produced many thousands of these cable hangers, which were quick and easy to install and held the cable up within it safely.

This fabricating business ended when the federal government that is known as MSHA mandated changes in the hanger that I could not incorporate into it.

Andy—in Salina

My brother, Andy, was still single when this little event transpired.

I was asleep when my phone rang for attention, very late one night: 3:00 AM to be exact. On the line vas George __ our local policeman, asking if I could come to Salina, our so called hometown, just 3 miles away.

I asked why and he said to take Andy home. Without any more inquiry I agreed to be there in a few.

Here, George patrolling around, had found Andy parked right in the center of the highway running through town, engine running, lights on, dead drunk, barely able to communicate upon being awakened.

DUI rules and regulations were not yet instituted way back then, so there were no consequences to speak of, unless it involved a serious accident or injury.

So, I took Andy home. We retrieved his car the next day, Andy having missed work. Of course, there had to be an explanation for something this bizarre. Here, Andy had attended a private party somewhere on the wrong side of Pittsburgh, had way too much to drink over an extended time and was finally shooed out the door by the host, a long way from home.

He admitted he had driven some 40+ miles from somewhere south of Pittsburgh, then through Pittsburgh Streets, there was no Parkway then, by heavily traveled Rt. 22, then by various state highways, somehow finding his way into Salina rather than home, just 3 miles away, all with no knowledge or recall whatsoever of any of the trip. None at all. That is where he ended up, obviously guided and directed by some unknown higher power.

Have I mentioned the presence Of Guardian Angels, anywhere?

Andy - Intellectual Discussions

When I was into early adulthood, living in the same house with my brother Andy, but not yet married, we would often stay up late, engaged in discussion of the mysteries of life, particularly in how and why some people were successful in life, in financial affairs, social and romantic and so on, while others were unable to find success in only some or few of those aspects.

We finally determined that, in reviewing recorded details of successful people's actions, there was a certain similarity in them all.

It appeared that they all had studied the great philosophers, the thinkers, the authors. Shakespeare, Aristotle, Plato, Confucius, Emerson, to name a few.

So, I bought a set of books that included many of these people's histories, and publications, and actually read them carefully, often pausing, pondering what did he just say, what did he mean?

I began to see more clearly where they were coming from.

In 1964, I bought the age-old book written by Napoleon Hill, Think and Grow Rich, reading and re-reading it numerous times.

There is a source of intelligence hidden in the safest place of all, deep within our own minds. This source is available to everyone, but you must pursue it yourself, no one can do it for you.

I have never stopped pursuing and applying the intelligence available on any subject perceivable to the human mind, sometimes winning, sometimes losing.

Brother Andy apparently applied the concept, as he rose to the top of his profession, a far cry from his humble beginnings as a timekeeper at a construction site.

Racing State Cop

Summer, 1953, returning home from my job at Alcoa in new Kensington one afternoon, on Route366, I caught up to a vehicle, and passed him at 45 or 50 mph, not an excessive speed for the lightly populated area.

Reaching a fairly long stretch, that vehicle then passed me, arousing that ingrained instinct of the young, a challenge, in my '53 Chevy convertible, so I then passed him, he retaliates by re-passing me in a dangerous area, at a much higher rate, probably reaching into 65 or 70 mph.

By now, we are at the infamous Camp Joanne stretch, a full mile of perfectly straight roadway, no one else in sight. I had raced there before.

So, I passed him, probably at 85 to 90 mph; at that time the top speed allowed anywhere was 50 mph.

By then we're at the end of the stretch at a stop sign.

I stopped, moved through, and proceeded on down the road, he now behind me.

That's when the light inside his car came on, flashing red, and the siren was blowing along with it.

Of course, it was the Pennsylvania State Police in an unmarked car.

We pulled over, he getting out of his vehicle, putting on his hat, then came toward me going through the usual ha-ha I got you process.

Yes, I had just been entrapped, suckered into a street race from the start, he not showing his police head cover.

In retrospect, I wasn't street smart enough to know I had been entrapped by the appearance of an ordinary driver, absent his trooper's head covering, and probably would have beat the charges by taking it to a court hearing.

So, I paid whatever the fine was, and got a 90-day suspension of license, but allowing me to go to work and back as a restriction.

I, a clean-cut young guy, with a reputation bordering on sainthood, simply ignored the restriction, drove as if the suspension didn't exist, quietly counting down the 90 days, not racing anyone.

Finally, I was exposed, when the owner of the local gas station I frequented mentioned to me that she had seen it published in our local newspaper.

After the suspension had already ended!

'53 Chevy Antenna

It was a nice Sunday afternoon, I, having nothing better to do, decided to go for a ride in my '53 Chevy convertible.

With the top down, I'm traveling along a remote back road, when all of a sudden, my radio antenna, about halfway up, changes from being vertical to horizontal, a perfect 90° angle, with practically no sound accompanying the event.

Stopping and parking, taking a closer look at the now bent over antenna, I found traces of lead on it, at the point of impact, proving, most likely, it had been hit by a small caliber bullet.

Listening, there were no sounds of shooting anywhere near my location.

I have wondered how far that bullet traveled, and what the mathematical odds were of it hitting the antenna.

I have also wondered what the mathematical odds were of it hitting me, just a few feet from the antenna.

Racing Joe at Perrysville

The cars we had when we were in our late teens were not particularly powerful, around 100 hp more or less.

When I bought my '53 Chevy, it had 105 hp, just a bit of an uptick from the norm, but it did run quite well, and I did my share of casual street racing with it.

One Sunday afternoon I was driving around, going nowhere in particular, when I passed a friend, Joe, a really good mechanic who favored the Plymouth, a mediocre, grandma going-to-church type of vehicle, of no real street merit.

Unknown to me was the fact that he had hopped that '51 Plymouth up to where grandma was something else, to be respected when turned loose.

So, the proper signals were made, and we proceeded to what was known as the Perrysville stretch on State Route 380, 1 mile of straight road, with two dips, before going uphill to a sharp curve.

I, in my hot Chevy, Joe in his beefed-up Plymouth, lined up at the intersection of Route 380 and another state road, and I flashed the go signal.

And, away we went, engines roaring, past the only house nearby at about 80 mph, and into the wide open, straight, slightly downhill road all we could go, side-by-side, occupying the entire two-lane road.

At about the half-mile point, at the top of the first down dip, I noticed out of the corner of my eye that he was beginning to edge up on me, starting to pass.

I glanced down at my speedometer, yes, I know it's supposed to be an odometer, and saw that I was going 105 mph when he passed me, I giving up at that point.

He pulled off at a wide spot along the road and we had our post-race review.

I said, Joe, do you realize that where you passed me at the top of the dip, you can't see if there was someone in the dip, out of sight from where you are at the top?

He responded with yes, but you can see on out if there's someone coming.

I said what if there's a kid on a bicycle already in the dip? Or a stopped vehicle, or a pedestrian on foot?

It was a sobering realization, and I never drag raced there again.

Was there a Guardian Angel there making sure there was no one in the dip?

Mom at 100 mph

I had ceased racing other cars at the Perrysville stretch because of the dangers in its roller coaster configuration, however, at that same stretch of road, a little later in life, I was in my brother's '56 Buick, a truly powerful car, I don't know what engine was in it, but, anyhow, I was returning mother from church that Sunday.

Turning onto Route 380 at the little village of Perrysville, heading east, I said to mother, would you like to see what it's like to travel at 100 mph?

She immediately erupted, no-no-no! as I was stomping down on the accelerator. I am already at 85 mph going past the last house, picking up speed, she still yelling no-no-no, not enjoying the ride at all, not appreciating that I'm giving her conversational material for her next coffee klatch, a once-in-a-lifetime experience.

Reaching the top of the first dip, I glanced down at the speedometer, approaching 110 mph, so I backed off, slowing to a normal speed.

She was so stunned, she couldn't speak; I, of course, laughing the whole way.

She squealed on me to my family, but they were also amused.

The next Sunday, bringing her home from church, I asked if she would like to see 100 mph again.

There was no response, just a wistful look. That said it all.

Boys will be boys.

Teaching Dolly to Drive

When I first met Dolly, she had just turned 16, ready for driver training, usually done by a parent, relative, or acquaintance. Being her new dreamboat, I offered to do it.

I not only discussed various safety related issues, but demonstrated how to handle some of the most common hazards she could encounter.

I dwelled specifically on one of the most dangerous hazards, the one causing numerous head-on collisions, the worst of all being often fatal.

Nearly all of the primary highways were originally built using concrete for the main body.

All too often erosion of the berm along the edge of the concrete would create a void, leaving a drop off that could be anywhere from minimal to serious, five, even six inches or more in many cases. This was common everywhere.

Typically, a vehicle crowding the right-hand edge of the road would drop the right rear tire off the road, causing the front end to swerve violently to the left directly into oncoming traffic at worst, across the road at best, requiring quick response in correctly steering the vehicle to regain control.

So, I had not only discussed the proper procedure for handling a drop-off, but physically demonstrated it in a safer setting, and had her practice it to some extent, under my watch.

So, this day I took Dolly out for a training session, traveling along the Rugh ponds near Slickville, where the type of danger being discussed was prevalent.

As we are moving along at about 35 to 40 mph, she, being too close to the right side of the road dropped the right rear wheel off the road into a 6-inch-deep void, the front end of the vehicle swerving violently to the left,

She shrieked, threw her hands up into the air, letting go entirely of the steering wheel.

I, alert for just such a situation, and since we were moving, suddenly, in the direction of the last big pond, located down over a steep bank 100 or so feet away, I grabbed the steering wheel, pulled it sharply to the right, and regained control very quickly. Thank God, no one was approaching us.

She recovered her senses quickly, pulled over and stopped.

I told her we would revisit the training in those situations later.

I drove us back home.

'

53 Chevy Convertible

At age 18 I had what I believed was a good, long-term job with a big company, having lost the use of my Brothers' 51 Chevy, since he was stationed in Kentucky, and had taken his vehicle with him there.

Having a beautiful girl friend, and a '37 Chevy pickup truck wasn't exactly a desirable social mix, I needed a car.

So, I went whole hog, I ordered one from our local Chevy dealer, a beautiful fire engine red, white sidewalls, chrome everywhere, biggest engine available, automatic everything, '53 Chevy convertible.

When it came in, and I took ownership in March, I picked Dolly up, my future wife, at her school at lunch time, going for a short ride, cold at 40 or so degrees, top down, she was the envy of all her friends .

Brother Andy talked me into allowing him to take it to his station, Fort Knox, in Kentucky, where he quickly became the center of attention of the local girls, one of whom became a sad story, ending in circumstances I'd rather not expose here.

Having lost my job when the Korean War ended and unable to make the high payments for the car, I traded my brother it, in exchange for his '51 Chevy, so life still went on, a bit less glamorously, for me.

This was just one of the setbacks, that life would have visit me through the many trials and tribulations waiting for each of us, prefaced by those all wise, all knowing, all-encompassing words:

Shoulda, Coulda, and Woulda. Life is so filled with those words, to us all.

Shoulda, Coulda, Woulda.

Mercer Hill

I was just sixteen, had just adopted my Brother's new '51 Chevy when he was drafted, sadly, into the U. S. Army. A friend, Bob, and I had gone to a movie in Saltsburg, and it had started to snow as we went in at 6:00 PM.

We left the movie at 9:00, and we now find the snow has accumulated to 3 or 4 inches, just enough to make the roads slippery and dangerous , pure ice everywhere.

I had not yet put winter tires on, so I had my choice, up a short, steep curvy hill, with summer tires on the car, or a long, straight steep hill to get back toward home, the hill being identified as Mercer Hill.

I chose the long, steep straight one, and with a bit of a chase, I was doing fine up to the halfway point, where I spun out, no hope of additional progress.

I have no choice but to try to get back down, try to go around, so, I put it into reverse and start backing down, on the ice.

Touching the brakes for control of my descent, the car took off, sliding faster and faster, totally out of control, backwards down the steep hill, moving towards a drop off embankment of 30 or 40 feet at the bottom.

I call it miraculously, the car, sliding backward, started to spin around, the front end ever so slowly turning like some giant hand was pushing it, till it was facing straight down where I was able to regain directional control very nicely, and drove back to the other short grade, and made it home safely.

I cannot explain or pretend to have personally directed the car to do what it did.

I can only suspect Who did, can you?

Evergreen Nurseries

For some unexplainable reason, experienced nursery owners and managers opine it was probably temporary insanity, I became interested in owning and operating an evergreen (pine trees) nursery, even though I lived in close proximity to what has been touted as the Evergreen capital of the world, Indiana County, Pennsylvania. If it's not actually the capital, it's close. There are numerous evergreen nurseries here and millions and millions of trees for sale.

Irregardless, l, a simple, ignorant teenager reasoned; all I have to do is plant a seedling, wait 7 to 10 years watching it grow, cut the tree in advance of the Christmas season, sell it, head for the bank to deposit X number of dollars. Sweet, repeat the process Ad infinitum. Life is good.

Sorry, it just doesn't happen that way. Through the years I have had nursery owners and managers as clients needing my survey services, during which I have seen the reality of nursery care.

Anyhow, in perpetuating my then current dream, I began clearing, by hand, a 10-acre tract available on the home farm in anticipation of planting several thousand seedlings as quickly as possible, so as to start the 7-to-10-year cycle going. After several days of severely hard work, I had about ½ acre cleared, a very long way to go.

Reality set in and my enthusiasm dimmed considerably, putting the proposed career move into temporary limbo.

After several forays into other dream worlds, touched elsewhere, the nursery dream re-emerged when, pending my being drafted into the military, caused me to think; while I am absent here I could have trees growing.

So, I went to a large, local nursery selling evergreen seedlings and purchased 5,000 seedlings, using up all of my available cash, then planting them in beds occupying what had been a vegetable garden in prior years. Mother, tolerant soul that she was, gave up her garden space for my trees without complaint, saying she was getting too old to dig dirt anymore. She even watered them for me while I was gone.

What I didn't know, in my youthful ignorance, was that the nursery selling me seedlings was not a big fan of helping future competitors to get a start in the tree business, and as a result, sold me 5,000 inferior seedlings, totally unsuitable for Christmas trees.

It took the two years I was in the military for the seedling's growth to physically show their true characteristics, which was for lumber and other uses, requiring 50 + years to mature, and be of any real value.

Trying to make the best of it, I planted them anyhow, hoping to recover some of the investment that I had so innocently made, and once again been taken advantage of.

What few trees survived over the next years that the deer, insects, windstorms or other issues didn't destroy grew straight as arrows skyward, competing with each other and native trees for sunlight. Some, after 67 years, reaching about 100 feet in height, now looking like misplaced flagpoles.

By chance, the remaining trees are located along one of my current walking trails, and as I walk by I admire them as survivors and as a lesson in life to me.

So much for career number ***

Masonry Career

After discharge from the military, I attended a technical school in Pittsburgh, funded by the VA, that offered training in various trades, including brick, block and other mortar and concrete related ones, with a group of veterans.

The instructor was a former journey man brick layer, the true focus of my interest. He soon discovered I was the only one in the class actually interested in learning the brick trade as a career. So, he gave me special one on one instruction, and answered my many questions. He actually taught me enough in a very short time span that I began offering masonry services to the general public while attending the school, knowing I had a knowledgeable source for questions I may have.

Bricking a simple, single-story house, with not too many offsets, insets, and so on, was easy.

Fireplaces could be tough, and my first one was white brick with black mortar. Deadly. Being an absolute amateur, I should have subbed it out to someone who knew what they were doing, but being the hardhead I was, I agreed to do it.

My instructor/mentor just about fainted when I informed him of what I had taken on, and out of pity, or mercy, agreed to work with me and teach me on weekends to prevent a certain disaster in a very fussy client's house.

This trade is not just about laying a brick that weighs less than 5 pounds, but what I quickly learned is that onto concrete block is where the brick is actually laid. These blocks vary in size and weight accordingly.

The two most common sizes are 8-inch and 10-inch used around houses. Quite heavy to start with, amazingly heavy as the wall gets higher, and at chest height you really earn your keep.

After quite a bit of experience I took on a lot of chimney work, Some were easy, when low to the ground, less than 20 feet. Above 20 feet they can be another story, especially as poorly equipped as I was. My ladder was an old 40-foot extension with wooden side rails and wooden rungs, along with some rickety scaffolding I built out of old pallets or whatever else was available.

The higher the chimney gets off the ground, the harder it gets, and increasingly more dangerous. Carrying hundreds of bricks eight or nine at a time in a handheld carrier, and following that up with 5-gallon buckets of wet mortar cement up the old extension ladder to a platform held up by the previously mentioned wooden scaffolding, 30 to 40 feet high was not fun.

Then build the chimney working from that shaky, narrow unguarded platform, oftentimes well into the night.

With a wife, four kids and a dog depending on me, my Guardian Angels, you will hear a lot about them as we travel through this whole life story, were kept very busy, and obviously did an admirable job since I am still here.

Goodbye career number *** other interests beckoned.

Home Repair

After the farming fiasco of 1952 faded, I let word out that I was offering home repair services such as in electrical, plumbing, concrete and roof repairs.

I didn't know much about any of the services I was offering, but studied how to do books on each trade religiously, and asked many questions of knowledgeable tradesmen that I would seek out. They were all eager to help a young guy get started, would be outgoing in explaining how things should be done, could be done and their secrets of how to get along with the people they were serving.

Then when I got a job to do, I would simply bluff my way through, usually coming out the winner.

It was not hard; most people are very good.

As best I now know, the switches and receptacles I installed still work, the plumbing still flows, the roofs I put on do not leak,(the ones that are still here), and none of the porches I built have collapsed.

I never did learn to like commode and sewer jobs.

I worked cheap, way too cheap, but I was desperate.

Nix career number ***.

Andy - End of Coon Hunting

I grew up with two Coonhounds, beautiful, congenial animals, always tied to their boxes, often just yelping, hoping for just a little attention which they never got, except for those rare hours spent hunting raccoons, their life purpose.

Brother Andy being the proud owner and caretaker of them, also was growing up, increasingly exhibiting signs of separation from the sport, into other new interests.

Cars, Girls, Bars, Life.

Weekends were the worst, long periods of absence, the dogs needing food and water, being attended to by me, and mother, our complaints falling on deaf ears.

Not having a telephone meant any contact to arrange hunting jaunts had to be done in person, and he started hiding when his hunting partners would show up at the house to schedule a hunt.

They, discouraged as that became ever more frequent, eventually stopped coming, and so did the hunting stop altogether, he having lost interest in hunting racoons by himself.

I had never developed any liking for it. I preferred hiking in the woods in broad daylight, not night.

Inevitably, the sad day came, when the boxes were silent, the dogs having been sold or given away.

An era had passed, we moved on.

Somewhere, an old song ends by singing, once you pass its borders, you can never return again.

He never did, a new world had opened.

Locked Out

Way back, when Dolly and I were dating, I was going home from Tarentum, late one night, when I had to pee, bad.

I knew the area well, knew there was an intersection ahead, with a wide spot, and a small building there.

I pulled into the wide spot, did whatever I had to do, and went to get back into the car.

Surprise, I had left it running, and somehow, I had locked myself out. Now what, I'm 20 miles from home.

Okay, I reasoned that the building would have electric, electric would require a meter, a meter would have a ground wire, exposed. There was even a night light, so I could see to break off a piece of the wire.

Sure enough, and it was big enough for what I had in mind. I broke off a piece, jammed it into a small opening between the hood and a fender, pushed hard creating an L on one end.

Vehicles in those days had a vent in the front part of the door window, with a round button to push when you wanted to open it.

So, I inserted the L into the car by forcing it past the rubber seal, twisted the L end over the release button, pulled, and I'm on my way home. Elapsed time, problem to freedom, less than ten minutes.

Once again, I 'm heading home, now remembering I had promised to pick up a six pack for my father.

So, I stopped at a bar close to home to get the beer, left the car running, as it was cold, went in and got the beer, then went back out to the car to go home, finally.

Guess what? I 'm locked out again, same scenario, car running, lights on , my L wire from the last time is inside the car, on the seat.

This time, I went back into the bar, got a coat hanger, redid the L process, and soon, I'm on my way again.

When will they ever learn, when will they ever learn.

Carolyn

As a major part of this story, I am enclosing parts of the final letter written to my beautiful Sister-In-Law, granting her freedom to detach from any obligation to me in the most congenial way I could envision. I will always love her and wish her the best. Her letters to me while in Korea always ended with P.S. I did not write my best.

I would always write back, ending with: Why not?

Dear Carolyn (and Frank):

I'm just sitting here on a cold, clear morning, allowing my thoughts to ramble wherever they choose, and you drifted into the scene.

Of course, distant past emerges, and reruns come alive, front, and center.

You were seven, I believe, when that tall, skinny kid arrived on the scene in January, 1953.

Even though you were a bit spoiled, you quickly became a favorite, just second to your beautiful big Sister.

After a wonderful lifetime with her, I will only repeat that which that which I have spoken many times elsewhere: She is a perfect candidate for Sainthood.

What a great group I became a part of. Aunts, Uncles, Father and Mother- In-Laws, and Frank, all super people. The pending relocation of Ted and Judy saddens me for many reasons, among them the fact that I will then become the sole link to the family point of origin, Avonmore.

But, life does go on, doesn't it?

And, finally, there's Thor, my beautiful German Shepherd buddy, ninety-five pounds of pure joy, my boyhood dream come true. He's with me 7 and 24, never more than a few feet away. He loves people and delights them everywhere we go.

Carolyn, it's okay if you don't respond, nothing will change. I used to communicate by letter to a former classmate who moved to California decades ago. It took her seven years to answer my latest letter.

Best wishes, best regards to you both.
P. S. your writing was very good.
Love, Chuck

I never heard from her again.

Drafted – U.S. Army

I was drafted into the U.S. Army in 1955. I was excited, anticipating high adventure.

Two years later, I was not at all disappointed, even a little sad to leave it.

The one major negative I can still feel, is echoed by that 8 ½ x 11 poster I saw, somewhere, that read: "If you believe you are indispensable, put your finger into a bowl of water, then see how big the hole is left there when you pull it out." Not really inspirational, nobody cares about you; you are in fact, alone, on your own.

Getting off the bus in Pittsburgh, I began to feel it; I was a part of something very big.

A crisply uniformed Non-Commissioned Officer herded a large group of us into a room, introducing us to a different world, one of you WILL, not, will you?

My initial meeting with the city guys was great, they quickly accepted me into their fold, seeing I was the true Country Bumpkin, unknowing of the ways of the city streets.

My perception of City Kids was totally reversed, very quickly. Growing up, I had believed it was the farm boys that were tough, the City Boys less than.

After an 800-mile ride on a train, we were in Columbia, South Carolina, where I saw my first real racist event, the details not important, here, but I, a Yankee, was utterly appalled, shocked.

I learned what cattle must feel like, herded from place to place, the age-old hurry up and wait syndrome, urged on by a now different level of temperament in the uniformed personnel.

Measured to fit, clothing was issued, along with a duffel bag. It was very hot and humid in South Carolina, and it was required you wear, at all times, the winter coat you were issued, the first taste of you will, or else.

Processing was slow, long lines moving, but barely, so it seemed, there was plenty of idle time, just stay in Iine, move when the line moves.

In with the mix with Pittsburgh and North, were young men born and raised in the South. One thing led to another, and sure enough, the Civil War was rekindled. A big, strong Southern boy insulted and then challenged one of my newfound Pittsburgh friends, and before the challenge had been fully issued, he found himself knocked down, flat on the ground.

Jumping up, he warned, now you've done it, and before the new threat was completed, he once again found himself on the ground, effectively ending the challenge, and the War.

Later, in conversation with me, he, now civil, told me that when the stars swirling around in his head slowed, he decided to end the restarted Civil War, but it did not last. After all, Boys will be Boys.

For me, Basic Training was not exactly fun, but not that difficult. Mostly, I felt sorry for the Training Instructors who had to march along with us, stand out in the miserable heat doing their best to pump some knowledge into less than interested, half-asleep clods, sharing the long hours, sleep deprivation and all right along with us.

I certainly did not envy them, for when this pack of monkeys graduated, ready to go out and save the world; another batch was already on the way, to do it all over again.

I was invited, but passed up Officers Candidate School, already seeing military life for what it is; unfairly competitive.

I returned home from the attitude adjustment realignment process called Basic Training a virtual hero, but only in my, and my dog Sandi's viewpoint, proudly wearing my fatigues around town, actually looking a bit silly. No one was impressed, telling a friend I had been inducted, he said oh, when did you leave. It was the same after final discharge, too. I still had 21 months to reach hero level.

Several weeks later, I found myself in Georgia, even hotter and more humid than South Carolina, in Signal School, a considerable advance from my early Compass days. There, I was taught enough about Communication that I qualified to go to Korea and serve the R.O.K. Army, stationed at the DMZ, the designated Neutral Zone between South Korea and the hostile North Korea.

After graduation from Signal School, I went to Fort Monmouth, New Jersey waiting for Orders, a two-month long vacation of sorts in a tourist haven on the Atlantic Ocean. Then, Orders were received, Korea bound.

Flying to Fort Lewis, Washington, I had one awful experience. I had fallen asleep on the long flight, awakening in intense pain in a tooth. I mean a pain crushing out all other sensibilities. Its origin was a mystery, as I had excellent teeth. Being on an airplane late at night, I had a real problem, with no ready or near future answer.

My only hope for relief was to appeal to the higher power, which I silently did. Once again, it had to be a fifth-dimension response, because the terrible pain suddenly disappeared, never to return.

Processing through Fort Lewis was done during a non-stop 21 days of heavy rain, nothing the likes of had I ever seen. Welcome to Seattle. Then, for me, a new experience was watching the coastline of the American Nation slowly disappear from view, heading for Korea. It was all just a part of the fun.

Door to Heaven Open

When I was stationed in Fort Monmouth, New Jersey, we had a group of silly guys who would do goofy things, just for the fun of it.

We were well known at this restaurant and went there frequently. We usually asked for, and got the same cute, friendly, humorous waitress. So, one night we ordered, then the usual wait till delivery.

Watching carefully for her exit from the kitchen approaching with the food, one of the guys jumped up and shouted very loudly "Hey! Someone left the door to Heaven open, and the Angels are all getting out - here comes one now!"

She loved it, and so did the other patrons in the restaurant.

Korea—Boss Dog

While I was in Seoul, processing into Korea, Reveille was at 6:00 am, we all assembling at a lot at the edge of the City.

There was a resident pack of dogs that would assemble with us every morning and participate in the event.

We were always amused how this one dog, not necessarily the biggest, was the boss dog.

He would actually line them up, Iike us, in some kind of social order, snarling and bumping any that were out of the line, back in.

After taps, they would dissipate, out of our area, till the next day.

I always brought food tidbits to them, and I'm sure others did too, quietly passing to them.

Korea – Mountains or Valleys

We had either mountains or valley bottoms, with a stream there that would overflow in Monsoon season, that features weeks of constant, heavy rain.

Korea - Roads

Roads in Korea were pothole free. They were kept that way by dozens of R.O.K. Troops, armed with long bamboo poles, who would sweep them every day.

Korea—DMZ

Being stationed at the DMZ in Korea, it was sort of weird to realize that just ten miles, or so to the North, there were also stationed, many thousands of North Korean and Chinese Army Troops, along with the usual military hardware.

Hundreds upon hundreds of big artillery, all pointed in our direction. In the event hostilities would resume, I knew Communications would rank very high as a target.

How long does it take one of those big shells to travel ten miles? Would they send just one, or hundreds?

Not long. Many.

Korea – Chinese Army

At times, after dark, I would see the Chinese Army flares shot up into the sky as part of their ongoing battle practice and training. A far cry from a Fourth of July fireworks display, and much more disconcerting.

Korea – Silent Now

Having considerable idle time, I would often take long walks up into the mountains where not that long ago, 3 years or so, fierce fighting was going on, people killing other people, and why, I wondered, for what reason.

Passing, or visiting, the still intact hand excavated machine gun placements, now abandoned and silent, thank God, The trenches where men from both sides died, and for what good cause.

Korea was cold, miserable, I imagining the hardship endured by fragile man.

Dentist in Korea

While I was In Korea, I needed some minor dental work, so I was in the chair when the dental tech came in, a sweet young thing.

There was an expected level of banter between them, he making some derogatory comments about her, and her family background.

She came right back in perfect Ukrainian with: if I strike you once, mightily, you will never recover, along with a full-blown torrent of humorous invective regarding his background and even projecting the venom into his future. I cannot print what all she said - in perfect Ukrainian. He not understanding a word at all. I, a first generation Ukrainian, grew up with the language, so was quite well versed in it.

So, I responded to her in perfect Ukrainian; well said sweet one, would you care if I had that published in the Army Times, the U.S. Army newsletter?

I'm sure he, the dentist, would give me your name!

She flushed bright pink, a look of total embarrassment on her face, hastily threw down the picks and prods she was holding, and raced out of the room, not returning the entire time I was there, he working without a tech.

I choking and gagging much of the time.

Chingo

Hungry Puppy

A starving, forlorn little puppy, no identifiable breed, shows up one morning at our Quonset hut, obviously desperate for something to eat.

He was instantly well taken care of, and in very short order was adopted by all 10 of us stationed in that hut.

He was absolutely full of life, inspirational in every way, giving his attention to everyone with no favoritism at all, visibly grateful to being rescued, then becoming an operative part of us.

We all agreed, then officially named him Chingo, Korean, for Friend. He was not allowed to travel with us in our military-issue vehicles, but there was always someone at the hut to occupy him.

His presence was pure joy; walks in the previous battlefields surrounding us with him were memorable.

But my time in Korea had just about expired, my time to go home. To tearfully say goodbye to Chingo, but leaving him in good hands, the best hands, the United States of America Army.

Sadly, several weeks after my discharge, a letter arrived informing me that Chingo had been stolen, kidnapped by the Korean guards assigned to our unit, his ultimate demise by their hand, a sad attempt to fend off their never-ending hunger.

In his honor and memory, we named Jim's collie puppy Chingo. His name is inscribed in my workshop's fresh concrete floor; it shows August 14, 1974 as the day of his remembrance.

May God Bless and keep him safe, always.

It is my fond hope that he too, will join us all at the Rainbow Bridge.

Korea—Power Unit

Independently housed In Korea at the DMZ we generated our own power with trailer mounted four-cylinder, gasoline engine-driven generators.

There were always two on site, to ensure no outage of any duration. When one would konk out, we would simply take our duece and a half to Seoul, 40 miles away and trade the dead one for one that did work.

Returning from Seoul, towing a power unit, I was just entering a small village along the way when I noticed a woman standing along the road, terror stricken, staring at my trailer, dashing off to the side of the road.

Here, the power unit had somehow caught fire in transit, and was shooting flames high into the air.

I stopped, quickly disconnecting the power unit from the truck, and watched it burn itself out.

Then I turned around and went back to the motor pool at Seoul, and traded it for another one.

The comment I got: Boy, a record. You're the first one to burn one up in two hours.

I agreed, but did not laugh, I'll never know how it could have caught fire, but with gasoline in the tank, who knows.

I wrote up a report, but there was no investigation. There was still trust, and truth, those days.

Korea - Power

Generating our own power in Korea, we knew we had to maintain a minimum amperage and voltage to properly power our receiving and transmitting operations.

None of us were electrically knowledgeable, but we did notice at some point was that the lights were dimmer than they should be, and the transmitter would stutter step at times, and the generator sounded like it was struggling.

We, the communication link between the U.S. Forces, and the R.O.K. Forces, were located in close proximity to the R.O.K. headquarters and the facilities for their operations.

And it was a good, professional level association.

I began searching for a cause of our recent power deficiency, tracing wires from the generator to our fuse panel.

I discovered a fairly big wire connected to our outgoing wire, coming from the R.O.K. Camp.

When I disconnected that wire from ours, all Hell broke loose. The lights at the R.O.K. Compound all went out, and before long, our telephone was ringing.

They had quietly tapped into our power some time ago, gradually increasing the demand and were now dependent on it to operate certain radio equipment, and lights.

When I disconnected it, their Commanding Officer contacted our Commanding Officer, demanding restoration of the power.

So, I reconnected it, but not for long.

Whatever transpired at much higher levels, I do not know, but we did not continue as their power source from then on.

Korea - Old Man Beating Woman

We lived in a Quonset hut, ten of us, some ten miles from a U.S. Center, and would travel every day to all or some of the meals served for all military personnel.

One day, in that journey, we came upon an older Korean man beating an older Korean woman along the road we traveled. Whatever compelled me to do it, I'll never know, but I yelled stop, to our driver, and he did.

I jumped down out of the truck, went over to the pair, kicked the old man, hard, on his butt, knocking him headlong into a side ditch running half full of water, this being the rainy season.

I signaled to the old woman to leave, while I prevented the man from chasing her.

When she was reasonably far away, I got back up into the truck, and we left.

I shudder to think what would have happened to me if U.S. Military would have seen or found out about my actions. It would not have been good.

Korea—Australians

On a gentler note, we, having our own vehicles, visited the Australian compound one Sunday afternoon.

The Commanding Officer himself greeted us, and showed us around, his charming, beautiful wife was equally cordial and welcoming.

I will always remember with warm respect, how absolutely nice everyone there was.

A nice memory to revisit.

Korea - Tanks

To buy miscellaneous personal items, we would go to a PX located near the DMZ, traveling the only road available, crossing via a bridge over a mid-sized creek.

Apparently, as part of their training, U.S Tanks would also use that road, but were too heavy to use the bridge.

So, there was a bypass just below the bridge where the tanks would cross through the creek, creating a big mud hole on both sides, and I mean a big mud hole.

From our high and dry viewpoint up on the bridge, we would watch those nice clean, diligently washed tanks approach the mud hole, go into it, and sink completely out of sight, turret, and gun, included, and then emerge like a big frog, muddier than all get out, continue on, badly in need of another wash job at their base.

We suggested they be happy in their work.

Korea – Two Columns South

I was not a part of this, but was related to me, our group, by our then Sergeant-in-Charge, who was a part of the event. He was there from the start and was part of the attack that pushed the North Korean Army to the Chinese border, a temporary victory until the Chinese Army joined with the North Koreans.

He was sitting in a latrine very early the morning of the initial counterattack, suddenly hearing widespread shouting, and other noises, and as yet, distant motor vehicles, tanks, mobile gun carriers, etc. approaching.

An overwhelming combination of North Korean and Chinese foot soldiers were on the move, this time going south, attacking, and not retreating.

The orders to retreat were automatic, packing up as best possible in utmost urgency, rifle fire exchange beginning.

Having superior air power, the retreat south was somewhat controlled by U.S. Forces, so the retreat fighting was limited to night activity.

Columns of attackers would move south in the dark, columns of retreating U.S. and R.O.K. Forces would also move south in the dark, avoiding as much as possible, enemy artillery from finding them.

He said one night as they marched south, on a road, they came to an intersection where another road joined theirs in a converging manner, the road also hosting a column of soldiers heading south.

No one was permitted to speak, converse with anyone, as radio silence was the rule in cases like this. No one violated radio silence.

So, they marched on until both columns reached another road, but this time, the column that had joined in some miles back diverged off into the newly encountered road, silently separating from the column he was in.

It was then discovered, the joining column was North Korean Army troops moving south.

The columns marched on till separation came, no recognition was divulged, no fighting occurred.

Korea – Trading Insults

At night, with nothing better to do, we would call other R.O.K. communication guys, and exchange humorous insults back and forth, we glorifying their women, denigrating their men, among many other topics. We would refer to Korea as being one big outhouse. They called us round eyes. It was all in fun, agreed to.

Korea—Day Of Reckoning

At the Quonset one day our phone rang, and it was our Officer-in-Charge, requesting me, and one other guy to come to headquarters to meet him.

He spoke with my cohort first, a very brief interview, then it was my turn.

He said sit down, relax, this is an Information gathering interview about operations at your site.

He told me that the Military Police had picked up our Sergeant-in-Charge at some woman's home in some village, and wondered how he could be in charge at our hut and be arrested in some woman's home at the same time.

So, I told him the truth. Sarge, as we called him, was a total alcoholic, had only two Interests in life, booze, and women. He had been living away from us the entire time, months, since I had arrived, in some home, only occasionally checking in with us, never staying, even overnight.

I, we, had taken charge of our operations; quietly carrying out all our duties, never failing, never creating a problem, things went smoothly.

The O.I.C. smiled, admitted their lack of oversight, thanked me, and I left, back home to KMAG, as we were known.

Korea – New Leader

Soon thereafter, a young, career-oriented sergeant arrived at our hut, announcing he had been assigned to us in place of Sarge, who had been demoted back to private, and reassigned elsewhere.

Very aggressive and progressive, he actually invited the top commander, a one star General, to come and visit us.

He took over all the managerial duties, which I had tired of, and wasn't that far from the end of my term in Korea, anyway.

Korea – Whirlwind Romance

One amusing facet was our new Sergeant had been in Europe, and had been reassigned to Korea.

Coming Stateside, he had landed in New York City, then left for home on leave prior to going to Korea.

He said that he had told a fellow soldier that he was going to marry the first girl he met after getting off the plane.

As it happened, he went to a restaurant for something to eat, and was assigned a waitress to take care of him.

I'll shorten a long story here.

He married her a short time later, and took her to his original home here in the U. S.

From all indications, it was, and Is, a happy, ongoing marriage.

That was 65 years ago, and I wonder how he fared in life, he was a real leader.

Korea – The Last Roundup – 16-Year-Old

And, finally, when we traveled from our Quonset hut to the mess hall, we passed through a small village named Pochun.

We traveled in our assigned duece and a half, a two- and one-half ton-rated truck, a flat bed, open top with bench seats on each side, through Pochun, clearly visible into, and out of the back.

As we would pass by this one house, I noticed a beautiful 16-year-old girl, who would always be at the door, waiting.

I admit, I was attracted to her, but, having a beautiful, faithful, wonderful girl waiting for me at home, I had to let it pass, never making any attempt to contact her.

Our houseboy, Mike, informed me she admitted she was in love with me from afar and wanted me to come and meet her.

I told him it was not possible, and shipped out soon after.

Life goes on, the mind forgets, the heart does not.

Goodbye Korea, never to return, I wish you well.

Lord, Help

I was on board ship, only God knows where, out in the Pacific Ocean, returning from Korea. We were in a storm, a real, never-ending storm that we were trapped in as it pounded us day and night, relentlessly.

The boat we were in was a hold over Liberty Ship, hastily assembled during the big war just a few years ago. It did not escape me to know those ships were made out of World War II steel, with World War II welds, with World War II welders.

The waves would raise the bow 55 feet up out of the water, then come slamming back down, burying it back under water with a horrendous wham, time after time, exposing the propellers spinning in open air, till the cycle repeated.

Being somewhat knowledgeable about structural engineering, I was very much concerned as to loading, stress resistance, when half the ship vas down in the water, the other half up in the air. The potential of it breaking in half, unimaginable center stress at that moment when the change in direction occurred.

This storm just went on and on, five days and nights, and on the fifth night, the human stress level was changed:

On board, we had the usual wise guy, a smart aleck who always had a sometimes cute, sometimes not so much, comment that could be heard throughout the sleeping quarters, wide open to all, when things were quiet.

He openly voiced contempt for ocean storms, claimed fearlessness.

He would usually groan or make appropriate noises and comments, sort of conversing with unseen participants in humorous exchanges, Always the Victor.

That night, after 5 days of beating, the storm had become particularly violent, the boat slamming, the shuddering vibrating ominously along its entire 600-foot length, repeatedly, everyone was fearful, uneasy, absolutely silent, including Mister Wiseguy, the fearless one. Then, a particularly violent upheaval and subsequent nerve shattering slam, suddenly Mr. Wiseguy's voice, clearly, loudly, beseeching, imploring, and petitioning the Almighty, crying ever so humbly, Lord, get me outta this one, and I'll get out of the next one myself.

Everyone relaxed, we still talk about it.

Airplane at Puget Sound

Returning from Korea in 1957, I was processed through Fort Lewis in Seattle then boarded an airplane for transport to Kansas City for final discharge. We had just taken off and were just a few minutes eastbound, when several of us saw a puff of smoke emerge from the overhead baggage carrier.

Then a second larger puff, and we were shouting for a stewardess, who came running, took a quick look, and hurried to the pilot's compartment.

Apparently panicking, both pilot and co-pilot came running back to where the smoke was, leaving the controls unattended.

Suddenly, the nose of the airplane decided to head for the Puget Sound, the ocean inlet, fully in view to me, and many fellow passengers, coming up fast.

The pilots, instantly aware of what's happening, turned, and raced back to the controls, quickly redirecting the plane from its power dive to Eternity, to level, then skyward where it belonged.

We were then grounded, switched to another plane, and flew uneventfully to Kansas.

Uneventful alright, except to quite a few of us who no longer had either breakfast or lunch in our bellies.

What was the big excitement? We still had at least a hundred feet between our plane and the water when the power dive was arrested and reversed skyward.

I wonder how many Guardian Angels were present, doing their job.

I am grateful for whatever was the case.

My Second Puppy – Pal

Returning from Korea in 1957, I learned my dear Sandi, had died of old age, leaving me with no personal canine companion, which I would not tolerate.

Sister Catherine, Kay, ever being the one eager to please, took it upon herself to eliminate that as a problem, and in short order procured a gorgeous, full blooded Cocker Spaniel puppy, one that simply melted your heart away when you were in contact with him, and we named him Pal.

He had those big, beautiful ears that draped down almost to the floor, and huge feet that were encased in fur reaching far out, especially when near any accumulated water, like a puddle, or the outfall of our spring, or even out in the rain, creating a real mess when going into the house, leaving a long, muddy trail for someone else to clean up.

He was an absolute joy to everyone, always willing to play, bringing toy after toy to be thrown, gleefully returning them time after time after time.

When we moved from my original home to our new, permanent home, he became confused as to where he belonged, so he traveled between both, spending the days here with the kids, then returning to his original home at night.

It never did become the typical Man – Dog relationship with him, since I always worked full time at a regular job, then always had side jobs that kept me away much of the time, but the kids gave him continuous companionship during his final years.

Sadly, at one point, a mining client, a reckless driving type, came flying up the driveway one evening, striking him with his pickup truck.

He did not recover from the injuries, and died at the age of ten, leaving a very large hole in my, and the kid's lives, along With my Mom, who was his caregiver over all those years.

It is my fondest hope that he'll be waiting at the Rainbow Bridge for us.

Wait till he meets Thor.

Mining Career at Seanor UMW

Just after my discharge from the military, I went to the aluminum company of America, where I had last been employed prior to my being drafted into the U.S. Army, to reclaim my old job.

Presenting at their employment office, I stated my belief there was a legal requirement for job reinstatement for a returning veteran who had been drafted, (conscripted,) into the military. They quickly informed me that law had expired at the end of World War II. There was no job, nor would there be one in the foreseeable future, due to deteriorating economic conditions. So, I left.

On the way home I happened to come upon a previous neighbor, an old friend growing up together. I inquired how and what he was doing, and he told me he was working at a local coal mine, earning a respectable hourly rate as a United mine worker. He said they were hiring, and I should consider applying for a job.

So, I did, and was hired immediately, since they like young men, and thus began a possible career in mining, but understanding it was not for the faint of heart, nor the weak of spine.

I started work the following Sunday night on hoot-owl, 12 to 8 am as a part of the resupply crew.

Never having been underground, it was strangely fascinating, riding in an open mine car, clackety-clacking several miles along a dimly lit corridor, with a well-supported roof, enclosing a railway. I tried not to be dwelling on the fact I was aware I was

300 to 400 feet below the grass and trees, with billions of tons of rock above me.

A coal mine, all mines, are a unique creation. To begin with, when you are inside of one, please understand; you are under untold tons of rock from the instant you enter until you exit; the air you breathe is, in my experience, all vacuumed in by huge fans that never stop, directed by walls of some type, steel, concrete, brick or whatever, to active areas, for the most part, a little to mined out areas, all of it allowed to flow to and through the fan, all power is carried in cables sized to meet their prescribed capacity just feet from you, and it is commonly about 55° inside constantly in there, and it is dark, very dark. Just your head lamp.

All mining machinery is electrically powered, and fairly quiet when it moves. You must always stay alert, danger is everywhere.

Finally at the transfer point, where several of us carried various types of materials and supplies from the loaded mine cars to a moving belt that normally carries produced coal out of the mine but was reversed to carry men and supplies into the active mining site.

Soon after, I was moved to the active mining areas, the face, as it's known, where I was assigned the job of roof bolter, arguably the most dangerous job in mining.

The roof bolter routinely goes ahead of the mining crew to maintain the integrity of the roof by installing steel bolts holding steel plates tightly to the roof, of whatever length is necessary, in a prescribed pattern to assure a relative level of safety for the miners.

One day, as I was struggling up a grade, physically pulling my roof bolter, a machine weighing about 500 pounds, I came to a person sitting along the way, waiting for me to pass.

It happened to be the mine surveyor, the person that is responsible for keeping the mining going in the right direction.

I stopped to catch my breath for a few minutes when I suddenly realized there was a much higher-level vocation, along with a much higher potential for advancement in general, as is the mantra for us driven, progressive entrepreneurs. Being a union bolter or any other union-job category, having its defined limits, was probably just a steppingstone for me.

So, I simply asked him how does one get a job like that, inferring, his.

His answer, stop in and see the mine foreman, my helper is quitting next week and I'm going to need someone.

That same day I stopped into the foreman's office, a personal family friend, and asked for the job.

It was well known, based on prior conversations, that I was quite proficient in math and various other technical considerations.

So ends my UMW mining career and begins my surveying career. What lies ahead? We'll see. Oh, will we ever see.

Sometimes I lament, I only need 18 more years in the UMW to qualify for a pension. Probably very unlikely at 88, and a dying UMW.

Coal - Early On

Becoming a coal miner in 1957, then a Surveyor, exposed me to various facets of the coal industry, from production to marketing, so I was pretty familiar with the whole process.

Parked at a Tastee Freeze one day, I met an old acquaintance, Lonnie, who had just begun to work with a coal processor buying and selling coal in the Pittsburgh area.

The unusual aspect of this dealer was that he accepted much lower grades of coal than any other coal handlers in the entire surrounding area.

The grade of coal involved was unsaleable at the time at any price, so having a market just meant the margin of profit was small, but, nevertheless, there was a profit to be made, so I hoped.

I, being knowledgeable as to the whereabouts of a substantial volume of this grade of coal, agreed to acquire the product, he would load and deliver it to the processor's yard.

The first problem surfaced immediately. He, having just one component necessary in this endeavor, a truck, rated as a one-ton, legal capacity, even hauling the usual illegal four tons, was simply uneconomical after all the operational costs were added up, barely anything left for the operator, and certainly nothing left as profit.

So, I bought him a much larger truck, one rated at nine tons, legal. Now, the next issue. The locations I had been sourcing the coal had loaded our truck as part of the sale, but suddenly changed policy, so that source dried up.

Other sources were just piles of coal, you bought it, you load it. Now we needed a loader, and a trailer to haul it around in. Getting in deeper and deeper, having seen no profit at all yet.

My partner finds a loader, a John Deere 2010 I believe, cheap, look out, with only one issue. It had been on fire, but he assured me the fire did only minor damage, it was ready to run.

Was the old adage Caveat Emptor showing up again? It sure was.

I bought it cheap, ready to run. Yeah, ready for the scrap heap. And run it did, into the first pile of reject coal, and that's as far as it got. The fire damaged transmission and rear end gears chewed themselves to bits, and now it's confirmed junk, and I own it.

Having a sizeable amount of coal reject committed, and too boneheaded to throw in the towel, admit defeat, we're off to our local friendly John Deere dealer, and as you might suspect – several days later, they deliver our brand-new John Deere 350, a track highlift, the answer to our loading needs.

My new loader, and my new payment book in hand.

We go through the usual market fluctuations over the next couple of years, profits still non-existent, never in the mix, break-downs common and often, typical struggle.

The market for low grade coal collapsed, but since there still is a market for higher grade product, I'm faced with a real dilemma. I'm getting ever deeper into this thing, the debt starting to take its toll.

It's clearly obvious, if high grade coal can be sold, I need some, a lot of that, now. How do I get it?

Not having adequate resources to go out into the producer's realm and buy it for resale; that being highly risky due to cheating methods I'm all too familiar with, or I can consider one other way.

Produce it myself.

I already had the coal bearing land under lease, but there was one more major step. You can't produce coal without real machinery.

So, I called my local, ever friendly (when you're buying) Caterpillar dealer, and by the next day I was much deeper in debt. I now had a machine that was the answer, or so I had been convinced by my partner. I had a machine that could do it all, single-handedly. A 977 track highlift.

My partner went to work; we're now officially strip (surface) miners. The 977 handled the removal of the topsoil and subsoil easily, then Mother Nature said, "Let's get serious, let's try some good, hard sandrock."

Several hours of roaring, clawing, and pawing later, there wasn't much progress toward the coal 40 feet farther down the strata, lots of hard rock in between.

The next logical step is to call in a truck-mounted drill, and prepare for a blast, blow the hard rock apart with a blasting agent.

The driller convinced me to try the newly developed blasting agent, in liquid form, so they loaded up all seven of the holes drilled, all 40 feet deep.

We watched from a safe distance, and after the "fire in the hole" outcry, we saw seven 40-foot-long streaks of blasting agent go shooting skyward, pushed up out of the holes by the dynamite detonator at the bottom.

The hard rock wasn't even scratched, much less shattered into small pieces.

Apologetic, the new guys left, no charge for the failed experiment. I called in the old tried-and-true blasters, and we then had loose rocks we could handle.

After an extended, tedious process, the coal was finally reached and marketed, but the cost far outweighed the return, so it was time to make a change.

I acquire one additional large pile of product, coal fines, in this case. No rock whatsoever.

Then I turn the payment book over to my partner, now ex-partner, and wish him well, exiting the whole deal.

Sadly, in a changing, deteriorating coal market, he was forced to take on other types of work.

Excavating underneath a house, a miscalculation of some sort occurred, and the house partially collapsed onto him. He was injured such that he could no longer operate heavy equipment.

Disposing of all of the equipment, he found peace in a successful wood working business until his passing a few years later.

He was a good and decent man; may he rest in peace.

Throw Caution To The Winds

As the demand for coal began escalating exponentially, the taste of honey I had, and was experiencing from the sale of reject coal, apparently inspired me subconsciously to enter the arena of production and sale of the higher grades of still widely available, the key ingredient obviously being the large scale equipment necessary to achieve this.

Having a net worth hovering just a bit above zero, but in offset of that negative, my debt burden was also minimal, creating something of a neutral scenario.

Already having a substantial reserve of marketable higher-grade coal, to ready marketing in having several coal dealers locally, I decided to, as is often said, jump in with both feet, and made the call to our local, friendly Caterpillar dealer, and ordered the first two of the many machines needed, a D9H Bulldozer, and a 980B Front End Loader.

This was done quickly, without the irritating inconvenience of a Financial Statement, or a substantial up-front payment.

Amazingly, within a few days, the two machines were on the site of my first open pit coal mine that was already permitted and bonded, ready to seriously begin the pursuit of my long-standing dreams of a secure future.

One day later, an invoice appeared in my mailbox for some three hundred thirty-five thousand dollars, the cost of the equipment.

An amount I could only Imagine existed, never mind I had committed to that debt, not really realizing the true gravity of having taken on such a humongous obligation.

In any case, the course of action was very clear, very well defined.

Get to work! Produce! Sell! Make that agreed upon monthly payment! On Time!

The rest is History, outlined in story after story in this, the Last Roundup. An old song says, Lord, you gave me a Mountain this time.

Thank you, I'll do my best.

Dick Weaver

I first met Dick W in the story told about my stopping to chat with the survey crew when I was a union laborer pulling a roof bolter along, underground, long ago, now.

He was a gentle, soft-spoken man, five good kids, good full blooded German wife, a really great guy with a really good family. Coming from an executive level background, he was down to earth, intelligent, unpretentious.

Living some twenty miles from the Seanor Mine, he rented a dwelling nearby, and I, having a one-ton flatbed truck in my masonry business also ongoing at the time, offered to help him move, lock, stock and barrel, here.

It was on Memorial Day, 1959 when I landed in New Kensington where they lived and commenced loading my truck. With sideboards I had added, we packed an entire five room house onto that flatbed, piled high and wide.

Moving tenuously, we must have presented an appearance similar to an Oklahoma Sooner Family heading to California, choosing the easiest possible path between there and here, the least steep hills, least sharp curves, the smoothest roads.

We only broke down once on the twenty-mile journey, a flat tire at the Beaver Run causeway. I had to mount the spare right on the road, as there was nowhere to pull off, narrow berm, then the lake. I prayed my jack could lift the load, and thankfully, it did, and we were once again on our way.

One more uneventful trip and we called it a day, 16 hours of hard work, and they were at their new home, setting up.

I was only 24 years old, and the big, wide, wonderful world of industry had just opened up on me, and I was absolutely thrilled. My first involvement was an already active project, a 750-foot-long hole slanting into the mine from the surface, to facilitate an advanced part of the mine with supplies and personnel.

All kinds of survey, engineering-related work was my experience over the next five years, my knowledge level expanding exponentially, to serve me in the future, as is evidenced in the exposure written in those many stories.

Dick and I worked together for over five years, and not once was there a negative exchange, never a harsh word between us.

He taught me much about many things, he was very smart. He would say, struggling with a tough question: Who knows what the turtle knows - but the turtle.

He preached, when lifting or pulling something really heavy, don't pull or lift with all of your might, save 5 percent, hold back because that's when you inflict permanent, serious injury. Go get some help instead.

I've adhered to that philosophy since, and at age 88, I'm uninjured anywhere.

Our boss, Rusty Lewis, was a really nice mining engineer; was equally personable and helpful, professional in every way.

It's a bit amusing, though, when eight years later, he was employed by me, after I had received a Professional Surveyor License.

Then, in 1964, a new mine neighboring the Seanor Mine turf had opened up, and they were in the market for a full-time surveyor to take care of the many projects forthcoming there.

I applied for the job and was hired, starting immediately.

So, Dick gave me a two-hour finishing course in operation of a transit, I already being familiar with the backup work, the math, etc.

And I was now Chief Surveyor in a coal mine, one within the proximity of my home, one projected for forty year's work. I'm set for life. Sure.

As an entrepreneur, previously often stated, I was manufacturing mining products and also in the business of sharpening mining tools for a number of mines. I was also providing surveyor services to the public without the convenience of a Surveyor's License – a bit illegal, when an old friend, Dick W. happened to see me at the mine he was now surveying for.

He made one suggestion, a suggestion that ultimately changed my life. The suggestion that I should study a bit and take the test for a Surveyor's License, which I followed up on, and within a few months I was a Licensed Surveyor, able to legally work for the public, and industry in general.

I kept in touch with him, informing him of my now having a license, and he made a request.

Would I sign and seal current mine maps for him, the regulatory agency requirement of providing maps to be recorded to allow the public access to the whereabouts of the underground mine, every six months. He, as yet unlicensed, couldn't do it, so I did, making me his co-worker.

At the honorary dinner his church was holding for him – previously mentioned in another story, I requested permission to rebut his telling of how appreciative he was of my saving his life, as he put it.

Absolutely gratified that I had an opportunity to speak in the presence of his most respected peers, I said:

I met this wonderful man, Dick W. many years ago, when I was a coal mine laborer with a future progression of unknown potential beyond an increase in hourly wages and a future pension.

Five years working with him gave me knowledge and experience far above and beyond that of a coal mine laborer.

Thanks, in great part to him, I am well on my way to an ongoing future of high promise, secure and already rewarding beyond my wildest dreams.

In his guidance I found patience, wisdom, and direction for a bright future. I want to publicly thank him from the bottom of my heart. Thank you all for listening.

Dick retired when the mine he was working for closed during a miner's strike.

I, very busy, totally occupied long hours every day, rarely took time to visit with Dick. He, now living in town with his wife Irene, happened to meet my daughter and told her that Dick would like to have me visit him, reasonably soon, at his house.

So, the next day I stopped in and had a memorable half-hour visit with him, reminiscing about the past history we shared, and so on, a very nice moment in time.

I bade him goodbye; he died a few days later.

He was 82, God Bless and Keep Him Forever, a truly fine man.

Smoke in 7 Right

I was the Surveyor's helper, and we were up in 7 Right in the Seanor Mine when word came through via telephone, there was a cable on fire upwind of that section, and a lot of toxic smoke was coming toward us, and we should leave, abandon the section, now.

Cable fires create horrible smoke in high volume that is absolutely deadly, a few minutes breathing it, and you're likely to meet your Creator, soon.

So, everyone working in 7 Right heads for the belt, getting out to a safe area. All except me.

I, supposedly an intelligent, high I.Q. guy, reasoned that if I retreat deeper into the mined section, the smoke wiII short cut, bypass where I would wait it out.

The sheer stupidity of that reasoning defies description, but there I was, committing certain suicide.

The smoke had not yet gotten into 7 Right, requiring travel time to get there in free flow. I'm sitting in as far as I can go, when it does begin reaching me, when, out of the blue, so to speak, a miners' light appears, he shouting, Charlie, come on, get in here.

It was George Hafer, barely known to me, who had noticed I had not gotten onto the outgoing belt.

Jeopardizing his own life, he got off the belt, ran back considerable distance to where I was and saved my life.

The smoke persisted for several hours, was more than needed to qualify me to begin my next life, somewhere.

Thank You George and May God Bless You Always.

No question, he was my Guardian Angel.

Cable on Belt

Back in the good old days, we used to ride the coal hauling belts into and out of the mine work area, sometimes for miles, taking upwards of an hour.

The belt that hauled coal out of the mine was simply reversed, so supplies and personnel would be taken in.

I believe that method is illegal now, battery powered tractors are used now, much safer in transport.

One morning, we were going in to an active section, riding the belt, I in front, when my miners' light showed me something was stuck on the belt ahead of me, I fast approaching it.

Here, it was a long, heavy cable the mechanics were taking in to the section to repair something, and instead of them taking the cable in after all men had gone in, they thoughtlessly put it on the belt ahead of the miners.

So, I was the lucky one to be right behind it, the worst possible place to be.

The anchor they had put on the front of the cable to hold it on had already fallen off, leaving an extremely dangerous potential, Which actually occurred.

The front of the cable had wiggled off the moving, bouncing belt, and had hung up, with the rest of the long cable piling up at that spot, blocking anything else from moving past, which in this case, was me.

Seeing I'm fast coming to the blocker, with just seconds to assess my situation, I reached for the emergency stop wire that is always along side a belt, pulled on it, and nothing happened, the belt was still moving, fast.

Down to practically no time left, I'm desperately aware I absolutely cannot get caught in the piling up cable.

In short order, I would have been crushed and cooked, the belt moving, but I am not.

And there are guys coming on the belt, soon, with nowhere to go. I could not jump off the belt on the right-hand side because a bad roof condition at that point demanded that posts be set very close together, leaving no room for landing, if jumping off the belt there.

But we've heard this before, providentially, suddenly, an opening of just a couple of feet appears, and I have a spot to bail off.

Now I can reach the pull cord and stop the belt, preventing anyone else from being pulled into that pile of cable.

With the belt stopped, we untangled the cable, took it off the belt, restarted the belt, jumped back on, and went on our not so merry way to work.

Another day in the pits?

Was my Guardian Angel present?

Kentucky Drillers

Working at the Seanor Mine in the early 1960s' as a surveyor helper, we were drilling a large hole, 6 feet diameter, for an air intake into a newly projected mining area.

A drilling contractor out of Canada had the contract, with most of their employees being young men from Kentucky.

As a group, they were unfriendly, non-communicative, hostile by nature, so it seemed.

I, a Bonafede Yankee, was not among their favorite people, especially being technical, I was viewed as less than a man, in their rough and tumble world. Drilling is a hard vocation, always wet, cold, dangerous.

Drilling a 6-foot hole had its problems, it's not like ordinary water well drilling, where the drill bit cuttings are simply blown back up the hole, easily shoveled aside.

Those days, a big core drill was the tool, that method cuts a channel around the outer perimeter of the hole, leaving the entire center in one piece.

In order to extract a section of drilled strata, fingers on the drill are activated closed, then the whole piece, 4 to 5 feet long, is carefully pulled up and out of the hole, deposited nearby for removal.

Standing watching this one day, as they were pulling the core out, it slipped out of the barrel holding it, and falling back down the open hole, then wedged itself crossways, stuck there about 50 feet down in the hole, close to two tons of rock.

The driller tried to carefully tug on the drill, to no avail. It was stuck, really stuck.

The foreman admitted to being at a total loss for a solution, the Kentucky boy drill operator was clueless, and in desperation, looked at me and said: Okay, smart guy, what do we do? So, I told him:

Take the hand-held jackhammer, drill stem and bit down there into the hole, drill a hole no more than three feet deep into the center of the core.

I'll get you an expansion shell, a 3-foot-long roof bolt with a top plate, and lower them down to you.

Put the bolt through the hole in the plate, screw the shell onto the bolt, insert the bolt into the 3-foot-deep hole you drilled, tighten it up with a hand wrench, tight, the shell anchoring the bolt to the core.

Then a cable was lowered, fixing it around the bolt, under the plate.

Now, driller, pull, real easy, pull.

Lo and behold, the core came loose, slowly brought to the surface, intact, a huge sigh of relief from everyone.

The look Kentucky and I exchanged was worthy of a camera.

This all transpired in late November, if I remember correctly, and right about the time the core problem was solved, it started to rain, the temperature was at around 35 degrees or so, very cold.

So, I said to my new-found friend, pointing to a tarp, I'll give you a hand setting that tarp up, give you some cover in the rain.

He looked at me derisively and said: Hell no, man, we won't maaaalt, and looked away.

So, I left and went back to our warm, dry office.

The next morning, going to work past the drilling site, it was still about 35 degrees, raining a continuous drizzle, and I saw my Kentucky friends out, drilling in the rain.

The sound of his comment echoed in my skull: Hell no, man, we won't maaaalt.

And they didn't, done and gone several weeks later.

Fast Belt

We, the Surveyors, routinely covered each section of the mine about once a week, sometimes missing a week if there's a valid reason.

A belt upgrade had been done in a section named West Main, and this was our first visit there since it had been completed.

Finishing quickly that day, getting ready to jump onto the new belt to leave, I noticed it was running faster than normal, but dismissing any concern, I get on, heading outside.

The way we rode was flat on your belly, head up so you can watch ahead for problems, or to see your exit point.

You must jump on, since the belt is already moving, and you quickly learn how to time it.

Already on, I notice how fast it really Is going, just as I slam into an air check, a fairly stiff rubber flap across the belt to guide air flow, that rips my helmet and miner's headlamp off, throwing them behind me, violently striking the support rollers, throwing the helmet and light up into the air, then slamming back down every four feet of travel over the rollers.

Now I'm in total darkness, no helmet, no light, flying at 800 feet per minute towards the dump point at the end of the belt, with no idea as to the makeup of it; as to how I would transfer to another belt going in another direction, in this case towards the coal silo, where the end, for me awaits.

In desperation, I reached behind me with an open hand, and I am absolutely sure, my Guardian Angel placed the bouncing miner's helmet, and the still-intact headlamp into my outstretched hand just before the moment when I had to get off the belt or die. Being able to see where I was now, and safely get off the belt.

Writing about it still gives me the shakes.

Kettle on Transit

My transit man, Dick Weaver, at the Seanor Mine was setting up his transit preparing for our next set of advance markers.

It usually took him up to 10 minutes to level up while I just stayed nearby, sometimes watching, sometimes not.

This day, I was fairly close by when I noticed a very slight movement in the rock just above him and the transit, and something compelled me to yell to him - Jump! Move! Now!

He, thank God, instantly reacted to my shout and jumped, clearing 4 or 5 feet away in a second.

Just as he jumped, a large kettle, some call it a pot, about four feet in diameter, a foot or more thick, dropped straight down out of the roof, smashing the transit into small pieces.

Had I not seen its first move, and had he not reacted to my shout, he most likely would have been killed by that rockfall, it weighing anywhere up to 5 or 6 hundred pounds, compounded by the kinetic thrust of a falling object.

Even though he was openly grateful at the time, I became fully aware of his appreciation some years later, at a Church Dinner being held in his honor, for services he had rendered to them, when in his after-dinner oration, he tearfully expressed his appreciation openly, relating the experience, in my presence.

Note: A kettle, as far as we know, is the original form of an ancient tree, filled in with sediment as part of the coal forming process.

Load Of House Coal

I volunteered to deliver a four-ton load of coal to a customer in the one-ton dump truck I had bought for this, years ago. A home high on the hill overlooking the drivers' testing center near Nev Kensington was my objective.

Being experienced at this, I viewed it as just a routine, most likely, uneventful event.

Oh yeah.

My not knowing, or realizing it, this home was not active daily, and because of that, the driveway access was neither well defined, nor readily travelable, especially in wet or soft ground conditions, which it was actually both.

That, combined with a sloping, severely steep ending at the house presented me with a real challenge.

Of course, I put the truck into four-wheel drive when leaving the highway, I was still confident it was not going to be a problem at the top, a long way up.

The first thousand feet or so went well, no issues, then it became steeper, a curve or two, a bit more tender footing, following some semblance of a roadway, ever more indistinct.

I still see that last leg in my mind's eye, even now. It was steep, all grass, slight right-hand curve.

An intense, brief emotional shot of fear passed through me as floored the accelerator, lunging upward, almost reaching the house, when the wheels lost traction and stopped moving forward, stopped altogether, spinning wheels but not moving.

In what has to be classed as fifth dimension entrance, I only remember starting to slide backwards, totally out of control, picking up speed, looking at a thousand-foot, steep down drop to who knows what, when, suddenly, the truck, going violently backwards, turns sharply upgrade, sliding to a complete stop in a spot wide enough not only to dump my load of coal, but to safely turn around, and head back out the way had come in, now empty and in complete control, not only of the truck, but my fate.

There is no question, the Guardian Angel(s) took over up there, and here I still am.

Thank you very much, my dear Angel(s).

Herb Under Rock

We were doing a routine survey in the Jamison Mine one day, advancing the mine, when I became concerned that my helper, Herb was taking far too long to return to me after having installed the markers in the roof, as usual.

He, being too far away to be heard, if he answered my verbal call; there were no telephones or radio allowed underground.

Appearing from his direction, I noticed a flicking of his head lamp, his miner's light, in a repetitive sequence, so I abandoned my transit, and went toward him to see what the problem was that he wasn't returning.

Getting near him, I heard a subdued - help, Charlie, help.

Here, in pounding the marker into the roof, he had caused a large loose rock 6 inches thick or so, weighing hundreds of pounds, to have fallen onto his back, pinning him in a doubled over position, unable to shed the rock, which was still being held in one corner by a roof bolt, only able to have made that circular motion commonly used to signal – come to me.

Quickly getting help, we were able to lift the rock off him, and then pulling it down.

Fortunately, he, being quite strong physically, had sustained no injury.

Mantrip—Steve

I was the Mine Surveyor for the Jamison Mine, and, having completed my work in the mine one day, was at the man trip station early, so I could sit wherever I chose.

There is that segment of society, especially in some occupations that are considered rough and tough, like underground miners, that believes that technical, professional people are something less than manly, clean hands, etc., only to be tolerated by the real men.

At the man trip station that day, I was sitting in the prime spot, such as it is.

At quitting time, the miners all come there, pile in anywhere space is available and go, no big deal, it happens every day.

Well, that day, here comes Steve ___, a big, unpleasant guy, who, seeing me in the prime seat, his seat according to him, approached me and said - you're in my seat.

I said, I don't see your name on it.

He took a few steps toward me, menacingly, and repeated - you're in my seat, move.

In my work as a surveyor, we commonly carry a bricklayer's hammer, ideal for what we do.

Sitting there, I picked up our hammer, gently tapping my open hand with it, and said:

Steve, I'm going to tell you a little story, one that happened long ago.

Steve is listening closely now.

I continued – Steve, when I was about 8 or 9, my Father had a fully grown bull, weighing about 1500 pounds or so.

A local butcher came to our farm one day, and my dad sold him the bull.

I, curious, said to the butcher, how are you going to get him up into your truck? The butcher, not a big man, said to me: Watch.

He took a midsized ball peen hammer out of his truck, lined up with the bull's head, and with one lightning-fast stroke, killed the bull instantly. He never knew what hit him.

I stopped tapping my open hand with the bricklayer's hammer and paused before setting it down beside my helper, watching Steve closely.

He never said one word, sitting down in an open spot in the man trip.

I continued to occupy that seat anytime I rode the mantrip, never again challenged for it by anyone.

Including Steve.

Gas Well at Jamison

My helper and I had finished our work that day in the Jamison Mine, and we're waiting for the mine foreman to come by, as he usually did around Noon on his way out of the mine.

He showed up, on his battery powered buggy, as expected, and said - come on, get on, let's go for a ride.

I said no, there's nothing I need to see down in there, go ahead, we'll wait for you here. I was in there yesterday and lined them up.

He snarled saying let's go, come on, get on here, let's go.

So, I got on and away we went, to an active section of the mine, and a few minutes later, we're there, next to a continuous miner grinding away at the seam, progressing at about a foot a minute into the solid coal.

Suddenly, I realized the miner was mining in the wrong direction! The day before, I had given the section foreman markers in the roof to go by safely, past a live gas well, but he took it on his own to grab some easy coal and turned the miner ninety degrees to the right of my sights and was already within ten feet of the well when I stopped him.

I am loathe to think of the consequences of a fifty-ton miner with a huge carbide-tipped cutting head powerful enough to routinely slice through rock hard coal, cut into the old, rotted gas well casing, then the tubing, spewing untold amounts of gas into a spark filled chamber.

At least 20 men would have met certain death immediately, or within a very short time.

Just writing this story gives me a headache and the chills, 57 years later.

Certainly, my Guardian Angel was on duty, faithfully tending to his/her duties on that day.

Post on Scoop

I was in the Jamison Mine extending the directional markers that day, and having completed the initial section, needed to do another area, some distance away.

In 42 inches of height, it can be just a bit trying, carrying a transit and bucket, so I stopped a miner driving a scoop, a battery powered unit that can either carry or tow a trailer.

In this case it was towing a single axle trailer filled with posts, 6 Inches in diameter and 42 inches long, going in the same direction as I was.

So, I climbed into the rear end of the trailer and signaled go. Mine floors are not uniform, so the movement of the trailer, being a single axle, was not just forward, but rocking up and down enough that the front of the trailer rocked up, catching the end of a post against the roof, and the continued forward movement, caused the post to be pushed backward, just missing my head and shoulders, flying out of the back of the trailer like a battering ram. The driver, oblivious to what had just transpired, continued on.

I just breathed a silent: Thank you God, Thank you, Guardian Angel.

End of Jamison Mine

The Jamison Mine was experiencing geological issues in the mid 60's, the coal seam being much thinner as we drove west. As the seam diminished, increasing amounts of methane gas was expelling out of the coal, making adequate ventilation a real problem.

In response to decreased production, and increased demand, management superseded the mine's normal projection, and mined an area they should not have.

In doing this, a large volume of water had accumulated in the worked-out area, and was trapped above the approved, active area.

As it happened, the mine foreman requested that I go to the active area and mark an absolute limit as to the current mining that would safely bypass the huge lake above it, created by the emergency for product earlier.

So, I marked it, spoke to the day shift section boss, solemnly warning him not to mine beyond my markers, and to inform the Hoot-owl shift of my warning.

Ever pressed for production, though, the second shift foreman figured I had left ample safe distance to the water, which I had, took just one eleven foot cut beyond my markers.

No problem, yet.

The third shift boss comes on, fully instructed as to what transpired during the day, and second shifts, and cautioned as to why there is the need to maintain a barrier of unmined coal from the impoundment.

Again, the boss, ever pushed for production, reasons, well, Charlie left plenty of barrier, second shift only took out eleven feet of it. I'll just take eleven more feet, it'll be okay.

So, he took out eleven more feet, and there went my entire 25-foot barrier, and while they were there, it was okay.

Here, the third shift had mined within 3 feet of the mined area filled with water, and it had just begun to trickle through underneath.

Saturday morning, the maintenance crew is met with a fast-flowing stream from the now broken barrier, passing into haulage and track transport areas, starting to fill a lower mined out area.

A dire emergency now, pumps had nowhere to pump to, the mine opening being several thousand feet away, much higher in elevation, and no receiving or treatment ponds in place.

The only hope is that the trapped volume vas less than the mined out area. It was but ran at a much reduced rate; although ultimately, it didn't matter.

I here note that all this happened at the same time I was planning to leave, to put forth a two-week notice.

Explosion

I believe it was February, 1967 that conditions In the Jamison Mine became difficult in one of the active mining sections. The coal seam encountered an area where strata turned into a sandrock primarily, a condition that often brought negatives with it. Thin coal, excessive methane gas, and bad top and soft bottom.

These conditions in combination also created difficulty in properly ventilating the work face, often allowing the buildup of dangerous levels and accumulations of methane gas, forcing stoppages of mining until clearance is achieved. Compounding these natural issues was the unhappy fact that the continuous miner and the receiving shuttle car (a buggy) had recently experienced an electrical arcing when touching during loading. A common event.

The night shift mechanics had addressed the problem but these issues can be extremely elusive to Identify, and it was believed the repair had been made. Mining resumed at the usual starting time in the subject section, and all appeared to be normal, and going well.

It is not known, nor will it ever be known exactly what went horribly wrong, but it is believed the buggy returned from the dump point to the miner creating an arcing of high voltage electricity in and around the pocket of methane gas that violently exploded, creating a fireball that engulfed six miners in close proximity to the explosion.

Thankfully, no miner lost his life in the conflagration, but much suffering ensued from the burns sustained.

The mine never reopened or produced any coal ever again. Over one hundred jobs were lost forever.

Morgan Strip

In recalling the Morgan Strip, I'm not only bringing back the many memorable events and people who were involved in my first, greatest, and longest lasting surface mine, beginning in the spring of 1974, and ending in the autumn of 1987, in the Ruth Kier property.

This was the mine I, we, cut our teeth in the mining industry. This was the mine where I had been friendly with the landowner and his great children, Don and Betty, from childhood, and have remained so throughout his, and their lifetimes to this day.

This was the mine where I met the first one of the finest groups of people in my entire life, the District Mine Inspectors. His name was Bernie Snyder, and the list of others since is a bit long over 44 years, and numerous districts in multiple counties, but they all were good, sensible workers focused on doing their job, help keep the miners safe, and kept a close eye on our precious streams.

I have only high praise for them all.

This was the mine where Chuck Morgan and I stood looking at the endless old highwalls left unbackfilled, and the pit holes left from ancient deep mining unfilled, the old mine opening unrestored.

These have been restored long since, with dozens of deer and other wildlife having a place to safely survive.

This was the mine where, in backfilling all of the open pits have prevented millions and millions of gallons of rain from entering the old deep mines, and being contaminated, allowing it instead to flow into the Kiski River clean and natural, mixing in with the once highly polluted river, creating a river now containing edible fish, and numerous other river dwellers.

We, alone, do not take sole credit for this wonderful upgrade of river water quality, as other operators also were a big part of this.

This was the mine where Tom F. had the basketball sized rock go through his "Hunting" Trailer's roof, past his bed while he was in it, and go through the floor into the earth underneath.

This was the mine where I, building a heavy-duty road out to the township road, accidentally dug into an old gasoline tank, about half full of gasoline, luckily (?) not causing an explosion or fire in doing so.

This was the mine where I had purchased an old steam shovel actually powered by a big diesel engine and hired a heavy equipment hauler to move it to the mine from a site several miles away.

A driver for the moving company, obviously high on something or other, came, and we loaded the 70-ton shovel onto a 40-ton lowboy, and away we went pulled by a big tractor onto a state highway, then crossing a 20-ton limit bridge, tearing down every low hanging telephone line because of the height of the shovel's cab, then turned onto a township road to my site, then discovering he was too long to safely navigate a sharp S curve, got the whole rig cross-ways, hanging the lowboy and its load up in the air over a culvert end about four feet off the ground, stopped, where he can't proceed or retreat. He expressed his opinion of the world of heavy hauling in no way related to Christian terminology, then got into his accompanying vehicle and left, saying something quite unholy as they pulled away, along with it's yours now, good luck.

An impossible situation was now mine, an absolute novice at this sort of thing.

As it happened, a friend of mine, Ben Elkin, was working his bulldozer at my mine, now just less than a half mile away from the hung-up lowboy, and learning of the dilemma, visited the site, then instructed me to leave, he would address it.

Somehow, someway, it had to be God and a couple of Angels, altogether in the form of Ben, but that night he had the shovel unloaded safe on the ground.

The next day I called the guy I had bought it from, and he came and drove it the rest of the way to the site where I could work it.

I never did actually work it. Instead, I bought a one-yard CAT excavator, which was much more suitable for what we were doing.

I eventually gave the shovel to a scrap dealer with the understanding, you take it, move it out, it's yours, no charge, no fee. I kissed one nightmare away forever.

This was the mine where I purchased my first big bulldozer and mid-sized front-end loader, then survived the shock of that invoice for $335,000 that came in the mail.

This was the mine where my then son-in-law, Calvin, was running the big dozer when the mine collapsed under him, leaving him stopped sideways at a 45-degree angle, desperately looking out a side window, mouthing HELP.

He was able to use the blade and the rear-mounted ripper to lift himself up; while we shoved dirt and rock under the dozer, filling the hole he had fallen into, driving up and out afterwards. He never did live that down, that look of desperation and that piteous cry for help, which we mimicked forever.

This was the mine where Chuck Morgan and I stood, looking at the old deep mine, long since abandoned, worked out of any safely reachable coal, a scar left on the ground, the opening unblocked.

He said, "What do you think? Can you believe in yourself, and your prayers to the point where you're willing to risk everything, devote all of your time to chasing a dream, a dream journey fraught with unknown dangers, toils and snares?", taking words out of an old gospel song.

Chuck had worked long and hard, day and night, yet had managed to accumulate somewhat short of his lifetime goals, turning his grocery store over to a very capable son Don, an equally hard worker, both honest as the day is long.

I am sure his, their, positive outlook for the mining to be successful was of great help, both to me and them, with royalties to be paid, month in and month out.

This was the man who cautioned me that there was an unknown, unmarked property line that caused me to pay royalties to him, rather than the rightful owner, which I needed to track down.

So, I immediately ran a survey and proved he was correct, discovering a man named Ralph Lytle who was the unknown rightful owner.

I contacted him, discussed the situation, and was surprised to learn he was long since aware of the unmarked property line, and was not at all concerned, believing the right thing would ultimately be done.

And it was. I gave him a substantial check for current royalties due, with future payments assured, in total agreement.

There were many aspects of that mine that were positive, in great part, the Kiski Township Supervisors let us use the road system without undue interference or demands, there being only one dwelling along the roads we used, and they were not concerned about our trucks.

As we were approaching the final part of the area available for mining, one unhappy ending did occur, which had to do with an adjoining landowner who had been isolated by a property line barrier; he owning a sliver of low-grade coal, just a few thousand tons, easily mineable, since we were right there.

I offered him a substantial up-front payment for permission to take it. He refused for no legitimate reason, and we continued on, away from the orphaned coal.

He later claimed that his refusal was based on his having erected a foundation for a future campsite there in this totally remote, unobserved area.

His regret was elevated when vandals and thieves came and stole a very expensive fireplace, and actually dismantled a chimney and stone wall he had built for it, then later the door and windows he had installed in the foundation. They stole them all.

So, after thirteen difficult, many times trying years, we restored the final pit, all per specification. We sadly, fondly, told the Morgan Strip thank you very much, we wish you well forever, and breathed our final goodbyes.

Hunter Strip

A former Client, long gone, had got a few samples, lumps of coal from a site, and had it tested for quality. The results were astounding, every critical parameter higher than high, truly mouthwatering. Are you sure?

Another operator had been told about it, and in all the fuss as to who had the priority, I was told to draft a lease agreement and release of rights, which I did, and he signed it but in the absence of a witness, so when he changed his mind, he claimed fraudulent terminology, restrictions, and reservations were part and parcel of the document, and so on, all of which I denied.

A legal skirmish then ensued, and after some trading and payment, I got the job site.

The permitting was rough, regulatory was nasty the whole way, revise this, revise that, change this, add that, ad infinitum, you 're near Loyalhanna Creek, the highest class of stream.

Finally, ready to start, we discover the access way is by terms not allowing heavy trucks on it, besides, it's too narrow.

Right off, we're building a thousand feet of high-cost road through clay-like strata, the high dollar stone disappearing into the soft clay, load after load. I'm off to a great start, to go broke. The negatives are escalating.

Another discovery also visited, the cabin at the property, long since a home site, had its own drinking water source, a spring right beside it, flowing clear and cold all the time . Working there preparing the site, several of us took a big drink from the spring.

By the next day, all three of us were behaving a bit differently, spending a lot of time frequently visiting the outhouse there, downright sick. Of course, the mineral content of the water was way different than our systems could tolerate. The negatives on this job just keep piling up.

Just about the time we are ready to start mining, to generate some revenue to cope with the equipment payments, the U.M.W. calls a widespread strike. It's well known; I operate non-union, but have an arms-length unspoken agreement to honor their actions, painful though they may be.

So, while the war rages, we sit, idle, and wait.

One day, my phone rang, and it was the State Mine Inspector, Jake L. He says, Charlie, do you know you have a big open pit, from previous mining by others years ago that is completely full of rainwater and you better get it out. That was all he said.

So, I borrowed a 4-inch diesel pump and enough hose to get to the end of the pit, and into the permitted downstream channel.

Then, I and my three boys started to pump the water out of the pit, which was 300 feet long, 60 feet wide, and 40 feet deep, full to the rim.

A four-inch pump at open flow can move close to forty thousand gallons per hour, and we pumped for three weeks non-stop before it was over.

We took turns babysitting the pump, I and one of the boys would run for 12 hours, then the other two would run for 12 hours, over and over.

To this day, none of the boys will listen to a John Denver record because I drove them insane with that tape while pumping, the only one I had.

I had just purchased two new machines for that job, a Cat D8K and a Cat 988B. Now we're on our way to fame and fortune.....sure.

The strike settled, we drilled and blasted a cut, and went to work. I hired an experienced "friend" to operate the 988B, and it only took him one week to destroy two tires – cost to replace at that time was $12,000.

Finally, we had our first cut of coal ready to go.

Now what? The buyer sampled the coal and said, "Charlie, this coal is junk, I can't pay you the agreed price, I'll give you half." The samples were lies. I had no choice; the payments were overdue.

So, I fired my friend and contracted with another former surface mine operator, Bruno, to take over the job, pulling my kids and me to another job I had acquired nearer to home, the Petro Job.

Bruno was a bit weird, kept loaded guns around nearby all the time inside the machines while operating, and kept three German Shepherds at the office trailer, all nasty and alert.

Contractor Bruno goes to work, and before you know it he needs another 5,000 gallons of fuel.

Time marches on, and enough production is achieved that costs are at or about break-even, when, way too soon, he needs another 5,000 gallons, then another, then another. Over the winter period I had bought over 30,000 gallons of diesel for the job.

Coming to my senses, I learned he had been selling my fuel to friends and acquaintances, taking 4–55-gallon drums out at a time in his pickup.

So, out he went, and another former operator needing a job took over. I didn't really know Mike Z, but he had some equipment, including a big drill, so in he came. Mike was pleasant, always agreeable. He had two employees, and he never left his ultraclean pickup, staying clean himself.

Soon after his arrival we made a deal where I sold him the job for one dollar, he assuming the permit and all liabilities that went with it.

In the deal, he agreed to buy a big front-end loader, a 400 Hough, from me for $80,000, payments to be made early on.

For the record, he never made a single payment, but what he did made up for it, and he returned it later anyway.

The first thing he did was to address the constant flow of water into every active pit, a big-time cost and pain, treating it before discharging it, if necessary.

Mike returned my loader to me, backfilled the last pit, made everything nice and legal, then went to Florida to live with his family.

Sadly, he was killed in a gangland shooting a short time later.

One night, late, very late, I went up that mountain to that job site for the last time, tore down all identification signs related to me, or us remaining in place, broke them all into small pieces, piled them in a ritualistic pyramid in the center of the township road, poured gasoline I had brought all over them, set them on fire, and left.

One last look in my rearview mirror featured a flaming pyre, a fitting farewell to all those years of torture there, now over, forever.

Drilling at Pymatuning

About 40 or so years ago, a mining engineer friend of mine owned a tract of land near a major reservoir, a natural wet land, extensive, covering many acres, with a coal seam in or around it, way north of here.

He directed me to its location, and told me to go ahead and explore its potential for surface mining.

So, I'm up there this fine day with a Davey drill, ready to check out the whereabouts of and coal characteristics for future marketability.

I was able to drill only a few holes, not finding any coal to speak of, well away from the wetland.

The driller looked at me and said, "Where next?"

Seeing how wet and soft the ground was nearer the lake, and not daring to stick a 40-ton drill in the mud, selected the only firm, dry spot In the area, and directed him to it, stopping in the middle of the township road we were traveling on.

He looked at me, puzzled questioning the wisdom of drilling in the township road. I forcefully pointed down, indicating to drop the drill bit and start drilling.

What if a car comes, he asked.

I said, what if it doesn't? Drill.

So, he drilled. It was easy drilling, soft, the primary drill steel sinking fast.

Suddenly, at 20 feet of depth, a full-blown deluge, as the bit hit an aquifer, the return air blowing water up 50 feet or more, spraying everyone.

The driller stopped drilling, and looked at me, looking for guidance. I immediately signaled up, up, up with the drill steel, and once up I signaled down, fold the drill into its resting place in the truck bed.

Once the steel was out of the hole, the water was free flowing up out of the 6-inch hole a foot high in geyser like form, a regular artesian well.

Spotting a round boulder about the size of a basketball, I grabbed it and jammed it into the hole, temporarily slowing the flow.

Then shouted, let's get the hell out of here. I haven't been back since.

Al Tenney

I met Al at the R&PCoaI Company headquarters in Indiana, Pa., the day I was given the deed for a tract of unmined coal they had sold me thanks to a guy named Wootsie Faulk, a great friend, located within my then-current mine, a real win for me.

There was instant camaraderie, we both being well versed in mining and knowledgeable in many other topics.

He was Vice President of Field Operations and had a firm grip on everything going on. He must have thought his Jeep Wagoneer was a big dune buggy, because in my many travels with him, he drove it everywhere a dune buggy could go.

To say Al was beneficial to me, us, is an understatement of monumental proportions, and too voluminous to list. Of course, I benefitted him and his company too, in many dealings.

Generally, he gave me well-paying contracts for various projects, always keeping me healthy financially when economics turned bleak, as they all too often did in the coal business.

He employed my boys when they needed work, during strikes or depressed economic times. He knew we were experts in circumventing certain regulatory rules and saved his company many thousands of dollars in cooperation with us.

We had an arrangement where I supplied him with permitted sites ready to mine, he supplied me with financing help in many of my sites. There was never a wrinkle, with a well rewarding ending for both sides.

When the R&P Coal Company was taken over and terminated operations, I purchased all their unmined Pittsburgh Seam Coal in my region in an agreement he and I hammered out that was absolutely fair and equitable, ultimately benefiting us and his successor coal company greatly.

He was unquestionably fair and honest in everything we ever did. He paid for every lunch, would not take no for an answer. It was an all too brief and pleasant association of 15 or 20 years, but, a health issue arose, and tragically, during a medical procedure something went horribly wrong, and the world lost one of its best and brightest sons.

If the world was filled with men like Al, what a wonderful world it would surely be. I will hold his memory at the highest level of respect possible, as long as I live.

May God bless and keep him in His fold for all time, he was the best.

Truck Driver, Boron

It was a busy time, mining coal two shifts a day, we were using a lot of fuel.

So, I contacted Boron company, a major fuel distributor, and contracted for fuel delivery by full tanker loads, 8,000 gallons per load.

One day a load arrived, right on time, the driver, to his credit, was in perfect order, immaculate in professional attire, spotless truck, neat tie, white gloves, impressive.

Son, Jim, and Bill met him, informing him that his 4-inch diameter hose discharge nozzle would not fit into the receiving tanks hole, which was only 3 inches in diameter.

No problem said the driver. He simply changed the 4-inch nozzle out, putting a 2-inch nozzle on the discharge hose from the truck. LOOK OUT!

Now Jim told the driver that he and Bill would climb up the ladder onto the tank, insert the truck's discharge line into the tank hole, and then both would climb up on top of the tank to anchor the hose down to avoid the chance of any spillage when filling the tank.

The driver mumbles yeah, yeah, okay, okay. He's now in a hurry to hit and get away from these hicks.

Jim and Bill are still standing on the ladder, already having inserted the hose nozzle into the tank because it's very clumsy, when the now impatient driver turns the truck pump RPM up high, throwing the discharge valve open, diesel fuel on its way, big time!

That's when all hell broke loose!

Those truck pumps are very powerful, made so as to be able to discharge a full load as quickly as possible.

Well, the now constricted 4-inch line, down to a 2-inch opening compounded the pressure way up, ripping the nozzle up out of the tank, diesel shooting out, hose whipping about wildly, soaking not only Jim and Bill but the impatient driver head to toe. It was absolutely wild, chaotic.

In mere seconds they were all soaked head to toe.

By the time the pump was stopped to be able to shut the nozzle off, many gallons of fuel were sprayed into the atmosphere, and onto them.

By the time the driver had everything under control, the boys were already near him, ready to maim, at best, kill at worst. The Hill District was safer.

The driver, pleading piteously for mercy, escaped unharmed, most likely vowing to never return here again – never!

I sent the boys home, needing recurring showers, now!

We never saw that driver again.

Bowling the Boss

When I was the Mine Surveyor at the Jamison Coal Company, I shared a general office with the Mine Superintendent named John H.

He bowled regularly in a bowling league and was, supposedly, an above-average bowler.

Since I was around average or better with my 185 average, I jokingly challenged him to, I believe it's called a frame – three sets of ten or more throws.

He would always refuse, for no reason, but since he was then on a two-week notice of departure, he agreed to meet the following Sunday at Lee's Bowling Alley.

When I arrive, he's already warmed up, I said I didn't need any warmup, having bowled within the past year, somewhere.

He throws first, a spare.

I throw, two strikes.

He throws, another spare.

I throw, two strikes.

He throws, nothing.

I throw, two more strikes.

And so that was pretty much how it went. I wound up with a 255, pretty respectable for my first game in months.

There was never a second game. He bagged his ball, shook my hand, and left, never to meet him again.

That was 56 years ago, and I remember it well.

Dan M

Dan and I became friends when I took over the regulatory requirements for his small deep mine, related to the guiding, mapping, and filing, along with certain federal reporting, etc.

He was a throwback to the hard times era, and was a rough, tough, gruff single minded type, unyielding in his beliefs and mannerisms.

He openly hated MSHA personnel, stating so, in their presence when they came to his site. They, in turn, wrote him many fines for various indiscretions.

He was a one man, one mule show, hardworking, relentless, 16 or 18 hour days were commonplace.

He had a wonderful wife, a truly gentle soul, disabled by medical issues, but cared for by Dan and his sons admirably, dying at an early age from the health problems.

Dan had two sons and one daughter. The sons receiving treatment such, that a strained relationship, at best, would describe it, one leaving and the younger staying in the original home.

His daughter, however, was the apple of his eye, he showering her with every kind of emotional and financial support, in every way favoring her.

Through the years Dan and I associated, our relationship was like a roller coaster, one day up, the next, down, always a guessing game.

I maintain a high level of respect for him in several ways, as some of the deals we made and were involved in were , and are, beneficial to me in the long term. There were promises made, but not kept, too, but in retrospect, probably a good thing for me.

One day he called and asked me to stop in at his house, which was highly unusual, as he was not at all social.

When I arrived, it was painfully obvious, there was a human being experiencing intense pain, indescribable suffering. He motioned for me to sit, and then he opened up.

He had just been informed that his beloved daughter had been murdered, by her thirteen-year old son, Dan's grandson, who had admitted and confessed his plan to do so, and who was now in custody.

He said he never wanted to see his grandson again.

Understandably, this wrecked his already chaotic relationship with his two sons.

I rarely saw him after that, as he had closed his mine and there was no social interaction at all. He was a visibly different man thereafter, and died at age 82, alone.

Dan had not informed his sons of the deals he and I had made over the years. One, in particular, was a property he had a fifty-percent interest in that required the payment of property taxes annually.

When he died the taxes went unpaid; as the heirs of his estate, the two sons were unaware of their inherited ownership of the property.

I, the owner of the other fifty percent, was made aware of the unpaid taxes due, overdue, and was offered the opportunity to pay them and thereby assume one hundred percent ownership of the property. It was the case where there was just one day left to pay the taxes, as the next day it was going up for Sheriff's sale.

So, I called Dan, Jr. and informed him of the entire situation; his inheritance and the unpaid tax due, mentioning that if he was not interested in following up, I would pay the tax and own it entirely, or at least protect it.

He thanked me profusely, immediately went to the courthouse and paid all tax due, saving a very valuable property;

rightfully he and his brother's, keeping it and its future, ongoing income where it belonged.

Thank you, Crabby Dan, Senior – sometimes good things do come in rough packages.

Hunter Strip 988B

It was well into winter when we began mining at the Hunter strip, and being up on top of the mountain, it snowed often, and in higher volume .

It was a fifteen to twenty-inch event, and the loader operator thought he would plow the snow off the narrow, steep township road as a service, not only for our own needs, but for the public as well.

So, he takes the loader, a 52-ton 988B, out onto the snow-covered roadway.

A heavy machine creates ice from snow, just by traveling on it, and that Is exactly' what he did.

Starting down a long, steep grade, he thought he should not continue, as it was getting ever steeper, so he shifted into reverse, and yes, the ice he had just created said no, you not going anywhere, all four wheels spinning backward, the loader started to slide frontward, down the hill.

Now he sinks the teeth of the bucket into the ground to stop the forward slide, the only thing holding him from slipping into oblivion.

There being no cell phones in those days, it was fortunate a traveler came by and called for help from a house phone in town.

A large tow truck came, but overwhelmed by the weight of the loader , and in such conditions, didn't budge the loader, also spinning out, even with chains on.

So, he called a second, really large tow truck, and both were able to pull him up to a safe place.

I recall the operator telling me he would not call me, the scenario being far too ominous.

I believe he was correct.

Just another negative experience at the Hunter strip.

The cost of the two trucks was 1,200 dollars for the rescue.

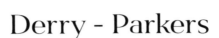

Derry - Parkers

At our Derry Mountain Job one night, Jim and Steve were working second shift, it is getting along toward the end of the lunch period,10 pm or so.

They were sitting in the big front-end loader, the 988B, parked at the far end of the strip pit, when a car with 2 boys and 2 girls pulled into the outside end of the same pit, parked, and made themselves at home, not realizing Jim and Steve were in there too, a hundred yards away.

The boys remained quiet for a little while, giving the parkers time to start doing whatever parkers do.

The engine on that big loader was really quiet, and well muffled even at high RPM. It being winter, and quite cold, the car's windows would have been up, keeping things even more muffled.

At some point, the boys started moving toward the parkers in the big loader, quietly covered the hundred yards from them to the parked car, and at about a hundred feet from them, revved the engine full bore, raised the bucket to full height of about 16 feet, snapped on all the twelve floodlights, and charged toward them in the car, horn blowing, slowly.

The driver of the car, not bothering to dress, then proceeded to set what has to be a record setting exit from the pit, never looking back or saying goodbye.

Boys will be boys, and girls be girls, but they must choose their parking spots more carefully in the future.

Phil B.

In the heyday of the late 70's, after an extended UMWA strike, the coal industry became wildly chaotic, the price of coal quickly rising from a depression level four dollars a ton, to twenty-four dollars, or more, per ton.

Demand was insatiable, generating stations were popping up everywhere, all needing coal for the expanding grid network.

Newly established surface miners were gearing up for prosperity everywhere, me included, selling previously unsaleable coal to eager buyers.

I was heavy into surveying and mining engineering at the same time, picking up new clients almost daily, really busy.

At peak, I had 26 surface miners and 11 deep mines depending on me for technical support services.

That was the setting for my introduction to Phil B.

Phil was unusual, special, not what was normally found in the industry.

Phil was a setup, a plant, something never seen by those of us knowledgeable in the business.

He was straight out of the big city, put there by powerful people, not only to hide him, but to join in the burgeoning coal world, a new source for big money, by them. They even gave him a new name, Phil B.

They bought a huge tract of land with a house and barn on it, over 500 acres, and moved him onto it. They even put some beef cows on it, a real farmer. It also had a very high grade of coal in it.

He knew absolutely nothing about coal, or in the extraction of it out of the ground, not a simple, easy process.

He was extremely smart, both street and general, leaving formal schooling for the dark side of society, and its activities, at an early age. He had spent 6 years in prison, but I didn't ask him why, or what for. He was an experiment , and it worked, for them.

An engineering company had done the necessary work to get him mining, but he wanted someone with more practical experience to serve him. I don't know how he found me, but he did, and by the time I got to visit his ongoing job, there was already a huge hole in the ground, ready to load some coal.

I had never seen It before, but he actually had a powered broom sweeping the final dirt off the exposed coal seam, qualifying it tor top dollar.

Traveling around with him and his hyperactive Collie Dog in his pickup one day, we parked above the pit to look at something, leaving the Collie in the truck, engine running as it was cold outside. Hearing a noise, we see the truck moving, and we watched it go over the highwall, some 70 feet to the bottom, crashing nicely. The Collie was unhurt, the truck totaled.

But the story doesn't end here, it goes on. As time passed, I became more involved with Phil. There was a discussion about a future business relationship, a deep mine with me in charge of it, having considerable deep mining experience; they funding it entirely, a major undertaking. We also explored going into a natural gas well development program, then oil wells.

I had reached the stage where personal protection was assured, and in several instances did have certain threats against us squashed. A group of underage kids, including my two oldest, were granted certain privileges and protection while visiting entertainment complexes they owned in town.

My wife and I would occasionally visit him and his family at their home at the farm, but she was always uneasy there, for no good reason.

Within this time frame I had been invited to work for, then join, another coal mining group within the same vicinity. Being trusting and naïve, I was not aware as to the true makeup of that group.

But Phil was, and in fact, he had been assigned to monitor their actions, and to make sure no harm came to me, an innocent participant in the mining activities, but not in their other, highly illegal endeavors.

Shortening a long, sordid chain of events, Phil extracted me from them, not only unharmed, but with a sizeable payment for my stock holdings in them.

As is all too common in the coal industry, things changed negatively, markets cratered, costs soared, regulatory became vicious instilling new, ugly rules difficult to cope with or circumvent, which was Phil's nature, so he hung it up, quit.

With an even bigger hole left open. He confided in me that the job had a net gain of $450,000 dollars. That was in 1980.

Regulatory then forfeited the bond placed on the job, which just happened to be $450,000 dollars. So, some lucky insurance company funded the restoration cost.

That whole scenario changed everything. Time and distance created a separation of our relationship, and all talk of future business ventures ended.

Phil finally bought a bar near his home, and to the best of my knowledge, drank himself to an early death at age 58.

I have only good memories of him and his associates and will always hold him in the highest regard.

So long, my friend, one of few.

Trucking

There are those times when, in a moment of silence, I question my own sanity in having entered into certain arenas in life where it became painfully clear I didn't belong there.

But isn't that the case with most of us, at one time or another.?

One such venture was my foray into the wide, wonderful world of trucking. My son, John, with the natural ability to sell Eskimos whole house solar heating panels for their igloos, convinced me it would require less than one year till could retire to Hawaii, live happily there, never need to work again.

It was a go! We leased several over-the-road trucks right away.

John could find the loads of dry freight, dispatch the trucks outgoing, repeat that process in reverse bringing the trucks back home. Good deal, get paid, going and coming, just a little time on the phone. All I had to do was make the bank deposits.

Wait, these loads are not that easy to find, it's a big world, you need to be contracted to a broker. That word should have frightened me.

So, we signed up with one out of Philadelphia, of all the corrupt places, we were in the worst.

Oh, they gave us loads, all right, but by the time all the fees were deducted, we owed them money.

Trucking is one of the toughest, roughest businesses of all, and I maintain the highest respect for those small guys that are in it, subjected to the killer instinct of the big boys.

There is no easy business, or we'd all be in it.

Somehow, we survived the broker, operating costs, and drivers. Insanity must have, once again, prevailed.

To get away from the exorbitant leasing costs, we should buy the trucks.

Wonderful! All you have now is licenses, inspections, insurance, repairs, and oh yes, tires, fines and the best of all – DRIVERS.

We got a great deal on four tractor-trailer units, big, over-the-road, ten-four, good buddy-style.

The problems never stop or even pause, much less end, even temporarily.

I had already disposed of two of the original four trucks, and this made three.

This was a never a love-hate relationship, it was a hate-hate relationship as far as I was concerned, and the sooner I was rid of the last one, the faster I would return to some semblance of sanity.

This was almost accomplished when the driver of the last truck was dead-heading home along one of the turnpikes, driving fast as usual; and was unaware the tractor had caught fire at one of the rear duals, possibly a brake hung up, easily spreading to the outside fuel tank.

Other truckers, seeing the fire burning, accelerated by the high-speed, tried to call him on their CB radios, but he, not was not hearing them since his was shut off and not responding, not slowing down.

So, two of them went into action. One passed him, got in front of him. The other came alongside, both slowing down, forcing him to also slow down, and finally, stop.

They and other truckers came with fire extinguishers and put out the fire.

After repair I sold it as quickly as I could, extricating a huge thorn out of my a** forever.

God Bless the truckers, our true lifeline.

Bee Hill

A former client of mine asked me to go with him to evaluate a property he bought, for possible strip mining.

There being no road access to it, we carried the pick and shovel in to it, and went to work, digging in the bottom of the old strip pit that was present throughout the site.

After several hours of hard work, we had a hole, about 6-feet by 6-feet dug, with no sign of any coal, it having been removed by prior mining operations.

That was quite a disappointment, since long standing rumor was that there was coal remaining over the entire 3 or 4 acres.

As a result, my client, aging, ready to retire, offered me the property, so I bought it, with only minimal coal remaining in deep-mined areas.

Once I owned it, I and my former son-in-law, Calvin, went to take a closer look at my purchase.

As we proceeded, we noticed a nest of bees, yellow jackets, at the far end of the pit, and our access. One or more of them was approaching us in a hostile manner.

Retreating, we hurriedly moved to return to my truck, when even more yellow jackets joined in the chase, then even more.

We made it to the truck, stung only a few times each. We, then and there, named the site Bee Hill.

Being long since qualified to do so, I obtained the proper permits to mine the site, my own company being busy; I joined with another company to do the mining there.

Since we had road access now, having acquired the rights-of-way from a public road to the site, we brought in heavy equipment.

The first move was to return to the hole that I and the former client had dug by hand, looking for the coal, this time with an excavator.

The surprise of the day was that the hole that we had dug by hand was the only spot in the entire 3 or 4-acre area that didn't have any coal; everywhere else did, the coal seam was intact, in place.

Continuing to open up around that spot, we uncovered several hundred tons that afternoon, of high-grade coal.

An interesting aspect of that job was that we mined a respectable several thousand tons of quality coal from there. There were at least 50 yellow jacket nests in trees along the outer perimeter of the mined area.

We never understood or learned what attracted and maintained so many bees there.

Another interesting fact was that, in the mining of that site, an additional mining site was discovered that adjoined this one, yielding many more thousands of tons of forgotten coal.

Sitting there early one morning waiting for coal trucks to arrive, I saw a form of a larger animal approaching me.

As it came closer, I switched on my truck's headlights and the most beautiful emerald green eyes flashed at me.

Now quite close, I saw that it was a fully grown, nearly all black mountain lion, quickly diving into the woods next to the mine roadway.

It had been seen once before this, and there were people claiming to have heard a cry similar to theirs, including my Granddaughter, in the general area. It has not been seen again to my knowledge.

After mining was completed, I sold the property to a young couple. Foolishly naïve, they had assumed that the right-of-way we had for the coal mining operations would carry through to them. That was not to be a road is always trouble.

In fact, their access was extremely difficult, severely steep, and needing to construct a bridge across a sizeable stream, which I had explained to them at the time of sale.

They said it was not a problem, this was going to be a camping site only, but they apparently thought that as long as we were still there, they could use our road.

The adjoining landowner refused to give them access, leaving them with a huge debt for an unusable, nearly inaccessible property, despite my warnings and explanations.

Frank – Russ

A mining client of mine, Frank K. growing up in abject poverty in extremely trying circumstances before and during the Great Depression, in my opinion after considerable association was that he was, in fact, mentally affected negatively. There was an evil side to him, at times it was ominous.

I avoided him when I could, but he always treated me well and paid my invoices when due without question. Besides, no one else would serve him.

He openly hated regulatory, and in particular, detested his current State Mine Inspector, Russ, and was going to fix his wagon, as he put it, he confided in me. What he had planned was to call the inspector, ask for a meeting at his garage, set the day and time.

Then, ahead of the meeting time, he was going to fill a coffee cup with gasoline, set it on a windowsill near the door, and wait for the Inspector to arrive.

Upon his arrival, he would pick up the cup of gasoline, pretend to be drinking the coffee, stumble forward, spilling the gas onto the Inspector.

Cigarette lighter in hand ready, he would light it, setting the victim on fire.

That's as far as he related to me.

Thank God, what actually happened, as he told me later, was that the plan was going well, except that when he pretended to stumble, his foot actually caught something on the floor, and he really did stumble, spilling the gas on himself, apologizing, saying he had been cleaning parts, no harm done.

He never mentioned it again.

I was always amused when we would return from a business visit to his mine, he insisting I drive, he ride.

Upon return to his parked vehicle, he would automatically review his vehicle where it was parked, carefully lifting the hood, looking closely in the engine compartment.

A world I had never known much about.

Small Rock—Highwall

There were four of us working that day at our mine, and it was lunch time.

In the morning's mining we had uncovered an opening into the big deep mine we were mining through, recovering unmined coal from long ago.

Only a small hole was opened, but big enough to arouse the curiosity of one of the guys, Bill, wanted to see what the inside looked like there.

The highwall above the opening, still loose from the recent excavating, was not safe, small rocks still falling down, at I warned him to stay away from the hole, but his curiosity got the best of him, and he went over to it to look in, bending way over to better see in.

Just then, we watched a small, basketball sized rock slips out of the highwall, about 30 feet high, and go tumbling down, konking him right on his unprotected head.

Helmet flying, down he went in agonizing pain, stretched out on the bench, holding his head. We are thinking he's pretending, but actually, he's not.

He finally struggled to his feet and came over to where we were, doing our best not to visibly be laughing, but we really were, silently.

Grim faced, angry, he said between clenched teeth: I'll kill the first one who laughs.

There was way more laughter the next day, he joining in.

Irwin Hill

It was late autumn, late in the day, already dark when the last truck was loaded, ready to leave.

It had been snowing, hard, and the road was dangerously slippery, the long, steep, curvy Irwin Hill waiting.

The driver admitted he feared going down that hill, but there was no discussing this dilemma, my then son-in-law Calvin, and I offered to help him go down that hill.

We agreed to get up onto the loaded truck, shovels in hand and become a cindering crew, throwing loose coal out over his truck's hood, providing some grit for his trucks tires to maintain continual effectiveness of his brakes.

The driver agreed, and there, in the dark of early December, snowing hard, slippery road, were Calvin and I frantically digging and throwing coal, keeping the loaded truck in control all the way to the bottom, he now safe, the rest of his trip on flat or gentle roadway.

Of course, and I had to walk back up that hill, but it was a victorious atmosphere.

How many times does my Guardian Angel have to keep me safe?

A very scary ride, one Calvin and I would occasionally revisit, again, grateful for a happy ending.

Dozer over Highwall Chatting with another surface mining operator, we were discussing his method of mining using a dragline, comparing it to dozer, loader.

My system was common, used by most operators, a simple block cut, where we measure out an area, say one hundred feet wide by one hundred fifty feet long, and move that overburden into the empty space left from the previous block, accomplished by bulldozers, loaders, and often, rock trucks. It's all close, contained.

His system was to employ a dragline, essentially a big bucket on the end of a long wire rope that is lowered from the original surface by the machine to scoop the loosened rock, then cast it aside, ultimately exposing the coal.

His job was such that it left a long highwall, isolating the dragline from the backfilling process down at the coal seam level.

I mentioned how difficult it must be to bring a bulldozer from the original surface down to work at the coal level, there being a highwall, a cliff of 70 or so feet high, in his case, between the two.

He said the highwall can be several thousand feet long on his job, and it takes an extended time to travel a dozer that far, from the mining area to the backfilling area.

So, he thought, I'll try something.

He then pushed about a dozen blades full of soft dirt down over the highwall, all in one spot.

Then, he turned the dozer around, and backed it out over the highwall, falling backwards onto the pile he had just made, and away he went, short cutting by a long distance.

He said he did this repeatedly, and one of his employees also began doing it.

Until the day he destroyed a dozer when it twisted sideways on the way down, and killed him In the process.

That ended the practice, especially after the MSHA, Feds, levied a huge fine. I mean Huge fine.

D9 Setup

This little story was, and still is, stupid. My guys were backfilling at the mine that day, I was busy elsewhere, but had said I would be there right after lunch to help spread topsoil.

When I got there, all four of them were still eating their lunch, but I noticed a furtive look on all their faces, when acknowledging my arrival, triggering me to think, watch out, there's something awry here.

So, I climb into the big bulldozer, alert, throw it into reverse, and start back, they're watching closely.

I noticed the area I would work in was way too smooth, like it was booby- trapped. My first pass looked too easy; level hard.

As I start backward, the rear end of the dozer sinks, deep. Now I'm stuck, they visibly laughing.

Do you have any idea as to the long-term potential for ribbing me about getting stuck has, if its legitimate?

What they had done was dug a trench, filled it with soft mud, and then coated the mud with dry dirt, disguising the mud hole, waiting for me.

Then, setting the dozer so the first move would sink it, and me, into the mud hole.

I got out, looked at them, said okay, now you can get it out. And, I got into my truck, and left.

I'm still laughing, at them.

225 Above Highwall

As others concur, when you're in a high dollar business, deep in debt, costs outrunning income, payroll, fees and taxes all screaming, demanding attention, people do desperate, sometimes foolish things.

Working a double one cold winter night, I was in my 25-ton excavator, preparing for another block of mining.

I was 60 feet above the coal in relatively easy digging, removing a foot of snow first, then the trees and brush, making a level bench for a drill to be able to safely drill a series of holes for blasting.

It was well into the night, and even with good, powerful lights, I did not notice a crack forming on the highwall side of the bench taking shape.

Suddenly, silently, a large chunk of the bench, all clay and soft shale, gave way, falling into the open pit, 60 feet down.

The collapsed section reached just short of my machine, but I couldn't know if it had ended there or was continuing underneath me. There was only a black void looking down the newly formed hole.

It's time to get the hell out of there, now. I put the bucket against a still stable part of the bench, pushed backward gently, and punched the reverse pedal, quickly moving back away from the collapsing wall, back to a safe spot, then going home.

Just another day in the pits.

When you are the one responsible and owe a hell of a lot of money.

Tom——Rock

My first strip mine was a very big job, for someone as small as we were in the mining world. We were there for 13 years, which is a very long time in this business.

An individual of questionable moral character had leased a spot from the landowner and moved in a full-sized trailer, which was in close proximity to our operations.

The stated purpose was for a hunting camp, but the real purpose was for something else. Let your imagination run.

We were drilling for a blast one day, when Tom and his girl-friend show up, expecting to spend some time in the hunting trailer.

We warned him of the pending shot that was scheduled for after lunch. Of course, he ignored our warning, and they went on with their business in the trailer.

It wasn't long after our blasters arrived, loaded the drilled holes, and ba-roooom, shot triggered.

Well, a round stone, closely duplicating a basketball, went flying high into the air, then, in a beautiful arc, came down, down, down crashing right through the flimsy roof of the trailer, down past the bed they were in, through the equally flimsy floor, finally embedding itself into the soft ground underneath the trailer.

He, raging, angry, half dressed, came flying out of the trailer, screaming.

We were thankful no one was injured, but highly amused; couldn't stop laughing.

Tom passed on years ago, but we're still laughing.

Rock at '75 Jeep

A personal friend, and former client, went into the blasting business, and had asked me if he could provide blasting services for me.

I agreed to it, and having holes being drilled for my next shot, I called and said I wanted a shot for the next day.

Watching them load the holes with blasting agent, I questioned why they weren't loading the holes as high up as I had seen other, more experienced blasters do. I was told this was a new, time-saving development, using a newly formulated blasting agent and method.

Okay, blast time near, I moved my Jeep away about 500 feet, blocking the public dirt road nearby from travelers.

Boom, the shot is triggered, I'm looking skyward. Way, way up high, a dark object appears, moving even higher, then begins a long arc, directly toward me, and my Jeep.

It's too late to move my Jeep; I take my chances and stay still. The object, a softball-sized piece of very hard white sandstone, coming directly at me like a meteor, slammed into the hood of the Jeep, imprinting itself into it very cleanly, but not breaking through.

It didn't affect the operation but did create a lot of comment until a new hood was installed.

If the new method of loading shot holes was revised then and there, as other areas were also showered with fly rock, a no-no in the blasting world.

Everyone laughed about how precisely the rock found the Jeep, but how about the fact that it was just about SIX feet from finding me?

J.D. 510 Slide

Our first strip mine was located just off a remote, un-improved township road.

I had a John Deere rubber-tired backhoe there as part of the mining equipment.

It had snowed quite a lot, and I wanted to move the backhoe into a shed about 200 yards away, down a fairly steep grade for the first 100 yards.

Admitting gross inexperience, along with a generous dose of stupidity, ignoring the fact it was pure ice on the roadway, no cinders, no nothing, just ice. I get in, fire it up, and away I go. Within 20 feet, I was out of control, sliding ever faster, just hanging on, flying.

10 or 15 feet either way, left or right, and a 25-foot drop off into a deep gully is waiting, but I'm sliding perfectly straight, holding my breath.

Finally, I am at the bottom of the steep grade, stopped, un-harmed, safe.

A little wiser, I think, but not sure.

Do Guardian Angels drive backhoes?

Mining Clientele

Once I received my Professional Surveyor License, and having ten years practical and technical experience in mining, it was natural that I gravitated to the mining world.

The fact I was just starting and worked a bit cheaper than established surveyors and engineers helped, plus I went out of my way to make life easier for busy operators.

My phone answered day or night, seven a days a week, 6:00 am to midnight.

At peak, I had 26 surface mine operators to take care of, from permitting to all the follow up, clear through final completion and bond release.

Most were long term, including myself and my other companies; many would last just one job of 3 or 4 years, then sell out, move to a less stressful life.

It is a known fact: mining is easy to get into, very hard to get out. Some marriages are a little like that.

I had 11 small deep mines at one time to take care of. These were tougher, underground is a different world.

You better know where property lines are, where gas wells are, where houses are when you are underground. Most mines are in thin seams, 40 to 48 inches.

You are the one who points them; you had better know where you are.

I would typically go into those mines after hours, so as not to interfere with daytime production and get back home late at night.

They all required servicing every six months, so there was never a lull.

Small mines are very expensive to operate, and most were soon history.

Underground there's ventilation, power supply and haulage to maintain, very costly necessities; and the more they advance, the more costly it is.

Hunter Lawsuit

My phone rings, one day, and it's the owner of the land at a former mine site of mine. She informs me that she is being sued by an adjoining landowner, claiming we had stolen numerous big trees from their land in the mining.

Being a Professional Land Surveyor, I had certainly surveyed the property to not only prevent such an occurrence, but to comply with permitting and bonding stipulations, so I was really curious as to the issues in this suit.

The legal process, in this case was the method where three learned lawyers are assigned to hear the case, and then render a final judgement, all in a relatively casual setting.

So, I appear in this courtroom, listen carefully to the sworn testimony of the Plaintiff, along with enlarged pictures, telling how all of these priceless trees had been taken, cut, and sold, then the stumps burled in the mining process.

They admitted they had hired another surveyor to check my property line markers, and found no problems with them; we clearly to have not affected the neighboring property in any way.

In observing these three lawyers, believe me, these lawyers are not stupid. I notice an ever so slight smirk on each of them, they know when they're being BS'D.

Now it's my turn to testify. I say, sirs, if you visit the site in the lawsuit, you will find:

1. My markers are still intact.
2. The other Surveyor's ribbons showing their past presence.
3. The restored mine site is well away from the property line.

4. No actual timber of any size on the adjoining property.

I don't know where they took the pictures they showed of those trees, but to me they have a strong resemblance to the ones down in Idelwild

Park, a mile or so from here along Rt. 30. I was here long before any mining was done, and they certainly weren't on, or anywhere near this site.

By now, the lawyers are visibly smirking, having witnessed outright blatant perjury.

That completed the witness testimony, and they rendered a decision then and there.

It took them less than fifteen minutes and they were back with their decision.

Case dismissed, with prejudice.

The war didn't end there; the hostile neighbor installed a steel gate denying her access to her cabin, even though it was a long-standing right-of-way.

There's another legal battle pending, but I'm not involved in that one.

She was not without success since we had built a road to haul the coal out and it was left intact for her future use.

In that other lawsuit, a judge ruled in her favor on the right-of-way, but even that didn't end the problem with the gate.

The early passing of the hostile neighbor did.

980 Breakthru

I was operating my 5 ½ yard loader, digging and carrying soft shale over burden from a block one day, knowing I was very close to the top of the coal seam that was mined out.

I dumped a bucketful off to one side, and before backing up, I happened to glance down, underneath my machine. What I saw caused me to freeze in fear.

Opening the cab door, I saw I was trapped, unable to exit to the ground, because there was nothing but open space between me, and the bottom of the mined-out coal seam, fully ten feet below the machlne.

Here, I had collapsed the remaining strata above the void, leaving all four tires perched on edges of the mined-out area.

Not daring to move, we filled in around the loader until it had support enough to move. If any wheel had caved in, serious damage to the loader, and possible injury to me would be certain.

This made quite a dinner story that evening.

OSM

I'm not sure what year it was, but around 1980 when the coal industry was booming it seems the geniuses at the federal government thought the states didn't know how to regulate mining, so they instituted another evil agency to oversee not only the states, but every operator in every facet of the mining process. It will live on in infamy, named O.S.M. for Office of Surface Mining.

The inspectors hated them, as did we.

They hired and trained rejects and misfits from other industries who were ignorant and arrogant, writing huge fines for the most ridiculous violations: a light bulb out, a horn they couldn't hear at a hundred yards. A two-thousand-dollar fine was written for a bulldozer track one foot past an arbitrary ribbon, hung on a bush indicating the mining limit, hung there by a miner, not a professional.

They would shut a job down for the least valid reason - a miner not wearing a hard hat while eating lunch in his truck.

It was all a part of the planned destruction of the mining industry, by the evil entrenched in the federal government.

We are seeing the results of their plan now, with the disintegration of the coal mining community, and power plant closures. Are the blackouts far behind?

Do people realize how awful a prolonged blackout is?

Apparently they've accomplished what they set out to do, as O.S.M. is now reduced to oversight-only status.

License

It is a hard fact of life, when you go into almost any kind of business, you automatically become either an adversary, or enemy, or both, not only to existing ones, but to certain members of the regulatory agencies that oversee your operation of the business and are friends in one form or other of your competitors.

During the wild expansion of the coal industry in the eighties, many new operators like me came into it when the opportunity to make a more prosperous life presented itself.

Small dirt-oriented contractors, along with major road builders, became surface miners.

Great resentment crept into the minds of some In the agencies, seeing coal operators buying helicopters and building those storied mansions on the hill. I happen to live on top of the hill, in a stone-encased home.

It always be my belief I was the subject in one of those cases, where certain persons in the Harrisburg offices, for reasons of their own, targeted me for ultimate elimination from the industry.

They zeroed in on a mine site of mine where I had a contractor doing the work.

The satellite office in Greensburg had been instructed to strictly enforce all regulations, and even go above and beyond.

In the permitting of that site, the water samplers had failed to identify an existing acid drainage from previous mining, and illegally, the DER, as it was known then, claimed my contractor created it, and I was not only fined heavily, but ordered to treat that discharge, for all intents and purposes, forever.

I hired an attorney, and an engineering firm, both of whom agreed I was not at fault, the engineer's from a geologic review of the strata, and the attorney from a legal standpoint.

DER at that time did not concern themselves with there being no law in place to justify many of their questionable tactics, simply made their own rules, calling them Policy.

My attorney set up a court hearing on the acid discharge liability, but I was warned by insiders at the DER that, even my having a strong case against my being liable; the long-owned landowner was willing to testify of the prior existence of the discharge, it was a futile resistance.

I was told by a former, disgraced, head of the agency, the courts were so corrupt I was wasting my time fighting the case.

So, I simply walked away.

They rescinded my License to Mine. They arrogantly said, one less, so far, so good.

That's what they thought. Look at me now a***holes. I retired after 37 more years of mining and am reasonably comfortable. No thanks to you.

In those 37 years I encountered many good, intelligent, conscionable, respectful, and respectable Field Inspectors and their bosses, and other personnel in DER and its successor DEP in our two reviewing offices.

There were just a very few higher-level managers I hope to never meet again. There can be rotten apples in every barrel.

Don - Gary - Hazard

My being a part-time partner, I happened to be absent from the strip job that day while my coal company partners Don and Gary were hard at work at our mine when MSHA, a representative of our beloved federal government safety enforcement saviors showed up to do another inspection of the equipment, jobsite, workers, and records of personal re-training requirements to be available for review.

He went through all the niceties, then proceeded to waste half a day re-inspecting everything, mechanical and site conditions, before getting into the personal stuff.

Knowing their required annual training had expired that very morning; the fact was, they were already scheduled to attend the usual, repetitive, so-called training class everyone had to go through, and which typically everyone slept through, the very next day. But they gambled that no Fed would come and be a problem.

They gambled and lost. The Fed asked for their training certificates, which clearly showed they had expired; it now being illegal to be on the job site.

So, he wrote up the violation of federal law, a fine of $200, and a written declaration stating: "I hereby declare Gary and Don to be a hazard to themselves", presented it to them and personally escorted them to the entrance gate, personally locked it and forbade them to re-enter under penalty of federal rules and regulations until they were properly re-trained and duly re-certified to enter and operate their mine.

We never did pay the fine.

Steve Pumping Hart Mine

Number three son, Steve, always ran our "other mine"; and of course, its operational problems were his to cope with.

There being constant high volumes of contaminated water in his job, he had set up the usual required ponds and treatment apparatus, and was pumping the water out, preparing the pit for the next cut.

The water level had reached the point where he had to lower the pump deeper into the pit to be able to completely empty it out. After moving it, he reconnected the hoses, started it, and stayed with it to be sure it was pumping.

All often, for who knows what reason, it would quit running. He checked it out, found nothing, plenty of fuel, restarted it, and pumping began. Shortly, very shortly after, it quit again.

Rarely do miners welcome the arrival of MSHA, Federal Inspectors, especially if you're having a problem, and, sure enough, there was that white plate, and a Federal Inspector getting out of it.

Now, you must stop whatever you are doing and meet and greet him, so Steve did. After the niceties are exchanged, the inevitable question, are you having a problem.

Steve explained the situation, and the Fed said, wait, don't go into the pit to the pump, I want to get something from my vehicle. He returns a few minutes later, with a device in hand, an oxygen level meter.

They both start going down into the pit, and halfway or so, his meter starts pinging. The further they go in, the more urgent the pinging.

He stops, looks at the meter, and says to Steve, go, get out of here, now.

The pit was loading up with Black Damp, carbon dioxide, coming out of exposed deep mine entry in the highwall.

So, they both got out of the pit, the wind picked up, clearing the C02.

The Inspector checked the pit once more, it was all clear, start the pump.

They're not all bad. Was he Steve's Guardian Angel? Very likely. God Bless him.

Dream Strip Mine

Small time strip miner's only dream of a mining site with little or no overburden to remove prior to the extraction, and I owned the coal, outright.

My dream had come true.

Or so I had hoped.

Additional positives were present at the site. A friend owned the surface, and was eagerly interested in the job, hoping the payments for surface rights would benefit him in his tough business, Farming.

A second positive was the regulatory agency agreed the mining should be beneficial due to an expected cleanup and restoration of the previously- mined peripheral area, so permitting was not an Issue.

There were also some very sobering negatives associated with the site. The greatest was the fact it was the natural end point of gravitational flow of acid mine drainage from hundreds of acres of old deep mining upslope, in all directions, reaching flows monitored nearby of up to 6,000 gallons- per-minute at peaks.

Removing the coal at the targeted site could potentially invite this flow to it since the entire area was almost flat, a huge pool of bad water currently finding its way out elsewhere but nearby, visible.

I had already drilled the site with a water well rig, leaving a number of 6-inch, Schedule 40 pipes at or below grade, so I could monitor what the coal was doing, if anything.

And, more importantly, what the water was doing, if anything.

So, permit in hand, along with all approvals, we begin, my million dollar dream underway.

Having the site prepared, $25,000 dollars later, we're ready to start digging. So, I tell the boys to hold off on calling for trucks to haul out the coal, just yet, let's go check the pipes, one more time.

That's when I find the water in the pipes is no longer dormant, laying still.

The ocean all around the pipe site is now draining, flowing fast across the top of the pipes, guaranteeing disaster if I open up the coal seam, it being impossible to treat such a huge volume to any level, much less to compliance.

The message was very clear: start digging and you're out of business and liable for indescribable environmental damage; there being a trout fishery just a mile or so downstream.

The decision was both easy and hard to make. I stopped the mining, the easy part.

The hard part was in telling the now devastated landowner, my friend.

His dream, along with mine, was now in ashes. He had hopes of becoming debt free from the royalty payments.

He passed on not long after that terrible shock.

Storm Water Pond

I had permitted a new site for stripping, and had moved in the equipment to build the usual, required sediment control pond, in this case with a capacity of about half a million gallons.

The pond was at the extreme head of a small creek that ran only during the wet time of the year, or during storm water run-off. The design of the pond was such that a maximum flow after a storm would be limited by a twelve-inch diameter overflow pipe, over several days, not enough to be of any great concern downstream.

So, I went about building the pond according to the specifications, installing the overflow pipe, but running out of time to line the emergency spillway with rock, or to properly anchor the overflow pipe down.

That would be Monday morning's work, first thing.

However, over the weekend, the rain came, lots and lots of rain. The pond worked well, too well. With no mining yet, there was no pit or other to intercept any storm flow, so it all went into the unfinished pond.

As the pond filled up, two facts became apparent; one was that the overflow pipe end had not been anchored down and was being floated up as the water rose higher, and the emergency spillway had not yet been covered with rock, leaving it unprotected from being eroded by the overflowing storm waters.

And, as the storm and rain continued, so did the rising water in the pond.

There was a building, a nice garage converted to a retail outlet of sorts, active daily, down below the pond, actually built straddling the small creek first mentioned, and a pipe of questionable capacity laid in under the garage to carry the wet weather and occasional storm flow, which it had done successfully for years, exiting well away from the building.

Well, the heavy rain filled the pond, floated the overflow pipe up out of the water, forcing all the water incoming to go out the unprotected emergency spillway, quickly eroding it, and a part of the dike, allowing a mini tsunami to head for the garage blocking the natural stream channel, and its underlying pipe.

In a matter of hours, a half million gallons of muddy water visited that garage, immediately plugging the pipe under it; smashing through a back door, then a front door, flowing out from it until the rain stopped, along with all the storm waters afterward.

To their eternal credit, the owners were amicable about the whole event, very understanding. Help, and a good cleanup, plus a fair insurance settlement returned harmony to the site.

I rebuilt the pond, anchored the overflow pipe down properly, placed the rock onto the emergency spillway, and lived happily ever after. Yeah, sure.

Then we stripped out the coal with no further incident.

Hornet Nest at Girty

Surface miners rarely stay at one site for extended periods. The mining sites that are or become available usually take less than 3 years to remove all of the available coal there.

So, it's a constant search for another site, this the ongoing process, competing with other operators for sites, in mining terminology, a piece of coal.

A survey/engineering client who owned a small tract of property with strippable coal on it offered it to me, so I went one day to evaluate it, and prepare the permit application.

A deep mine had been located there for some number of years prior to my involvement, now abandoned, with several small sheds still there, intact.

Curious as to possible contents, if any, of one of the sheds, I swung its door open wide, still holding onto the latch, discovering I was exactly eyeball to eyeball with a huge Bald-faced Hornet nest.

Apparently, the suddenness of the move caught them unaware, because even the usual guard bee didn't immediately react.

It's well known, multiple Bald-faced Hornet stings can be fatal, and they are a most formidable adversary.

My Guardian Angel must have taken over, as I instantly slammed the door closed, even a quick twist of the latch to secure it.

And, I retreated, and I mean I retreated.

Coal Markets

Throughout the 49 years I was Involved in coal production and sales, I dealt with buyers ranging from very small one-man-shows to major corporations, most who have disappeared from the scene. None that I dealt with continue to buy from outside producers, now down to just a very few.

I said many years ago, the day would come when the coal industry would be reduced to just a handful of American producers, and we are there now.

The dealers l dealt with, except the major corporations, who accept delivery at consuming facilities, power generating stations, all had a coal yard, where they stock coal and blend it with other coal before sale.

All coal yards have scales to weigh both the incoming and outgoing resale coal. This is where we separate the sinners from the saints.

Some, not all, were so blatant in the cheating game, that after one sale, the producer vowed he would bury the coal rather than sell anymore to that yard. Everyone knew who they were.

Others were expected to short weigh at least one or two tons. Very few didn't. That, we always would offset by loading one or two tons of black rock or other inferior material into the load, so it was usually sort of a draw. After you've done this 10,000 times, you can look at a loaded truck and be close on the tonnage.

A common scenario would be: I would routinely load 24 to 25 tons at the mine, that load would be weighed and credited as 23 tons on my weight ticket, then that truck would travel around the scale, through the yard without stopping, come back to the scale, reweigh the load, now showing 26 tons on that weight ticket, and off it would go, to its market.

Somehow it grew 3 or so tons right in the truck, but I was paid for 3 less tons. Depending on the relationship with the weighmaster at the point of destination, the load could be even heavier after it was weighed there.

Some people served time in the big house for that after they were caught. This was never the case with major corporations, though, it just didn't happen.

I had a tandem dump truck, legal load at 16 tons. My oldest son was driving it, hauling coal to another yard.

The normal procedure when hauling is, if it's a single load involved, the incoming truck is gross weighed, moves to the dump site, then light-weighs to get the net weight.

If it's continuous hauling, the truck is light weighed just once, using that weight for every load of the day, and is only weighed when loaded.

Well, my son, always in a hurry, would weigh loaded, go dump, then leave with the bed lowering as he traveled away.

This one day the weighmaster happened to watch my truck leaving, bed not quite lowered, when he saw that the bed was still half-full, the wet coal having hung up, and did not empty completely out.

He screamed on the CB for my son to return, then weighing him, now empty, but there was still over 8 tons in the bed. There was no way of knowing how long or how many loads were hauled with that condition.

We could only invoice for the weight as shown on the weight slips. One buyer was also my surveying/engineering client. Street smart, he would counsel me about stupid mistakes we all make. He would tell me, "Bucky, it's a whole lot easier to get into trouble than outta." How true, how true.

He had hired a young, aggressive in-house accountant. The accountant decided to directly violate my sales agreement with my buyer/client and sent me an invoice for over $400,000 dollars for supposedly unpaid royalties or some other imaginary reason; that didn't fly, either.

Chatting with my client, Bud, he said the IRS was coming the next Monday to do a complete tonnage audit.

Of all the unexpected possibilities, on Sunday night, in the wee hours, a fire of undetermined origin permanently postponed the audit. The records all went up in smoke. At least, the ones that weren't hidden offsite.

Again, chatting with him one day, he confidentially informed me that he was closing up here, leaving the area for greener pastures down south.

He said no, he had found a huge site with long-term, unlimited reserves, and he felt that was the way to go, even though it was far from home.

I challenged the wisdom of the change, being aware of the remaining potential in staying in place, here. Further, I knew the area he was talking about. I said, "Bud, you're ignoring your own advice about getting into trouble, that area is a trap, it's already been mined, a lie you've been told and swallowed. It's all worked out with nothing but trouble waiting for you."

He firmly said: "No, Bucky, I've got three million dollars that I don't know what to do with, so we're going, soon."

I will skip over the dozens of horror stories he experienced down south, and end by saying; he died broke and deep in debt to many good people.

I never met or spoke to him again.

The final coal buyer, Drew ___ I sold coal to was a welcome relief. Honest, personable, paid on time, and his scale was never ailing.

Selling to him, we slept well.

And, we said goodbye to the Coal World, after 44 years.

What a ride it was.

20-Inch Gas Line

One of my strip mines had an inherent feature that was not exactly desirable, but such is the strip miner's life.

That feature was a 20-inch high-pressure gas line running the entire length of the job.

That pipeline was monitored weekly by air, so there was constant overview of our mining near it.

Well, the pilot must have fallen asleep one week, a holiday possibly creating some confusion because he didn't notice our mining was quite close to the line. Our operator at the mine, Bill, being very diligent, was mining near the line, and found solid, high-grade coal that extended underneath the pipe.

Our permit restrictions did allow us to mine within 25 feet of the pipe, but Bill, ever watchful of compliance with all regulations and permit conditions, worked through the holiday, chasing that solid block of coal, greatly contributing to the cause.

The pipeline was about ten feet above the coal seam at that point, and in the process of taking out the coal, he undermined it, and upon his arrival the next day, lo and behold.

The fill around the pipe had caved into the pit, exposing all 20 inches of it, hanging in the open air beneath it, not a thing of beauty in any case.

Reestablishing priorities quickly, Bill had the spot backfilled ever so pretty for the next monitoring flight, no problem, no on ground visit.

Boys wiII be boys, Bill was the best at it.

Meet Jack Miles

It was always my pleasure and compensation to meet and interact with high-level management in the coal industry.

Jack was superintendent over several deep mines, and he became a permanent fixture in my life, along with his delightful wife, Jan, we being about the same age and train of thought.

Going to meet him; his office being above a garage, close to twenty feet up, accessed by an open grate stairway, fairly steep.

Of course, my constant companion, Bori, my big, friendly German Shepherd had to lead the way, until he came to those stairs, stopping short at the bottom.

I coaxed and pulled him up onto the first two steps, where he bogged down, terrified, shaking, spread-eagled legs, struggling to climb at my urging and pulling.

Finally at the top of the landing, he didn't need coaxing to go into the long, narrow row-house style of offices, ten, I believe, in a row.

He proceeded to visit Jack first, then uninvited, went door to door to everyone; all were pleasantly surprised at the intrusion by such a distinguished visitor.

He returned to Jacks' office, laid down, keeping a wary eye on him, having seen wolves in sheep's clothing somewhere in his ancestral past, but was soon sound asleep.

Bori revisited each office prior to our departure. The trip back down those open grate stairs was less eventful than going up.

Woodie's Prize Job

A former fellow strip miner and client told me he had one last tract with strippable coal on it, the likes of which you've never seen, a final job, then retirement to anywhere you choose, firmly entrenched in the lap of total luxury, for life. It sounded too good to be true.

Time passed, he aged, got tired and weary of the hassle, finally called and said he was hanging it up, and if I was still interested, he would show me the property, and lease it to me.

Of course, I was still interested, and in the company of my two then- partners, we went to see the dream job.

I being the one who spent a lifetime procuring work sites for mining, was well acquainted with disappointment, but this was the one that took the proverbial cake, won first prize, the blue ribbon, in disappointment, and more.

Within minutes of arrival at the site, we saw there was already a large discharge of acid mine drainage, showing the coal had been previously mined, strike one and two.

The water problem was real trouble, a high cost while doing additional mining, long-term liability that is disastrous and most likely trust fund that you must establish, cost $100,000 dollars and ongoing treatment, forever.

Strike three, I'm out.

That was enough to tell us to run, don't walk from this future hell hole.

As a courtesy to my former client, coal stripper, who had offered this site to me, I felt we should do just a little follow up evaluation. So, we stopped at the house nearest to the property, a neighbor I would have to contend with, if I took on the job.

So, we casually knocked on the door, and an older man and woman cautiously opened the door and the man greeted us in a friendly manner, as you would expect, but not his wife.

Explaining who we were, who directed us here, and our purpose in stopping.

His wife had disappeared shortly after the opening of the door, but now she reappeared, shotgun in hand, and pushing her husband aside, yelled, quite convincingly: "these are the same sons-a-bitches who were here last week, the ones I told to get out of here and never come back."

That was all the convincing we needed, and as we moved away, she came out onto the porch, loaded a shell into the shotgun pump, that easily understood harsh clack, clack, clack, and said, "I'm gonna show them." Her husband stopped her and pulled her into the house.

We retreated to the truck in record time, and without saying any goodbyes, departed.

It was the first time I had ever been told to leave in such a compelling manner.

Text – End of Mining

Through the 44 years we mined coal, startup time was 7 am, rain, shine sleet, snow.

A combination of inadvertencies, Market, Federal Government, Equipment ageing, State Government, Regulation, finally brought us to the point where it was time to conclude the mining business entirely, in 2017, gradually selling or moving all of our heavy equipment.

After 44 years of every imaginable adversity, which I choose not to itemize here, and also many wonderful, positive experiences providing so much for so many, it was necessary, yet heartbreaking moment in our time, especially in mine, the originator of the whole life engaging program, outlined in great part within these many stories.

In a melancholy mood one morning, it being 7:10 am, just about when the big machines were already warmed up and beginning the workday.

I texted Cindy, who was the President of the Coal Company, K.M.P.

Associates. The text was:

Me: Now 7:10, the big engines roar
She: Hmmmm.
Me: Silent now, forever more. Could bring one to tears.
She: What happened?
Me: Life.
Sad. Not funny. Not dramatic.

Siren Song

It was early evening after a hot summer day, and I was trimming around the beautiful Knockout Rose Dolly had planted several years before leaving us, and was just a bit melancholy, thinking of her and all those wonderful years we shared. Silence dominated the scene.

Hark, What is that I hear? Out of the distance comes the most beautiful sound, a siren-like melody, faint but clear.

There is that school of thought, emanating from the fortunate few who have experienced that which is referred to as Heavenly Music, music so profoundly beautiful that it defies description, music that once heard, creates such absolute joy as to render the Listener speechless in any attempt to describe its purity and splendor, a peek into Heaven itself.

I cannot help but wonder if what I heard was a prelude to such, just a taste of what was yet to possibly come.

It is my understanding that one must not necessarily be on your death bed to be eligible to receive that Heavenly gift.

Was it someone expressing pure joy, or its exact opposite, extreme emotional distress, a duration of only a minute or so, then fading away till its source became inaudible, leaving me with just the memory, a haunting presence now indelibly etched into my subconscious mind, wondering if Dolly had momentarily reappeared.

About a week later, in somewhat similar circumstances, I heard a sound similar to the earlier one, but this time I get into my truck and drive down to the public road, where a young girl of about 18 is walking, away from my house.

I pull alongside her, and after identifying myself, ask if she was the one producing the beautiful resonance I heard recently.

She nodded yes, inquiring as to why I asked.

I told her how beautiful I thought it was, and how much I appreciated it, and that she was welcome to return anytime.

She simply said, "I love Life, and I love to sing." And, suddenly, she was gone.

I did not ask her name, nor did she offer it.

I said God Bless You.

I never saw or heard her again.

Life Lesson - Survey

I had received my Professional Surveyor's License, and was called by the President of the Avonmore Bank to contract a survey for one of their clients.

Having grown up near town, having been a member of the Avonmore Boy Scouts, and a classmate to many Avonmore High School students, I was pretty widely known.

There had never been any negative incidents of hostilities with anyone, plus being married to an Avonmore girl on good terms with her well-known family.

In conversing with the president, he informed me that a local family had recently brought in a completed survey done by some other surveyor; I being the only one in the area.

I bluntly stated that I wondered why they had not called me to do the job, being local and known to them.

I admit, his answer was not only a wakeup call to me, but a sobering fact of life, a lesson I have never forgotten, but have accepted.

He looked me straight in the eye, so to speak, and said: "Charlie, not everyone likes you."

Sometimes, the truth hurts, and educates, all at the same time.

Jake

Jake called me for a major surveying project he had in mind, a hundred or so lot subdivision, just after I had received my license in 1967.

He was quite a character, able to see the promise in housing far into the future, a smart man.

The Armstrong County Planners were great to work with, and in time, we had an approved layout, and Jake was on his way to much greater things.

He had two sons, intelligent and cooperative, one was a CPA, and had joined the ranks of the owners of the Steeler Football Team.

Brilliant, progressive, he soon became a key in their operations, advancing quickly.

There was discussion about opening a coal mine, with me as the head, but economics and circumstance discounted it, and we remained client and friend.

With unlimited funding available, Jake and family rapidly progressed in the housing industry successfully and began expanding into other businesses.

They became a major coal producer in surface mining and opened a limestone quarry which operated for many years; while at the same time entering the gas and oil world, ultimately acquiring and/or drilling well over a thousand wells.

Operating through at least 32 different corporations, while promoting a CPA firm in-house.

Then an outdoor advertising venture, now a brine treatment facility.

And, who knows what else.

I cannot help but see a certain parallel between me and Jake, with different early features. We were both non-stop thinkers as to how to make a better future for ourselves and our families.

An almost humorous comparison can be made. We both quit good jobs to go out on our own.

We both had good wives and children.

I designed housing subdivisions; he built the houses to put into them.

I was in the coal business; he became a major producer of coal.

He owned and operated a limestone quarry; I also owned and operated a limestone quarry.

He went into the gas and oil industry; I did extensive permitting of both and installed 82 gas wells for a major producer.

I treated acid mine drainage for years; he now treats brine from gas wells.

He operates an outdoor advertising business; I operated a sign business.

I operated numerous small ventures; some successful, some failures. He operated numerous corporations that I do not know in what service or product.

He had a billionaire backer from the start; I had no backer but my Wife and God.

He died a billionaire, the only one I have ever known. I will not, and it doesn't matter at all, does it?

And here is something to think about:

Once upon a time, I asked a very wealthy mafia client: Frank, why do you pursue more money? You already have far more than you or your family will ever need.

He replied: "Charlie, you can have enough to eat, enough to drink, be warm enough or cool enough, be as comfortable as you want to be. But, you can never have enough money."

Surveying - Farmer's Dog

Back in my startup years, during a meeting with a kindly old farmer to discuss what needed to be done in a survey for him, and also in subsequent meetings as the work progressed, I had pointedly noticed his nice, friendly collie-type dog, that every time we would stand and talk, would not only stay close, but would actually lean on the farmers one leg or the other, usually on the one being downslope of him, and place his head tightly against the farmer's leg.

If the farmer moved, the dog moved, if he stopped, the dog would immediately sit down next to a leg, settle in as usual, leaning closely against him.

Finally, I said to him, "boy that dog must really like you."

The farmer looked directly at me, cocked his head to one side, lifted his hand slightly, twisted his wrist in a half circle move, pointed his index finger heavenward and said, devoutly, "son, this dog thinks the sun rises and sets, right on my arse."

I trust they're in heaven together, forever.

Frank - Sign

Mining client, Frank K was a genuine character, called and asked me to accompany him to his current mine site.

So, we met, and when we got there, I said, "Frank, where is your identification sign?" You know you're required to post it within one hundred feet of a public road.

He said, "It's here, don't you see it?" I said, "no, where?"

He pointed to a tree nearby, and there was the sign, a 3-foot by 4-foot placard, nailed to the tree 20 feet up. He claimed vandals had destroyed the first one he put up, down at eye level, this one they couldn't reach.

It stayed there the whole time the mine vas active, satisfying the legality of its placement.

And all the inspectors knew him too well by then, and didn't choose to aggravate him.

It was well known he had already attacked one of them, driving his vehicle into him – accidentally.

He used to brag to me about his cash stash.

He used to run a coal yard for many years, at a time when houses everywhere burned coal, creating a huge demand for small loads of coal, mostly paid for in cash.

He claimed the government didn't need the cash, but he did, so he didn't bother to turn in the proceeds for tax accounting.

Anyhow, he told me he had a million dollars stashed somewhere, he being the only one that could ever find it.

Well, he died one day, and his son only needed one day with a backhoe to find it.

The new Mercedes tattled on him.

He was also the one who wisely preached to me about being in the coal business, selling your product, being paid monthly, sometimes to shady customers.

His advice: Charlie, watch out for that laaaaaast check. It may never come.

Chal--Rifle

A contractor acquaintance, wanting to expand into surface mining, asked me to visit a potential mining site for discussion with the landowner, and evaluation of regulatory issues, always present.

There were already a number of problems there, a major one being that a township road had partially collapsed into the ever-present ancient deep mine.

The question of economics came up, of course, the cost versus recovery, including royalties to the goofy landowner in the mix.

I, thoroughly versed in all aspects of mining, legal, regulatory, and economics, tried to talk sense into the hothead landowner, who single-mindedly was focusing on his payday, and nothing else.

One thing led to another, always more negative, when he paused, went to his truck, pulled out a high-powered rifle, loaded a shell into the barrel, and came over to where I was standing.

At ten feet, or so, he stops, gives me a hard look, and says: "You've got 30 seconds to be in your truck and out of here."

I didn't bother to check the make or caliber of his rifle; I just left the scene.

I didn't even bother to report it to the police; insanity is hard to prove.

And probably very messy.

Axle in Road

Long ago, when I had just started Professional Level (legal) surveys, I was at a job site where a kindly township supervisor said he would show me where he was positive the lot corner was, in the center of the road we were at.

We set there, and he says, there's an axle driven in here, close by, he affirmed he had watched it being driven in.

So, we mark out a 3-by-3-foot square, and start digging in the hard road surface.

We dug for about an hour, and saw it was lunch time.

Getting up out of the now 3 or more feet-deep hole, I stuck my shovel into the road at the edge of the hole to help spring me out, when the act of punching the shovel into the road caused a loud ' 'ding" , obviously metal to metal sound.

I had hit the axle we were digging for, just four inches from the edge of our excavation, right on top, clearly visible.

Not one of us had seen it the whole time.

Larry - Hornet

My helper, Larry and I were surveying a tract completely covered with small trees and brush.

At lunch that day, he brought up the subject of bald-faced hornets, had I ever been stung by one, and how does a hornet's sting differ from other bee stings.

Knowing far more on the subject than is healthy, I genuinely expressed reluctance to even discuss the matter, with my inner convictions that we create what we focus on, so we dropped the discussion, going back to work.

So, Larry is cutting a visual path for me through the brush when, bending a small sapling partially over to get a good angle to cut it with his machete, he exposed a basketball sized hornet nest, face high to him.

The guard hornet immediately nailed him, right smack on the tip of his nose, fortunately only once.

In excruciating pain, nose already swelling bigger and bigger, he stumbled back to me, and we quickly left the scene, heading for the nearest emergency room.

The pain was so severe he missed several days of work; even his vision vas briefly affected.

It took over six months for the pain to subside enough to where he could touch the end of his nose.

Be careful what you focus upon.

Oklahoma Survey

A part of surveying, sometimes an undesirable part, is property line disputes.

Most property line disputes usually begin with some seemingly minor, real or imagined infringement by one party or the other, and before cooler heads prevail, serious problems can arise.

A call for a survey clearly stated there was a dispute, no love lost from either side over years of non-Stop bickering, now escalated into near physical confrontation.

Foolishly, I agreed to enter into this maelstrom of hostility, and went to the site, ready to work.

The combatants were already there, exchanges, barbs, and threats already underway, both anxiously waiting for my arrival, to settle it, once and for all.

As I proceeded with the field work and calculations, the arguing became more vicious, violence not that far off.

One of those rare times when I was able to establish the property line with certainty, unquestionable, I began to install the steel pins, marking one corner first, then the line towards the other corner.

Apparently, the placement of the line was so counter to one of the combatants, so disappointing, overwhelming, he then collapsed onto the ground, and died, then and there, before an ambulance arrived.

I learned later he had experienced cardiac failure to the extreme.

It's part of the role we assume, not a happy part.

God Bless him anyway.

Two Bulls - Surveying

At one time, I had a two-man survey crew, and I sent them out to survey a property line between two farms one day. The transit man was told by one farmer that 'there was a bull with several cows in the next-door pasture, so watch for him, don't irritate him or he could be trouble, he's high-strung.'

So, the guys are running this long line between the pastures, watching the bull and his harem; they are curious, not hostile, staying near the fence, as did my guys. All was going well.

When the cows began looking back behind my guys, they too looked back to where they had started. There appeared a second bull and a few cows, but this time, on their side of the fence; and they were fast approaching, led by that big bull.

At that point, my guys hastily abandoned the project, and ran for their truck, parked outside both pastures.

The farmer met them, and admitted he forgot to warn them of the other bull.

Being told about this, I called the client, suggesting he find another less cowardly surveyor.

We were too young to die or be maimed. Besides, we used mighty expensive equipment.

Polish Electric Pole

I was in the process of preparing a permit application and upgrade for an oil well near Oil City, PA.

There being numerous oil wells in that area, I was unable to locate that particular one readily, so once I knew I was close, I started asking local residents for help in finding it.

Most had no idea, but finally, I saw an older man working in his garden and I stopped. He came over to me, and I stated my problem.

His eyes brightened, a smile crossed his face, and he started, saying: "Yes, you're not far, it's just up around this hill, then watch for a Polish Electric Pole on the left. It's just past the pole on your left. You can't miss it."

A bit puzzled, I said, "what's a Polish Electric pole?"

He said, "you'll know when you see it." I thanked him, and away I went, up the hill, watching intently. Then, there it was.

A typical pole, installed with the small end down in the ground, the large end high up in the air.

Whether installed by some comic intentionally that way, or inadvertently, I'II never know.

I found the well I was looking for.

Elders Ridge Garage

A client of mine, logger heading with a neighboring farmer over a big Iimb that had fallen into his small lot did a stupid thing. Instead of simply cutting it up and disposing it, he threw it out into the farmer's hayfield, and of all times to do that, while he's mowing the hay there.

The farmer didn't see the Iimb in the tall grass, and subsequently, ran into it, damaging the mower.

That's when all hell broke loose, culminating in a lawsuit, the farmer claiming that a recently built garage by my client was built partially on his land.

I, having surveyed the lot, knew that the critical issue was the fact that my client's lot did stop short of where the garage had been built, but existing fences had been installed there long ago, at least 50 years.

My client, depending on the 21-year rule, built the garage outside of his deeded lot dimensions.

In Court, after the testimony and Court actions, the Judge ruled in my client's favor, based on the 21-year rule that generally says if a property is marked, used, and maintained for over 21 years without any legal challenge, it becomes part of the user's ownership.

Note: I am not a lawyer, only quoting the law as I have experienced it.

Anyhow, the farmer disagreed, and took it to a higher Court.

That Court asked my client how long he had owned the lot his deed described, and how long he had occupied the extra land where he had built the garage.

It was 15 years, not 21.

It was also goodbye to that part of the garage that was encroaching onto the farmer's land, affected by the farmer's chain saw.

The remaining 10 feet of the garage is on my client's deeded lot.

Gary In my Survey and Engineering business I employed a bright young man, Gary, for several years.

He was smart, computer savvy, and did excellent work, both in the field and office. He had a college background, but was a bit short in practical aspects, as I saw it.

We often had friendly debates, among them was the question, how do trees grow?

I argued they grew from their outer limits, the end of a limb, the top of the tree. They extend every year, growing up and out.

He argued the tree grows from the ground, moving enmasse straight up.

I told him that when I was a kid, each Spring we would renew the barbed wire fence we had in the tree row. Why isn't the wire moving up with the tree, if the trunk is, if you are correct?

In ten years, for Instance, wouldn't the first wire put on be way up in the air, moving up with the trunk?

To the day he took on a better job, he never conceded that I was correct.

While taking some classes, later, Indiana University offered him a job as a professor. He refused.

Glenn—Pin in Creek

There had been heavy rain, and the creeks were running full bank to bank.

We had returned to the survey site to install the final line and corner pins.

Set up and ready, I pointed in the general direction, and told my helper, Glenn, to head toward the corner area, pin, rod, and hammer in hand.

He stepped off to about where he figured the corner would be, stopped, and held the rod while I measured it, he being at the creek bank.

I radioed that he needed to go backwards at least ten or twelve feet, knowing that much would put him into the big creek, in four or five feet of water.

Without thinking, he acknowledged, then turned around, saw where ten or twelve feet would put him and stopped.

He turned to me and said: "Hey, buddy, you'll know I 'm crazy if I go in there myself, but not if you come and hold the pin steady while I drive it in."

We put the pin on top of the bank, instead.

On another survey, we were again putting in a final pin corner, Glenn heading toward the spot, when, getting close, he turned toward me to guide him in the final few feet, going backwards.

Final adjustments made, I said "good, put her in." He bent over, set the pin down at the point, and started to pound it in. Suddenly, he dropped the hammer, jumped up and moved away, quickly, slapping himself, repeatedly.

The corner was exactly the same spot as a big Yellow Jacket nest, and they did not appreciate the pin going through it.

We had to go back that night to retrieve the hammer.

Glenn only got stung five times.

One day we were out doing the preliminary work for a survey that had both open fields, and dark woods to run through.

It being a bright, sunny day, there was a sharp contrast in that situation.

Under normal conditions, I would track my helper when he's going from open to woods since trees between us would cause me to lose track of him once he's in there.

So, on this bright day I was set up out in the field, Glenn moving into the woods when I lost sight of him. He just disappeared.

I called him on the radio and told him "Glenn, you're moving too fast, I can't see you, where are you? Wave your arms."

He came back with "I'm over here."

I said, "Glenn, I can't see radio waves, get to a spot where I can see you."

Angrily he said, "I can't see you, so which way should I move?"

So, I said, "Glenn, if you can't see me, how can I see you?"

He gave up, came back out to the edge of the field, and started over.

Survey in Conemaugh

I received an invitation to bid on a survey of the Conemaugh River at Johnstown, PA, as a part of a stream study, so I bid it, and was awarded the job.

The Corps of Engineers, a Federal related Agency, was involved, and I wondered why there was an absolute deadline for completion of the work, so I scheduled a next day start.

As it was, that day dawned bright and clear, but wickedly cold, like ten below zero cold.

We went and started anyway, since it was a sizeable contract, and there was no time to waste.

A man exited a car with a white plate, and he identified himself as the Corps of Engineers representative for the project.

He explained I was not executing the job correctly, as I was locating the bank of the river and recording its elevation alright, but the requirement was that my helper had to wade out into chest deep water and locate the center of the river along with its elevation, not just the outside bank.

Since it was ten degrees below zero, he agreed it was a bad time to go into the river, contract deadline or not.

So, we left.

When I got back to my office, I called the source of the contract, told him he had fraudulently suckered me into that contract, and that I quit.

He said, "I'll sue you to fulfill the deal."

I said, "I'll countersue on grounds not only of fraud and deception, but reckless endangerment, considering the conditions involved here, generally.

I never heard from him again.

Final Wish

My phone rang, one day, and a barely audible voice said, "would you be willing to talk to my daughter about doing some surveying for me?" I said "yes, have her call."

She called minutes later, explaining that her father wanted to divide his property among his children, but there being some family controversy, no surveyor would take the job, and time was of the essence.

Having weathered numerous family issues through the year, one more was of no real concern to me, so I accepted the job.

I carefully followed her father's wishes in the layout of each lot, made sure there would not be any question as to neighboring lines, untangled some existing issues, and took the finished product through the entire subdivision process, including the final deeds, signatures and recording finalizing the whole involvement.

That ended the family controversy, once and for all, according to what was said, later.

The next day, his daughter called, asking me to stop in and meet her father, at his home.

So, l did, as a courtesy, and being a bit curious as to the unusual behavior in this entire engagement.

He greeted me warmly, and with great physical effort, gave me a check in payment for the services, then clasped my hand, holding on for a few extra extended moments, and said "Thank you, goodbye."

I left; he died a few hours later.

His daughter told me a few days later, he knew his time was near, and appreciated that I gave him the ability to follow through with his final wish, before he died.

May he rest in peace.

College Professor

In the never-ending search for mineable coal, I arranged to meet a college professor who owned various tracts of land with coal, most of which had long-since been mined, but there's always hope of finding an overlooked tract, no matter how small.

My ever-present German Shepherd, Yuri, in full shed-mode, was with me of course, so I warned the professor that my Jeep with cloth seats would have fur all over them, typical black and tan, and that German Shepherds are notoriously generous with their fur at shedding time.

No, he insisted I drive, he would direct our travel, he better able to point out potential mining sites, and their previous history in greater detail.

We traveled for miles, generally striking out everywhere, my interest fading fast.

I noticed he kept checking the time, and finally, he said, could we travel to his attorney's office, not far away from our location at the time.

He then admitted he had an important meeting with his attorney and a bank president regarding some serious financial proposition that was pending.

I had no issue with that, and in a short time, we arrived at the attorney's office. It was quite elegant, with high-level accommodations, bronze memorials and all.

The furniture in the waiting room was equally tasteful, and we were invited to sit down for a few minutes until the attorney was freed up, ready for the professor.

When I met the professor that day, it was just after his last class for the day, and, understandably, he was well dressed.

He was decked out in a beautiful blue suede suit, starched white shirt, highly polished black shoes, the whole deal.

The receptionist leaned out of her enclosure and announced the attorney was now ready to see him, so he got up from the chair to go, his backside to me and the receptionist.

Now, realizing he had just spent several hours riding in my Jeep with its cloth interior thoroughly coated with Yuri's German Shepherd tan fur, the entire back of the fine blue suede suit was covered, giving him the appearance of a mountain goat, unbeknownst to him, as he proceeds into the presence of his high-dollar attorney, and his bank's top official, certainly hoping for a favorable impression in this, their initial meeting.

When I saw this as he moved away into the attorney's office, I burst into uncontrollable laughter, the secretary joining me when she saw it.

The door closed; it was too late.

Driving back to his parked vehicle later, there was no mention of anything abnormal having been said at their meeting.

I don't know if he ever got the loan.

His coal holdings were of no interest to me, and I never saw him again.

Surveying Conflicts

In the 63 years of my professional land surveying career, it has been my good fortune to have experienced just three, believe it or not, three, confrontations with hostile adjoined owners of a tract or lot I was in the process of surveying.

Certainly, in that length of time there were challenges to property line location, but always settled amicably, or in a courthouse.

I have found houses, both existing old ones, and recently built, to be located on the wrong lot, some half, or partly on a lot, and the other half or the remainder on a neighbor's lot.

I found an entire subdivision of 15 lots, with houses occupying every lot, to be completely scrambled, with houses on the wrong lot, houses partially on one or more lots, and in every imaginable way incorrect. All the lots were laid out, marked, and all of the houses staked out by the same surveyor, who had recently moved to another state.

I located him and made that dreaded call to give him the terrible news. A truly unpleasant experience. His errors and omissions insurance policy covered a very costly series of errors if he had insurance.

I have found commercial buildings physically located completely off their deeded lot, many encroaching onto road rights-of-way or neighboring lots. Houses and porches, especially in towns, were very commonly found to be encroaching into street boundaries.

The first case of hostility I experienced was a neighbor to a lot I was surveying who didn't really disagree as to where I had determined the property line went, but simply trailed us the entire time we were there, making sure my helper did not step or stand on her sacred soil to install the line markers and corners into the ground. She finally realized she had gotten a free survey and thanked me as we left.

The second, less pleasant case was somewhat more dramatic.

In this case my client was part of a well-known, rather nasty group (organization) that pretty much controlled things around there; politically, socially and on the streets. The client's group, owning a small tract of land of 10 or 15 acres, planned to lay out a subdivision there.

I was in the process of starting the survey that was required, when the adjoining owner, a wild-eyed middle-aged female, came flying out of her house, shouting obscenities, waving a pistol, demanding to know what we were doing there. She made it very plain that she did not care why we were there or whom we were working for, but that if I was not gone really soon, and not to come back, she was going to blow me to kingdom come.

Being only in my 30's at the time, I felt I was not yet that interested in finding out where kingdom come was, so I beat a somewhat hasty retreat from that site.

I called my client to inform him of what had happened, thanked him for the opportunity to serve him, and said I most likely won't be back.

He shrugged, apparently, and said not to worry; he would take care of it. Another surveyor was hired; a police escort came and stayed with him while he was doing the initial survey, and while he was installing the final markers and whatever else needed to be marked.

Conversing with my former client later, I learned the subdivision had been completed; the hostile neighbor committed to some type of care, and her property was purchased by the group and developed.

The third and final, I hope, confrontation came when I was surveying a group of town lots my client had purchased at a county tax sale and wanted them identified and marked on the ground.

The town they were located in is well monumented, so I was confident I was correct in my establishment of the lines and corners.

Having just completed the installation of a corner marker at the westerly endpoint of the purchased lots that bordered the hostile neighbor's lot, I am confronted by a definitely unhappy neighbor demanding to know what the hell I thought I was doing, trespassing on her land (we refer to such as sacred soil), and that she was going to pull the pin we had just put in and then turn her Malamute (very big dog) onto me.

I politely asked her to please calm down, this was not the end of society as we know it, that I have the legal right to enter a neighboring property to install markers, and that it is illegal to remove a marker installed by a licensed surveyor, and that I would have her arrested and prosecuted if she pulled that pin out.

Then, I would also have her arrested for the dog attack and let her know that if she turned the dog on me I would fight back, being well armed with a 24-inch machete, a hammer, long steel pins and a strong helper. The dog would most likely be confiscated and probably euthanized.

Besides, I informed her, she was getting a free $600 survey by default, her lot being an ad joiner to my client's lot.

After which, I would sue her for all kinds of personal trauma, real or imaginary.

All this visibly calmed her down, and she turned pleasantly social, asking what she should do with her burn barrel on my client's lot; I assured her it was not a concern, to just leave it there.

We parted on friendly terms, she wishing me a good day, and I wishing her well.

My 63-year long surveying career is about over anyway, so this was a fitting part in the process of winding it down.

God Bless all my previous wonderful clients, and their decent, friendly neighbors.

Fool Me Once...

Engaged in the never-ending challenge of tricking our animals, in this case Thor, into actually swallowing whatever evil smelling- according to his super sensitive nose – apparently life-threatening chemical poorly disguised as a beneficial pill one morning recently, I baited him with a small portion of chipped ham lunch meat, which he expertly caught and swallowed, immediately whetting his appetite, eagerly watching wide eyed for more, the sooner the better.

The next serving of lunch meat had an innocent looking pill carefully concealed in it, wrapped so as to be undetectable by that super sharp nose. Dropping the now generous portion into his open mouth, he wasted no time in directing it toward his stomach, to be ready for another dose, just in case.

One final, small portion ended the process, so as to leave him satisfied.

Score: Human, 1, Canine, 0.

Now the dinner hour on the same day, and time for another pill.

Yes, contrary to all elevated social mores I "feed" him at dinner from the table. And, as circumstances arranged it, dinner was soup and sandwiches.

Thor, of course, was parked next to me on the left side, and as it occurred, I had consumed half of a half-sandwich of the same chipped ham as was for lunch and gave him the remaining half in his bowl.

This time he carefully sniffed the offering, obviously suspecting something could be amiss, not grabbing and swallowing like he had done at lunch. Refusing to take it, walking away, changing sides, away from the suspect sandwich.

Whoever said dogs weren't smart?

Fool me once, shame on you.

Fool me twice……..

Six Children Growing Up

When there are six children in any family, especially one with minimal parental guidance or oversight, there are going to be many different opinions on any number of topics. This mix of personalities in fairly close proximity will, and did, create any number of squabbles, some serious, none of which carried beyond the reaching of adulthood and the dissemination into different interests, and of the gradual scattering into different geographical locations.

Gatherings as adults were normally congenial, individually sporadic, or continuing annually in a reunion, until aging created a gradual separation, and finally, a one-by-one departure to eternity's final rewards.

Godzilla

I don't remember, nor do I want to remember the year this happened, but I do remember the kids were between ages 6 and 12.

Long ago, having seen that all-time classic movie, Gone With the Wind, I felt it would be good for not only me and Dolly to revisit it, but the kids would enjoy such an all-time great movie, early for them or not.

This one week, it had been advertised in the local paper that the movie would be shown at the Vandergrift Casino Theater at 1:00 o'clock.

So, we pack up everyone and head for the Casino, get there, get seated, and here we go.

Well, every movie was prefaced with previews of coming attractions those days, so as the cameras started unreeling the first future attraction, or so I thought, what started to play was Godzilla, that awful Japanese production of absolute garbage suitable for morons to be entertained by some equally moronic producer without any chance of including anything sensible in any way.

So, what I thought was a preview was actually the feature show, I am suffering with an ever-growing intensity of frustration, knowing that since nothing lasts forever, this too would soon end, and the real show, Gone With the Wind, would then be shown.

I should have realized that Gone With the Wind is a 4-hour movie that could not have followed the preview of almost 2 hours of nonsense. What little religion I had left soon evaporated, just as the lights came on.

Well, stupid or not, I was, to say the least, incensed at having been fooled into attending that sorry production of a movie, and having laid down whatever number of hard-earned dollars for the privilege.

So, I tracked down the manager, and in unashamed fury, I unleashed my disgust on him regarding the false belief that Gone With the Wind was the feature shown, not Godzilla.

His defense was that it was an honest mistake, not having time to acquire Gone With the Wind, and that the Godzilla show was, in fact, a quality substitute enjoyable to everyone.

I, at elevated decibel levels, gave him my opinion: GARBAGE!

He refused to concede, trying to convince me it was a good replacement, to which I firmly, loudly, reiterated my opinion: GARBAGE!

By now, quite a few observers were gathered around, including my wife and 4 wide-eyed kids, just listening, staying out of sight.

Again, I not so cordially shouted GARBAGE!, some of the onlookers nodding their heads in agreement.

He offered me the ticket fees back, I said stick them, so he walked away before it got any worse, and he'd call the cops.

We never did get to see Gone With the Wind.

Ambulance Trial and Error

My oldest son, John, became an Emergency Medical Tech as soon as age minimums were cleared, and formally joined with the Avonmore Life Savers, the local ambulance service.

Until he reached driving age, Dolly and I would take turns taking him to calls, day and night. After reaching driving age, he was able to take one of our vehicles, ending that problem.

It only accelerated it when he reached Paramedic status, being the lead tech on calls.

As my businesses began to prosper, John left my family partnership and joined others to become big time coal operators and contractors.

The group he had joined, all undesirables, promptly named him President of the corporation, and promptly blamed him for tens of thousands of dollars in penalties issued for a number of serious environmental violations they had committed.

The ensuing war with regulatory finally ended when the Chicago based corporation filed Chapter 7 bankruptcy, setting him free.

Having learned a lesson, he returned to our involvements, where we would brainstorm any number of varying possibilities, I equally responsible for delving into such, not only agreeing to give it a try, but to provide the capital for startup.

His first, of course, was to start an ambulance service for the Saltsburg area, where he lived.

We examined every possible reason why it could not fail and assumed it would endear us to everyone in the tri state area, be awarded hero and savior status, along with undying gratitude from the natives.

Somewhere in this period, we agreed to take a flyer into the over the road trucking world, which ultimately proved to be a genuine disaster as told herein elsewhere.

Then we became dealers in portable telephones. He sold them by the hundreds, offering group packages to various organizations and employers everywhere.

The sad part is that when they defaulted, and many, if not most, did, there was a clause in the agreement that we were liable for unpaid obligations.

It cost me, big time before bailing.

Then, we got into selling used cars. A local Ford dealer gave us a really good deal.

He dumped a whole bunch of unsaleable junkers on us, which became a nightmare of repair issues when sold to unsuspecting buyers.

I finally gave the remaining unsold ones to employees, as is, where is, no warranty, no comebacks, no lemon law protection.

Then it was a tow truck, a tilt bed that was the simple answer, just drag the disabled vehicle on and go.

Towing is quite competitive, and when we were allocated the towing of a vehicle involving a triple fatality, it was all I could take, and I got rid of the tilt bed.

Then it was high-pressure washing of heavy equipment. Oh yeah, want to have some fun?

Get on the end of the hose and nozzle with five-thousand pounds of pressure pushing hot, soapy water onto a greasy excavator or other piece of heavy equipment that can be 12 to 15 feet high, splattering you in your rain suit with slop for seven or eight hours a day.

So, the glamour wore off quickly, and guys willing to tolerate this disappeared equally quickly.

So did the pressure washer and its trailer.

We tried renting our small box truck; found we were lucky if it came back in one piece.

While all this was going on, I'm still surveying and engineering coal mines, doing lot and house surveys, operating one or usually two strip mines, overseeing a wood fixtures laminated panels operation: all only using 18 hours a day.

I never worked on a Sunday, and I had quit golf as it no longer had any real meaning to me.

And while all of the above is happening, I'm being continually hammered to go into emergency services, in effect, and ambulance company. Did we? Yes, we did, for better or for worse. John named it Lifestat; it's quite a story. Here goes: just a small part.

First, you need qualified personnel. We had John, a licensed, experienced Paramedic. We had Don, and EMT available full time. We had Debbie, available part time – excellent beyond description. Several potential future EMT's. That was it.

Next, you needed mobile equipment. John found two ancient ambulances; Dodge vans formerly fitted as ambulances, at a local junk yard.

I bought them, and we were on our way. I should have left them in the junk yard.

Then, we were actually the laughingstock of the emergency medical community for miles around. And we deserved it.

Early on, the principals of a widely established, well-known successful nearby service called and requested a meeting.

At the meeting they made an honest proposal for me to assess my out-of-pocket costs, add a percentage, and they would take over in providing the service in our prospective area.

Convinced we could achieve the same end-result; better serving the need based on proximity, not some 20 miles, I said no. I was the fool.

We were now officially enemy number one; and to date, it has never really changed.

We were already confirmed enemy number one by the Avonmore and Slickville services, so that rounded it out; even though staffing for those two was hit and miss, as they were purely voluntary, and substandard.

Eventually we took over both Avonmore and Slickville, as they diminished in great part due to our superior service – being always staffed at high levels around the clock; they unable to do so.

To say this was, and is, a difficult business is an understatement of monumental proportions.

It would take pages and pages of writing to cover all the negatives that are involved – with more being added constantly.

Equally important to fire and police, I am amazed at the resistance by the public to support the ambulance service, so vital to a healthy community.

Few know the actual cost of operations; a properly equipped ambulance costing around $400,000 dollars, mandated by medical authorities, and you must have more than one unit.

I personally became an EMT, then a licensed Paramedic, and ran calls 24-hours a day, 7 days a week for seven years as a volunteer; never taking payment for my time to help keep it alive.

In the 34 years since my initial outlay of funding, the service has seen many changes, all negative.

Primary is in the attitude of the public in general; that the service is not worthy of its support – vital though it is.

Despite 34 years of 24/7 coverage, I have grave fear that its survival is in serious question, leaving local coverage to distant providers.

There is no other way to end this story.

Pittsburgh EMS Baby

In training for becoming a paramedic, I ran with the famous, or infamous, Pittsburgh paramedics, Homewood station, circa 1990, a great bunch of guys.

I experienced an endless flow of calls, everything from serious cardiac issues, to beer bottle battles, to absolutely asinine emergencies, like a call to an 18-year-old female for, yes a stubbed toe.

A call came one evening for an imminent childbirth, the usual countdown underway.

So, in the normal 100+ mile per hour, red lights blazing, sirens screaming, cross-city manner, we went flying to the call.

Reaching the caller's address, we – the three of us, found the caller up an open stairway, five floors up, patiently waiting.

Ascending the steps two or three at a time, we were at her side in seconds.

The caller, quite young in appearance; the patient, obviously born and raised in the deep South judging by the Southern dialect in conversing with her.

Very calmly the patient, looking down at the ambulance five floors below us on the street said, "how are you-all going to get me down from here to the ambulance?"

One of the Pittsburgh medics came right back with "how did you-all get up here?"

She said, "I walked."

He said, "that's how you're going to get down there."

So, without any visible difficulty, down she went, us flanking her so as to prevent a slip or fall.

We soon had her inside the ambulance on a gurney, where immediately – yes, immediately – here comes the baby, number 6; she at age 22, and I got to catch it. My first, and probably my last.

Route 22 Birthday Celebration

I had completed my paramedic training, and was running calls for our ambulance service when, late one night, the tones go off, and I'm rolling down the road to a motor vehicle accident.

This was on Rt. 22, a major four-lane highway, on a cold winter night, snowing hard.

A young man, celebrating his 21st birthday, had gone to a local bar along that road, and after having been served an unknown, supposedly, number of hard drinks, decided to go to another bar, to continue celebrating.

There was a wide four-way intersection very near the bar, at the bottom of a long, steep downgrade.

As best we could tell, he, possibly being in an altered condition from drinking, and confused by the falling snow, drove across the intersection from the Eastbound side into the Westbound side, directly into the path of a fast-moving tractor trailer, effectively ending the 21st year achievement, along with the celebration.

It was very sad; there was no medical attention necessary, just the Coroner.

Last Call

As a paramedic running ambulance calls, I was involved in a number of them where I will not divulge any details beyond the point of decency, and limited in number, only for the purpose of exposure of what emergency medical people go through, at times.

A call for a motor vehicle accident, a head-on collision from very high speed by a small car into a loaded triaxle, a crossover into the truck's path resulted in the near total vehicle compression so violent, the driver of the car disappeared; no trace of him was visible.

I do not know the disposition of that, as it was in a neighboring service's territory, and it was their responsibility once they arrived on the scene.

Another scene I will not describe was in the room where the subject caused his self-appointed exit from this world with a twelve-gauge shotgun.

That ended my participation in the response to emergency calls.

Besides, I had other businesses to run, and help support the Emergency Medical Service.

Dept. Of Labor

As the Lifestat Ambulance Service was just exiting its infancy, and beginning to expand, we were hiring additional personnel, and among them was one Scott ___ a former medic of our Eastern neighbor.

As we were operating temporarily as a partnership with no benefits and partnership rules, there was an immediate clash of attitude between him and us, the management.

Early on, he began undermining the system, convincing certain existing members of the partnership to rebel, and demand a change of structure, which was totally out of line in any case.

Scott was only the forerunner in this story, as he was the one who invited the U.S. Labor Department to investigate us and the system we were operating under, not being financially able to operate as a regular 501C Corp. not yet legally established.

So, the Labor Department landed one day; surely it was the Devil himself, or at least, his right-hand man that arrived here, flashing his badge and announcing his intent to destroy us, based on the complaint he had received from Scott and whoever else had cosigned it, former loyal, now adversarial members of the partnership.

When stated we were a legal partnership, he immediately launched into a tirade as to how he represented the Almighty Federal Divinity, and how with their unlimited resources, they would quickly squash us under their heel, even press for fines and punishment for me, and the rest of management including the possibility of prison time for me.

I let him rant till finally, I said, "Okay, what's the alternative?"

He said He would write up certain requirements and demands and return in a few days.

Return he did, with a legal document outlining the Labor Department's results of his investigation, and how the whole issue could be remedied, if agreed.

The details of his settlement proposal are unimportant for this telling, but what is noteworthy is that his proposal gave me freedom from legal reprisal by the disgruntled soon-to-be-former members of the partnership.

Best of all, certain timelines he incorporated into the final settlement benefited me, and Lifestat; many thousands of dollars these disgruntled ones would otherwise have received as partner's share of earned revenue.

Scott and certain others were invited out, and soon departed for greener pastures.

The Devil's protégé will never know how much he benefitted me.

1975 Brown Jeep

Emergency medical personnel were in short supply, as is usual, so any qualified person was always welcome for an interview.

A young man from a local town about 20 miles away showed up one day, said he was a licensed paramedic, and would like to work for us, having just moved here.

The interview went well but hiring him had some issues.

First was he had no vehicle to commute with, and had no credit strength in this area to purchase one.

He had two beautiful kids with him, about 4 and 6 years old, and admitted he was in desperate financial condition, he and wife living in an offbeat trailer court.

Appearing and sounding respectable, just down on his luck, I said that I had a good 1975 Jeep I would sell him at a reasonable price.

He flat out said, I couldn't give you 50 dollars for it, just don't have it.

I, the ever-compassionate fool, and badly needing a paramedic, ended the problem when said, I'll just give it to you, if you agree to go to work immediately, and stay indefinitely.

He agreed, but did I really solve the problem?

The next day we met at a Notary's office, title in hand. Once in the office, he says, "you're going to have to pay all the fees, license, notary, title transfer, and sales tax. A pretty good hit. Gritting my teeth, I wrote the checks.

Now he's mobile and can begin to run calls, his performance less than hoped, or expected.

A week goes by, and he begs for an early payday, he's in really bad shape for some money.

So, we advance him a two-week check, and all is well. It's Friday, we'll see you here Monday.

Monday morning, where's Robert? No show, after one week.

The phone rang within the hour, it's the State Police.

"Do you know a Robert B?" a voice says, "Yes, why do you ask?"

"Well, it seems that he went to ___ Bar, got drunk, left the bar, came to our DWI check point, panicked, drove around it, and being pursued, wrecked, went into a deep ditch where the 1975 Jeep caught fire, burned to a total loss."

"He is in custody, requesting you post ball for him."

"Tell him he can rot in there; he can go straight to hell."

I never saw or heard from him again.

It was the first, but not the last personnel issue; oh, what fun, and educational.

But you're never smart enough.

Slickvllle Ambulance

A neighboring volunteer ambulance service in Slickvllle was on the verge of Bankruptcy and repossession, I contacted their principals and asked for a meeting.

Melda, the President, came to our office to discuss the situation, and it was agreed we would take over entirely, including their accumulated liabilities.

We set up a base station at Slickville and provided paid staff, and things went reasonably well for a while.

Then, personalities began to conflict, township supervisors got into the chaos, and a large competitor began making overtures to take over the territory we had assumed in the takeover.

It turned out ugly, harsh inferences being cast around, finally we were replaced as the primary provider by the township supervisors.

Then, a slimy lawyer joined forces with the hostile element, and filed a lawsuit against us.

The basis for the lawsuit vas that we were not a legitimate 501c(3) Corporation, nor a corporation of any kind at all.

Presenting a printout from the Department Of State indicating we were in clear and complete legal standing was ignored by not only that lawyer, but also a county court judge whose name I don't remember, but I think her first name was Donetta, who approved the continuation of the suit by them against me.

That county court judge was slated to become a judge on the Federal Bench, and was, a short time later. Any corruption here or judiciary brilliance.

During the trial, I was openly aggressive in my style of response, and defensive, understandably, since I was under attack, after having been generously benevolent to a failed entity, at great personal cost.

I don't remember that lawyer's name, nor do I want to, but it had a sound reference akin to a Southern Intellectual, Yokel.

Upon conclusion of my testimony, my daughter, Cindy, was called, and being seated and sworn in, the lawyer, Yokel, or whatever his name was, addressed the Judge with the motion to cast her as a hostile witness. The kindly, soft-spoken Judge asked her to face him, and after his perusal of her, said matter-of-factly to the lawyer, "she doesn't look very hostile to me, motion denied."

And then she tore the attorney's case apart, giving him one final hostile stare, returning to her seat, fighting the urge to stick her tongue out at him, or worse.

The trial judge didn't take long; my defense was very simple. "Read the State Department Letter, stupid."

I and my daughter were designated as hostile witnesses, and we were.

We only had one thing to tell – the truth, bluntly.

It didn't take long for a sensible, honest judge to throw out the whole mess, and their poor excuse of a lawyer out, with prejudice.

It was all part of the fun, in a miserable business, with corrupt, evil people.

Nevertheless, it cost me five-thousand dollars in lawyer fees to defend – all a part of their evil scheme.

Lobo Wolf

In the recital of today's story, I am borrowing a page out of a letter written to my dear friend in California, several years ago. That letter will appear at some future time in its entirety.

November 26, 2020
Thanksgiving day, cool, cloudy.

Dear Joan—

Another pleasant surprise from California; a letter and a card picturing one of my lifelong loves; wolves.

My affection for them all originated in the early teen years when I was a voracious reader.

Jack London's book, Call of the Wild, so inspired me that, to this day, I still enter into a dream-like state encompassing that world in the far North where the wolf is king.

Sometimes I believe I was a wolf in an earlier life.

There is no question I subconsciously patterned my life, in part, in the lifestyle of the wolf, in effect; the male is king, the female is queen, each granting the other mutual respect and adoration, and each fulfilling their respective roles in the obligations to family and community, and in the raising of their children.

Time has not erased my vivid recall of a trip Dolly and I made to the town of Kane, Pennsylvania in 1958, to where the last surviving remnants of a once-proud, once-dominating, never domesticated canine group, the Lobo Wolfpack, was being kept in protective captivity, staving off the inevitable fate they faced: extinction.

Former Kings over creation, rulers of the forest, playing a vital role in maintaining the balance of nature.

Hunted to near extinction by ruthless, uncaring man, just a few endured.

Alone, I advanced to the edge of the enclosure, stood quietly at the fence, watching, as this magnificent animal approached me, one deliberate step at a time, slowly closing the gap between us until he was within a very few feet of me.

He stood fully 4 feet tall, perfectly proportioned; he was the alpha wolf, the unequivocal leader of the pack.

Unblinking, we stared at each other for the longest time, in what I will always commemorate as a subconscious connection between two soulmates, inscribing forever into me a primeval link into perpetuation.

The recall, the reply of that scenario haunts me still, and I expect will continue to, forever.

Perhaps someday, somewhere, there will appear a reason for it to end.

The Rainbow Bridge??

I named my first German Shepherd Lobo, in honor of him.

Paul W - Kitten

In 1964, I worked as a surveyor at the local coal mine, returning home each day via the township road passing by my neighbor, Paul W's house.

Oftentimes, he would be out and about the road area when I was passing by, so we would visit for a few minutes, exchange ordinary, neighborly interests.

One of our conversations centered on cats, having grown up with them on the farm, and how, at the moment, I did not have a cat, and would like to get one for the kids.

Well, It just happened to be that he had a kitten I could have. He said he would round it up out of the barn, and it would be ready for me to take the next day.

Next day, I stop on my way home, and Paul is waiting for me, with the kitten.

Oh yeah! kitten all right. I'm expecting a kitten, you know, a tiny seven or eight ounces of adorable feline.

The kitten, about 3 feet long nose to tip of tail, probably weighing in at least 20 lbs. with a mean, uncompromising look in its eyes, resembling a real mountain lion, reluctantly came to me, I put it onto my left arm, cradling it against my body, headed up the hill, it being just a short distance to the house, where the kids were eagerly awaiting its arrival.

The short ride was routine, except for the low growl coming from the kitten, soon arriving at the house.

Stopping, opening my door to get out, the kitten, seeing freedom beckoning, abruptly launched off my arm, I 'm sure matching the level of thrust of a jet fighter taking off of a carrier achieves, disappearing rapidly towards Pauls' barn.

The four long, deep grooves Its claws left in my arm did eventually heal, thanks to much care by my RN wife.

I quickly went inside and called Paul. Picking up the phone, without saying hello he said, "he's here already." End of conversation.

Soon after, we found an actual kitten for the kids.

Pokey

My brother, Andy, was living alone at the time, in our original house, and having grown up with dogs, missed their presence as both watch and companion, so he decided to be on the lookout for one.

As it happened, people, for whatever reason, were abandoning their dogs right and left, and one morning Andy found a puppy at his door, having been dropped off during the night.

He accepted it immediately, providing it with all the comforts of a real home.

For no really good reason, he failed to name him, and time moved on, the puppy growing fast into a fair-sized dog, 60 to 70 pounds, fairly tall.

I, having moved into our partially completed house – there remained much to be done – and one Summer day I was working on the driveway building some sort of cabinet or other, my electrically powered saw laying on the ground.

The saw, quite aged and worn from my having used it in the construction of two houses previously, had reached the point where it had a short-circuit situation, and would bite you hard if you handled it improperly: a one-man saw.

It was common for Andy's dog to come up to our house and go into the basement to cool off on the concrete floor, staying for whatever length of time it took to satisfy him.

So, this hot summer day I am at work on the cabinet, watching Andy's dog coming up the driveway, panting hard, tongue hanging down, aiming for the basement door.

Between him and the door, though, was my saw lying on the driveway.

He, ever curious, wanting to check out that bright, shiny object in his path, poked his nose firmly onto the hand grip, his extended tongue slapping against the saw blade, flush.

Well, the saw was ready to bite anything touching it, and bite it did – hard!

His tail shot straight out; he leapt away from the saw instantly, yelping and screaming, turning away, he hightailed it down the driveway, back to his master's house, in record time.

However, it was still very hot, and the next day he wanted to cool off, so here he comes up the driveway again, heading straight for the basement door.

By chance I had once again laid out that evil saw in the same spot as the day before.

This time, though, his memory of the prior days' experience with that bright, shiny object directed him to come just to the beast, turn hard right for several steps, then hard left for several steps, then hard left again, back onto the direct path into the basement, then the final right along that path, and he's home free, in the basement.

I then and there officially named him Pokey, for the obvious reason.

Pokey, being a free-spirited runner, was struck by a car several years thereafter; and did not recover from the injuries.

It took years for Andy to recover from his loss.

Jim and Bear

On another visit, Jim and a friend were very late in returning from a day of fishing.

What had happened was they had been fishing, and getting late in the day, decided to go back to camp.

The track they chose was through some very dense vegetation, briars and so on, chest high, rough going, poles held high to clear the brush.

Suddenly, a bear stood up on its hind legs, saw them, briefly charged them, then stopped.

They, abandoning the poles to the bear, took off, running back towards the creek, finding a tree of about 6 inches in diameter, and both climbed up as fast as possible, the bear not far behind.

The bear milled about around under the tree for about ten minutes, then left the scene, disappearing into the woods.

They stayed treed for a short while, mustering up as much courage as possible, then came down, taking off towards camp, all's well that ends well.

But it didn't end, just yet.

When bear hunting season came in that next Autumn, Jim, determined to avenge the incident in fishing season, bought a bear hunting license, and went back up to that spot, this time armed with a high-powered rifle, looking for Mr. Bear.

Walking down to the site along an open logging trail, in four inches of fresh snow, he saw a set of very fresh bear tracks, huge bear tracks, recently made.

That's when and where better judgement lit up his brain, and he said to himself: "Wow, what if I get him? Worse yet, what if he gets me?

That ended not only any thoughts of revenge; it also ended his ever hunting bear again.

Lobo and Kitten

Lobo, our first German Shepherd, was a real sweetie. 130 pounds of gentle giant, pleasant demeanor, the peacekeeper when babysitting the kids out in the dirt piles, or anywhere else.

He was, generally speaking, king of our big two-car garage, the absolute unchallenged ruler.

One day, we decided to get a kitten for the kids to expand their animal behavior horizons a bit. So, we brought a kitten home one Sunday, set it on the garage floor and called Lobo over for an introduction to his new friend.

Bo took one sniff of the kitten, then proceeded to lay down a streak of pee, dividing the garage about in half, crying piteously as he went: Kiyi, Kiyi ,Kiyi-ing the whole way.

Then he sniffed the kitten once more and left.

Bear at Y

A surface miner client of mine, Ben, was evaluating an area he was planning to lease for mining, and asked if I would accompany him since it meant going underground in a remote area.

There being a mine opening allowing access to the deep mine further into the hill, we, of course, went in, flashlights being our only light source.

We only went in a short distance, perhaps 300 feet, the length of a football field, when we came to a 45-degree left hand turn, and a 45 degree right band turn, probably for access to separate parts of the mine; now abandoned.

For no real reason we opted to go to the left, then traveling for a short distance, finding the old deep mine workings, now caved in, preventing any further penetration.

So, we turned back to leave, and soon we were back at the Y previously mentioned, but now there was an odd smell there that hadn't been there when we first were there. So, we looked around to try to identify the new smell.

And identify it we did!

There, just in front of us, was a still steaming pile of bear dung, apparently from a bear whose den was in the entry we did not choose to go into.

Never did the cliche, there's light at the end of the tunnel carry more significance than that day, as we scurried to the light at the end of the tunnel.

Loyal Creek Coal Mine

I started what may well have been a career in 1957, at the Seanor Deep Mine; placed on the supply crew first, then in a few months transferred into the production division, then into a Surveyor Helper.

All positions, understandably, the bottom of the totem pole, a beginner. Union domination kept me at the bottom of the pile while I was in their realm.

As a Surveyor Helper, though, I was part of, yes a very small part of, management, therefore non-union.

Carrying a reputation of certain elevated intellectual capability, I was often drawn into problem solving by other managers, primarily the Section Foreman directly involved in the coal production.

I actually was awarded savings bonds, and other financial awards for submitting various cost saving suggestions to high level management, the only one out of 200+ employees to do so.

Of course, this was known to the top boss of the production division, and he was not particularly enthused that such a low-level peon was being recognized with new, workable ideas to help the cause.

One day, he confronted me about my actions, not in praise or appreciation, but in contempt and derision, ending the verbal assault with: "Charlie, you ain't nuthin but a chain boy, in other words, nuthin, mind your own business."

Understanding human psychology to some extent, I refused to either respond to him in kind, or to let it affect my relationship with him, remaining friendly, if not friends.

I left the Seanor Mine a few years later, but kept in touch with him, and became quite friendly with his son, a mining engineer.

The Seanor Mine closed in the interim, and then he worked in the Jamison Mine, where I was the Mine Surveyor, as a Section Boss, one notch lower than he had been all those years at Seanor.

I, the entrepreneur, planning to open my own deep mine, knowing his skills, invited him to be a partner in the mine I was planning.

He accepted, and what do you know, I was sort of his Boss, by agreement after all those years.

Finding myself overwhelmed with work in my already active businesses, I cheerfully sold him my interest in the mine when his son, the mining engineer joined in with him.

They, as a family, mined there for some number of years till, sadly, a younger son was killed by a rock fall there.

He's long gone, now, but maybe we 'll meet again, in that great coal mine in the sky.

Bear / Feeder

I've lived up on this hill for a long time, and have maintained a bird feeder forever.

For convenience, I kept it low, about 6 feet off the ground, for easy refilling.

There was no issue for years, but one morning I found the feeder laying on the ground, emptied of the sunflower seeds I kept in it for the birds.

I didn't think much of it, refilled it, and hung it back up.

The next morning it's down again, this time it's partially caved in, obviously by something pretty strong. Yes, a bear; we do live in the country, after all.

This time, I put a steel pole, made for hanging flowerpots onto, into the ground, firmly, and up higher, about 8 feet.

The next morning, I 'm greeted with a rainbow shaped steel pole, empty feeder. He, or she, had reached up, pulled it down to the ground, bending it completely over.

So, I move the feeder over to a big maple tree, to a 5-or 6-inch-thick limb that's at least 11 feet high.

In order to be able to refill it, I rigged a pulley to the feeder to be able to lower it, and raise it back up, then tied the rope to the tree.

Overnight, he/she ripped the rope off the tree, and down goes the feeder.

Now, this time I get a ladder, and tie the rope 15 or so feet up the tree.

No problem for him, he simply climbs up to the rope, tears it down, and down goes the feeder.

Next, I rigged a system where the feeder is hooked into a fixed hook on the high limb, I, using a long pole to unhook and lower to the ground to refill it, eliminated the rope.

That baffled him, but not for long. Since the feeder was now hung from a 5-inch-thick limb, too small to climb on, 8 feet away from the trunk of the tree, too far to reach from the ground, he had a problem. Now what?

He climbed the tree up to the limb, then reached out as far as he could, and started chewing off the limb.

He made it halfway through the limb, before giving up, finally.

When my refilling system became inconvenient, I started over again.

This time, I dug a small hole right beside the heavy corner post of my grape arbor, made up a hangar for the feeder on a 2-inch steel pipe, buried the end of the pipe next to the post, and anchored the pipe to the big post with a chain.

To refill it, I simply unhook it, lower it down to fill it, then raise it and re-chain it.

The bear finally gave up, never returned; but the squirrels didn't, easily climbing a 2-inch pipe.

The only answer I had for them was Thor, my German Shepherd. After he dispatched the third one, they even gave up.

Birds can't eat acorns or hickory nuts, squirrels and bears can.

I get millions of them every year from all those big oak trees growing there.

Bear at Hart

Bori, my second German Shepherd, and I were evaluating an area for the permitting of another strip mine.

We were about a half mile into deep, dark woods when I came to a big, partially decayed tree laying in our path.

Climbing over it, I noticed a big chunk of bark, about eight feet long, obviously torn off that tree, laying alongside of it.

The underside of it was fresh, too fresh, not yet dried.

Nov there's only one thing that I know of that can tear a piece of aged bark that big, off a decayed log.

I kept on with my work, but was now uneasy, Bori not really any help, sticking fairly close to me, too close, inhibiting my forward advance.

So, I turned around, headed back toward my parked truck, even accelerating my pace just a bit.

Finally, I was at the road, not far from my truck.

Still uneasy, turned around and looked back to where we had just been.

Just then, a mid-sized bear came out of the woods where I had just exited, paused, looked at me for a few seconds, then turned away, leaving me and Bori, now at the truck. He had followed us out.

Now at ease.

But a mid-sized bear is really BIG.

Bears at Weimer's

I was opening the road from a township road into a newly- permitted job site one day, using one of my 25-ton excavators, when lunch time struck. It being a sunny, but cool day, I stayed in the cab out of the wind, quite comfortable.

A neighbor's beagle was there with me, just nosing around. With the engine off, it was quiet there,, when in the distance I heard what sounded like galloping horses, that tarump, tarump sound that thrilled you as a kid watching westerns. I thought it was very strange because I was completely surrounded by woods, no open trails, so who would be riding horses in there.

As the sound came closer quite fast, growing much louder, the little beagle ducked under the excavator, and I stood up in the cab to get a better view.

Suddenly, there they were. Two mid-sized bears galloping at full speed, heading straight for me, not paying any attention to the excavator, just missing it by four or five feet from the cab where I was sitting.

The silly little beagle charged out from underneath the excavator, challenging them as they passed, and then actually chasing them.

Their running speed was downright astonishing, as they flew by me, jumping effortlessly across a wide stream bed, then climbing straight up an old spoil pile like it was a level field, quickly disappearing into the brush and trees.

I remain in pure awe of the awesome power I saw in those two bodies as they came and went by, totally unaware of my presence.

Yuri – In Memory Of

Yuri, being the German Shepherd Dolly was the closest to, and developed a special affinity to, is featured in today's offering in his memoir.

In follow up of my last presentation featuring Dolly's presence in my life, I'm disclosing the memoir I wrote upon the passing of her favorite German Shepherd, Yuri, as the one she spent so much time with, staying by her side while she worked in her flower beds, garden, and grass chores.

She also stayed with him, giving comfort, in his final moments here on the earth.

~~ In Memory of Yuri Boris Starr of Kravet ~~

September 1, 2005 ~ July 21, 2010

An old man pauses, and pensively gazes out over his recent companion's burial plot into the distance, closes his eyes, scanning back over some four years, eight months, twenty five days, and SADLY REMEMBERS:

A disheveled, muddied, little puppy, separating from his group, waddling toward them, making the decision easy for them.

A disheveled, muddied little puppy converted into a beautiful, bright-eyed little furball by a bath and dryer at the kennel.

The long, joyous ride home with their sleeping little angel.

The rapid change from a baby into a companion demanding endless attention in care and play.

The razor sharp teeth and countless cuts caused by them in play and in training.

The day many of those sharp little teeth came falling out, and finding them hither and yon.

The complete love of "going somewhere, anywhere, anytime ~ wanting to be with the old man wherever he went ~ happy in knowing that he was a part of the work to be done each day.

His eagerness to reunite with "His Mommy" at their arrival back home, content to be with her the rest of the day.

The total exhaustion and collapse between "His Mommy's" feet at the end of another day. Immediately puppy dreamland would engulf him, secure in his safe haven.

~!~

His early and enduring affinity to all people, especially to Bill and Cindy, along with Bailey, the ever tolerant senior dog, and later, Missy, all of whom he visibly adored throughout his brief stay here.

His total dedication to duty, and ready acceptance of his ordained job of guarding them, whenever and wherever they may be.

His manner of intently listening when spoken to, including his conversations via cell phone, the endearing twisting and cocking of his head, trying so hard to understand.

Placing his entire nose and head onto the old man's arm every morning as he sat in his chair at breakfast, asking for something to eat.

How he would come back in after eating his breakfast re-energized, select a toy from his vast supply, and WOOF at them to "not just sit there" but to play a little.

How, night after night, he would insist on a game of tug-of-war with the old man, and then some playful combat, with the toy or toys of his choice.

How they played "Ring Around the Rosey" after supper, uncaring that they were disrupting any conversation or discussion being had.

The spirited charges up and down the hall, chasing "that stupid red dot" that he never did capture.

The numerous times he and Bailey chased that same red dot 'round and 'round the yard, out into the night, into the snow. They never caught it, either.

How he so loved chasing a Frisbee, refusing to give it up. All the Frisbees, along with his host of toys being taken with him, to share with his many friends in puppy heaven.

How a beautiful township/fire department secretary brought him a whole basketful of toys ~ some of which survived the years, and were taken with him.

How he loved centering himself within any group that was assembled. Was it related to some sense of duty, or simply his love of being around people of all walks.

~2~

How the rushing air would cause his lips to flap furiously when he stuck his head out of the truck window going down the road at fifty miles an hour.

How he would vacuum in the cool air from the truck's air conditioner in the summer when it was hot, and then not understand why that same vent didn't cool him when he got too warm in the winter.

How, in his daily travels, it was routinely understood that half of the old man's lunch was his, and meals were to be shared at home, too.

How, on those days when he couldn't go with the old man, he would know it was time, watch and wait, then come bouncing down through the field to the end of the driveway to greet the old man, claim his half sandwich, and then guide the old man up the driveway (at walk speed.)

As a fully grown mature dog, when it came time for a little rest after play in the evening, he would lay his head on "His Mommy's" feet, and soon be off in dreamland.

How, for more serious sleep, when it was announced that "it's time to go to bed," he would dutifully escort them to their bedroom, and then proceed to his.

How, on many occasions, a well rested German Shepherd would decide he had had enough sleep, and would poke his wet nose into the old man's face at any hour of the night, and say "will you let me out?" Little humor was found in that.

How he loved the visits by Cindy and Bill, along with Bailey, and would wait and watch nightly for their arrival, joyously running to meet them at the end of the driveway, making sure they knew the way to the house, to play. He seemed to understand when they said "it's time for Bailey to go home now," and would sit contentedly and watch as they left.

How he loved going to the office, where Missy spoiled him, big-time. A fresh drink was always waiting. He would start to squirm and pace impatiently a mile away.

How much he loved Beggin Strips and Pupperoni.

Upon their arrival, how he would threaten "Pooch", the Quarry guard dog, with dismemberment or worse, from the inside of the truck, but once let out to meet "Pooch" it was "hey, Pooch, how's things here at the Quarry ~ care to play some?"

~3~

How the crows were too smart and fast for him, but the racoons, possums and squirrels were fair game, to be chased up the nearest tree, forced to stay there all day long, waiting until he went inside for the night.

The Bear was a standoff.

How he slowly drew in his circle of operations, a ball chased only to the curve in the driveway, chasing a Frisbee only a short distance, staying close to the truck on work trips. Refusing to share lunch, being selective in food, drinking less, ever shorter play periods. More and more lay down and sleep time, less and less energy, developing a limp, losing weight, becoming ever more distant and isolated.

The trip to the vet for evaluation, and the results of the blood test. The valiant effort by good and highly knowledgeable people trying to ease the pain. The ominous warning. The final effort to provide care and comfort.

The kindness of so many in hoping and praying for the best, and being blessed with an extra month of his presence. For this we are truly grateful.

The final goodbyes by those who cared so much, and then he was taken away.

Yuri was laid to rest alongside his predecessors Lobo and Boris, in our burial plot under the grape arbor, where they can forever share in being "Kings of the Hill."

Yuri, you were here for just a little while, but the myriad wonderful memories you provided will last us into eternity. We will never forget you.

Thank you very, very much ~ we will always love you.

The mysterious rainbow that briefly appeared in a rainless sky, shortly after his passing. Is there, in fact, a Rainbow Bridge? We hope so, and if there is, we hope it will include people, too.

Dear Reader ~ Thank You for Caring,

Chuck and Dolly Kravetsky

Ivanhoe

Ivanhoe was number four in a long line of German Shepherds, and Ilke the others was always happy to be with me, wherever we went, unless Dolly was not feeling well, when they would usually stay at home with her.

I had moved an excavator to Jim's house to clear an area, and, of course Ivanhoe was with me.

The noise, and violence of crashing trees made him uneasy, and he stayed clear of the activity area.

When several pickups arrived, woodcutters, chainsaws in hand, he really became nervous.

Having taken a drink break, I was walking away from the truck, towards the excavator when he barked, loudly, standing by the truck door.

When I stopped and turned around and looked at him, he lifted his nose skyward, and howled, woo, woo, woo, signaling he wanted in the truck, where he stayed till lunch break.

It was May 30, Stella's' birthday, and Ivanhoe was sleeping outside in the garage while we ate her birthday dinner, oblivious to our activity.

At exactly the time for the birthday cake to be cut, Ivanhoe beats on the kitchen door, comes in, sits down, and howled with us in singing the happy birthday song, ate his piece of cake, then left immediately.

Like all German Shepherds, Ivan loved to ride. Oftentimes, he would move to the front seat, sit looking out, extend his paw for me to hold, for miles.

As Ivanhoe's' disabilities increased, I bought and built devices to assist him in mounting and dismounting the back seat of the truck, giving him riding presence to within just a few days of his passing.

In addition, I'm including the memoir I wrote for him shortly after his departure.

In Memory of Ivanhoe Yuri Boris Lobo of Kravet

June 18, 2010 ~ November 18, 2018

The refrain "Only Love Can Break A Heart, Only Love Can Mend It Again" courses gently through my consciousness as I recall how the arrival of a beautiful German Shepherd puppy restored and uplifted a wonderful woman, my wife Dolores, whose heart had been broken by the passage of her beloved German Shepherd, Yuri, some eight years and three months ago.

As was the case, this puppy had been the payment for services rendered by a child psychologist to someone unable to pay otherwise, causing the separation of it from its mother at age six weeks.

Due to this, or some other unknown reason(s) he developed an independence early on, which never really left him.

Now, at age eight weeks on our initial visit, when first viewing us, he ran and hid from us. Something higher must have said "take him", so we did. On the way home he only threw up twice in Dolly's lap.

I named him Ivanhoe, after the flamboyant literary character, and life with him commenced.

What joy he brought to us, but especially to Dolly, who soon considered him as a fourth son, and I'm sure he considered her as his surrogate mother.

In the time she spent with him he reignited her life. He was a shining light in mine.

His independence and bullheadedness began to show more and more, so at the age of eight months I hired a professional dog trainer to teach him obedience and proper manners. His name is David Fait, and we immediately dubbed him the "Puppy Professor."

Ivanhoe was essentially hard headed in many aspects, and somewhat aggressive. The Professor insisted dogs can best be trained by reasoning and verbal direction.

The weekly training sessions went on, and in observing the ongoing success, or lack thereof, I injected some of the methods I've developed over the years training animals into what I call the Charles S. Kravetsky School of Pain and Suffering, which more quickly and permanently effect the desired result.

Anyhow, the application of both methods resulted in a well mannered and highly disciplined puppy in one year. Initially Ivanhoe thought he was the only creature that should be allowed to occupy this planet.

He had, somehow in the process, learned that there is room for us all here, and to love everyone.

His devotion to duty dictated that his primary attention be focused on protection of home and family, and thus, he preferred to be outside most of the time, watching, watching.

He kept the deer, raccooons, opossums and squirrels at distance from the house, but the chipmunks and bear were another story. The chipmunks were too small and fast for him, so he ignored them, and the bear was way too big and dangerous to mess with.

Every morning he diligently watched for any vehicle movement, to be sure he would not be excluded. He lived, fervently, to be going somewhere, anywhere, anytime of the day or night, and be a part of the daily activity, joining in whenever and wherever he deemed it necessary, or just lounging around throughout the day.

Wherever we went, upon arrival, he would demand to be let out of the truck and join me so that he could inspect every nook and cranny there. To the people there it was usually amusing and positive, but sometimes a bit unnerving. One hundred thirty five pounds of big dog running loose in your store?

When traveling and reaching the Kiski Curve just West of Saltsburg, he somehow knew if we were going to Saltsburg, or to our office and Jim's garage. If it was to Saltsburg, he remained calm and collected. If it was to the office or Jim's garage he was up and fussing, fretting, whining and pawing to get me to hurry. The urgency to get there was overwhelming.

Once there, inspection of the pee point and other equally important areas was done immediately, then into the garage or office to meet and greet the resident canines. That done, he was ready to get back into the truck and move on to other adventures.

Wherever we went, if only I could go inside, he patiently waited, greeting me happily upon my return to the truck, irregardless of whether it had been ten minutes or hours.

If I stopped at Burger King for lunch, he insisted we share the french fries, one for me, one for him. No ketchup on his.

When we returned home from a long day somewhere, it was usually Ivanhoe's supper time. While I disembarked and parked, Ivan would wait, impatiently reminding me he needed his supper NOW, by elevated non-stop Woo, Woo, Wooing until I delivered it.

Then, some rest and a nap while we ate our supper, and it was time to PLAY. German Shepherds LOVE to play.

His absolute favorite was chasing sticks. I had fifteen or twenty of varying sizes which I would throw for him. Throw after throw, after throw. He chased them tirelessly, drop them and watch for the next throw. Frisbee catching and big green tennis ball rated high too. He never tired, but I did, and would call it a day(or night.)

He took several sticks and his big green tennis ball with him to be sure Dolly had something to throw for him.

On days that he couldn't go with me for one reason or another, he was constantly by Dolly's side. Outside, if she moved, he moved (into the shade, of course.) If she went inside, he went inside. He was always in sight, never far away, always alert for any danger.

He was terribly depressed for weeks after she passed away.

If my cell phone rang, he would howl along with it. Sometimes I held the phone to his mouth and let him answer the call, usually to the amusement of the caller. He had such a beautiful drawn out wolf-like howl. The memory of it is ingrained within me, and will always generate a chill.

He would howl along with you if you sang Happy Birthday to him, even if it wasn't his birthday. What a happy memory, too.

He thought it was great fun to destroy, sometimes eat, stuffed toys, squeaky toys, balls and so on. He had little concern that those toys cost a lot of money.

Through the years on days off, we would go for long walks in our beautiful one hundred eighty acres. There are old roads, trails, open woods and fields, small streams and small ponds to experience.

I'd say "Ivan, would you like to go for a walk?" He would jump for joy, and away we would go, returning hours later, exhausted and thirsty. He would take a big drink and collapse, totally spent and content.

And then, sadly, my knowing of the hip dysplasia common to German Shepherds, I began noticing how, in walking, Ivanhoe would occasionally buckle, partially collapse to the ground.

It slowly became more frequent, to the point where I felt I needed professional evaluation. A DNA test by the University of Missouri confirmed my greatest fear. He was diagnosed as an affected carrier of the dreaded degenerative mylopethy disease, for which there is no cure. The typical prognosis from onset to final is six months to a year. Ivanhoe was blessed with almost two years.

Our long walks became ever shorter and less frequent, then ended entirely when he was no longer able to walk. Renovation of vehicle access, seats, ramps, lifting devices and great effort by us both allowed him to by my constant companion for an additional year, plus.

Finally, primal instinct apparently directed him to stop eating altogether, only drinking copious amounts of water. Visibly diminished strength, the inability to move or to even bark at visitors caused me to experience severe frustration at my being unable to alleviate his pain, or to successfully encourage a peaceful, natural passing. The emptiness in me began to grow exponentially.

And so, after all the years of his going with me almost every day, and now being physically unable to get up to help me get him into the truck, he was confined to a bed in the garage. It was so hard having him watch me leave without him, facing another long, empty day alone.

On the eve of his passing, in an attempt to assure him it was permissible to leave me, and the confines of this earth, I engaged him in an extended conversation.

In the eight years and three months of his presence, he had never once responded verbally, as if in conversation, to me. This time, however, with great effort he raised up, turned painfully and looked directly into my eyes and clearly and audibly responded with an extended series of muffled WOOF, WOOF, WOOFS that I will forever believe was his way of telling me "It's okay, It's okay, everything is gonna be okay."

The final goodbyes by those who cared so much, and then he was taken away.

Ivanhoe was laid to rest alongside his predecessors Yuri, Boris and Lobo in our burial plot under the grape arbor, where they can forever share in being "Kings of the Hill."

Ivanhoe, you were here for just a little while, but the myriad wonderful memories you provided will last me into eternity. I will never forget you.

Thank you very, very much - I will always love you, God Bless You.

The beautiful basket of flowers placed at his grave by some beautiful soul will always be appreciated and remembered.

The mysterious blooming of the Forsythia Bush at the shed road gate shortly after his passing.

Is there, in fact, a Rainbow Bridge? I hope so, and if there is, I hope it will include people, too.

Dear Reader - - thank you for caring

Chuck Kravetsky

We Remember Bailey

This story memorializes a wonderful dog Cindy rescued and provided for, over some 13 years, in exchange for his unfailing loyalty and companionship.

I hope you enjoy the telling of his life story.

~ ~ *We Remember Bailey* ~ ~

May, 1999 ~ February 20, 2012

Once upon a time, at the house on the hill in Bell Township, in May of '99 on a warm Spring evening, it was said:

"Cindy has to go home, now" - - - - -

The cars' engine was about to be started - - - - -

A faint whimper from under the car was barely audible, and because of it, the engine remained silent, and the car didn't move.

A frightened, apologetic, hungry little white and black puppy was found hiding underneath, hoping against hope to find someone to care for and love him, who he could, in turn, serve and love for a lifetime.

After his apparent abandonment on the Township Road, how terrifying was that long trek up the driveway, tiny step by tiny step, to the big house on the hill, well guarded by a huge German Shepherd Dog.

Or could he and that German Shepherd Dog become lifelong friends, and play and play and play together through the years to come.

And, as it came to be, he did indeed find good and kind people who welcomed him into their lives, and who named him BAILEY.

Bailey quickly worked his puppy magic, and helped them heal from an earlier loss of the their dear friend, Bernie.

And so, too, began an association that provided many laughs, much joy, and comforting companionship, along with the occasional need for firm guidance and reprimand.

There were sleepness nights providing comfort every little puppy needs, to feel welcome, and at home.

There were trying days when no effort seemed to calm a hysterical baby.

Then there were the times when a puppy would fall asleep curled up on a lap, or at their feet, blissfully unaware of any of lifes' trials and tribulations.

Learning early on, always asking to be let outdoors for personal needs.

And to terrorize the blackbirds in the yard.

And to remind the community cats that the yard was off limits to them.

How he loved going to the Firehall, and playing ambassador to the world.

Proudly riding in a Fire Engine as the "find the fire hydrant specialist".

How he loved next door neighbors Ruth, Gene and Timmy Platko, along with their Grandchildren, often visiting them, and lying on their porch.

How Lynns' treats were graciously accepted.

Anticipating the evening run to play with Bori, then Yuri, up on the hill.

Being the Alpha Dog, with just the lip curl, low growl, and occasional nip to keep them understanding the correct pecking order, never mind they outsized and outweighed him by twenty or thirty pounds.

Flying through the grass and up into the air, expertly catching a Frisbee, showing them all how it should be done.

Returning to the "launch pad", eagerly waiting to again chase the thrown Frisbee, racing to get to it first.

Chasing the "Red Dot" round and round in the snow, time after time, but never really catching it.

Drinking gallons of water, summer or winter, from all the exertion.

Accepting the decree: "Bailey has to go home now", and jumping into the back seat, satisfied in the evenings' visit.

How he loved just riding with Bill.

How he loved going hunting with Bill.

How he accepted Missy as his sitter, and loved her as his "Other Mother".

How he kept her safe and out of harms' way in their outings and visits to Jim's shop.

Going to the office with Cindy, and being "Guard Dog" for her and Missy.

Occasionally making his presence known there, by causing the need for whole-house fumigation.

Keeping the German Shepherd visitors in their place at the office.

Always being friendly to everyone.

And the years went by, as they must inevitably must.

~ 2 ~

The awful sickness came, and stayed.

Bailey bravely persevered, tolerating unknown pain and suffering, yet always ready to greet someone with his tail wagging.

Then it was "time for Bailey to go home, now".

And now, when Ivanhoe visits the office and searches for his friend, we must tell him: Ivan, he's not here, he's gone to Rainbow Heaven. He's playing with Yuri and his friends now, up there.

Thank you, Bailey, so very much, for so many wonderful memories.

Cindy and Bill
Charlie and Dolly
Missy and John
Engine Company 55
Ruth and Gene and Timmy
Jim
All who knew him

~ 3 ~

Bear at Shed

Several years ago, Winter just would not quit, and so I was buying corn to feed my animal friends. I don't know who Is eating it, but it kept disappearing, so continued to set it out.

Along the driveway to my shed, there is a large, flat stone, which I used as a feeding point, a nice smooth table-like surface.

One day, I finished distributing the corn, and went into my shed to turn around, and go home.

Starting to back up, glanced in my rearview mirror, and saw a movement by something, being several hundred yards away, not very distinct.

So, I paused, now watching the mirror closely, and I saw something was approaching me.

I sat still, now watching aa a sizeable bear was getting ever closer, apparently unconcerned that I was sitting there, truck idling.

Finally, he was right beside me, standing just looking around.

So, ran my window down, leaned out just a bit, and said, firmly: "Hello, Mister Bear."

Suddenly, he comes alive, and took off like a cannonball shot out of a cannon, not looking back, nor exchanging greetings.

I was amazed at the power and speed of his rapid departure, a new-found respect.

I still occasionally see him, or her, descendants, and, one night about Ten pm, my German Shepherd was out, and I heard his low growl.

Grabbing a flashlight, I went out onto the porch and saw him staring and pointing across the driveway, still growling.

Shining the light in that direction, I saw those big, yellow eyes looking at him, unblinking, barely 20 feet away, not moving.

The bear ran when I yelled at Yuri to come to me, and all was calm again.

My brother used to refer to these things as Gracious Country Living.

Hey, they were here first.

Niece's Visit With Dog

A rare visit by one of my niece's family, along with their dogs, always welcome here, was moving along quite nicely.

Talk was of the attraction of me by the one pup, and I instinctively liked it, too.

Maybe too much attraction, as it came over to me close, then jumped up on my lap, snuggling in for the long haul.

I really did not mind, and gently stroked its head in appreciation.

His reaction, then, was to effect a sudden change in the immediate atmosphere, and the smell was atrocious.

The pup's prize winning, room clearing natural essence captured not only my air space, but also those within the room.

In self-defense, I dumped him onto the floor, opened several windows while holding my breath.

That did not negatively affect my affection for him, only my acceptable proximity to him.

Dogs will be dogs.

Thor

Out on one of my daily walks with Thor, a deer was spotted, and Thor, not allowed to chase deer, took off after it.

I whistled and shouted, "Thor, No, Thor, No," as he disappeared into the woods in hot pursuit of the deer.

More whistling, more calls, no Thor. He had openly disobeyed me, his Master, or so I think.

When he finally gave up the chase and returned, I continued on my walk, totally ignoring him; I would not speak or acknowledge his presence, or even look at him regardless of the pleading looks he directed at me, the attempts to get my attention and approval.

I put him to bed as usual in his cage without saying a word, nothing, no routine good night sendoff.

The next morning, I maintained my silence, no greeting, ignoring his usual early morning ritual, no speaking, no touching, no response from me.

As I began to dress, put socks on, he jumped up onto the bed, straddled my pillow entirely, refusing to move when I began to make up the bed. He ignored my sharp order to move, resisted even when I pulled him physically, flattened down on the bed, adamant in refusing to move.

So, I relented, said, "Okay Thor, I forgive you for disobeying me," patting his head softly, then one stroke across his shoulders and back.

He immediately jumped off the bed and went out into the hall, where he usually waits for me, and the usual trip to the kitchen for breakfast.

In Memory Of Skylar

Skylar, a mid-sized Aussie, was part of a three-puppy litter, the last born, docile, lovable, duty-bound. Constantly on watch, giving fair warning to cats, squirrels, and robins to stay clear.

In the eight years of his presence, he easily won the heart of everyone he touched.

The descriptive poem sums up how he affected all those who knew and were around him in his brief stay here with us.

Be careful when reading the accompanying sheet.

—In Memory of Skylar—
January 20, 2020

Yesterday, I said goodbye, after all these
    years, my Friend.

So many good memories, I hoped they'd never end.

The very first day we met, you completely won
    my heart.

Your little nose, your perky ears, your eyes so full of
    fun. I held you in my arms that day, I held you when
    life was done.

Rest now, there's nothing left to chase. No guard duty,
    barking or running at your constant puppy pace.

No sharing of sleep time, in someone's warm embrace.

And though you've gone away, you will always be-
    my Puppy, my dog, my best Friend, you have meant
    so much to me.

That Life goes on, though saddened it will be.

I know you will be waiting, at the Rainbow Bridge,
    for me.

With endless love, forever.

Cindy
Bill

In Memory Of Silas

Silas was a puppy my Grandson and his Fiancée brought to live with them to help fill in those empty gaps when a life presence is felt to be necessary or desirable.

He was the nicest pup you could imagine, accompanying Jim everywhere, disarmingly friendly to everyone he ever met.

He loved to play with balls, begging for just one more throw, a perfect companion to the other two dogs at the Transmission Repair Shop, and a perfect companion to the guys at the shop.

Tragically, he died very young in an unfortunate playtime mishap when a ball he had chased down jammed in his throat, choking him.

He now shares space forever In the hallowed company of the four German Shepherd predecessors already occupying the grape arbor, up on the Hill.

—In Memory of Silas—

Yesterday, I said goodbye, after all these
    years, my Friend.

So many good memories, I hoped they'd never end.

The very first day we met, you completely won
    my heart.

Your little nose, your perky ears, your eyes so full of
    fun. I held you in my arms that day, I held you when
    life was done.

Rest now, there's nothing left to chase. No guard duty,
    barking or running at your constant puppy pace.

No sharing of sleep time, in someone's warm embrace.

And though you've gone away, you will always be-
    my Puppy, my dog, my best Friend, you have meant
    so much to me.

That Life goes on, though saddened it will be.

I know you will be waiting, at the Rainbow Bridge,
    for me.

With endless love, forever.

Jim, Jr.
Shana

Pair Of Cardinals

I have a pair of Cardinals that nest just outside my living room picture window.

The male must have been absent the day brains were being installed, and wages an endless battle with his reflection in it. Last year I discouraged him somewhat by hanging an 8" by 11" picture of a yawning lion at the usual point of attack, but I lost the picture over the Winter.

I've hung pictures of eagles diving, cats crouching, freight trains coming straight at him, nothing is really effective.

I have finally given up on discouraging him. It's been five years, ongoing , so now it's a contest of will, to see who outlasts whom. I wish him well.

Oh, Oh, it's 4:28, and Thor just reminded me he eats at 4:30, and it's a cardinal sin if I don't fulfill my duty and obligation in a timely manner.

Thor Gift

Thor, my German Shepherd buddy, goes everywhere with me.

At a local restaurant recently, a former client of mine was there, with her German Shepherd beside her. An adult beautiful male.

Thor, ever the social butterfly, insisted we go and meet his canine counterpart, so we did.

His owner, a pleasant middle-aged woman, exchanged the usual niceties, and of course, Thor and her shepherd went through the usual doggie niceties, sniffing, poking, strutting, whatever, everything going well.

The meeting over, Thor went around her, pausing at her back, lifted his leg and let loose a generous portion of his morning coffee all over the back of her leg, as her German Shepherd casually watched. By pure chance, my daughter was photographing the scenario, and caught this deed, perfectly.

We titled that picture: I just want to give you something to remember me by. Glancing at her soaked leg, she graciously left without saying a word.

Boys will be Boys.

In the Memory of Lobo

Upon the passing of Chingo, our big collie, my desire for a German Shepherd dog came front and center, and we started watching for one in our daily newspaper.

Soon, one appeared, and after a call, we headed for the advertised puppy's kennel.

Arriving, the puppy, a beautiful German Shepherd much larger and older than usual, greeted us, tail wagging vigorously, along with the owner of the kennel.

He was the last of the litter, not taken because of his being firstborn, and very big. No one wanted him but I did.

And what an extraordinary find!

He adapted quickly to his new environment, just loved the kids, adopted them instantly, and life went on.

Like most dogs, he soon became addicted to riding in a vehicle.

I, very busy, usually away from home operating a coal mine and surveying/engineering for my many clients, could not take him with me much of the time, so he accepted staying at home with the kids, refereeing their squabbles, not allowing physical confrontations, getting between adversaries when necessary, or even pushing them apart.

A real babysitter: otherwise, he stayed with Dolly.

He also became a bit of a problem at times, going away from the house in pursuit of a female in heat somewhere in range; we are getting phone calls to come and retrieve him.

He loved traveling with me in my '85 Dodge 1-ton dump truck, preferring to lay his head on my lap while moving down the road, reveling in the sound and soothing vibration of the truck's motion.

As he aged, he would signal to me he needed help to get up into the seat; it being too high for him to reach, his front paws up but needing a lift for the rest of him. He would turn his head and look at me wistfully, with the clear message – please help me.

On the date of our wedding anniversary, he wanted outside, went to his box, laying down, opened his eyes and looked straight at me, licked my hand, and left us forever.

He was 11 ½ years old.

My hope is that he will be at Rainbow Bridge waiting for us. God Bless Him Always.

Bori--Coal Slime

My number 2 German Shepherd was Boris, Lobo Lupus Of Kravet, officially; Bori is what he responded to.

He, like his predecessor, Lobo, was a genuine sweetheart, always with me, making life brighter most of the time.

I used to go to a print shop in Greensburg, PA. fairly often, to have large prints of my surveys made; and of course, he would go with me into the shop and all.

In the shop, he would sit up on an inner level, 4 steps above street level. Incoming customers were told he vas the new security system, an impressive 105 lbs. of canine presence.

He loved people and would always go and greet anyone who extended any overture to him.

He won so many hearts of the shop personnel, that I had an 8 ½ X 11, full-size picture of him in a frame made as a gift.

That was 25 years ago, and the picture is still on the wall. His story is often related to inquiring clients there.

One day I took him to our groomer for a bath: 3 hours, and forty dollars later, he's all shined up, ready to go with me to check out a potential mine site for a client.

We're climbing all around a former strip-mined area, with piles of old spoil all around, along with depressions filled with rainwater and coal waste.

At one point, Bori was out of sight, so I went looking for him. I found him, alright, standing neck deep in a slime hole, an exclamation point to his recent bath.

To make it worse when I hollered at him, the look on his face, was: What!

Bori died in my arms at age 10 ½. It is my fondest hope we meet again at Rainbow Bridge.

I include my memoir for him.

In memory of Boris Lobo Lupus of Kravet

April 15, 1995   -   September 17, 2005

It is with a heavy heart we inform you that on September 17, 2005, our beloved Bori left us.

He had fully recovered from surgery, and had enjoyed an extension of life free of all aggravation. But, time caught up with him, and , peacefully and painlessly, his spirit passed on.

His first, and last, love was people. People like you, and including you (all.)

We will never forget the numerous kindnesses extended to him by you (all.)

The joy he brought wherever he was is too voluminous to detail, but it was just great. He will be a tough act to follow.

He rests here under our grape arbor, on "his" hill where he was king, alongside his predecessor, Lobo.

With kindest regards,

Chuck and Dolly Kravetsky

Thor Kisses Woman

I was parked in the Shop-n-Save lot, ready to leave, when a car with an older woman passenger pulled in close to me.

Thor, as usual, his head hanging out the back window, observing.

My truck is higher than a car, so he was well above her, as she got out.

As she stood up, she came face to face with him, and he gently reached out to her and kissed her right on her lips.

She looked at me, just a bit surprised, but smiling, and said, "OOh, I love Dogs, I really liked that", and left, not looking back .

Crow on Tree

From my office's North facing window, I have a full view of a huge Poplar tree reaching far into the sky.

Sitting here at my drafting table, I happened to look out just as a crow was doing a perfect two-point landing on one of the highest tiniest outermost branches of the tree, assuming a post out on the edge, momentarily secure.

Why it selected that flimsiest of branches will never be known, nor matter, but that was the choice.

It being quite cold, 20 degrees or so, there was no insect in flight for possible interception, and no other crows were on the tree for company. The wind was just moderate, just enough to bounce it mildly ,keeping it alert.

Suddenly, a burst of wind lifted it high, the rebound back down causing the limb it was sitting on to snap, break off, dumping the crow suddenly downward.

Never fear, crows are excellent navigators, and was in freefall only briefly, then spreading its wings, expertly correcting the downward movement back to complete control, gliding effortlessly away, unconcerned as to the recent forceful eviction off its perch.

Oh, that life for us mere humans could be as easy to recover from life's mis directions.

Did I learn anything from watching that crow?

Did I learn to choose your landing spot carefully, a spot not prone to sudden collapse when the winds of life erupt suddenly?

Did I learn to have an escape plan and route, then use when necessary?

The crow did.

Thor – Close Call

Late Autumn was underway, with the usual influx of undesirables invading the premises in anticipation of Winter's hardships in the great outdoors, so, I bought some D-Con, not only to discourage the movement, but to eliminate those already here.

With the danger this presents to pets, Thor in this case, I was careful in placing the deadly cubes where he couldn't reach them, in behind the trash barrels In the corner of the garage.

Seeing the barrels were full, needing to be burned, I loaded them into my pickup for transport to the burn enclosure, momentarily losing sight of Thor in the process, leaving the poison exposed, unbarricaded for several minutes.

It had to have been while was loading the first barrel into the truck, that Thor had reached in and grabbed one of the cubes, carrying it out into the yard, dropping it when I signaled for him to saddle up, get in, we're heading out, he, ever eager to ride, anywhere anytime.

So, I unloaded, lit the trash on fire, and returned to the house, where I parked, letting Thor out of the truck, he goes over into the yard, paused, and then came running over to me, flipping something out of his mouth at my feet, then giving me a look that could have said, look what I found, you can have it.

It was the poisonous cube he had taken, somehow, when I was loading the trash barrel into the truck, he now apparently realizing it was trouble, returning It to me.

Even though it did not appear to have been even partly eaten, I still spent a very uneasy twenty-four hours watching him for any sign of his having ingested any part of it.

He had not, Thank God, He is fine.

His Guardian Angel was on duty that day.

Cletrac

In surface mining we are required to backfill our excavations, reclaim and redistribute the topsoil that had been removed and stored, then reseed the entire area with an approved mix of grasses and legumes, then cover the seeded area with suitable mulch to stabilize and protect the new growth.

Many of the areas we mined were severely steep and difficult to travel over with conventional mining machinery.

In order to better cope with this, I determined it would be much easier if we had a small, low to the ground bulldozer style track machine, it would simplify and speed up the process.

An acquaintance just happened to have a machine that fit that need perfectly, an Oliver Cletrac, for sale.

Contacting him, we agreed on a price, and I bought it. It being just a short distance, I opted to drive it to its new home at my machine shop.

You guessed it, I had only gone about a quarter of a mile when that sound you don't want to hear – was heard.

Yes, engine failure, clack, clack, clack, stop.

Go get my other tractor, tow the carcass of my new purchase to my shed.

Now what? Do I demand my money, $2500, back and create a big fuss?

The seller, a long-time acquaintance, the husband of a girl that grew up around me. Bob – often mentioned by me in these stories, is her brother. Their mother was my lifetime friend.

So I decided to say nothing. Did he know the engine was ready to blow? Maybe, but I doubt it, because it ran well for the 10 or 15 minutes that I drove it.

Since the block was undamaged, we rebuilt the engine, taking the Cletrac to our mine site.

It served us well in my original need, but then another issue appeared.

The machine, being very old, was totally non-compliant with federal government, MSHA standards that require certain safety regulated features on all equipment at coal mines.

As a land surveyor, I knew a lot of people.

One person I knew was a caretaker, a guard at a major water reservoir serving a suburb of Pittsburgh.

The reservoir was well-known, verified by some of my trespasser friends – there were plenty of big fish in it: walleye, pickerel, bass.

Of course, the reservoir was off-limits to fishermen.

The caretaker, in a conversation with one of my coal haulers, mentioned he was looking for an Oliver Cletrac to have as a keepsake, having had one on his farm years ago.

The Cletrac, no longer having any use for me other than as a tractor, no longer had any value to me. So, after contacting him, we made a deal.

The deal was, I get a couple hundred dollars, he moves it, I get to fish all I want – out of sight, of course, and it's yours.

Fishing was good for years, and then he retired and moved away.

I never saw him again.

Calvin at Bar

My former son-in-law, Cal, was in a bar one evening. Striking up a conversation with a guy sitting next to him, the topic became home security. The guy mentioned he had been a green beret in the military, and his expertise was in breeching security systems in buildings, including private homes.

So, a friendly bet was made, that he couldn't get into Cal's house, as it had been thoroughly secured personally by him.

Cal went home and slept peacefully through the night. Upon awakening, he noticed something pinned to the footboard of his bed. It was a note; did you sleep well last night? it said - initialed by the guy he made the bet with at the bar.

Cal never saw him again.

Wagner House Clearing

There were at least a hundred people gathered in response to an invitation to assemble to observe, even contribute, to the opening of the wedding gifts for my oldest Son, and his charming wife, Tammy, at her parent's home here in Saltsburg.

I, the Father in-Law of course, was there, and had inadvertently brought a special gift for the entire gathering.

It was a miserably hot afternoon, very high humidity, no air movement at all.

The house we were at was a typical two story, multi-room structure, not yet equipped with an air conditioning unit capable of coping with this extreme of a condition, so everyone did the best they could under the circumstances, the atmosphere hanging heavy indeed.

As usual, great, and plentiful food was provided, and everyone having eaten their full, was invited to the opening of the gifts, inside the living room, central in the house.

Even though this event transpired over 40 years ago, I personally claim what might be classed as a dubious record, but unchallenged as best I have heard. Not exactly fit for the Guinness Book Of Records, but a real record, nonetheless.

Here's what actually happened. The faint of heart may well stop listening or reading, whatever, at this point.

The room was packed with interested people; more were in nearby rooms, observing from there, children were playing, romping about, even upstairs in the bedrooms.

Well, the gift that I brought originated from some unknown source; some claim I had consumed an overly generous serving of roadkill; others said it was a long-standing digestive issue. I 'm not sure.

Frankly, I don't know where or what created it, but when it was released, slow developing pandemonium broke out, clearing out the area in close proximity to me, first.

Then, as the good news, or bad, depending upon your perspective, spread room to room ever so slowly, like a plague, permeating every cubic foot of the house, the exit of the entire gathering accelerating outward, was some thing to behold, something akin to a herd of buffalo stampeding.

Even upstairs, where children had been playing, was completely empty, silent, the atmosphere trapped. No one dared take the time to open any windows, the whole house stood, abandoned, empty of humanity, life. I'm told even the spiders left.

I dubbed it "whole house fumigation, 101."

The house eventually recovered, but needed days, not hours, to clear, be livable again.

Four decades later I still claim the record mentioned, and it still provides a raucous reaction when recalled from memory.

Will this be my legacy?

Boys will be boys.

Cat Stench

It was Christmastime; we had been to Youngsville where Grandma and step-Grandpa lived for another great dinner, and gift exchange.

I had a 1965 Chrysler car at the time, and we had used it for the trip, it being big enough to easily accommodate all four kids, now growing, and of course, Dolly.

The visit concluded, we're on our way home, 3 kids in the rear seat, Dolly and Steve in the front - Steve in the middle next to me.

At the intersection of Route 66 and Route 322, a very busy road, I was stopped, waiting for a break in traffic on Route 322 so I could cross over.

Suddenly, the engine roared to life, surging into busy Route 322, certain trouble.

Fortunately, I keep my left foot perched above the brake pedal; instinctively I jammed down with it, hard on the brake, arresting the forward movement of the car, traffic swerving away from me barely out onto Route 322.

What had happened was Steve had been asleep, and when stopped at the crossing he partially awakened, and in doing so, stretched his legs straight out, one onto the accelerator pedal, flooring it, causing the engine to explode into high rpm, the transmission still In forward drive.

It all happened in a few seconds, but the after effect lasted much longer.

So, we continued on, another 70 miles to go, finally arriving at home.

I stopped, began unloading the car, the kids, anxious as usual to get inside, quickly ran in.

And just as quickly, came running back out coughing, gagging, groaning, making all kinds of noises, shouting, opening the doors and windows, now.

Alarmed, I ran into the house to see what all the commotion was about and I immediately discovered It.

That morning, before we left for Youngsville, we forgot to make sure our male cat was out of the house, and sure enough, he had been locked inside all day.

As nature dictates, sometime during that long day, he had to pee, and did he ever.

The stench was indescribably overwhelming, unbearable, and worse, the entire house was so filled with the smell, it was impossible to know just where he had done the awful deed.

The kids abandoned ship, leaving it up to Dolly and I to find the location, hoping it wasn't in multiple places.

Searching, dreading it to be under a bed or behind heavy furniture, we kept on, dearly paying the price of stupidity, until, finally, there it was.

Of all places, right under the decorated Christmas Tree, his gift to us, and better yet, puddled in one spot on a plastic sheet that had been laid down to expedite future cleanup.

Now a simple matter, I carefully removed the entire sheet.

It only took a week of open windows to clear out that awful, all-pervading aroma.

Sometimes, we learn the hard way.

Dolly at Camp

Me and my family were long-time friends with the great family who had a hunting camp near the Northern border of Pennsylvania. We would occasionally go to for a weekend, stay for trout fishing and deer hunting every year.

We loved the mountains and the terrain, clean streams, the isolation, and the people there.

After convincing my wife, Dolly, into a weekend away from it all - upon arrival she goes into clean mode. No, Dolly, just relax, you're here for a break, the mice will stay off the counter as long as we're here, so just relax.

It went downhill from there. Her Registered Nurse training and instincts at war with the atmosphere, all the food she brought was tightly sealed in lockable containers.

The camp house was reasonably modernized, with running water, electric, and heat from a huge wood burning stove. It was peaceful, quiet, nice.

You don't really need much more, or do you?

There was an outhouse. Located for convenience at the time of installation, it sat right along the pathway from the parking area to the camp. She, having to visit a never-before experienced facility, an outhouse, had misgivings before reaching it.

In there just long enough to properly present to the hard board seat she screamed, immediately ejecting from it, heading for the camp house.

Investigating, I found not one, but two, fair sized black snakes, comfortably lying along the walls; I'm guessing waiting for next meal to appear.

I chased them out; she came back, as one would necessarily, sooner or later, I standing guard.

She vowed that If she ever came back, she would bring her own private chamber pot.

She never did return, said one visit was enough in the mountains of Potter County.

Iselin Lawsuit

Over the years I had acquired ownership of a huge pile of coal-related reject covering some 14 acres near the Village Of Iselin, which, through the years, and ongoing, was contributing to the pollution of a sizeable stream at its outer perimeter.

So, I acquired the necessary permits to remove it, and to restore the 14 acres to a suitable wildlife habitat condition, a very desirable intention, certainly with all the blessings of the D.E.P.

As it was, there was this so called, self-anointed lawyer living in Iselin who, not surprisingly, for a lawyer, filed suit against me, and our coal company and the permit-issuing agency, the D.E.P., in objection to their issuing a permit to remove the reject (boney) by the coal company, on grounds of his opinion that l, the owner of the reject, should be held solely liable for the removal, at my sole expense and action.

His presentation before the Court in Pittsburgh was so ridiculous; many statements were outright lies, under oath.

A bright young secretary from the County Agency in charge of these things quickly proved him a liar and perjurious in certain claims.

That Judge didn't take long to throw him and his ridiculous suit out, never to return.

Yes, there are good lawyers on this planet; refer to my story regarding my farming career at age seventeen, but this surely isn't one of them.

Assigned Value

A very wealthy, long-term client, a high-level member of the other side was retiring, and asked me to do some cleanup work for him.

Even though it was, and had been, a sort of an arm's-length adversarial relationship through the years, but as a matter of convenience, it had endured, and was now ending by his retirement and leaving the area.

My fees had always been paid in a timely and businesslike manner, so I was a bit puzzled when my final invoice for $125.00 went unpaid.

Months, a year went by. I had never re-invoiced him in the past, and did not consider it in this case, as that would enter pride and appearance into an insignificant issue.

But, as happened, his son-in-law hired me to survey a property for him, and in the ensuing follow up socializing, certain improper and undeserved remarks that his Father-In-Law, my retiring client, had made about me were passed to me, there obviously being no love lost between them.

So, I thought, it's time for contact.

I penned a short letter to him, it read:

Dear ___

Please be informed, my final invoice rendered to you, some time ago, does not represent much in the world of finance; be assured in your apparent decision to refuse payment will not greatly affect my economic survival, nor will it's retention by you, fully ensure continuance of your maintaining the lifestyle you have grown accustomed to.

However, there is one consideration.

In life, there are certain values we assign to certain things.

One of those things is the value we assign to our name.

Obviously, you valued your name at $125.00, much to my surprise.

If that is the number you are comfortable with, I'm fine with it too.

Please consider the Invoice for $125.00 canceled, with my thanks for the association in the past.

Yours truly.

It took less than 48 hours till I had a letter of apology, and a check for $125.00 in hand.

I never met or spoke to him again.

Thor Won't Speak to Me

Oh, Day Of Days, the Holy Grail, the long awaited pinnacle of Pigskin adoration, by one and all, including, according to the following, my German Shepherd, Thor.

The final determination of superiority, pitting one Billionaire's Millionaires against some other Billionaire's Millionaires assemblage concluding the annual half year of unceasing brutality, determining the final two combatants who will, disguised by modern medicine's best pain killers, run out before a hundred million adoring fans to take away a Holy Trophy, the Lombardi Cup, that possibly, in the distant future may be available to the highest bidder, in that one-day Proverbial Mother of all yard sales, along with other less coveted best of this, best of that prizes.

Anyhow, it was Super Bowl Sunday, 5:30 pm. I had fed Thor evening staples, and he typically wanted out, so I left him go out. Since it was cold, the doors were closed, so he was unable to let himself back in.

I, being Human, and Male, decks all cleared, of course, turned on the TV to the broadcast of the game.

The unforgivable fact was that, immersed in the awe-inspiring action on the field between those two giants, I completely forgot Thor, being outside, was unable to share the observation with me, of such a classic performance.

What I did observe, in, of course, my sole opinion, just ahead of half-time is an all-time brilliant maneuver by a half billion-dollar genius; a not so apparent ankle hit, instantly creating a well-defined limp, as he hopped over to his bench, where, in full view of the cameras, grimacing very convincingly of the presence of great pain, setting into the minds of not only of the many millions of viewers, but the minds of the opposing team that he was not going to be able to continue in the second half, a monumental loss for his team. Better yet, if he did try to play, no opposing team member would want to forever be identified as the one who may well have ended the career of one of football's truly great players by tackling him, possibly reinjuring him seriously.

I had presumed early on that half-time would be a less than memorable show of weirdos on parade, for which I shut off the TV at that time.

Half time is over, second half about to get underway.

So, a full starting lineup is out on the field, ready to rumble.

The second half opens, all appears well; we, simple public, assume the same potpourri of chemicals as usual have been injected where needed, and he's ready to resume battle.

The second half was like a second life; ball movement for one side great, the other side listless – they should have thrown in the towel and gone home to accept the fact that they were both outplayed and outsmarted.

The half-billion-dollar boy functioning well, throwing well, scrambling well, and when things got really tense late in the game, a hard run gaining 15 plus yards, getting them close to the goal line, reasonably guaranteeing a win, with no pain or injury apparent.

I'm not sure, but I don't think there were any more sacks in the second half, or no really hard hits on him.

Smart coaching and smart play ended the game with his team once again winning the exalted trophy, leaving me and many millions in absolute afterglow.

Anyhow, more importantly, getting back to Thor, nowhere to be found.

Then I heard a big SCRATCH! at the front door, find him alive and well, but very disgruntled. He had missed the entire game and was obviously very unhappy about it.

He bypasses our regular Good Night routine, and runs to the bedroom, jumps up on the bed, and completely straddles my pillow, all 100 pounds of him.

I ordered him to move, get off the bed, and my pillow, with no reaction. He won't even look at me.

He refuses to budge, so I grab his collar and pull hard. He just flattens down, no go.

So, I say, "OK, Thor, it's OK, Thor, it's OK," and pat him gently on his head.

He immediately jumps up, gets off, and disappears into his cage.

The next morning all is well, all is forgiven and forgotten.

And oh, yes, the game. I silently congratulate the winners, not for any superior play, but for superior strategy, turning an almost sure loss into a sure win.

Letter to Stella
January 24, 2012

Dear Stell,

We may have been considered poor, but we didn't know it, and were happy anyway.

The process of visiting the cows, horse, chickens, barn, granary, and spring; every January 6th, Christmas Eve, and repeating the Lord's Prayer at each stop.

The Christmas Eve dinner of boiled potatoes, prunes and halupkies.

How cold and snowy it usually was.

Mom's birthday being prayed over.

The excused absence from school.

The introduction to St. Matthew's Church and the nuns who took us to Hlywiak's basement for Catechism.

The chocolate milk we shared when I was in Second Grade and you were in Third Grade.

The shows, stage performances and what-not that required a dime to attend.

Being in the group that didn't attend.

The pain of exclusion really wasn't that bad, and was soon forgotten.

The deep snows of February slowly giving way to sheets of ice that made the trip to the bus a real adventure.

Trudging up over the hill through the deep snow to catch the bus.

Shoveling a path up over the hill that immediately blew shut.

The softening of the air as Spring gradually replaced Winter.

Watching the Hepatica and Johnny Jump-Ups compete with the grass for space.

Shedding the winter coat.

The new leaves bursting out all at once.

The awful moment when it was announced that we were at war with Germany, whatever that meant.

Then Pearl Harbor.

The air-raid drills in school.

Pulling the window blinds down when an airplane went over.

Monday mornings when war bonds and stamps were being sold.

When you had a dime to participate.

The excitement of Valentine's Day, and the box to put the cards into.

Not being among the rich who had one for everyone.

Not getting one from everyone.

The unforgettable sweet smell of the Crabapple blossoms in the woods along our path.

I say that is what Heaven smells like.

Daffodils and Dogwoods we'll never forget.

Singing 'Carry Me Back to Old Virginny' as we tromped along on the way to the bus on a beautiful sunny morning.

Having a complete family that, with its faults, was still a true blessing.

The anticipation of the final tests prior to the end of the school year.

Taking the tests and getting the results.

Reflecting on unevolved romances.

The birthday that coincided so closely to the end of the school year.

The last day of school, Grade _____.

New House, 1957

In 1957, making decent money in a good paying job in the coal mine, I determined it was a good time for us to upgrade our living standards, closer to the modern normal, since I, our parents and brother being the remainder of the original family living at home.

So, I designed a very simple new house that I would build for myself, my parents and brother; the 4 sisters all had flown the coop, and were set up in Big Town, all employed.

Knowing dangerously close to nothing about building anything, much less a house, I set out anyhow.

As a fast learner, I started, selected a spot, evicting the cows from a part of their pasture, sadly, cutting down an old, wonderful, highly productive pear tree in the process.

The house was to be 24 feet by 24 feet, 576 square feet, close to the original house, with four rooms and a bath, plus one bedroom in the basement, and Father had his shanty.

Brother and I went to work, after our regular jobs. I hired an excavator and dug out a partial basement. I had to buy dynamite at the local hardware store to loosen the ground for him to be able to dig it out.

Brother and I formed a footer, the mason who came to lay the concrete block found it out of level and had to redo parts of it. Oh, well, then lay the block.

Speaking with experienced carpenters and other builders, I was guided as to the usual steps in the construction.

An electrician took care of that end.

Plumbing and drains we were familiar with.

We made lots of mistakes, but in 6 months, we moved into our brand-new house.

This one had an indoor bathroom, but Mother had a hard time in forgetting her upbringing and refused to use the indoor commode. Till it got really cold. Mom, there's a window, and an exhaust fan, just push the switch. And, Mom, this is not the Ukraine.

Siding and brick went on the following year.

Total cost. I contributed $2,000 dollars; Father contributed $1,000 dollars, 4 sisters contributed $2,000 dollars.

A new house for just around $5,000 dollars, if you can believe it.

Brother contributed much labor.

We were now modern, or close.

Masonry
Two Little Girls in Slickville

When I was offering masonry services, my part time partner and l were laying a slate deck onto a porch one day when two young girls about eight or nine came strolling past.

They stopped, watched us for a while, then one girl said, are you the best carpenters in the world?

My partner responded, we don't know if we're the best in the world, but we don't know of any that are any better.

They left, apparently satisfied.

Wedding

January 25, 1958 dawned cold and cloudy; a fresh eight Inches of snow having fallen overnight.

My and my Family's timely presence at the pending wedding assemblage being somewhat important, it was more than a bit daunting to be facing almost a half mile of mostly uphill, snow-covered driveway to the public road.

Andy and I, both being seasoned mud and snow drivers; plus, I feel certain with some Divine assistance, we arrived at the church in Avonmore in good time.

The Ceremony went well, routine, well-attended by the wonderful friends and neighbors invited who had braved the hazardous conditions and honored us with their presence.

As life and time dictates, many, if not most of those attending are long gone to their own reward now, just pleasant memories.

After a brief, well-executed lunch served by the good church women, we all gathered at my ever-gracious Mother-in-Law's home for gift opening, and socializing.

Then, it was off to the Holiday House (now extinct) in Monroeville for a complimentary (the four Sisters) steak dinner and stage performance.

After a great night's rest and breakfast, it was off to Washington, D.C. (complementary, four sisters) where one of the ever-present Visitor Guides, for the modest fee of, I believe, fifty dollars, took us to every major noteworthy feature In the Capital, giving enough time at each to thoroughly enjoy the visit.

I still marvel that the man, a total stranger, was completely trustworthy and honest in his services and promises.

I question if I would repeat the same experience today.

We returned Home to our basement apartment, Dolly back to work at the Allegheny Valley Hospital where she had trained to be a Registered Nurse, (and was class valedictorian) for Ten dollars and Ten Cents an hour, I am on temporary layoff from the Seanor Coal Co., waiting for a pending call to return to work.

Upon my call back shortly after, we moved to my original home, joining my parents and brother, until moving to our newly built home in 1962, up on the hill, named Heaven.

The rest is a long history, outlined in these four hundred some stories.

It's been fun, oh, has it ever been fun.

1967 D.C.

I believe it was In October, 1967, when the demonstrations were going on in protest of the Vietnam War; there being a major one scheduled in Washington, DC.

We accepted an invitation from my Brother-in-Law, Ralph, who worked there, and lived in nearby Silver Springs, to come and visit, and then to attend the demonstration.

Dolly and I, and Cindy, then nine, went, and joined the thousands of protestors, it being a beautiful autumn day.

We passed by three nuns, attired according to protocol, standing by their rented car which, perhaps by Divine dictate, had disabled the car, parked there, hood up, radiator mimicking Old Faithful, preventing them from reaching the central point of the protest, several blocks away.

The National Guard was present, the soldiers standing at Parade Rest, not allowed to interact with anyone in any way.

I, we, happened to be close by, and by pure chance, witnessed the event that went worldwide, when the young protestor who ever so carefully stuck a long-stemmed Rose into the business end of a National Guardsman's rifle as he stood motionless, and silent in his assigned position.

I was, at best, amused by it, only realizing later after seeing the picture had gone viral, that we had witnessed a historical event.

If recall correctly, there were a few minor skirmishes, but nothing of major significance was accomplished towards ending that horrible conflict.

Car up Kings Hill

One snowy winter day was going home from work at the Seanor Mine, when going up a long, winding, steep dangerous hill with a drop off of several hundred feet on one side, appropriately named Kings Hill. I had to come to a complete stop, a vehicle ahead, unable to continue in the deepening snow.

An ongoing heavy snowfall had made the road almost impassable, but I, a long-time experienced driver, had put on chains before I left our office, so I was in good shape.

I went up to the stalled car to learn what I could, as to the problem.

It was a fairly young girl, trying to get to her job in Saltsburg, a couple of miles away, foolishly venturing out in such terrible conditions so, I, ever the helpful one, said to her: "Take my car to the top of the hill and park in the wide spot up there. I'll drive your car up and you can go on safely from there to work.

And away she goes in my well-equipped car; I take a quick look at hers, stuck on the steep hill.

What do you know? The right rear tire on her car is bald, bare. Now I'm in trouble.

I got into her car, start it, and try to go forward. No go at all. I put it into reverse and start back down, I touch the brakes to stay in control, and away I go, the brakes useless with the bald tire there, and I'm already totally out of control, sliding backwards, picking up speed, unable to steer effectively, or at all.

I am convinced, to this day; I entered into another dimension at that point, a total blank mentally, sliding backwards down the steep winding road for at least a thousand feet until, the car, now turned completely around, nose first, came to a very small vide spot on the side of the road, and came to a complete stop, looking down at a straight stretch to a level area.

I apparently came back from wherever I was, drove the car down to the bottom, parked it at a wide spot, then walked to the top of the hill where my car and the girl were waiting.

I took her to work; she recovered her car the next day.

I never heard from her again.

Consider: What could have been her fate if I had not interceded? Only God knows.

Going Home, Sweet Home

December 24, 1962, Christmas Eve, early evening. A cold clear night, beautiful full moon shining brightly, and we, our entire family, were going home for the very first time to stay, leaving a tearful grandmother, a solemn grandfather and brother/uncle behind, never to return, after four years of cohabitation.

We were only going half a mile to our new, partially finished house, needing the additional space badly for the six of us, so it really wasn't the end of the world for them.

Our moving van, a quite basic single axle farm trailer, was loaded to the gills, so to speak, being towed by our little Farmall A, with all the appearance of pioneers heading west, absent the oxen and cattle.

We were our own welcoming committee, and the ceremony was brief, in fact, imaginary, but we had landed, looking for a very long term, fruitful experience in our new, permanent home. We, now actual homesteaders, proceeded to unload our somewhat meager belongings, practically losing them in the vast, or so it seemed, open spaces of the big new house.

The bare walls echoing the excited outbursts by the kids. The floors were still just the subfloor, bare plywood with no covering, no doors anywhere, including the bathroom, except exteriors; no kitchen cabinets or countertops, just a long piece of plywood with a cloth covering the open front. Major appliances just covered the absolute basics – stove and refrigerator.

Beds were set up, and exhausted kids soon were in dreamland; parents scuttling about, preparing for the future.

There were both positive and negative experiences as life in our new home progressed.

Immediately positive in having a full basement for kids to play in, open space on the ground floor, an intercom to allow monitoring of kids at play or asleep.

And wide-open spaces outside, at the time 14.7 acres.

The most significant negative reared its ugly head in an incident with the coal boiler.

The immediate negative was in Dolly's having to learn how to fire the coal boiler.

A coal boiler is a bit different in firing; and then its control, so as to maintain a desired water temperature and subsequent whole-house comfort.

The house being located on one of those dream-like locations, high on top of a hill with a full circle, 360° view, was also subjected to the full force and fury of an unforgiving, often relentless wind that creates a nearly uncontrollable vacuum, pulling far more air through the fire pit than is desirable or safe.

What I didn't know was that when the plumber installed the new coal boiler, he mistakenly set the water temperature sensor to STOP the distribution pump at 130° F, instead of STARTING the distribution pump which circulates the heated water through the radiators in the house, cooling it to safe levels.

Shortly after moving in, it became quite windy, and one morning the boiler went wild, heating the water to perilously high levels; the thermostat sensor, set backwards, shut the distribution pump off instead of leaving it running, and the water temperature shot straight up, building up to a very high pressure in the pipes leading away from the boiler, tripping the pop-off valve that protects the entire system.

The second mistake the plumber made was to direct the pipe from the pop-off valve out into the open basement instead of down to the floor, as is ordinary and usual.

As circumstance dictated, at precisely the same time as the pop-off started to shoot boiling water and steam away from the boiler, Dolly happened to be passing by, heading for the laundry area just past the boiler, narrowly missing her.

The bonehead plumber came back very quickly and reset the sensor correctly after my less than friendly call.

The coal boiler and hot water heating system continued to be a serious problem throughout the years, especially during times of high wind when the water temperature would reach dangerously high levels, overheating the house. I often stayed up late into the night cooling the house down by throwing ashes onto the fire pit to slow down the burning.

I finally solved the problem by removing the hot water system entirely, replacing it with an electric hot air furnace, and later gas, which also facilitated an air conditioning unit to be installed.

As time passed, I gradually updated the house, adding a big garage, office, and laundry on the ground floor; eliminating a 12-year ordeal for Dolly which was:

Having installed the laundry at the extreme west end of the basement originally, directly under the master bedroom – and the steps to the ground floor being located at the extreme east end of the basement, it necessitated her to carry all accumulated laundry 60 feet from the bedroom to the steps, down 11 steps, then 60 feet to the washer and dryer. A repeat in the reverse direction when recovering the finished product.

Also, I now had an exclusive office to work in without disturbing anyone.

Sometime after the major addition I bought 58 tons of natural quarried stone, which the boys and I chipped for good appearance, preparing it for laying around the entire house and a fireplace.

We installed the stone in the dead of winter by building a movable enclosure, large enough for two Masons to work in, and us moving it as work progressed until completion.

It was and is a thing of artistry and perennial beauty, an everlasting testament to the two wonderful Masons who formed and fit the stone so precisely and professionally.

In that same time period, having acquired additional acreage adjoining our 14.7 original acres, I converted some 30 acres of farm field into finished lawn, which I humorously argue is Western Pennsylvania's biggest private lawn.

Mowing it ever since is no small deal. I use three mowers; an 11-foot and a 14-foot drag behind, and a 6-foot underbelly, all finish mowers – requiring 10 to 12 machine hours to complete a mowing.

The house, having a double flue chimney, I brought in a freestanding wood burner to help offset the cost of electricity, trading the pain and inconvenience of cutting, splitting, storing, carrying, and handling ash residue for the purported cost savings.

One windy winter day I went to the basement to feed the wood burner and heard this awful roar when I got down there.

Here, the high wind, creating a strong vacuum to the wood burner, caused its smoke exhaust pipe, apparently coated with creosote, to catch fire, spreading to the main chimney, where it was burning fiercely.

The clean-out door at the bottom of the chimney was already glowing red, turning orange. Had it burned through there was no stopping the fire, with dire potential.

Hearing my shout of fire, my son-in-law at the time, Calvin, grabbed a big fire extinguisher, sprinted to our shed, grabbed the ladder, set it, then raced to the chimney, and with several strong blasts from the extinguisher, put out the fire, saving the house.

Have I mentioned Guardian Angels somewhere before?

Being high on a hill, during thunderstorms we were often bombarded with lightning strikes, losing water heater elements, pumps, and televisions constantly.

We hopefully solved that problem by installing eight lightning rods, one at each corner of the house.

We have not lost any of the previously mentioned appliances since, thank God.

Gratefully, life in the house has been a pleasant routine, with just the occasional loss of a roof shingle, peeling paint, and caulking; along with the occasional water pump needing attention.

One deer season, an unknown hunter sent a high-powered bullet through a window into a bedroom, which buried itself in the wall.

No harm done; life goes on.

God Bless Our Home.

Andy Ice Cream

We had moved into our new home, with my salary as a surveyor helper able to cover the costs of a family and a small mortgage, but not a whole lot more.

My brother Andy had started a humanitarian gesture for our 4 kids, now 1 to 5 ages. That was to bring to them, us, a half-gallon of ice cream every payday, which they eagerly looked forward to. They soon learned when payday was, and would watch down the driveway for him, we all ever grateful for the practice. This went on for years.

Some years later, he came to me, asking for a little help.

An unforeseen series of crushing problems had occurred, and he reached the point where he was unable to cope with them on his own, now in jeopardy of losing long-held assets.

Fortunately, I had become a reasonably successful businessman by then and was able and willing to help him overcome the problems, no strings attached.

Andy – Vitamin Enriched Kid

In those years we lived together with the remainder of my original family, Andy was quite fond of Cindy, my daughter, at age 3 or 4, and so on, and often times right after dinner, he would sit on the sofa, which was an automatic signal to her to run and jump up onto his lap, hugging him prior to playtime with him.

It just so happened that right after dinner is when Cindy was given her daily dose of an evil smelling liquid vitamin, at which time coincided with her happily running to jump up on Andy's lap.

It was quite amusing to observe that he never rejected her, allowing her to get close to him, she is huffing and puffing; he would pick her up, stretch her out to arms-length, while proclaiming "Oh, you vitamin enriched kid" and hold her away briefly till the smell diminished, then returned to begin play.

She gleefully laughed at the whole process every time it occurred.

The House 1962

Spring, 1958, an agreement is reached between me and my good, lifelong neighbor, Paul, to sell me the top of that most beautiful hill situated between my original home farm, and a major part of the parent tract of the out sale.

This was my dream come true, as had often, over the years, come to this place, sat for hours in silence, become one with the setting sun as it concluded another day on this wonderful planet.

Having no money to immediately pay for this gem, he most generously extended open credit and I was able to pay in full a reasonable time later, working day and night.

My great work associate, Dick W and I then surveyed it, and I and Dolly soon were the proud owners of a truly beautiful 14.7-acre tract in Bell Township next door to my point of origin.

Now, the focus turned to that most revered, most dreamlike topic, a house of our own, a secure place to raise, and grow, God's most favored entity, a family, already started.

April 21, 1962, the decision has been made, the bank loan of $10,500 dollars has been secured, the excavation has been done, and the foundation has been built by local masons, and me.

I, and Brother Andy, both working full time jobs, are the work force challenging this project.

This project being a house planned to be a Structure 30 feet by 58 feet, initially, in frame, eventually encased in brick.

We had previously built the four and a half room house we were living in, so we weren't total beginners to the building process and were rapidly progressing our knowledge.

I subcontracted out the basic framing to two experienced carpenters, and very quickly, we had an enclosed frame to work in.

Working till midnight every day, I was progressing well, brother and other limited help pushing things along nicely.

December 24, 1962 was the big day, or night, as it happened, outlined in greater detail elsewhere.

We had moved into our dream home, albeit sparse, but our dream realized.

There was a long way to go to reach the final point of building, but the original loan of $10,500 had us moved in, on our own and a mortgage payment of $102.50 a month in place.

I will be forever grateful for the two wonderful carpenters who came here almost daily for over two years, part time, and not only finished the building, but extended the house to its current 105-foot length.

And, to the two ultra-professional stone Masons who encased the house within absolutely beautiful stone pattern only an inspired professional could achieve.

And so it remains to this day.

I brought in heavy equipment and cleared the entire hill, preparing it, then seeded it all in grass, which is maintained as lawn. Trees were planted, creating the storied shady lane access to the house.

It is my firm conviction that the former owners of this land they put into my trust would be pleased with its ongoing park-like beauty and atmosphere, the walnut trees Annie W planted so long ago, highlighting the existing public roadway.

This is the house I, and Thor, live in, and will die in.

Tinsmill Dust

The Jamison Mine was underway, getting ready to produce coal, and a critical facet of the market was that the coal had to be washed and dried.

Management, experienced, very intelligent, designed and built the washer-drier at the pit mouth, which was directly between the two towns of Salina and Tinsmill, with a combined population of about 1,200 people.

It was a well-designed plan but had one major flaw; there was no dust filter/collector ahead of the exhaust pipes. On still evenings, a huge haze and cloud would form; and linger for hours, all night at times.

As a result, when prevailing wind was West to East, Tinsmill's 70 or 80 houses all got a nice, sticky coating of black, ultrafine coal dust all over every exposed surface; and whatever amount of dust furnaces and air conditioners vacuumed and dispersed inside. It was very hard to clean off.

Never mind, all over cars and lawns. If the prevailing winds were East to West, Salina was the recipient. Needless to say, even though my employment was provided for a few from town, this did not at all endear the coal company to the citizens, especially the women.

Back then there were no real regulations regarding such, and the people had little to no recourse and continued to suffer.

The problem was ended when a methane gas explosion in the mine injured six men, closing the mine forever.

It was a sad ending all around, with promised long-term employment for over a hundred now gone away.

Runaway Buggy

Having completed our required work in the J mine that day, my helper and I were chatting with the section boss, just loafing waiting for the end of the day.

We were sitting in an entry where a coal hauler, a buggy as it's known, was hauling coal from the machine digging the coal, to an outgoing belt, then returning for another load, repeating this process trip after trip all day.

His travel way to the miner was the same entry we were sitting in, but he was turning to the right just before reaching us, which kept us well out of his path, about 50 feet away.

Conditions there were typical in underground mining of that particular seam of coal, 42 inches or so of height, mined out 18 feet wide, air guides posted along the side, restricting widths down to 14 feet or so, making it tight, very close.

The buggies are about 10 feet wide, long, just clear the roof, at times it's difficult to see easily where you are going when driving one.

So, we're sitting there chatting, my transit set up right beside me, my helper and the section boss close by, when suddenly without warning of any kind, the coal buggy is coming fast, directly at us, the operator failing to make the usual right turn.

Here, he had lost the brakes on the buggy, and traveling quite fast, thought he didn't want to slam into the solid wall of coal, and opted to direct the buggy straight down the entry we were in.

Having only seconds to react, all three of us leapt out of his way, he just missing us, but not my transit, smashing it to bits.

After he stopped and walked back to where we were; we asking him why he decided not to make his usual return, he claimed not to have seen us, an outright lie, because we had been there for quite some time prior to the event.

I shudder when I remember this event, what a horrible disaster that could well have been had we not been alert.

Obviously, my Guardian Angels go underground too.

Steve – Grass Fire

Number two son Steve, age 8 or so, developed an attraction to fire, and I caught him several times, playing with matches, learning how to strike the match without burning his fingers. My firm admonishments to the contrary didn't seem to register adequately, though.

At the time, we had no actual lawn, it was still just a big field around the house, and when the grass grew tall, I would hook up the old sickle bar mower and knock it down, no raking it, leaving it to dry naturally, eventually fading into the ground, become topsoil in 10 thousand or so years.

Anyhow, acres and acres of dry grass did create something of a fire hazard when dry, and, with a strong puff of wind, could easily spread into hundreds of acres of dry woods.

One evening, I noticed Steve was missing from the group playing In the dirt piles, so I asked if anyone knew where Steve was. Someone said yeah, he's out behind the house. No one knew, doing what.

So, I went looking for him. Sure enough, he was out back, matches in hand, trying to set fire to a small pile of the now dry grass.

As I approached, he looked up at me and said: It won't burn, been trying, but it just won't burn.

Reaching him, I said, it's gonna be burning really hot, real soon.

I grabbed the matches, and him. The real burn began right now.

He never played with matches again.

Apple Pie

One of Life's greatest pleasures for me was undoubtedly the apple pie that my wonderful wife, Dolores, would prepare, a thing of absolute beauty in the just-right crust, filled with the delicious, properly assembled and cooked down ingredients, then baked to perfection.

In the ongoing search for commercial duplication by modern technology, none has come even close to matching her result with their computer controlled blends and equipment.

Sometimes, I wonder if they needed help in Heaven with their baking, and she agreed to show them how it's done.

It will be interesting to see if that is, in fact, the case when – if – I get up there.

You Gonna Live

Four kids growing up, there was no end to the medical emergencies popping up out of nowhere, day after day.

Dolly, being a Registered Nurse, was fully qualified to assess, determine and apply the remedy for survival of the wounded one.

I, a licensed Paramedic, veteran of numerous dire, distressful contingencies, could step in when the Nurse was overwhelmed.

Scraped elbows, thorns, splinters, bee stings, nicks and cuts one quarter of an Inch or less long, bumps, bruises, even stubbed toes; along with other equally life-threatening mishaps were all collectively handled initially in the same manner by us, the medical providers.

When the tears subsided, sufficiently, the first medical inquiry was: Are you gonna live?

At times, this produced a resurgence of tears, but then, usually, a burst of laughter by the unfortunate victim.

Most of the time, this was an adequate cure, followed up with soap and water, mercurochrome, a bandaid and assurance that life never was in jeopardy.

Silly though it may be.

That same initial treatment still dominates the medical action taken in most cases.

At least here in our households.

Choke Cherries

My three boys became very accustomed to having tricks played on them, but never learned to be alert all the time.

This one summer day we were out in the woods, when we came to a cluster of true choke cherries, as they are known in our area.

These cherries, when fully ripe, are actually an edible food, but the fact is, they are so sour, so constricting they could seriously pucker up a crocodile's mouth, requiring hours or longer to recover.

I said loudly, oh boy, choke cherries, I loved them when I was a kid, and I'm going to eat a bunch of them right now.

I took half a dozen, threw them into my mouth, not daring to chew, even break the skin of any of them, just pretending to chew and swallow, echoing how good they were.

They just couldn't wait to try some, so I said okay, but they're the best if you all get a mouthful, and chomp down all at the same time hard.

Okay, the scene is set.

I said at the count of three, all bite down, and then I did the countdown.

They did the rest.

We still laugh about it 60 years later.

It is still so funny, those wrinkled up faces, the remarks.

Boys will be boys.

Ed. B.

It started out with the typical professional - client relationship, gradually escalating into a partnership, another mistake in life.

Someone much smarter than me coined it: Fools rush in, where Angels fear to tread.

First, it was property line identification, then property development. Then a partnership in the painting business, painting big tanks, buildings, barns, whatever.

First of all, he needed money. Six thousand dollars to be exact, to buy the equipment.

Against the best advice from a good man, the President of our little bank, who tried his best to discourage me; but I had been sold the proverbial bill of goods, and I jumped in. In short order, I would be rich beyond my wildest dreams.

Our first bid was a flop. We had traveled to Cincinnati, 360 long miles to look at some big, very big, tanks, taller than the empire state building, that smelled of stale oil to high heaven. I took a dim view of me hanging on a pair of ropes up there, applying an evil smelling goop onto the outside of it.

We didn't get that bid, but we did get the one for a large school district, half dozen schools to paint, both grade and high school.

I was temporarily put in charge of a motley crew of so-called painters, young kids, old men, none with as much experience as I had, which was none.

He did have one experienced painter; we soon discovered why no one else would hire him.

He was an alcoholic pervert, but we needed somebody who knew which end of a paint brush you dip into the can of paint.

Oh, what a crew. Some were afraid of ladders and would not paint anything higher than they could reach, others would not wear a mask, some, gloves at all times.

Where the quality control dude couldn't see, they wouldn't paint, and so on and on. Outside, half the high windowpanes only got wiped down, they only looked painted.

Finishing up at one school, he, Ed, found there was not enough paint to finish the gymnasium.

It was a light green, sold by Sherwin Williams only, unavailable since a special mix had to be preordered.

Not a problem for Ed.

He brought two 55 gallon drums the next day, assembled every partial, unused container of paint that we had, various colors, then began a community mix, blending every drop of whatever paint we had, watched the developing product in the drums, adding some kind of dye to make it greenish.

When all the leftover paint was mixed in with what good paint we had and were still short of the required amount to finish the gym, he simply added kerosene to the mess, stirring it in till there was enough. It came out a perfect green, visually acceptable to the quality control guy.

Since the gym was high, no one ever checked anyhow.

Using our high-pressure air sprayer, it was applied in a matter of just a few hours, and we were out of there.

It was widely known Ed was really goofy, but brilliant, unorthodox. He had this inborn ability to focus on something he wanted, and it would magically appear.

When I questioned him about how he did it, he shrugged and said, "I don't know, I just think about it, and it comes."

After many years of study, I understand what he does, and how he does it.

Painting in one of the schools we had, Ed came upon a young school employee doing janitorial work that had just finished his lunch and was sitting at a desk out in the hallway smoking a cigarette.

Ed yelled FIRE! He's on FIRE! chasing him down the hall, heaving the bucket of water on him, still yelling FIRE! He's on FIRE!

I thought I would die laughing.

The painting ended when we were doing the final school of the bid.

That was where there were several female students preparing for the first day of school.

We were about completed with the painting when our previously mentioned alcoholic employee, claiming it was all with playful intentions, grabbed one of the girls, threw her over his shoulder, and carried her outside about 500 feet, until someone physically blocked him and forced him to set her down.

The school administrator was informed, and upon his arrival we were invited to pack up and leave, permanently, before the police were called.

That ended a truly sorry adventure for me.

I not only lost the original $6,000 dollars I invested, but a lot of valuable time, and cost in the operations.

I was never given one dime.

Another former client called me one day and asked if I knew anything about my partner Ed, who, having bought a gas well from him, and did I know what, if anything, he had done with it.

I said I didn't know anything about him buying a well from him, but why did he ask.

Well, he said, the well was very old, and had reached the point where his monthly sales to the buyer of the gas had been yielding very small checks, less than $10 dollars a month, so he decided to sell it to Ed B.

Several months after the sale to Ed, the buyer called him, asking if he had upgraded the well, since they were now buying a much higher volume of gas from that well, and were wanting to know why.

So, the buyer and the seller agreed to meet at the meter where the sale is measured and recorded.

Very quickly they saw there was fresh digging around the meter. What Ed had done was install a new pipe, connecting one end into the buyer's main line: the other into the pipe coming from Ed's well going into the meter.

So, he was selling the buyer their own gas by routing some of it over to his pipe, adding to what his well was producing, and sending it through the meter.

A criminal investigation was supposedly done, but nothing ever came of it that I am aware of.

Goodbye Ed. Partnership over, but for some weird reason, still friends.

Did I say that somewhere – fools rush in – you know the rest.

Runaway Volkswagen

Teaching our boys driving, the Volkswagen Beetle was perfect.

Often times, when we all would be at home, I would allow them to take turns, one lap at a time.

The routine was;

Start the car, drive it backwards downhill at a -10% grade, for 700 feet down to the township road; stop, return to the house, stop, and park.

That was it, over and over, they learned, they loved it.

One day, we were all present, when youngest son Jim, took his turn, came flying back up the driveway, stopped, pulled on the handbrake, and got out, leaving it running as the next driver was eagerly waiting to take his turn.

Before he could get into the vehicle though, the handbrake cut loose, and the Volkswagen began slowly rolling backwards, driverless.

Seeing it start to move, I ran after it, caught up to it, grabbed the left front wheel and sharply twisted it to the left, redirecting the Volkswagen to roll towards the level part of our yard, where surely, I thought, it would stop.

While we're watching, laughing, instead of it continuing to roll towards the level part of the field, for some unknown reason the front wheels straightened out, then reversed their direction, directing the car to go sharply back down the steep part of the hill, picking up speed, crossing the driveway, just missing a big tree, and disappearing out of sight, ever faster, heading for my pond at the edge of the woods some 600 feet away.

By then the laughing had stopped, and we were all tensed, poised, waiting for the sound of the Volkswagen crashing into the water or the trees if it missed the pond.

The crash came, and we went down to assess the damage.

Here, several weeks before, I having cleared a considerable amount of brush around the pond, had piled it in front of the pond for future burning there.

The Volkswagen, after traveling a thousand feet downhill, had landed precisely onto the pile of brush, with the exhaust muffler being the only mortality.

My Ford tractor easily retrieved it from the pile.

You Already Told Me That

There are those times in conversation with someone, usually someone you know quite well, where you begin relating something to them, when they suddenly cut you off and blurt out: Oh yeah, you already told me that, or I already know that, or I already told you that.

At best, it's mildly embarrassing, at worst, it's downright ignorant and rude, and you feel like ending the conversation and walking away.

When I am confronted with such a situation, I simply stop, let the other person continue their comments, suppress my inner reaction, and pretend not to be affected, and do not return to the original topic.

It all happens in a flash.

Show and Tell

It was Show and Tell Day, and son, Jim, caused a bit of stir with his presentation.

When I first began to strip mine coal, I needed to blast strata as part of the process and had a license and the equipment to do it.

This included a detonator, a small wooden box housing a small generator, with a handle on top, the type you may see in the Wile E. Coyote and Road Runner cartoons.

Jim brought it in and set it down in the classroom, then explaining what it was, and its purpose, demonstrating the bite when touching the wires coming out of it when the plunger was pushed down.

He further explained that that was what triggered the explosion of dynamite. He received quite a response from both students and the teacher of the class.

Enough so, that the teacher Invited the principal to come and see it.

Irregardless of the detonator being completely harmless in and of itself, the expected paranoiac reaction came, and Jim was instructed to carefully remove it to a closet, and to be sure to take it home at the day's end.

DUI Checkpoint

At age 10, or so, as our boys were reaching the age and stage of motor vehicle interest, I began the process of teaching them the fine points of driving, along with the rules and regulations that come with it. Well, some of them.

Having a Volkswagen beetle at the time, it being small with good visibility and handling, along with a conventional stick transmission, it was ideal for the training.

Often times, if I needed extra help in a survey; I would take them with me, and upon completion of the survey allow them to drive us back home, each taking a turn.

It was already dark when one night we were returning from a rather distant job, and of course, they were reveling in the fact they would each get a chance to drive.

As we rounded up over a small hill, we could see in the near distance red lights flashing down our path.

Sure enough, it was a highway DUI (driving while intoxicated) checkpoint.

Jim, age 10, was driving, and closing the distance between us and the checkpoint was happening rather fast; there were just a few vehicles left between where we would be stopped, in close proximity to the police.

Thinking fast, I ordered Jim to drive to a point fairly close to the last vehicle waiting in line to be checked, then pull off the road on the right side, park, and quickly slide over the gearshift into the passenger seat.

As soon as he was stopped I jumped out of the passenger seat I had been in and ran around to the driver's door, opened it, and began coughing wildly, doubling over as if I was in a coughing seizure.

To his credit, one of the officers, seeing my action, came running over, asking "are you alright? are you alright? do you need help?"

Slowing the cough to a stop, I assured him I was going to be okay; I was on medication and would be fine soon.

I was fine soon after easily passing through the checkpoint.

I drove the rest of the way home.

Steve Saxophone

Number two son, Steve, was in seventh grade when he developed a strong desire to learn how to play the saxophone.

My belief was there a girl in band at school that he wanted to impress, since she was already taking lessons in saxophone.

After days of whining, l, not a great fan of that music, claiming it was more effective than water boarding, finally gave in, and we went to a musical instrument outlet and rented a high dollar instrument.

Reality soon set in, endless practice dominated his time; it was a slow learn, possibly years to achieve an acceptable level of proficiency, among other discouraging factors.

Finally, as the length of time between practices extended, we canceled the rental agreement and returned the saxophone.

In response to inquiry by his peers, friends or relatives as to why he gave up on a potentially rewarding musical career, the story that was left out, not really challenged by me was that, in view of my unexplainable, irresolute disdain for the sound of a saxophone practice, the foo foo foo, I had restricted his practice location to an area at the banks of Wolford Run, deep in the big woods, some 2,000 feet away from the house at the bottom of a long, steep, slippery hill about 300 feet lower in elevation than the house; inaccessible by a vehicle.

And, of course, only when I wasn't at home.

Most extended their condolences.

This has been a source of amusement ever since.

Cindy Hayride

Next door neighbor Paul W., still in possession of one horse, and needing to prepare for another winter feeding, had cut some grass for hay, not far from our house.

It having cured adequately for barn storage, was raked into a wind row, and was ready for harvesting, Paul opting to haul it to the barn loose, without converting it into bales, as is usually done.

So, Paul connects his steel wheeled wagon to his new tractor, the Farmall BN, and drives up to the prepared field.

The field, relatively level for the most part, slightly to the fairly steep downhill, where the bulk of the wind rowed hay is located.

It being a one-man job, our kids are still quite young and small, were no help in such an undertaking, just watching from a safe distance.

Aligning and parking the wagon with the wind row on a level part of the field, Paul goes to work, picking up the hay with a pitchfork and throwing it into the wagon, the load slowly growing bigger.

As it grew bigger my daughter Cindy, who was watching the whole process, thought it would be great fun to go for a hayride, the one forming right in front of her.

Assuming it would be for just a short distance to the end of the field, Paul agreed; she climbing up onto the piled hay, Queen of the Hill.

Moving the tractor along the disappearing wind row, reaching the point where the field is no longer level, but downgrade, he stops, pressing the tractor brakes on, securing them with the pin made for that on the tractor.

Paul returns to picking, throwing, and piling, when for some unknown reason the locking pin releases the brakes and the wagon starts rolling away, down the slope, slowing increasing its speed. When Paul realizes what's happening, he drops his fork, sprinting towards the moving wagon, finally catching up to it; desperately, dangerously leaping up onto the tractor, bringing it to a safe stop.

Cindy, unaware as to the gravity of the just terminated event, was calmly lifted down from the wagon, simply assuming it was the end of the hayride, totally oblivious of its true potential.

She left, happily running home to tell her mother about the exciting hayride.

John Guitar

John was a born salesman. He probably would have sold the Brooklyn Bridge locally, if given the chance.

This time it was a guitar. Where that wish originated, I have not the slightest idea.

He was relentless; life itself wasn't worth living if he didn't have a guitar.

And the day comes; we're off to your local, friendly guitar dealer, to buy, not rent, a guitar suitable to take him into the Country Hall of Fame, no question.

As is the case, all too often, a young boy's central focus can shift, very quickly.

The guitar teacher was an incompetent, irritating in her impossible demands, stays on the telephone during my lessons, and so on. Yeah, Yeah.

Soon, the lessons went by the boards, whatever that means, he could do it on his own. Look out Country music world, John on the way.

As expected, the dust was readily Visible on the guitar that day when John S., his Grandfather by marriage came for a visit with his Grandmother Toots.

My son, John, soon brings up about his entry into the music world, and John S., very interested, says he, too, had been a guitar player in his youth, asking to see the instrument, taking it into his hands.

As an old pro would typically do, John S. strums the guitar, wrinkling up his nose, wisely stating it needs the strings adjusted.

He got through the process, strum and listen, twist those knobs that tighten or loosen the strings, then repeat the same, involving far more time than you usually see when real players do it.

Finally, he says, "It's impossible," hands the thing back to John, turns away, changing the subject.

The strings were in total disarray, like he said, impossible.

The guitar never played again, joining the deceased predecessors in guitar land heaven, I guess.

So much for the Country Music Hall of Fame.

Truckers - Dolly

My Wife, Dolly, was taking the kids to visit her Mother in Youngsville, PA one day, in our 1965 Volkswagen.

The roads normally traveled by, included a short section of interstate 80, a major East - West highway heavily used by over-the-road truckers.

For some reason, three of them, catching up to her, apparently thought it would be fun to play a game with her.

One moved In front of her, one close behind, and one close beside her.

The one behind came up close, forcing her to speed up, the others, probably in contact by CB, kept the same pace.

To put it simply, she was terrified. A woman in a small car with four small kids, being assaulted by three huge, roaring monsters at ever increasing speeds, the perfect formula for a disaster.

The relief finally came when her turn off point came into sight, and she got away from the bastards.

That was 50 years ago, there were no cell phones yet, to call police for help.

Her relating that experience that evening was horrifying, the recall of it writing this story still gives me the chills.

Strangely, that evening, news reports told of three truckers arrested and charged with driving under the influence, and other charges, near the Ohio line.

We' II never know who they were, and don't really want to.

I might wind up in jail, they in a hole.

Golf Tournament

I was in only one Golf Tournament In my life. It was in 1970, at the Oak Lake Golf Course.

I, and one of my few friends played there regularly, so it was not exactly like the U.S. Open, but pretty much among the regulars. I was not a really good golfer, consistent Iow 80's to high 70's, with a handicap of 8, nothing to really brag about.

As luck would have it, my regular partners all had to work that day, so I was put into another foursome, one that for some unknown or unstated reason, just didn't like me, and didn't like them either.

Of course, I teed off last on the first hole, a decent drive within 50 feet of the green. Again, hitting last, I sank it for a birdie, one under after one. That didn't help the relationship at all, now hitting first. Another decent drive out of my $29.95 set of clubs. Being closest to the green, I 'm back to hitting last. This time, I'm on the green in two, sinking a 15-footer, two under after two. No applause, no attaboy, silence from my foursome, visibly irritated.

Third hole, a par three, I'm still first, on the green again. This time, a par three. There's some muttering, mostly silence, the rest of the group typical. They stunk. The next six holes were somewhat routine, some good, others not. I believe I was plus two after nine. The course was just nine holes, so there was a break, announced by the other three after nine. They also told me they were taking an extended break and that I should join some other group, a threesome needing a fourth player.

The parting was absent of tears, or hand shaking, no actual goodbyes, or it was nice playing with you. The second round of nine was much more pleasant, the scoring pretty much in sync with my record, winding up the 18 holes with a 76, and taking away my handicap of 8, I scored 68, nothing spectacular.

I never did see a complete rundown of all the golfers' scores, but I was announced as the winner of the tournament a week later. The first, and last one, ever. There was no congratulatory outburst, no recognition whatsoever, none. There was no plaque, no framed placard, no gold or silver cup. My prize: 6 Wilson staff golf balls, handed silently and privately to me.

Ed B. - 2

My one-time partner in the painting business was a genuine renegade, and a character of undefined limits. We remained friendly, even after the painting fiasco ended.

Ed was aware, from ordinary conversation, that I had a problem with potable water, as my spring, being at an elevated location, was about to dry up for the summer. Also, knowing I had a perennial spring some 2,000 feet away, with power available there, he, without any prompting, set out to remedy my situation.

Ed lived about ten miles from me, and one morning here he comes on his backhoe, demanding to know where the running spring was, then proceeded to dig a 2,000-foot-long trench, telling me to go buy the pipe for it, which I did. He had brought a helper, and within several days, I had a second, dependable water supply.

After lunch on one of those days, he and his helper were here at the house, and he called his helper, a teenage kid with a long, black, scruffy beard, over to him where he was petting our big, black, furry Collie, Chingo.

The kid went over to him there, and Ed said to him, "Hey, Scruffy, do you want to see a perfect picture of yourself?" The kid was confused and said nothing. Ed then reached down, grabbed Chingo's tail, lifted it high as it would go, exposing Chingo's rear end, full view, and held it up for a few seconds. We observers cracked up, and we still do.

But there was another side to Ed. All I ever knew was that Ed, owning several cash-oriented businesses, had admittedly played some games that weren't exactly kosher with tax law, and as could be expected, Internal Revenue was coming next week to take a peek. His accountant warned it could get nasty.

Sunday night, the week of the confirmed visit on the next day, his wife, for no explainable reason, awakened at 2:00 am, noticing that Ed was not in bed. That was not unusual, as this was not uncommon for him.

She said that something kept bothering her, and was unable to return to sleep, so she got up and went out to the garage to see if his vehicle was present.

It was, and he was in it. So was the end of a garden hose, connected to the running truck's exhaust, sending deadly carbon monoxide into the cab where he was. She jerked the hose out of the cab, shut off the truck.

He refused medical attention, having just begun the incident.

I never heard the outcome of his visit with our favorite agency, but he remained out of jail, as far as I know.

I have not seen or spoken to him since. Sometimes our friends can be more dangerous than our enemies.

JD 350 - Clearing

I had purchased a John Deere 350, a fairly small track hilift around 1972, a part of the original start of me going into the coal business. There being considerable brush and small trees growing between the township road and our house that I wanted cleared, I brought the hilift home to do the clearing myself.

Many of the trees were locust, 4 or 5 inches in diameter, slowly spreading into the previously farmed land around the house, taking it over.

I only had the night to operate the tractor, and I went to work pushing over the locust trees with the bucket, backing up to get a clean bite at ground level, creating a pile.

This went on for several hours, the cleared area expanding ever so slowly, but progress visible. Being dark, I turned on the lights, continuing pushing, repeating the process, push over, back up, push, pile.

Sometimes, the small trees that were pushed over would not stay clear down, flat to the ground, and would recoil, lifting part way back up, creating a big spear that I had to maneuver the hilift around to avoid ramming it with the rear--dangerous, but doable.

Preoccupied, not thinking, stupidity, whatever the cause, after I did a push, bending down a number of trees, I failed to look backwards before starting to back up. Moving backwards, one of those spear-like trees, the top broken off, about 4 inches in diameter, suddenly slid sharply between my rib cage and arm, quickly bringing me to my senses. I stopped hard, petrified, spear protruding out over the instrument panel.

I am loathe to consider, one or two inches further over, into my back, and my problems are over, but my familie's are just beginning.

Thank you very much, my dear guardian angels.

Lesson learned.

Dirt Pile

Building this house was hit and miss from the start. The original lot of 14.7 acres was purchased in 1958, and was fully paid for by 1962, when I commenced building.

The excavation was completed the year before, with the top-soil having been put to one end of the future building location. The house being over a hundred feet long by thirty-five feet wide, made quite a bit of soft dirt, sort of scattered about in smaller piles.

Every family with kids should have a pile of topsoil, or piles available for playing in. It was amazing how much time they spent there; it was the perfect babysitter.

We bought them all the toy heavy equipment there was: trucks, bulldozers, excavators, etc. Did this greatly influence them into a lifetime of involvement with those machines and activities? Very possible, very likely. We eventually duplicated every one of them and then some, in real life, with real equipment. It has served us well.

Cindy played in the dirt, too, a lot of the time, a real mudhen.

Ratty Golf Clubs

My friend, Leo, and I were out golfing one day, and in the usual manner, when we caught up to several foursomes, I dropped my clubs, which I carried, on the ground, making a noticeable rattling sound, attracting some attention.

One of the other waiting golfers looked at my clubs lying there and said derisively, "Is that the best you can do?", which was highly offensive to me, a total stranger.

The simple truth regarding the clubs being the fact I had paid $29.95 for the set, including the bag, some years ago, and having used them quite a bit, the bag had become, to say the least, downright ratty, with gaping holes along the bottom often allowing clubs to fall out--admittedly really shabby.

Further, my having grown up in borderline poverty, it was not in me to be overly concerned as to appearances of affluence. In other, plainer words, "I don't much give a damn what anyone thinks of my bag and clubs", was my attitude.

So, in response, I said to him, loud enough that everyone present could hear, "Sir, you may be interested to know I own a coal mining operation, where I have two Caterpillar bulldozers, two Caterpillar front end loaders, and a big Caterpillar excavator working right now—what do you own?"

There was no response, only silence. "Would you like to tour my mine sometime?", I asked.

He never said a word and turned away. I never saw him again.

Calvin

My former son-in-law, Calvin, was a true enigma.

Growing up in an early American style suburban atmosphere, somewhat central to three populated communities, he had plenty of town-oriented interaction, a certain glamour that was attractive to a farm raised girl with like kind social involvement.

She having been raised in a closely controlled environment within a close circle of moderate friends limited by a higher standard of social behavior.

Calvin had a sporty car, was active in his father's auto repair shop, was in high school chorus, and performed occasionally as part of a singing group, was well known and widely popular, so there was a certain attraction to him.

However, due to proximity and availability of alcoholic beverages, not only in a home atmosphere but other gatherings, a habit was developing, but only beginning to show itself, which should have been recognized as a red flag, but was not, especially by me, having been raised in a somewhat similar setting.

No, I didn't interfere, to my eternal regret, a personal policy with our kids.

Time passes, there was dating, parties, graduation, whatever.

I really never asked about the details, but sometime in his junior year, he was involved in a terrible vehicle accident, where there was a fatality, for which he blamed himself, not directly, but indirectly. The pain never left, even though everyone knew he was not at fault, just being at the wrong place at the wrong time.

The relationship continued, and finally, they were married.

Upon graduation, I hired him to work at a new mine near Punxsutawney, with me; we staying in a rented apartment. Calvin, never really conversant with me, preferred a bar, which he visited nightly.

Then he and Cindy found an apartment near Punxsutawney, and she moved there, with me still being close by.

Calvin suddenly developed an interest in coaching a softball team, a girls softball team, with a girl coach already in place. Calvin was always unhappy, moody, argumentative. Things went from bad to worse, and he became increasingly despondent, depressed, and tried to end it all, ramming a wall with his pickup, unsuccessfully.

Then, a strange incident occurred, where a puppy that was about to be killed was saved by Cindy, by agreeing to move to the then puppy's owner's house and apartment complex as a rental, in exchange for its life.

That puppy lived with Cindy for 14 years thereafter, happily. She had named him Bernie. That move to a house precipitated the setup for the next saga. Calvin set fire to his pickup in an attempt to exit the scene, out of continuing severe depression.

Things went from bad to worse, again, and Cindy booted him out of their house, so he went to live with his new girlfriend, the coach of the girls softball team—she is already three months pregnant with his child. The child was born, but sadly, its mother had developed a rapidly moving cancer, and was gone in just a few months. Calvin went back to his original home, the child taken and raised by its mother's parents.

Calvin's return home was not exactly a replay of the biblical prodigal son's return, and things did not go well. Somewhere, he found a candidate for his third wife, and after marrying her, he went to live in her home, but he was out of a job, and with no income, another child was on its way.

Long ago when he first arrived in my circle, and I was told of his quiet, continual suffering from the memory of the accident previously mentioned, in which he had no fault, had done nothing wrong, I told him, in confidence, "Calvin, if you ever reach the point in life where you feel it's hopeless, nowhere to turn, feel free to give me a call."

Well, on a dreary, foggy, rainy day in November, 1995, my phone rang. It was that dreaded call, and I said, "Hello", then listened. A barely audible voice said, "Chuck, do you remember long ago when you told me that if ever I was really down, to feel free to call?" I said, "Yes, how can I help you?"

He said he was in desperate shape all around, and needed a job in the worst way, and was beyond dead broke. As was the case, I had just opened a major long-term strip mine and really needed some competent, trustworthy help with equipment operation, so I said, "Start Monday, 7:00 am, as usual."

Things were better then, for quite a while, but with the drinking once again beginning to show up negatively. Then there was a divorce from wife number three, and more financial problems.

Then a fourth wife came along; this one owned the bar where trouble was always waiting. One day, a vicious argument between him and his not so sweet wife broke out. He ran to his pickup, grabbed a loaded pistol, and came racing back in, where a physical confrontation ensued. The gun discharged, and Calvin was on his way to a hospital with life threatening injuries.

To complicate things, over the past few years, he had developed a serious hyper-extension of his belly, bordering on elephantitis, to the point where he was unable to climb steps, or walk on rough terrain, so he could no longer work for me in mining, from a medical viewpoint. I urged him to apply for medical relief, which he did, and was granted full disability.

His affairs were subsequently assigned to his competent sister-in-law, she clearing up past financial issues.

Sadly, he died alone, a troubled soul, of cardiac failure, at age 62. May his next life be less troubled, Oh Lord.

Thank you.

Mom - Rudy

Mom was living in Pittsburgh with sisters Ann and Stella, needing some additional care as she aged, but was in good condition, generally.

Sister Mary and her husband, Rudy, lived just across the hall in the apartment building, so there was continual interaction.

Dolly and I were visiting one Sunday, when the subject of Rudy came up.

It was a widely known and accepted fact, that in the Ukraine, where Mom grew up, there was ongoing hostility between the Ukrainian people and the Italian people, for reasons long forgotten, but perpetuated anyway.

Mom thought about Rudy for a bit when his name came up, then, in her infinite wisdom, said, "You know, Rudy is a really nice guy--for an Italian."

He really was a nice guy, never changed. He's gone now.

D9 to Derry

After a short, vicious legal battle, I obtained a lease for a sizeable tract of strippable coal on Derry Ridge, way back when.

From the outset, there was an undertone of ominous future involvement, silent subconscious warnings unheeded by me, hopelessly naive.

Irregardless, I obtained the required permits and called for a move of my D9H, a 52-ton bulldozer, from home to the Chestnut Ridge, some 50+ miles via the permitted route.

The first thing I encounter is the guy moving the dozer, is a full-blown renegade in his own right, immediately contradicting the permit condition that the blade must be removed for the move, automatically making the load ten tons heavier, and six-teen+ feet wide, rather than just ten or so feet wide.

So away we go, big tractor, 55,000 rears, big lowboy, big dozer loaded.

We travel right through the town of Indiana illegally, with lots of traffic and many lights, clearing a path as he flew along, then by various routes through another town, Blairsville, then Derry, then finally to Route 30, where the truck breaks down, parking it and the load at a wide spot.

The next morning, he shows up with a different tractor that's much smaller than the one the day before.

He assured me the truck would handle the load, and off we go again.

The roads traveled till now were all high-grade highways but now we're at the bottom of Derry Mountain, on an unimproved, narrow, twisting township road, already a steep upgrade with no guide rails, two miles of hold your breath navigation to the top, where my job is.

I had followed the truck from the start of the move, but the driver, Ben, came over to me, and clearing his throat in a funny way, said, "Charlie, you better get ahead of me, go to the top and block any traffic."

So, I did, and waited up there.

In about 15 or 20 minutes, sure enough, here he comes, pulls in and we unload the dozer.

Being a personal friend, as he's preparing to leave, he says, "Charlie, do you want to know why I didn't want you behind me climbing up the mountain?" I just stared.

He said, "This truck only has 37,000 lb. rears – way, way too light for the 65-ton load. One misstep, one pause, one missed gear, a soft spot, or a stop, and it's all over."

With a 130,000 lb. load resisting me, pulling me backwards, you may never have found the pieces at the bottom.

Did I say ominous forebodings somewhere? There's more, later.

Cindy's Cooking

Three boys and one girl meant things could stay out of balance, pretty much all the time.

As Cindy was growing up, being the first born, she was the constant target of the boys pulling all kinds of pranks and insults, usually producing a comical end result, and at times, not exactly.

Her initial outreach was, of course, in meal preparation, and desserts.

Dolly soon bought her the world-famous Easy Bake Oven, of her time, and she was off and running.

Successes ranged from acceptable to terrible, but didn't really matter much in either case.

I was equally guilty of having fun at her expense along with the boys, and would often cooperate in antics emphasizing her failures much more so than in her successes, such as they were.

We knew when she was making cookies, for example, and would agree to accept several cookies for our dessert after dinner, and all take a bite about the same time, and all collapse to the floor, moaning and groaning in agony, calling loudly for medical attention, each saying their final goodbye to earth and family, all lamenting the decision to eat the cookies.

These comments did not sit well with Cindy, and she would threaten to never again offer any of her efforts to such unappreciative dolts.

Another time, she gave out little pastries, which we promised to keep for supper dessert. In the meantime, they partially soaked the goodies in vinegar, then drying them before supper time.

Then, after supper, the family dogs would be called in, and a pastry set down before them, watching as they refused to eat it, turning up their noses and walking away. They laughed as they watched, but not really funny.

Somehow, we all survived the learning process, no harm done to either her ego, or our digestive systems, and, along with time passing, finally ended it. Cindy grew up to be a wonderful, well-balanced cook.

Thank God, in view of life events.

Fire of Undetermined Origin

In the years that I was fabricating cable hangers for area deep mines, I had a distributor who was also an entrepreneur of sorts, and a risk taker. Doing well financially, in frequent conversations, we would discuss various ways of making money.

He, being a heavy drinker, reasoned ownership of a bar was something he would do, at some point.

So, a place became available, and he bought it, heavily financed by some questionable acquaintances, as no bank would touch a previously failed saloon, the location being in an undesirable area.

He admitted early on, the business was struggling, and when his wife and kids told him they'd had enough and walked out, he knew he was in real trouble.

I repeatedly warned him, half joking, "Andy, I don't want to hear about any fires of undetermined origin in the news." There was always some nervous rebuttal.

One day, the morning news was ominous. A fire of undetermined origin has been reported at the saloon, his.

Several days later, the news was again talking about that saloon owner. Andy has been arrested and charged with arson.

Additional news reporting as the days went on told all the details: the night of the fire, very late, the local fire department chief happened to be going home from a fire elsewhere, in his car.

Traveling past my friend's saloon, he noticed orange flickering through the windows of the dance hall part.

Curious, he stopped and went for a closer look, seeing small flames rising up near the walls of the room.

With his department's engines still out, not far away, he called one to his location, it being there quickly. So, they broke into the building, went to the fire area, extinguishers in hand.

They found a bizarre setup. My friend had filled numerous gallon jugs with gasoline, set them a few feet apart along the walls, connected the jugs with some kind of rope soaked with gasoline, and either lit it himself, or set up some type of fuse to start the fire.

They quickly put out the fire, as the system apparently hadn't worked according to plan, and had not yet done much damage.

I don't know whatever became of the saloon; I'm assuming his financiers took it.

Even though he had been arrested and charged, with his connections, some judge must have considered this a prank, levying no punishment at all, as far as I know.

Andy, Andy, Andy, no fires of undetermined origin, right.

I never saw him again.

Evenings at Home

I worked practically every evening, mostly at home, welding or fabricating in my shop, paperwork in my office, or sharpening mining tools in my basement.

I would always break from whatever I was doing, to help put the kids to bed. We would play games, I would tell them stories, I would listen to theirs.

I would read books to them, often reading backwards till they realized it and hollered.

Strangely, one may say, or admit, but I never kissed them goodnight.

I can't and won't try to explain why, but it had to be some kind of a follow through from another lifetime.

I know, weird.

When I was fabricating, I was in my shop, a hundred yards away from the house, so there was no noise to interfere with sleep.

But when I was sharpening miners' tools, bits, it went on in the basement right under their bedrooms and it was loud, a big fan ran the whole time, vacuuming out the deadly dust from grinding carbide steel creates.

The grinding would go on for hours, then I would load up the finished bits, and deliver them to the mines, 8 miles away, rain, shine, snow, sleet, whatever, for their use the next day.

Office work till midnight was quiet, but the lights were on, and routine.

It was a hard life, but a great life, never a dull moment.

I would not want to repeat it.

Mount Pleasant Mine

In providing professional services to the local mining community, I agreed to accompany a client to evaluate and sample the coal, in a feasibility study of surface mining an abandoned deep mine roughly 30 miles from home, in a remote area.

Having routinely done this same activity numerous times through the years, there was no known reason to assume a need to inform anyone as to where we were going, and how to get there.

So, one day we gathered together, myself, my client and his four sons, to go to the mine site. My client brought the tools, pick and shovel, to dig the coal sample with, and the boxes to put the sample into.

As an afterthought, I prepared my methane gas detector, lit the flame inside that indicates the presence of methane gas by its expansion, rising up.

In mining, these are referred to as bug lights, or lamps, and have the appearance of a common lantern to some extent. Putting the lamp into the cab of the truck, we departed to go to the mine.

A typical abandoned mine in the Pittsburgh seam usually has an opening, or more than one opening, large enough to walk or crawl through, and hopefully, travelable openings inside thereafter to walk through to be able to determine the percentage of coal remaining unmined in justification of future surface mining at the site. The samples of coal, after laboratory analysis, show coal quality and specifications for its marketability.

We found the site had been partially backfilled to just above the top of the coal seam, but not completely closed off, their having left an opening of roughly 8 feet wide by 10 feet long, with a vertical drop of about 10 feet to the bottom of the mine.

The opening into the mine being visible, access via the hole easily doable, my client prepared to be the first one into the mine. He threw the sample boxes into the hole, secured his tools and light, and climbed up onto the backfilled ridge forming the top of the hole, to begin his descent into the hole ahead of his four sons, and me, going last.

It is well known, the Pittsburgh seam of coal in this area has little, if any, methane gas in it, so I was not overly concerned, especially in a deep mined site--any methane would long since have bled off.

After preparing my methane detector prior to the departure, I simply left the flame inside burn the whole time, so it was still burning when we got to the mine.

Watching my client preparing to enter the hole to go into the mine, I had set the detector onto the same ridge of spoil (backfill) my client was climbing onto, a few feet away.

As he was set to slide down into the hole, I happened to bend down to tie a shoelace, and noticed that the flame in the detector had gone out. This is common, as sharp air currents like a puff of wind, can blow the flame out any time.

So, I relit the flame, and it immediately went out again, so I shouted to him to stop, don't go into the hole, and so he stopped. I relit it several times with the same result--it would just go out.

It struck! Black damp! Carbon dioxide, pouring out of the mine. Death in a few minutes is assured, due to lack of oxygen in heavy concentrations, which was surely the case here.

No one went into the mine. The sample boxes are still in the hole, as best we know. Had I not seen the flame out, and not double checked, finding the carbon dioxide, and the client, the father of the four sons, gone into the hole and quickly collapsed, would the sons, in panic, have jumped into the hole to rescue him, exposing themselves to certain death? Would I, also in panic state, have jumped in to join them? When would we be found in such a remote place? I still shudder at the mental replay of the event.

There is a God, and guardian angels, trust me.

Andy - Darkest Africa

Andy was not all seriousness or negativity, and often exhibited certain amusing characteristics.

I recall his telling me of his initial, and early meetings with what turned out to be his future in-laws.

He said, "Boy, you ought to hear them, they're such hypochondriacs.

I'll guarantee if they heard of a fresh, new disease in darkest Africa, they'd immediately charter a boat to go and get it."

Andy - Huggers

Andy was not all seriousness or negativity, but often exhibited certain amusing characteristics.

I recall the telling to me his initial and early meetings with what turned out to be his future in-laws.

After marriage to the same family, now living with his own family in our original home.

One day, his in-laws were coming for just a social visit, and he spotted them arriving, still some distance from the house on the long driveway.

He proclaimed loudly, so everyone could hear, "Everyone run, hide, here they come, here come the huggers, here they come, you could be crushed to death, run, run for your life!"

UFO

Son Jim, and son-in-law Calvin, were working a second shift at our mine, when Jim called Calvin on the CB. He said, "Do you see how close that helicopter is to us, right over your head?" Calvin stops pushing dirt, gets out to look, and says, "Yeah, I wonder what's going on?"

Shutting down both machines to better analyze what's happening, they notice there is no sound at all coming from the now suspect group of blinking lights, red and clear, up just a hundred feet or less, hovering in one spot.

After about five minutes, the object lifts upward, soon disappearing into the night sky.

The next day, I called the State Police barracks, relate the incident to them as it was seen, and inquired if they had been in the area the past evening.

The response was totally negative, so I hung up.

To this day, the boys swear it happened as described, no one questioning the story.

There were a few isolated reports from others that the group of lights were seen, of all places, in the big cemetery just a few miles to the west, near Avonmore.

I'm now the president of that cemetery, and I haven't seen any strange lights.

Yet.

Ole Swell Fellas

A primary feature between me and the Ole Swell Fellas, was an ongoing, humorous exchange of proclamations regarding myself when going to the Ole Swell Fella's, a camp in Potter County. It became a tradition of expectation, providing material for response.

I would write in the camp logbook, and, in Potter County, it being widely publicized by the news media, and even the local town crier, that Charlie Kravetsky would be arriving at the Ole Swell Fellas campsite this Friday afternoon. That attendance of this sacred, solemn event is mandatory by all local social and political dignitaries, and all local church choirs and pastors must also attend.

Upon my arrival, after the sirens and fireworks have ended their signaling, the choirs would break into joyous song, singing "How Great Thou Art", "How Great Thou Art", among other songs of praise and adoration. Then, a police escort and band parade recital to the camp house. Of course, this was always in good humor, coming and going.

This went on for years, there always being an appropriate response to my egotistical, self-laudatory claims, refuting such as hearsay, imaginative achievements, or outright lies.

On the day of departure for home, usually a Sunday, I would take pen in hand, and summarize the weekend's events, some being funny, some not, trying to include something about each one there, creating intense interest as to the content of my writing in the logbook.

Included in this telling is the final response, in letter form, received from the principals, theoretically taking me to task for a nefarious act I was wrongfully accused of actuating.

BE IT HEREIN NOTED

A

S U M M O N S

STATE OF PENNSYLVANIA
COUNTY OF POTTER

CIRCUIT COURT OF THE 10th.
JUDICIAL CIRCUIT
(CRIMINAL DIVISION)

THE GRAND JURY OF SAID COUNTY CHARGES THAT, BEFORE THE FINDING OF THIS INDICTMENT BUCK RUBERTA AND ELEVEN OTHER GOOD AND LAWFUL MEN AND CITIZENS OF SAID COUNTY, HAVING BEEN EMPANELED, sworn and charged to inquire in and for the body politics of the County of Potter , State of Pennsylvania, upon oath present and say: That on the 2nd. day of February in the year of our Lord One Thousand Nine Hundred and Seventy Nine, Charles Kravetskydid go to, walk to, crawl to, amble to, wobble to, stagger to, peregrinate to, or otherwise wend his drunken way to, a certain building to wit, Ole Swell Fellas' Lodge situated in said County where at approximately eight o'clock P.M., in the evening, standard time, various and sundry people of both sexes, namely men, women and childrenm were assembled in large numbers for the purpose of education and/or enlightenment and/or entertainment.

And the grand jurors aforesaid, upon their oaths, do further present and say, that on the date and day aforesaid, in the County and State aforesaid, and in the presence and hearing of the people aforesaid, the said Charles Kravetskydid speak, utter, expound, bellow, bawl, or in other manner make use of the following vain, vulgar, filthy indecent, improper, unbecoming and ungentlemanly language, to wit:

"All those who cannot swim will please mount the
benches, scale the walls, climb the stove pipe
or flee to the hills, or other places of refuge,
for I, the great He-elephant of Westmoreland
County, am going to piss on this here stove."

And the Grand Jurors aforesaid, upon their oaths aforesaid, do
further present and say, that on the day and date aforesaid, the said
Charles Kravetsky did then and there deliberately, premeditatedly and
with malice aforethought, pull out, drag out, jerk out, snatch out, or
otherwise extract, unwind, uncoil, or unreel from his trousers, pants,
breeches, pantaloons, drawers or other wearing apparel, a long crooked,
snake-like and formidable looking prick, peter, pecker, tool, organ,
whang, toody, joy-prong, Johnson Bar, tally whacker tea kettle or
shillalay, and did then and there premeditatedly and with malice aforethought as aforesaid, piss, wee-wee, pee, piddle, pee-wee, urinate or
make water, around, about, into, and upon, a certain red hot Franklin
stove then and there situate, causing said stove to fizz, fry, fume,
smoke, steam, scald, sizzle, and stink, thereby creating a malodorous,
nauseating, obnoxious and otherwise objectionable and disagreeable
stench, odor, smell, aroma, to the manifest corruption of his own and
the public morals and the wicked and pernicious example of all others
in like cases offending, and AGAINST THE GOOD ORDER, PEACE AND DIGNITY
OF THE STATE OF PENNSYLVANIA.

Solicitor of the 10th. Judicial
Circuit of Pennsylvania.

Foot Note: I live with a certain regret regarding the final communication to me.

Recall and dates are hazy here. To the best of my knowledge,
a terrible tragedy regarding one principal when his son was killed
in a coal mine accident, casting a pall over the entire ambience.

After a lifetime of humor and jest, I simply could not respond in kind.

He, having promoted his son into the highly dangerous line of work (mine electrician), lived with the pain until his recent passing in 2012.

May he rest in peace; a fine, fine family.

After the passing of both principals, both close to my age, the camp ownership was transferred to surviving children.

Even with many fond memories of the Ole Swell Fella's Camp, it just wasn't the same. I never went back. I wish them well.

Frank – Flowers

I'm not sure if the Aluminum Company of America had its original office in New Kensington, PA, or not, but I do know there was a major office of theirs here while I was growing up, and during the Great Depression.

One of my clients, Frank K., grew up in that area, and he has told me of an ongoing practice he was a part of.

Alcoa, a prosperous company, had a gardener who maintained beautiful grounds around the office building that covered a greater part of a block, with flowers everywhere, carefully cultivated, and beautiful.

As a kid, Frank would watch the development and progress of the flower beds, and when they were at their peak, he would sneak in, after hours when no one was around, and select the prettiest ones; carefully pluck just a few.

The next day, he would go into the upper-class section of town, knock on a door, and put on his most angelic persuasion to the nice lady who had answered and opened the door, hold up the flower or flowers, and shyly say, while partially covering his face, "Just a dime, lady."

It worked, but he never overdid it. The ladies nor the Alcoa gardener ever caught on.

He died a wealthy man but had not enjoyed any of it.

Tall Tales

When my brother Andy and wife Pat's kids were growing up, they would occasionally stop here at our house, just to visit.

They all being very intelligent and humorous types, it was natural that a good uncle would tell them stories about his illustrious past, of his observations, activities and achievements.

They were not totally gullible but didn't really question some of the purported facts related, at times.

They posed intelligent questions: Was I ever in athletics?

I said, "Yes, in high school I went out for football. Here's what happened." All candidates assembled for tryouts, and I was up first, trying out for the position of punter. I kicked the football straight up, and it went up, out of sight.

It took five full minutes for it to come back down. They all grumbled having to wait so long. The coach said for me to punt it again, so I did. This time, the football just exploded. He grimaced. Next, he said try to kick off. When I did, the ball went through the goal posts at the far end of the field and flew out of sight. No one could find it. I was then disqualified as creating too many delay of game penalties.

I was not interested in the other sports.

I tried farming. I planted a field of corn. It grew so high, the airplanes flying to Pittsburgh complained, because they had to fly around it. I tried gardening. I planted a watermelon seed over there, where the valley is now. It used to be level over there, but my melon grew bigger and bigger.

It drank all the water in the creek and grew bigger, its weight making the valley deeper and wider.

Finally, it stopped growing, so they put in a big pipe from it to the newly built Beaver Run Dam, and filled it up, like you see it now. The animals ate what was left, and I never planted any more watermelons.

They still laugh at my whoppers. There were many more.

Lake Erie Trip

This was it, the big day, Jim, I, and Adam ___ are going fishing for walleye in Lake Erie.

Bright and early, we leave, arriving there well after daybreak, drop the 16-foot boat into the water, and we're off to adventure, fame and misfortune, as it turned out.

It started out as a nice, sunny, cool day, but Adam said it can change very quickly out on the lake, and did it ever.

We, totally inexperienced in the vagaries of the big lakes, did not realize, in the absence of any noticeable wind, the water was actually moving us away from the U.S. shore.

Watching for the other fishermen clustered where walleye is found, we discovered there weren't any, none. Should that have been a warning.

The outlines we were heading for that we thought were fisherman's boats, were actually trees on the shore of Canada, we unknowingly getting closer to the Canadian borderland.

The penalty for fishing in Canadian waters, their half of the lake, is boat confiscation and only God knows what else. At that point, it was determined to turn around and point the bow of the boat toward the U.S.A., out of Canadian danger. That's when several issues came to light.

The skies had darkened ominously, had turned an ugly gray, an uninviting atmosphere, beginning to sprinkle rain, the wind picking up, blowing us back toward Canada--a very unhappy thought.

The temperature dropped into the forties, miserably cold when you are wet.

The waves increased to 5 or 6 feet, dangerous to such a small boat.

Then Adam admitted he had not filled the boat's gas tanks above on half full.

We were at least 25 miles from the U.S. shore, in now extremely hazardous conditions.

And, to top it all off, once we turned around, moving towards home, a huge wave swale swallowed the bow, then popping up when the next wave picked it back up violently, showering Adam, who was driving, with enough force as to induce an asthmatic attack on him severe enough that he shouted, "Charlie, grab the wheel, you have to drive from here," he collapses into his seat.

It flashed into my head, I could be at home, 150 miles from this predicament, safe and sound, minding my own business.

That dreadful feeling of fear, in anticipation of what lies directly ahead, became borderline overwhelming at that moment.

I had never driven any kind of boat, much less when three lives are involved in it, under the suddenly horrendous circumstances I'm facing.

Me now asking God for all the help I can get; I open the throttle of the 125 hp outboard motor wide open, fighting the endless assault by the oncoming 5-to-6-foot waves. The bow constantly dropping into the swales, popping up with the next wave, showering us with a fresh batch of cold water.

The splash water now accumulating in the bottom of the boat, and guess what. The bilge pump never worked, and certainly isn't working now. So here I go, grimly praying that the big outboard motor doesn't run itself out of gas, keeps its forward motion against those frightful waves.

Finally, the U.S. shoreline begins to take shape through the fog and mist, and we all are breathing a bit easier, the waves are a little smaller and less frequent.

I push on, wide-open throttle, every inch now precious, the shore getting closer.

At about 500 feet from shore, I run out of gas, now drifting aimlessly.

A passing boat ignores our cries for help, possibly tow us into shore.

Having just one paddle, and drift, we make it to shore, and fuel. And life.

Squirrel at Alcorn Crossroads

On a trip to visit my sisters in Pittsburgh, all six of us were piled into our 1975 Volkswagen one morning, traveling Rt. 286, a through road, at about normal speed of 40 – 45 mph, just short of its intersection with Rt. 819, it crossing Rt. 286, locally known as the Alcorn Crossing.

As I'm moving along, a squirrel, sitting along the side of the road, suddenly jumped out onto the road, directly into our path.

Not ever wanting to hit anything, especially any living creature, I swerved gently to the left, to avoid hitting it, when it made another jump, again into our path. I swerved left again.

Now I'm slowing down some, approaching the intersection, not knowing which way the squirrel may go, so I swerve back to the right.

Now the squirrel retreats, jumping once again into my path, and I'm hard onto the brakes, slowing even more, almost to a stop, almost into the intersection.

The squirrel jumps completely off the road, as a vehicle, running through the stop sign on Rt. 819, goes roaring through the intersection at very high speed, just missing my now stopped Volkswagen, which most likely would have been in its path if the squirrel wouldn't have been in the picture.

I, we, incredulous, just sit there for a few minutes, thank the guardian angel or angels that, once again, protected us from a horrible oblivion.

Note: That intersection, unprotected with 4-way stops until a recent fatality, has 8 ghosts to its credit. None since the 4-way stops were installed.

Truck Stopped

Cruising my childhood stomping grounds one day in my pickup, I was traveling along a dirt, unimproved back road, slowly, passing by a house with a fence around the yard, an open gate, and two big dogs sitting on the porch, just looking around.

Once past, the two big dogs, alerted, sounded the alarm, charging out of the gate, make a hard right, and then in hot pursuit of the would-be intruder commencing.

I, watching them in my rear-view mirror, continuing down the road at slightly varying speeds, a little faster, slow down, a little faster, slow down, inducing the dogs to greater effort, letting them believe they were driving the enemy away.

At about a hundred yards or so, they were both hard on my tail, when I slammed on the brakes, coming to a complete stop. Watching, I saw both dogs come to a screeching halt, their demeanor instantly changing from aggressive pursuit to puzzled astonishment.

The truck had stopped!

I'm watching in the mirror, their look now is confusion, what now, it's not running away anymore. And do you see how big it is, man it's really big.

Maybe we better think about this, oh, oh, look!

I put the truck into reverse and began backing up, ever so slowly.

They wistfully look back towards the house, where they were peacefully sitting just a few minutes ago, minding their own business, like, none.

Now I start moving backwards a bit faster, directly toward them, and they begin to retreat. I speed up, they speed up, we go faster and faster, I keeping close to them in hot pursuit.

Finally, they make it to the gate, turn in and race onto the porch, I now stopped, watching. They, safe now, one looks my way, but not approaching, barks just once, then turns away.

Is there a life lesson to be learned here?

Lobo – Receptionist

I had an original-style transit for years, and it finally needed some upgrading.

I took it to A.B. Smith in Monroeville and left it, being told to return in a week to pick it up.

So, a week later, I return there, and park my pickup right in front of the building, a very short distance from the receptionist just inside, a nice, friendly young lady, about 40 or so.

My 135 lb. German shepherd, Lobo, was with me, of course, and it being a hot summer day, his window was clear down, his huge head, tongue hanging out, big teeth completely filling the window, was watching me as I opened the door, approaching her desk.

Now close to her I said, with a very stern face, "Is my transit ready to go?

Do you know what happens to you if it isn't?"

She said, "What?"

I, pointing to Lobo, as described, said, "You get to deal with him. I turn him loose."

She remained silent, staring intently at him for a minute, then looked up at me and said, "Awww, he's nothing but a creampuff. I know because I had one just like him for 14 years."

He would have loved her.

70 Chevelle SS-Super Sport

This story will resonate more with knowledgeable car nuts, but stay with me, please.

Around 1980 or so, youngest son, Jim, talked me into buying a 70 Chevelle, the SS, Super Sport.

It is needing upgraded, or so we thought. He, a pretty competent mechanic, went to work. I have no mechanical abilities to speak of personally, and don't claim to have any. I'm a good observer, then I act like I know what I'm talking about.

It having an original big block, a 454 engine, he removed the entire drivetrain, then starting with the 454, he drilled it, honed it, shaved it, put in oversized pistons and so on, solid lifters, upgraded the ignition, and installed an 800 Holly carburetor.

Then a three speed click shift transmission, 411 rears, chambered pipes, aluminized headers, big tires all the way around, high dollar fire engine red paint job, chromed everything that could be chromed, braided hoses, and tinted windows.

It was outrageously beautiful. I egotistically loved the thumbs up I would get in town, when passing other car nuts.

It was a beast! As best we could tell, it had well over 500 hp.

Being a reasonably good driver, I was already approaching a million miles under my butt, in every type of conditions. I was king of the local hill for several years, quietly, virtually unrecognized, unnoticed, except in the car nut society.

There were negatives inherent with this level of a streetcar. Because of its features, I couldn't park it anywhere in town for fear of theft, not only the car itself, but parts.

Insurance for a muscle car was $1,000 extra per year.

It had to be garaged, pushing my pickup outside, where the snow and ice met me on winter mornings.

It required the high dollar gasoline, due to the high compression engine.

In summer heat, I roasted, no AC, and a lot of heat from the big engine, the pipes, and so on.

And of course, being a favorite target for police, the tinted windows, speed watch, and the, to us, beautiful sound of the chambered pipe exhaust.

I, we, slowly lost not only interest, but time to play with it, due to an ever increasing workload demanding so much time.

Sadly, I finally sold it to another car nut, but not without some regret.

Slickville House – Cindy

In the early 80s, my daughter, Cindy, was looking for a permanent home.

A big, beautiful house became available in Slickville, which is located reasonably close to our surface mining area of operations, our primary business.

We visited the house, finding it well-maintained, and appeared to be suitable for a permanent home, with ample local infrastructure, along with 18 acres of land that came with it.

After a somewhat abbreviated inspection, all appeared well, so I bought it. After the final settlement, in preparation for occupancy, we visited once again.

This time, we began a much more careful inspection, beginning with the outer perimeter, where we soon discovered the entire easterly end of the house had been extended some 12 to 14 feet to provide space for a modern bathroom and more bedroom space on the second floor and more living space on the first floor.

Somewhat disturbing, we also discovered a pronounced separation, a vertical crack in the siding, signifying a pulling away of the addition from the house had, or was, occurring.

In all of my pre-purchase discussions with the previous owner, the current seller, a single woman and former classmate in high school, living in a distant city, there was no mention of the addition that we found, or that there was any knowledge that a movement, or breakaway had begun. Now, being the proud owner of the property, it was my baby.

Now a bit disillusioned, we headed for the front door, preparing to enter the house.

Cindy was first in the door, but as she entered through the front door she stopped, pausing for a few moments, then stated that she had just felt a pronounced chill, like as if a wet towel or blanket had wrapped itself around her momentarily.

Contrary to other previous visits, the atmosphere inside seemed to be somewhat less inviting, much darker. However, there being huge rooms with very high ceilings, and small windows, we dismissed it. We agreed that furniture would alleviate all that darkness.

Neither I, nor her husband, Calvin, had felt anything out of the ordinary and passed it off as to her being pregnant and due soon, possibly giving her a higher level of sensitivity to a new or different building's interior environment.

However, in continuing our more detailed inspection, in the basement we discovered a fresh crack in a major supporting beam and paint chips on the floor along the one side. Continuing on to the second-floor bedrooms, we noticed an area of floor in the one bedroom that was spongy to some extent but dismissed it as simple aging, the house being at least 100 years old.

We also discovered some of the electrical outlets didn't work. As we exited from the bedroom with the spongy floors, we all heard a soft creak from one wall, but dismissed it as just a harmless noise.

Even though our re-inspection dampened our pre-purchase enthusiasm, she moved in anyhow.

Were these discoveries subtle warnings, an ominous premonition of potential danger?

Having moved in, some upgrades done, life moved along. A baby girl was soon born, two stray dogs had joined the family, and things were typically normal, for the most part, but:

Within the several years she lived in the Slickville house, prior to moving to Punxsutawney, PA, a number of unusual events occurred, once again, were they possible warnings of impending disaster, in urging them, indirectly, to leave the house?

Their infant daughter Tanya, at eight or nine months old, had just reached the ability to crawl. One evening, after dinner, Cindy was cleaning up, Calvin was elsewhere, having failed to follow through with his assigned duty to watch the baby.

Upon finishing the cleanup, Cindy looked for the baby, who was nowhere in sight. Calvin had fallen asleep, and also did not know where she was.

A frantic search of the first floor found no baby. Turning on the light in the stairway to the second floor, there she was, perched clear at the top, having somehow, in total darkness crawled up at least 18 steps, up a very long stairway. Cindy raced to the top, reaching Tanya before she could tumble back down the steps.

A second incident involving the baby was somewhat similar in setting, except when she was found, she was found in her stroller at the top of the long flight of stairs leading to the basement. Someone had left the door to the basement unlocked, and apparently a draft, or something, had opened it, exposing the stairway.

The two dogs that they had were routinely left inside the house while they were both away at work, with never an issue. One day, upon returning home, they found that for some reason, the dogs had broken through a barrier erected to keep them in the living room, then smashed a window out of the French doors between the living room and the kitchen, and in apparent overwhelming fear, had chewed off a large section of the door jamb on the front door trying desperately to get out.

The dogs were both given to friendly next-door neighbors, immediately afterward.

One day Cindy, having washed a load of clothes, was preparing to transfer the load into the dryer. Leaning against the washer with one hand, and reaching to open the dryer, a severe shock pulsed through her when she touched the dryer door. She was sick for days afterward.

An experienced electrician was called and came the next day. What he found was unbelievable.

The washer and dryer were both typically wired, and used for some time, at 110V, plugged into separate receptacles, on separate circuits.

He checked everything out, and replaced the receptacle that appeared to have had faulty wiring.

He then proceeded to check out his work and when he plugged in the dryer, all hell broke loose. Flames shot out of both receptacles, blowing both fuses, being on separate circuits.

Somehow 220V had found its way into one of the circuits without blowing any fuses.

Could this have caused a fire? Was this a warning?

He then rewired the entire washer and dryer system, bypassing the existing one completely.

The 18-acre lot the house was on was between the village of Slickville and the smaller village named wind town. Slickville had a store and post office, so people would often shortcut through the house lot when walking from one town to the other, which was a permissible long-standing practice. It was a well-worn path that just happened to be located alongside Cindy's garden. Cindy and Calvin had activated the original garden and it was growing normally, but with an issue created by a groundhog who thought they had done all this planting for him. Since he had nothing better to do, he ate more than his rightful share of the vegetables, so it was decided to eliminate the problem, which was him, since all the other deterrents tried did not discourage him at all.

One day, a young man, 13 or 14, who used the shortcut often, always carrying a boom box on his shoulder, was traveling along the path, nearing the garden. About the same time, Cindy spotted the groundhog in the garden, shouted to Calvin who grabbed a rifle, lowered a window, and shot at the groundhog.

The bullet kicked up the dirt directly in front of the young man, and he thinking it was him being shot at, terrified, dropping the boom box, and sprinted away as fast as he could.

Knowing the boy's family, Cindy quickly called them and explained what and how that had, in fact, transpired. There was no issue, all was forgiven, but the boy never took the shortcut again but went the long way around.

A new job location was in the process of being made, so it was the autumn of 1984 that Cindy moved out of the Slickville house, and experiencing truly unbridled relief in leaving, and as she so aptly expressed it: "I leave with sadness and joy, relief, and regret. If all the negative experiences were truly warnings of some future disaster, I regret not having accurately interpreted them, possibly leaving some future would with a looming danger at the house. Relief that the dark clouds gathered there are being left behind me forever. The joy is that the sun is rising for me, beginning a new, bright day for me and my daughter, Tanya. May God bless the Slickville house forever."

Dear listener: read on, or listen to the follow-up to this story in Chimney – Slickville House.

Cindy has always been considerably intuitive, and would, without rhyme or reason, experience vivid dreams of burning houses, but never even remotely site specific, and we have wondered if these recurring dreams were part of the entire scene: someone, something trying to discourage us from getting involved, The dreams ended permanently when her departure from the Slickville house occurred.

Addendum: Cindy moved to Punxsutawney, PA, and rented an apartment there. The day of the approval of the rental agreement with her new landlord, there was a beautiful, white sheepdog puppy running around under foot.

The meeting over, the landlord said, "Well, I am going to go and get rid of this dog."

Cindy immediately shot back, "Whoa, you're going to do what?"

He said, "I am gonna kill him, I don't want him."

She said, "No, you won't, I'll take him."

He said, "He's yours."

She named him Bernie. They had a wonderful 15 years together until he peacefully passed.

Is there something eerie in all of this, in the whole Slickville story?

We'll never know.

Chimney – Slickville House

In the early 80s, I bought a large frame house in Slickville intended originally for a dwelling for my daughter, Cindy. The house became vacant and unoccupied when she moved out, following her and her husband's work, leaving working heating systems, but needing a new chimney.

Previous owners had installed a typical oil burning furnace years prior to my purchase of the property including a 300-gallon oil tank that was placed in the basement, nearby.

I, being in the coal business, installed a new coal burning furnace, and left the oil burner intact as a backup, since it had its own exhaust system.

The coal furnace needed more exhausting capacity than the original chimney had, so I, being an experienced chimney builder, decided to build a new one, with adequate capacity for the new coal furnace.

It was an unusually warm end of December in 1984, so weather being favorable, I went to work building, day and night. Things went well, and I, knowing time was of the essence in late December, due to winter's probable return, proceeded as fast as possible, working into the night routinely and was not as diligent as is usually done for an outside client in maintaining good, straight vertical rise, and I discovered I already had a few prominent curves in its ascent at about 20 feet of height. Strapped to the wall, it didn't really matter to me since I owned the house.

Then, weather forecasters predicted a rapid change was forthcoming soon, and so, on New Year's Eve, 1984, a beautiful, warm 70 degree day, I vowed to finish the job, irregardless. I ate lunch and dinner at the chimney and kept on going. I bless my sons to this day, for having stayed, helping with carrying brick and mortar cement up that long, dangerous ladder, much of it in the dark.

I worked feverishly until well after midnight under light from the miner's lights I had bought years ago, for this type of purpose, and we finished the job.

The next day, winter roared back with a vengeance, bringing heavy snow and bitterly cold temperatures. I connected the coal furnace to the chimney, and all was well.

As it stood, I had committed to a rental and a move-in by month's end to a young couple born and raised in Slickville, wanting to return to their original home area. I called and told them the house was ready whenever they chose to move in, which they began their move on January 24, 1985.

In advance of their move, I filled the 300-gallon oil tank, turned on the original oil burner, and also started a fire in the new coal burning furnace to expedite the warming of the house, there being two small children involved.

It was January 25, and they had unloaded their first load, and had gone for a second, so they were absent from the house.

It was 18° below zero, I was watching the Super Bowl when I got the call; your house is on fire, big time, firemen are on the way. A truly awful call to get, any time.

I went there, sat in my truck watching the valiant firemen futilely battling against the conflagration, while the dauntless Red Cross and Salvation Army angels served hot food and drinks. I, helpless to do or be of any help, just sat there.

The actual gist of this lengthy story is, after all the smoke was gone, the only thing left standing was the 40-foot-high chimney I had so diligently built.

The actual appearance now was similar to a moving boa constrictor in motion, ever snaking up and up. I had sold the now empty land around it and the chimney stood tall, all alone, reaching skyward, a testament to the builder, resisting winter's wind, and summer's heat, year in and year out.

In the interest of public safety, the local fire department finally blew it down with a powerful blast from a fire hose.

To this day, I have no plausible explanation as to the true cause of the fire, whether it was the old building settling due the extreme cold, or it was the old oil burner malfunctioning, or somehow a new coal furnace glitch or some weird electrical quirk. Was it providential that no one was there, in view of all of what may be viewed as warnings?

We'll never know, but I thank God no one was hurt throughout the entire experience.

My Keratotomy

I believe it was late 1984, while reading the Reader's Digest one day, I came upon an article about an accidental severing of the cornea of an individual's eye, in Russia, and how in the healing process it was discovered that the cutting actually improved the victim's vision to some extent.

Thus, the study of the event precipitated a whole new medical procedure, named a radial keratotomy.

The process, forerunner to modern methodology using laser, was in a highly skilled surgeon, with an extremely sharp razor knife, making a series of cuts into the cornea, thereby correcting myopia, nearsightedness, which was my condition, and others to a variable degree.

I had heard of a seminar regarding this process being held in Pittsburgh, so, I attended it, asking many questions.

Convinced it was potentially beneficial, the risk being minimal, I signed up for it, then and there, being scheduled for the surgery a short time later.

The surgery done, a patch put over the eye, and a good night's sleep in the hospital came next.

Upon awakening, my wonderful wife, Dolly, a long-time registered nurse, having spent the night watching me, slowly removed the patch, and shared with me the revelation, wonder of wonders, my 20-400, nearly blind eye, was seeing at a near perfect 20-20, seeing sights I had never been able to see. Looking out of my hospital room's window, I could see street signs, bus destinations, people, in detail, and so on and on. It was truly wonderful.

I was completely overjoyed.

37 years later, I still maintain a near perfect 20-20 in that eye.

Having a healthy left 20-100 eye, aging, I have never seriously considered having it done, it always having been reliably proficient, and still is.

You know, if it ain't broke, don't fix it.

Wood Shop

It was in the spring of 1985, I was surveying a property with a building on it, as was common. In that building was a one-man business, a laminated cabinet fixtures supplier to one major distributor.

Conversing with him, I learned there was a huge potential in the business, but he, undercapitalized, was unable to produce the volume of the product necessary to achieve any real success.

Ever entrepreneurial me was impressed. Is this my long-lost pathway to success, fame, and fortune?

I had a building with plenty of space, adequate infrastructure, close proximity, and a credit strength strong enough to get me into trouble.

I told him we would be partners in a revival of his struggling start-up, and with his knowledge, and my support, we'd soon be up and running.

I was not yet aware he was a semi-reformed alcoholic, and an incompetent.

He had limited equipment: a saw, some hand tools, spraying guns.

There was minimal material inventory; he was flat broke. I said he should itemize everything, I would reimburse his original cost. It bordered on amusing, but it was simply pathetic. He even emptied his trash barrel, charged me for every piece of scrap, useable or not; most of it I immediately threw into the dumpster.

I bought everything that could possibly be used in the business, the best, all new.

At a very high price.

I will skip over the ensuing unhappy, unprofitable two years of operation, except for several factors and events.

Right off, Jack's wife openly disliked me, for her own reasons. Even though I saved them from a certain bankruptcy, loss of house and home, she had a visible disdain for me.

Next, Jack didn't like dogs, and at the time, my big German shepherd, Lobo was with me constantly. Compounding that, Lobo liked to lay on the chair Jack had for visitors. Well, Lobo really didn't care that he was unpopular.

Employees were a daily problem, like everywhere. Someone's winter coat was stolen, along with the winter shoes.

I announced I would shut the business down if they didn't reappear soon, very soon.

Magically, the next day, they were back.

Working with highly flammable glue and primer, fires were a constant threat.

One day, Jack called me in, proudly announcing he had hit a home run.

Dealing with a major manufacturer of office equipment in Pittsburgh, he had signed a contract for product delivered to them, monthly, in the amount of about $35,000.

Having been at, or near, a loss, most of the time up to then, I was suspect of Jack's mathematical abilities, and on an order of this magnitude, I felt I better double check his numbers.

At my office, I ran the costs, everything involved. Since I already had Jack's bid in hand, I could compare my cost figures to his bid to the manufacturer.

I was absolutely astounded.

My out-of-pocket cost, just for materials, was almost $28 per part, exclusive of labor, delivery, or profit.

His final price bid was exactly half of the real price it should have been.

So, the next day, I went in early, to wait for Jack's arrival; surprisingly, he was already there, running numbers.

No usual niceties were exchanged, and I said, "Jack, where did you get your numbers? Here are mine", placing the sheet before him. He took one look, threw the pencil he had been twirling up into the air, jumped out of his chair, never said a word, and went out the door.

I have not seen or spoken to him since.

Now, I find myself with an ongoing struggling business not exactly in my trained background, almost a half million dollars in debt, and my next serious challenge.

The first thing I did was calmed everyone down, said, "I will not let the ship sink."

Never fear, for Charlie's here.

Then, I called every creditor, explained I was now in charge, and they would be paid in full, in time, as we recover.

All but one agreed to cooperate with me, and that one came to regret their refusal, later.

The simple fact was that I was not broke. I had other substantial income.

I was playing opossum.

Concentrating my attention and efforts to this business, I immediately instituted cost cutting and other efficiencies into the mix, and within one year, had everyone paid up, and a profitable business running, but I actually hated it.

I then turned it over to my knowledgeable, competent sister-in-law, Pat, who ran it well over the next five years, at a nice profit.

As a humanitarian gesture, at the request of a friend, I hired a mentally challenged young man.

On his first day, I instructed him, and demonstrated how he should carry out the scrap laminate out into the dumpster, among other janitorial duties.

Checking on him a half hour later, I discovered him crushing the tenth full sheet of new laminate into the dumpster, not the scraps I had pointed out. At $200 a sheet, do the math. Sorry, I had to end his short-lived career at Wood Products, Incorporated.

Then the certified letter came. Our principal buyer had filed for Chapter 11 bankruptcy, and almost a $60,000 loss for me.

They went out of business a short time later.

So did we.

1985 Dodge Truck

I had decided I needed a single axle, four-wheel drive, one ton dump truck to better serve my house coal customers back in 1985.

So, my super salesman son, without my knowledge or consent, made a deal on one for me, a 1985 Dodge. Having been a staunch Chevy guy for forty years, the Dodge was not my preference, but the deal was already done.

My ominous, inner forebodings didn't take long to show up. Working at a job 65 miles distant, I took it on its maiden voyage, hopeful that all would go well.

It didn't. It had a dual battery system, and as I got to Punxsutawney, at the job site, one of the two batteries came loose and fell down into the engine compartment, breaking it, leaking. I gathered up the remains, threw them into a dumpster that happened to be nearby.

Proceeding on through town, just as we were crossing a railroad track at the edge of town, we lost the steering mechanism. The bolts that held the gear box to the frame had all fallen out, rendering the truck helpless.

We babied it to a large parking lot close by, bought some bolts, and were on our way again, four hours later.

That was just the start. Still new, going down the road, it would just quit. Engine dead. I learned several electrical components would simply quit working, no known reason.

It loved flat tires, always the inside dual, always with a load on. I carried two, sometimes three, spare tires, and a heavy-duty jack. If it wasn't one thing, it was another. I reached the point I would not go farther than a few miles from home with it, even with all the spare parts I was carrying.

Then, after the warranty expired, it decided it liked new engines.

They would either scatter or blow big smoke.

Our ambulance crew borrowed it, and parking it on the side of a hill, the parking brake broke its locking pin, letting the truck roll backwards till it hit a bank and upset.

Then, another engine, this time a used one. Big mistake. Disgusted, I gave the truck to my son, who needed one in his construction business.

He experienced the same thing, breakdowns anywhere, anytime, another engine, maybe two.

He finally sold it to a local body shop operator, a good casual guy, a good mechanic, good body work. He's had it now for at least twenty years, same engine, drive train, body, all is well.

He must have the magic touch to be able to keep the Dodge demon at bay.

I should have touched it with a sledgehammer on day one.

It's no wonder they changed the name. To GOAT.

Best Shot at Camp

I and our family were longtime friends with a great family who had a hunting camp near the border of Pennsylvania, which we would occasionally go to for a weekend, stay for some trout fishing, and maybe some turkey hunting, every year.

We loved the mountainous terrain, the clean streams, the isolation, and the people.

The camp house was reasonably modern, running water, electricity, and heat from a huge potbellied wood burning stove, peaceful, quiet, nice.

You really don't need much more, or do you?

There was an outhouse, located for convenience at the time of installation.

It sat right along the main pathway from the parking area to the camp house. Located on a fairly level spot, good grass all around, not too far or too close to the camp house, parking nearby.

It was a natural area for group gatherings to converse, debate, even argue in friendly fashion.

As it happened, a group was converging for the annual deer hunt, standing around the outhouse, talking, and of course, drinking beer.

As they were conversing, they saw that the guy who was the camp's joker, Blake, the guy who created fun at anyone's expense, half-drunk already, went into the outhouse for rather urgent business, by the sounds emanating from within and the groaning.

Always looking for entertainment, a couple of guys set the stage. The joker's already in the outhouse, indisposed, not at his best.

Two guys, already half drunk, get into a heated argument over who is the best shot with a high-powered rifle.

One loudly accuses the other, you can't actually hit a deer at 50 feet, in fact, you can't even hit that shithouse from here, at 20 feet.

The accused hunter grabs his rifle, pretends to load it, typical sounds of a bolt action, clickity, clickity, clack, and shouts, "Oh yeah, well, watch and see if I can hit it."

Mr. joker, in the outhouse, hearing everything that's been said, panics in absolute fear of his imminent demise by rifle bullet, bursts out of the door, pants pulled barely halfway up, choking, gagging, unable to speak, able only to make weird noises, one hand holding onto his pants, the other indicating stop, stop, don't shoot, staggering toward them.

It took hours for the laughter to die down. Years later, it still hasn't, has it, Blake?

1967 VW – Lonnie, Jr.

One of a former partners' sons, Lonnie, came to me one day with a sad story of how his vehicle had died, and having finally landed a job as an insurance salesman, he was without wheels, understandably necessary in the new job.

Always the compassionate fool, I keep mentioning, I said, "Well, I have just bought a new pickup, so I could loan you my 1967 Volkswagen until you're able to either buy it, or something else."

He said great, he was certain that within a few weeks, or a month, he would be in good shape, and he'd be in touch.

That was in or around mid-1986.

I haven't heard from him or seen my Volkswagen since.

I should give up hope, then, shouldn't I?

Bought the Garage

It was early 1983, things were going fairly well, the entrepreneurial spirit and tendencies are beginning to awaken, starting to look around for new worlds to conquer, caution being relegated to a back room, more and more out of the picture.

Add a little financial strength, and you have a dangerous combination.

What is the key word here? Future. Yes, it's the future.

Someday, the mining will end, either by total exhaustion of available mineable coal, or by as yet unknown, unexpected, unbridled environmental, economic, or political forces.

And, sadly, that time has come, and remains, only getting worse by the day. So, to prepare for a reasonably secure future not only for myself, but the young people now in our fold, something must be done.

It is. I buy an old, large building in Saltsburg, in filling the primary requisites for future expansion, jobs for any number of people, proximity, infrastructure, and space. It being about a hundred years old, it needed considerable repair and upgrading of structural components, which was soon completed, and continues to stand the test of time.

This was the location of an original Ford Motor Company dealership for decades, ending upon the passing of the ownership. At the time I bought it, it was housing a colorful business. It's what is known in some circles as a chop shop.

For those who are unaware, it was a shop that they brought stolen vehicles into, cut out certain parts, exchanged them for other stolen parts, creating a vehicle difficult to legally identify.

Or it was common for a wrecked or damaged vehicle to receive parts from a stolen vehicle, painted, and sold to unsuspecting buyers. And the stolen vehicle disappears from the face of the earth.

That, of course, ended when I bought the building, and more mundane styles of businesses were then considered for use of the space.

The first was a mechanic shop, gradually switching over to a mostly transmission repair service, still active now, but moved across the river.

Then, the Wood Products Company, making laminated parts for office furniture operated, with up to seventeen employees.

Various truck related businesses were headquartered there, along with my survey and mining engineering office, along with several other small business ventures.

Finally, some of the businesses were either abandoned, or failed.

The survey and engineering moved across the river, as did the transmission repair into a new facility, and in 1989, the Lifestat Ambulance Service was brought into the entire top floor, where it is to this day.

I sold the building to son John, who operates the ambulance service out of there.

Summing up the past 39 years, I gave it legitimate life in the creation and centering of many businesses along with all the employment within them, and it continues on.

For how much longer, with all the negatives swirling around the emergency medical services arena?

Only God knows.

Rebuilt Transmission

Son, Jim, rebuilt a transmission for a then close friend, in my garage, spent four weeks and considerable cost that I paid, for parts, being a nice guy.

The big day comes, the transmission is installed, his friend is mobile again.

That same night, John F., his good friend, goes out, gets drunk, tries to come to Jim's house, shortcutting through a field, since there were police on the lookout for drunk drivers, including him.

As you might expect, he got stuck in the mud, flogged the engine trying to get free until he blew up the freshly rebuilt transmission, utterly destroying it.

Then the cops came and gave him a free ride to the police station.

He used his one call to call Jim, informing him of what had happened to the transmission, and that he needed bail money to get him out of jail.

Jim said, "I hope you rot in there", and hung up.

So much for the great friendship.

We've never seen him since.

Jim, Steve – Old Man's Vehicles

Over the years, I have given away at least eight drivable vehicles, and one that was deemed not drivable but is still being driven around.

Three of those have unhappy endings, written about elsewhere, three are noteworthy in the near total absence of any appreciation of my gift, and the final two are featured in this telling, last.

The drivable undrivable was, is, my 1999 Chevy pickup. When plates, wire, and bolts would no longer keep the frame in one piece, I had a body expert evaluate it for possible professional repair.

One quick look, and he declared, "Tow it home, or to a junk yard. Don't drive it." He guaranteed that if I continued to drive it, not if, but when, I would find myself in the cab with the whole back end somewhere behind me, laying down on the road.

Talking to our local junkyard shortly after, I was offered $150 for it, so I signed the title over to him. Somehow, he patched it, and it's still going up and down the road, but carefully.

Now we're down to the last two.

This is where the word ungrateful comes into full display.

I decided with my kids, getting too much free stuff was unhealthy training, so rather than give them each a vehicle, I would sell them each one.

I don't remember the selling price of either one, but Steve got my 1975 Jeep Wagoneer, with only 195,000 miles on it. Jim got my 1978 Chevy Blazer with only 210,000 miles--easy, old man driven miles on it. Both in tip top condition, ready to run.

Whatever the price was, I assured them it was a bargain. Right away, the squawking began.

Hey, this doesn't work, that doesn't work, it won't start, it won't run, these tires are worn out, blah, blah, blah, ad infinitum, ad nauseam.

"Did you not ever hear of caveat emptor, let the buyer beware? Everyone knows that when you buy a used vehicle, there will always be little things needing fixed."

"Yeah", they said, "but needing a complete rebuild is just a little above that."

I will spare you of the hundreds of additional complaints that I still hear about.

I tell them, "You just don't appreciate the education you got, not only financial, but mechanical, and psychological. How much you improved your auto repair skills, the knowledge that has remained through the years, now visible in your present repair business and prior mining involvement."

One example of their training was when they bought an old Chevy Nova and went over it, fixing whatever needed fixed, then taking it for a ride for a test drive.

Going down a fairly steep grade at 40 or 50 miles an hour, they watched a fully inflated tire go rolling past them, the Nova then sagging down accordingly, then sliding to a stop.

What they learned was that lug nuts should be tightened before going for a drive.

All is well now, though I believe they have realized the school of hard knocks is sometimes the one that teaches the most, the quickest.

However, they still tell anyone who will listen: "Never, ever, buy any vehicle from the old man."

See, they learned something.

New York - Cops

My son, John, was taking a load of antifreeze into some suburb or other in New York City, getting there just after dark.

Typical city, traffic not moving, in this case because of an accident up ahead. Another tractor trailer just ahead of him was also stopped, unable to move.

As he sat and watched, a pickup backed out of an alley, onto the sidewalk then up the sidewalk to the truck just ahead of John.

As he watched, 5 or 6 guys went up to that truck, pry bars and bolt cutters in hand, broke open the trailer doors, and started handing out, in fire brigade style, boxes of microwaves, VCRs, whatever, as fast as you could imagine, loading the pickup truck full.

As it all happened so fast, the driver wasn't aware of it immediately, getting out while it was in progress. John couldn't hear any exchange, being too far away, and noisy idling of engines, but, after an apparent exchange with one of the thieves, the driver quickly got back into his truck.

With the pickup fully loaded, it retraced its path and disappeared. The accident was finally cleared, a friendly cop advising John to never stop, run the light if you must, in areas such as that.

He said they're always waiting, ready.

I never dispatched another load to New York City again.

IRS

When you are in business, you should expect to be audited. Being in multiple businesses, I was audited a number of times.

The first thing you better realize, is that the auditors you are facing are all intelligent, street smart, they know what they're about, and you're already looking at strike three, if you've overplayed your hand, somewhere along the way.

Having an experienced CPA prepare your return is a good idea, but they will only use the information you give them, so it's still up to you. They will only take your return to the legal limit, since they study the law, and you should, but don't.

One audit was already under way when my CPA arrived to sit in, answer questions.

The agent took one look at him, bluntly said, "What are you here for? We don't need you. You should leave." And he did.

Two days later, I owed the IRS $16. I said, "Now what?" He shrugged, said, "Forget it." So, I did.

Several years later, he came here again. He said, "We met before, didn't we?" I agreed. One day later he was done. Clean bill, no problems.

Another time, a young lady. It took her less than two hours, and she said, "What's this about?", that being a shortfall in the income I had reported, when I explained I had picked up a sizeable check at a client's office for a months' worth of coal purchased, then proceeded directly to my bank for deposit.

Being involved in multiple businesses, all high stress, high activity, the recording of the then deposited check was simply overlooked, lost in the shuffle. She thought for a minute, then said, "Yes, that sounds plausible."

I paid the tax due; she waived the penalty.

Another time, a phone call indicating a visit on the next morning, I was waiting at my fixture manufacturing facility.

The auditor arrived, I and my beautiful German shepherd met him.

As it was, he had a special liking for German shepherds. He was former military K9 unit.

As we entered the office, he noticed a big picture of the American flag in the front window, with the inscription "We Love Our Veterans" across the picture of a military person within it.

He paused, then asked, "Who put that in there?" I said, "I did", and we moved on. He asked, "Were you in the military?" I said, "Yes, Korea, 14 months."

We went through the building, he is making the expected comments and asking typical questions, and then we went to my office, a separate section of my house for continuation.

"How much depreciation are you taking for this office?" he asked.

I told him $13,500, and he just nodded.

He was quite a character, smart as smart is, way beyond me, asking tough questions.

He worked for four days at a desk I provided for him. I sat nearby, answering more questions, he muttering "yeah, yeah" to himself.

Or, he'd say, to himself, "Just a big penalty, community service only."

He'd say mutedly, "I see two years, no, maybe three, not two", inferring that would be jail time for me, never smiling.

He'd ask if I had a can of Pepsi, insist I take the half dollar for it. We watched my wife leave for work as an RN, stating his admiration for the profession.

I admit, on the morning of the fourth day, when he arrived, I actually said to him, "Why do I look forward to meeting the man, but not the event?" He just smiled.

The fourth day was wind down day. He finished up the paper shuffling and we sat down for a talk in the office.

He opened a folder of his conclusions, and giving me a direct, firm stare, said, "Charlie, tell me you are forever through with the trucking business; never do it again."

I swore it was gone forever. I had run that business for several years in a conflicting legal manner, using one set of standards and methods, having been restricted by recent changes in the tax law. And he knew it.

He slammed the folder shut, and said, "Good, I don't want to destroy you."

Then he said, "You're all about family, aren't you?"

The audit completed, he said, "Let's go for a walk, German shepherd, too."

Passing by my machine shed, he asked if that was where I'm hiding the Mercedes. I said, "Yes, do you want to see it?" He said no and we kept walking, it was such a nice day.

I did not get off easy, though. He called me a few days later and said, "Charlie, can you handle an assessment of ____?"

I said, "Yes, it was really nice knowing you."

That was a long time ago, and when I think of him, I always say, "God bless you, you're a good man."

I never saw him again.

Joan Letter - Iselin Church

Today, I'm narrating a copy of a letter I wrote to my friend Joan in California.

Dear Joan,

In reviewing my last letter to you, I am somewhat shocked it's been over two months since I wrote, even though nothing of any substance has transpired, things here have been somewhat chaotic, as per current octogenarian requisites.

What an unusual winter, ongoing. The grass is still bright green, groups of robins are still passing through, no wild geese are flying south, and no snow to speak of, temperatures in the 40s and even higher.

I am very uplifted by your expression of our friendship. I like it. It's natural and honest. Also, it provides a link to a shared past. This friendship will go on until we move on and possibly resume, up there.

Thanks for the Christmas card, beautiful. Some years ago, not being a party-type any longer, I officially declared myself exempt from all parties: one-year-olds, two-year-olds, three-year-olds, and so on, due to advanced age--70, 75, 80--whatever age is convenient to use as an excuse.

I recently extended this to cards for any occasion, so I have quit sending cards.

One day some years ago, I was surveying part of a 700-acre tract I had purchased from the R & P Coal Company, a tract completely surrounding the town of Iselin, near Indiana, PA.

A car with two older women stopped next to me and the driver said, "Would you survey our property?"

I asked her where it was, and she said, "We don't know, but we were told it was the church", located about 50 feet from where we were standing.

So, I agreed to do the survey since it was obvious they were financially distressed, and had a real problem.

I went to the county courthouse to get a copy of their deed, so I could mark the border.

Lo and behold, they had no deed. They didn't own the church they were attending all these years. No one knew who gave them permission to use the church.

I first called the coal company I had purchased the property from, and struck out there. Then I called the salvage company who had purchased the entire town of Iselin long ago from the coal company when the coal mine was closed.

I knew the vice president in charge of real estate, and told her my story, ending with, "Judy, do you have any idea who owns the church?" She came right back with, "Yes, you do. You got it when you bought the 700 acres around town. The coal company had failed to except and reserve the church from your deed, so you got it by default."

Since I owned everything around the church, I cut out as much land as they would ever need, marked it, mapped it, wrote a deed for them, recorded the deed, and as it happened, the day I was marking the corners, the same two ladies pulled up next to me.

"Well," the driver said, "What did you learn?"

I said, "There's bad news and good news, which do you prefer hearing first?"

She said, "What's the bad news?" I said, "You don't own the church."

After she recovered from the shock, she said, "Well, who does?"

I said, "That's the good news. I do." She said, "How is that good news?"

I said, "I'm going to give it to you for one dollar."

I handed her the recorded deed with all fees and taxes paid, and told her they owed me a dollar.

A week later I got a silver dollar and the thank you in the mail.

My kids will inherit that dollar.

Andy – Turning the Car Around

There is a very long driveway from a public road to the house where Andy lived, early and late in his life. Part way there, it narrows where a culvert takes storm water under the road at this time, but some years ago, before the culvert was installed, a big mud hole would form there, making it a very narrow travel way. If you were off to one side or the other just a little, you very likely would get stuck in the mud. The mud hole was in the narrowest point, one side reaching into the ditch that brings the water to it, the other side a drop-off into the woods, where you didn't dare be.

One night, late, my phone rings, and it's Andy informing me he has a visitor, a young man asking for help, since he's stuck in the mud, at the usual spot.

I, the resident rescue official, of course agreed to come to the site just a short distance from my home.

Arriving there, I find the stuck car with 2 guys and 2 girls in it, all from the Pittsburgh area, having been out just joyriding in the country, seeking adventure, all in fun, and now they're stuck, badly, in the swamp.

It presented a real dilemma. The car was the typical 18 or so feet long, the available space it was occupying was barely 18 feet wide, so in their attempts to turn around, they were hopelessly crosswise in the entire mudhole. Only a big crane could extricate the car from its position, it blocking an active driveway, and you're still 40 miles from home, or wherever you came from.

I don't know what, but something prompted me to tell the driver, get out, I'm getting in.

I got into the driver's seat, started the engine, flogged it hard, set the car into motion frontward, then backward, repeatedly, wildly, dangerously steering vigorously as needed. Within less than two minutes, I was out of the swamp, the car on the solid part of the driveway facing out.

I got out of the car, glanced at the awestruck occupants and told them not to ever come back.

This was actually the second time in my life where I believe I was able to function from within the fifth dimension.

I was totally out, mentally absent while that was happening. There cannot possibly be another explanation.

C65

I don't remember the year, but son John talked me into buying a dump truck, a 1960's something tandem axle, a Chevy C65, a 16-ton legal payload for him to haul our coal.

Amazingly, it developed a transmission growl on the way home, and only required $1,500 to fix it.

Oh yeah, it needed inspected, and among other minor issues, all those cute clearance lights needed replaced, along with all eight rear duals.

I was quickly rebuilding the truck but do not panic, soon the payloads will more than cover these little things. Little things already in the low thousands.

Finally, it was generating some revenue, but barely covering the cost of labor and fuel for a full week.

Friday evening coming back home, he heard a skronk, skronk, coming from the back. Yes, a differential had gotten tired, and needed to be replaced.

That's when I refused, parked the truck, where it sat for several months, before I decided to give it one more try.

In go the torn-up gears in the rear end, and this time, I personally am going to make a run.

I only load it half full, about 8 tons, and head for Apollo, the market.

I make 5 or 6 miles before there is a most awful whack, whack, whacking underneath my feet. I stop, pulling off at a convenient wide spot, and crawl underneath to take a look.

This time, it was the front U joint came apart, disconnecting the drive shaft from the transmission, a most unhappy breakdown, the whipping drive shaft does all kinds of bad things underneath.

We repaired it where it was, and limped it to my shed at the house, once again parking it.

Being in the way, I moved it up into my field.

One day, son Jim was standing outside of the house, looking at the tandem sitting out in the field, said, "What are you gonna do with it?" I said, "I should junk it, but it's still whole, runnable."

Just then, for no explainable reason, it set itself on fire, the flames shooting out from under the hood. It was a gas job. Jim grabbed a fire extinguisher from the house garage, ran to the tandem and blew out the fire.

I said, "That's it." I offered it to a true mechanic who loved GMC products, and he bought it. He ran it for years, no problems, and still is.

Was the difference that I hated it, and he loved it? I'll never know.

Tonto – 65 Cadillac

My son, Jim, needing help at his transmission repair shop, hired this guy who had hitchhiked fifty or sixty miles to apply for the job, hearing there was an opening.

He was quite the character, claiming to be a full-blooded Native American, independent, a competent mechanic. We named him Tonto. I, often in the shop, got to know him reasonably well, a likeable type, then.

Living with an acquaintance, walking to work, I knew he had no vehicle.

I also learned of the level of poverty that had been his lot, bare survival from past prejudices and slights through no fault of his own.

I had bought my wife, Dolly, a new Chevy Tahoe for Christmas the prior year, so I had her 1965 Cadillac sitting in my shed, unused.

Before presenting it to him as a gift, I put a new radiator in it, four new tires, new battery, whatever it needed, to be in top shape.

He seemed to be truly appreciative of the gift, but, oddly, his personality changed.

He moved back to where he had come from, commuting the 50+ miles to his job here. This went on for a week or so, before, surprise, no show, missing for several days. Then, the following week, there was no show at all.

Returning once again, I notice all four of the new tires I had put on the car are gone, bald tires replacing them.

He walked away when I asked him about it. I found out that he had sold them, for drug money. He missed the next day, and the next, then not returning at all.

We heard later; he had gotten into an altercation with police who had stopped him, driving drunk, ran, got into his car and drove wildly away, crashing into a pole, totaling the car, then being arrested and jailed.

I never saw him again. Good riddance.

Payday in New Ken

Mack, a mining client, had made a deal with a certain un-named group, for a sizeable tract of land they wanted, to build a soft ice cream stand, along with a mini golf facility--both high cash generators.

After the survey was done, we went to collect my fee, along with payment for his acreage.

His check, so we thought, would be much, much bigger than mine.

Puzzled, we agreed to follow the instructions as to the location of the office for rendering the payment.

It was: Go to ___ Alley, use the outside stairway down to the basement, ring the bell twice, someone will let you in, possibly him. The IRS has cameras on the front.

Following instructions, we're now in the office, a basement room, with a full-sized pool table in it. No office equipment, no secretary.

The man, both invoices in hand, throws the cover off the pool table, and looking at the invoices says, "Ok, let's get you paid."

On that pool table was stack, after stack, after stack of cash, in small bills, mid bills, and large bills, bundled, filling the table completely.

After payment, he flipped the cover back over the remainder, "to keep the dust off", he said.

We had barely scratched the surface.

Mirrors on Bridge

My 1985 Dodge one ton dump had extra wide mirrors on it, to better see backwards when delivering house coal in tight quarters.

This one night I was on the Avonmore Bridge, crossing the Kiski River, when a big truck, a triaxle, entered the bridge from the other end, and was approaching me at a normal speed, we both slow down, as the bridge is a bit narrow, especially for two trucks passing.

As we met, and passed by, I heard three sharp clicks, very close together, just a split second apart.

What had happened, was that in passing, I had moved precisely to the place where my right-hand mirror just nicked the bridge superstructure, and my left-hand mirror just nicked his left hand mirror, while his right hand mirror just nicked the bridge on that side, as he told me on our CB radios minutes afterward.

This had to be one of those fifth-dimension moments.

What were the odds, no damage done?

This rates a major HUH.

Jon

Mining in the Punxsutawney area in the mid 80's, I coordinated with a really fine young engineer, Jon, from the big coal company buying the produced coal, an ongoing, almost daily contact in one form or another, a great, clean, honest relationship serving both sides well.

We were long gone from that location, back to jobs I had set up here, near home, he losing his good job shortly after his company was taken over by a major producer, ceasing their operations altogether.

Being friendly with his great wife, my daughter was able to stay in touch, knowing how he was handling unemployment.

It could have been better, he a superior person, hard worker, conscientious overall, idleness was not a good fit for him. Having been exclusively in mining, he preferred to stay in mining, but no openings were available in range.

At times, he was somewhat despondent, depressed and unhappy thoughts were sometimes expressed. I had just been informed that my floor foreman in my wood products laminated fixtures shop was leaving soon, so that opening was pending.

Calling Jon, I invited him to come to the shop, and its 17 employees, for a talk.

Explaining the situation, I offered him the job, and started immediately. Jon was very smart, had some experience in carpentry and building, plus managerial background from his past employment, said he'd accept my challenge.

That evening, his wife told my daughter Jon was like a new man, uplifted.

Jon was everything I could have hoped for in a working foreman: personable, productive, and a safe leader. He simply took over, gave me a much needed freedom to attend to my many other ventures, along with the ongoing, established ones.

Then, due to a Chapter II bankruptcy filing by my principal buyer of wood fixtures products, the closing of the shop was imminent, and suddenly, Jon was offered a great job, in, of all possibilities, the coal business.

He took it, and worked there for years, happily, until he retired, to share life with his wonderful wife, LuAnn.

Andy - Pulling Him Up Driveway

It was one of those days, when a sudden warmup in February turns everything into a sheet of ice, that Andy called me early one morning.

Heading out to work, he was unable to navigate up past what we call the breakthrough, being nothing more than where there was an original property line, denoted with a row of trees, with our driveway snaking between two big trees. The road being an absolute sheet of ice.

That's where he was stopped, at the narrowest point.

I, having a good four-wheel drive vehicle, a Jeep Wagoneer, having been through many similar experiences, agreed to come to the rescue.

Confident, in fact, overconfident I could pull him up through the narrow, steep spot he was located in, I jauntily approached his vehicle traveling faster, way faster than I should have.

Realizing I was closing the gap between his front end and mine, I applied the brakes to slow down, and quickly discovered I was not slowing down, but sliding headlong toward his grille at an accelerating pace. He, thinking this was normal, began moving to connect the tow strap.

With disaster looming, the rescuer soon possibly needing to be rescued, something (??) clicked in my skull, prompting me to throw the Jeep's transmission into reverse and stomp on the accelerator.

Almost immediately, I had halted the downhill slide directly at him, into a controlled move backwards, giving me the space to turn completely around, stop, move forward then backward into a position for connecting the tow strap to him, and ever so easily pulling him up out of danger onto a safe public road.

Only I realized what had actually transpired, and I'm not sure I deserve to get the credit for averting a certain family disaster.

Who, then, does?

Next Door Neighbor

In 1958, I purchased the original 14.7 acres tract around our house, from my next-door neighbor, Paul W___, with no apparent controversy at all.

Paul, a good person, leader of a fine family that my, our, family closely interacted with over our entire lifetimes, especially with their 3 boys, my brother, and I.

We exchanged visits constantly, did various things together: target shooting, touch football, swimming, building dams, helped each other farming and so on and on.

In later years, Paul would ride his beautiful white horse to visit us almost daily, always a congenial visit, until one day after visiting, he went home, sat down in his recliner, and died. He was 78.

One day soon afterward, we, my family, were playing ball near the house, when the oldest son, Tom, came driving up to us on his tractor, the now old Farmall BN, highly intoxicated, demanding to know where the one corner of my 14.7-acre tract was.

Since I had surveyed it with my original surveyor partner, Dick W___, I was familiar with the corner location.

Fortunately, the corner marker he was demanding to see was beside a huge white oak stump, clearly visible standing by itself.

Apparently satisfied, he left with no other inquiry or comment. After Paul's passing, Dolly and I would take the kids to visit his wife fairly often, until she put the farm up for sale, and left to go live with her daughter and husband.

On one occasion when we were visiting Annie, she made the statement, that Paul had said long ago he would never sell me another square foot of the farm, in apparent reaction to a statement I had made, that I hoped that someday, I would own the whole farm. It hurt then, and still hurts in view of the decades of apparent friendship.

As time passed, one night, late, I came home from a business trip, and still outside, I heard a vehicle horn honking, about a quarter of a mile away from the house on the township road, just sitting in one spot, honking away.

There are no other houses nearby, so it was a complete mystery to me. I dismissed it, and went inside, and to bed.

Our house is located within 300 feet of the township road at its closest point, so ordinary road traffic sounds are rarely noticeable, especially when inside.

However, after the night I had heard the horn honking at a distance, I began to be awakened by that same honking, coming from a vehicle sitting at the closest point to the house, continuing for 30 to 40 minutes, interminably.

It became more frequent, and I became more concerned. Finally, one night when it was happening again, I loaded up a pistol and shotgun, and went out to the offending vehicle without showing a light, nearly invisible.

I firmly knocked on the driver's window, and discovered it was Tom, the oldest son, apparently very drunk, honking away. It was likely he was the one who had been doing it on his way home from a nightly visit to a local bar.

It is my conviction he, harboring an inordinate resentment of my purchasing the prime part of his original homeland, was punishing me for it. With his window down, he recognized me, and without a word, sped off toward his home, a quarter of a mile away.

I also purchased an additional 12 acres of the farm, after Paul's passing.

I never saw Annie again. She lived into her 90s, a good woman. I bear no ill will to any one of them. Tom died a short time later, at about age 55.

A sad truth emerged afterwards, as told to me by the real estate agent who handled the sale of lots from the farm.

I, a professional land surveyor, surveyed, partitioned, most of the original farm, including the additional 12 acres I bought, but, I learned, not the 10-acre tract adjoining my 12 acres.

After a lifetime, I was being checked by another professional surveyor, to see if I had cheated on my 12 acres, stealing extra land somehow.

He proved I had not cheated anyone.

Friendly Adversary

I met Wayne Z. way back around seventh grade, when we were about thirteen. I always had some sort of a team, baseball, softball, touch football, made up of my nearby acquaintances, and Wayne was always a part of the Kiski Heights sandlot make-up, so occasional school contact, and competitive play in ball, plus he was employed briefly by me. We were fierce competitors in ping pong at the Kiski Sportsmen's Club for years, each claiming to be king, always friendly but highly competitive.

The same went for golf, where even though I was reasonably proficient, he was better, being naturally gifted athletically, both in stature and strength. I rarely beat him.

Time marched on, I pursued my entrepreneurial involvements, and we rarely met or spoke for years, although on those occasions, we would always hurl adversarial comments to each other, each trying to outdo the other.

So, one day recently, after a very long hiatus, I was leaving a little country store with my jug of tea, almost to my Jeep, when just a short distance away, approaching me was Wayne.

We both stopped cold, each assuring correct recognition, then that pregnant pause, waiting for someone to speak.

I did, first, breaking the silence. I blurted out, "I thought you were dead!"

He never responded, just laughed and we went our separate ways, until, if, we ever meet again. I'm 88, he's 89.

Hairvey Company

Working with steel in my businesses, I bought a lot of welding related products: oxygen in big bottles, acetylene and so on.

The primary company I dealt with was named Harvey Company.

There was never a problem with invoicing and payment thereafter, until the invoices to me had a horrendous misspelling of my name, which I realize can be tricky, but not impossible.

So, I sent several notes back with my payment, noting my name was grotesquely misspelled, and that I would appreciate the correct spelling in the future, and plainly printed it out for them.

To no avail, invoices are still badly misspelled, for several months.

So, I thought okay, I'll fight fire with fire. The next payment by me, the check was made out to Hairvey Company, with a note attached that said:

"When you learn to spell my name, I'll learn to spell yours."

So much for the spelling lesson; it never happened again.

In Memory of Andy

My brother, Andy, was a prominent part of my life growing up, and within the span of 7 years between us creating differences in many aspects of life, there were those good times, and of course, the bad times, both of which are displayed in numerous stories involving him.

From a sometimes hostile, tumultuous start, our relationship stabilized completely, notably upon his being drafted, then induction into the Army in 1951, when I assumed total control over his new 51 Chevy.

Many good letters were exchanged, especially in the 24 weeks he was in basic training in Hawaii.

The war in Korea being hot and heavy, there was great concern that his being trained in infantry tactics would result in his being sent there.

Apparently, his listed experience in civilian life as a timekeeper in the construction industry qualified him for an opening in Fort Knox, Kentucky, as a supply sergeant, so he was transferred to a place of fun and frolic, rather than a place of hell and fury, a futile war.

He spent the remainder of the 2-year term there, actually considering re-upping for a second go but returning to Bell Township instead.

He was reinstated into his old job in the construction industry, and gradually progressed to higher, executive level positions, and, tragically, died at his desk, of cardiac failure, leaving a very big hole in our, and his beautiful family's world.

Perhaps we'll meet again, somewhere, somehow, and until then, may he rest in peace.

I include a copy of the original letter I drafted to his employer, a really superior group.

February 14, 1991 A.D.

Dear Friends of Andy Kravetsky:

Sometime in our journey through life, we may pass by a sign that declares: "Through these portals, pass the finest people on earth, our customers".

That sign, revised to read: "Through these portals, pass the finest people on earth", should be permanently placed at every entrance to Swindell Rust International, and its associated business fraternities.

After all these years of dispassionate association with the people Andy worked for and with, and of whom he often spoke, we have finally learned the reason he never uttered a single negative word, of you.

To you, the personnel of the Swindell Group, the manufacturers reps, suppliers and all the thoughtful individuals who so unselfishly provided to us that greatest of all gifts in a difficult time : <u>Your Presence</u>, we say sincerely, thank you.

The impact you have made upon us is hard to explain with words, and I choose to make no further attempt to illuminate it.

We're glad to know you're on this Planet with us, and will remain forever proud to have known you, be it but briefly.

Wishing you all the very best that can be in the future, we close this chapter in life.

With kindest regards,

Charles Kravetsky (Brother)
and
The entire Kravetsky Family.

Tire Sealing
at the Canterbury Mine

During a United Mine Worker's strike at a local coal mine, non-union workers took over production of coal, and non-union truckers were hauling the coal out, going through the union picket line.

The pickets were throwing jack balls, nails, and other puncturing-type objects onto the roadway, interrupting the outflow of coal by puncturing truckers' tires, a real pain to cope with for the truckers.

Being acquainted with management of the mine, I received a request for any help I could give in counteracting this problem. Accordingly, I designed and built a device with which to pneumatically inject a sealing fluid, available on the market, into the tires at minimal cost, and very effective.

The strike, and the need for my system ended several months later, when the coal company closed, and has never reopened, since no activity there allowed the mine to flood completely.

The strike effectively ended 140 high-paying jobs, permanently.

Tony C. - Inspector

My helpers came and went; most were short-term or part-time, as I, working alone, was involved in multiple directions, all the time, unable to devote continuous time to surveying, or anything else.

Tony was unique. Very smart, had three years of pharmacy schooling, unable to continue after a family tragedy, going from a low-level job to lower job, thereafter, winding up laboring in a coal mine.

We met by chance at a time when I needed help for a major job.

Tony drove me nuts. He was too good of an employee.

Because of my expanded and ever-expanding business life, I theoretically started my day at 7:00 am, but Tony would be at my office at 6:00 am, looking for something to do.

I would openly accuse him of having some screws loose, maybe dropped too many times as a child. He always took it in good fun but didn't change.

Once, in an open field, going to make a station, he encountered a swale, a dip deep enough to drop out of sight of me. He became confused, and got lost, following the dip rather than going in a straight line away from me.

Out of sight for too long, I radioed him, "Tony, where are you?"

He answered, admitting he was lost. I said, "Don't move, I'll come and find you."

So, I did; he was a hundred yards off to one side. This happened again, and again. One time in deep woods, going behind some closely bunched trees, he disappeared. Contacted by radio, I had to go hunt him down, that time far downgrade on a steep hill.

One thing after another, and I decided he needed more guidance than I could provide. I suggested, urged him, to apply for a position with the Mine Safety Administration, and he finally did. Having had past mining experience, and a high level of intelligence, he was quickly accepted, and trained by them to be an inspector.

He was a top-notch inspector for years. Sadly, he died young from a genetic disorder. He was a good man and will have my respect forever.

In Memory of Kay

My oldest sister, Catherine, preferred Kay, but growing up, we kids called her Cus, a short version of the Ukrainian pronunciation of her formal name Catherine, which was Kasha.

She was a bit more progressive than the other three by nature, puzzling, since she followed Mother genetically, and was as docile as could possibly be.

She was the one who would be the first to welcome a new neighbor, the first to seek employment at a very early age, helping neighboring women with ordinary chores, finally staying with one who practically adopted her.

Within hours after high school graduation, she was employed by Bell Telephone Co., staying with them her entire working life, retiring from them.

She bought a beautiful house at age 69, working endlessly in fixing it up with numerous plants, trees, and flowers.

Her original intent in buying a house was to provide a permanent home for sisters Ann and Stella, but that didn't work out too well, as she was stricken with an arachnoid hematoma, and left us without recovering.

She was, and in memory, remains a most beautiful human being, a wonderful part of my life.

A copy of my original memoir is included here.

In Memory of Catherine "Kay" Kravetsky
January 18, 1929 - December 11, 2006

At 11:10 P. M., December 11, 2006, the world suddenly became a quieter, lonelier place.

Our beloved Sister and Friend, Catherine "Kay" Left us.

She had enjoyed her final years tending the house and gardens, and apparently, it was decreed her work here was done.

Perhaps a greater need elsewhere had arisen, and she was called to it.

Her first, and last love, was service to people, friend or stranger, without asking of or expectation of thanks.

Her selfless generosity within, and outside of the Family, was an ongoing, lifelong practice. Specific occasions are much too numerous to list.

For the privilege of sharing a lifetime with this gentle soul, and her generous ways, we are eternally grateful.

To you, the kind and thoughtful individuals who unselfishly provided to us one of the greatest gifts in a difficult time, _your presence_, we say   sincerely, thank you.

We're glad to know you're on this Planet with us, comforted in the knowledge that we are in the company of so many truly good people.

Wishing for you all the very best that can be in the future, we close this Chapter in Life.

With Kindest Regards,

Charles, Ann, Mary and Stella Kravetsky

Church

I was just five when all six of us kids were first introduced to the Roman Catholic Church dispensation, by both nuns and priests.

By word of mouth, we were drawn into a local group who met weekly in the basement of a private home for Sunday school, the early indoctrination into the system.

After Sunday school, we were ferried to the church at the outskirts of Saltsburg, just a short distance away.

There we, I, would suffer through an hour or more of presentation, in Latin, except for an equally boring sermon to an illiterate, me, then a four, yes four, mile hike back home, rain or shine.

As I grew older, the continued use of the Latin language prompted me to various mind wandering, not really benefitting much from the whole program as presented.

There were good priests, and questionable priests, most positive and likeable, some negative and not at all lovable. I welcomed their leaving, some bordering on the "do as I say, not do as I do" instructive philosophy.

We, Dolly, and us, as a growing family, attended faithfully, supported the system generously, and embraced the philosophy, in great part, for decades.

As the kids grew older, independent, they gradually drifted away, embracing their own beliefs and methods toward salvation, leaving Dolly and me for some number of years, going alone, Sunday in and Sunday out, rarely failing to be there in our accustomed spot, left side, front row, seat space once occupied by kids, now available.

The memory of interaction with so many fine people, numerous social activities all present, but fading, as news of the now unacceptable, unforgiveable activities within the church came to light, a sadness of unforgettable dimensions settled in on both me and Dolly.

And so, we abandoned the Roman Catholic Church.

Now, some number of years later, in the writing of this life story, and revisiting that sad moment of truth, I can't help but to recognize the fact that, after sixty+ years of unfailing attendance, numerous services provided with no charge, generous financial support, and decades of personable relations with other church members:

Not one priest, no bishop, no single member of the church council has ever so much as reached out, inquired, as to why we walked away, which would, presumably, escalate into the obvious question.

We walked away with no regret; I will never return.

Chingo - School

A mail flyer offered training in a plumbing profession at a school in Pittsburgh, and my number three son, Jim, sent in a response signing up Chingo, our Collie, as a joke, for the classes.

He reasoned that since Chingo was really good at plumbing action at posts, trees, fire hydrants, and others, he could benefit from some training, whatever that might be.

A few days later, our phone rang, and I answer it, and a male voice says, "This is _____, from _____ School, and we've completed processing Chingo into our system, but we need additional information, is Chingo there?"

I immediately suspected something, so to buy time, said, "Yes, but he's indisposed, not available for a few days." He said he'd call back later.

That evening, I asked Jim about it, and he admitted he had filled in the application as a joke.

Well, the school failed to find the humor in it, and continued the pursuit, calling back.

I asked what the course actually taught, and what cost and time involvement. I stalled the caller; said I'd consider it and call him soon.

When he told me the high cost, payable up front, and stumbling on course content, plus a very short time involvement, I became really suspicious, and researched the history of the school, discovering they were a total scam, a fraud with a history of cheating other innocents of their money. The training was a farce, no real training at all.

He called again, this time insisting a payment by credit card be made, to enroll. He said they'd qualify him for commercial work, and assured he'd have a license very quickly.

I'd had about enough of this, and said, "He's already got a license", and I read him the number off of it. He said he'd get back to me.

He did, the next day. He was angry, said, "Hey, that number you gave me was a dog license number, what the hell are you trying to pull?"

So, I let him have it, said I'd already called the Feds, and they said they would see you soon.

So much for Chingo becoming a plumber.

Pole Caddy

A former co-worker and friend, Herb, now retired with time on his hands, enjoyed fishing at nearby Lake Erie.

What he didn't like was difficulty in finding a suitable location to set one or two fishing poles that could be easily monitored and readily accessible in case of a strike.

Being innovative, he designed a pole caddy made up of inch and a half diameter PVC pipe that by its design was stable on the ground, and held one or two poles securely.

After reviewing a prototype, we agreed it was a workable device, needing just a bit of tweaking to make it more user friendly, which I set out to do.

Having made some changes, it was ready for public opinion, and how marketable it would be.

So, I made up ten pole caddies and gave Herb five, keeping five for myself.

I consigned one to a local bait store and waited. Time went on, with no takers. Herb was experiencing the same public reaction, no sales.

Finally, my local store had a customer, granted a money back satisfaction warranty.

Well, it was just a few days later that the highly disgruntled customer was back at the bait store, demanding his money back. Questioned as to why, he explained.

He had taken the pole caddy with him to a local lake known to have large fish, set up shop, so to speak, loaded up a very expensive rod and reel into it, and sat down, watching.

Suddenly there was a violent yank on the line, jerking the high dollar rod and reel out of the holder, dragging it into deep water in a few seconds before he could grab it.

So much for the fishing gear, and so much for the caddy.

I did sell one and have had no feedback from that sale.

I have not heard of any sales by Herb, or if he is using one himself.

Just another broken dream, for me, one of many.

Leak in Pipe

Having hired a plumber friend to do some work for me, in conversation I said, "Ed, do you know I'm a miracle worker?"

He said, "Oh yeah, how?"

I said, well, a few months ago, a pipe sprung a leak, and I didn't have time to fix it, so I just went over to it and said, "Please stop leaking."

And it did stop - and has been fine ever since.

He asked which pipe it was, so we went over to it, and I pointed to the spot.

At precisely that moment, it started to leak again.

I know, I need to get my halo checked, and recharged.

6 Ton Bridge

The township road we hauled coal across, for many years, from my first major strip mine, had a bridge with a six-ton weight limit posted at it, a fairly big creek flowing under it, about 15 feet below.

We hauled across it for years with triaxles and tractor trailers carrying anywhere up to 30 tons payload, plus the weight of the truck, for a total up to 42 tons, plus or minus.

We never hurt the well-constructed bridge in the 13 years we used it, but a new township administration clamped down on its being allowed heavy loads after we had finished that job, so that was it: six tons, or go around some other way, or post some ridiculous bond.

The simple fact, there was no other way that was feasible. I still had a big front-end loader weighing 62 tons to get onto the other side, so I made the decision. I will drive it across the bridge, personally.

I drove, the picture my son took of me, and the big loader on it, proves all went well, the bridge held up just fine. I'm sure that's not a record.

Boys will be boys, an old song says.

Sometimes you gotta fight when you're a man.

I know, I should have bonded it.

My response, it starts with the letter _____ and ends with you.

Antenna & Josie

At a contracted jobsite, there was an abandoned building with living quarters available within it.

A recently divorced guy, along with his friend and companion, Josie, a full-blooded Saint Bernard, moved in, shortly before our arrival.

I, noticing an unusual sight, asked him about it. Here's what I saw: there was an ordinary, average-sized television antenna clearly silhouetted in the clear sky, near the top of a dead tree, way above ground level, close by the building.

He told me that, being in a deep valley, there was no reception in the old building when he moved in. He said he could have done without it, but Josie liked to watch TV, so he mounted the antenna on the building, with no luck at all. So, he tried a flag pole with equal results, none.

Looking up the steep hill above the site, he saw a big tree, dead but sound, having died just a short time ago, long enough to have lost its bark.

Having some climbing experience, he carefully checked it out, then, confident of its integrity, bottom to top, made the decision.

So, he put on his climbing gear, such as it was, tied a rope to the antenna, and up he went, climbing to near the top, stopping when the tree was just six or eight inches in diameter, so he said, up about 80 feet, he guessed.

He then pulled up the antenna, and strapped it to the tree with multiple big hose clamps.

He and Josie lived there for quite a while after we were gone, the TV reception was fine.

I stopped one time later, curious, and measured the height of that antenna, with my range finder.

It was 51 feet to the base of the tree from the ground at the building, another 87 feet up the tree, a total of 137 feet, which is downright scary.

I trust Josie appreciated his efforts, and risk.

They later moved to Avonmore, a few miles away, where Josie lived happily with cable reception for several more years, dying of old age.

Don and Gary - Road Trash

Several years ago, I was working with the owners of a coal company on a joint strip-mining operation, good people, a lot of fun.

One morning as we assembled, I solemnly announced I had good news for them.

Don said, "Good, we need good news."

I said, "You will be happy to know I signed you up to pick up the trash the traveling public throws out along Route 981 between Saltsburg and Latrobe, only 16 or so miles, and the good news is that PennDOT has accepted your generous offer, starting now."

"Oh, by the way, it's a five-year, irreversible contract, which I don't see as a problem."

The response was less than unprofane.

Note: In Pennsylvania, D.O.T. has a program where anyone can volunteer to pick up trash along a designated road and distance, in exchange for a posted sign identifying the volunteer.

Bell Township Affairs

I was elected a Bell Township Supervisor in 2002 for the usual 6 years, but I only lasted until 2006.

I got along well with one of the other supervisors, but not that well with the other one, a long-entrenched politician.

First, I was instrumental in having a long-time secretary replaced, she overdue for retirement after my having discovered a number of reports and submissions to various state agencies undone, and so on.

I was accused of wanting to run the township like Walmart, not like a good old boy.

Monthly, I would make a list of concerns, failures, or deficiencies, and then have an informal discussion over lunch, or some seemingly legal forum on the same day as the evening monthly meeting, usually involving at least some shouting and weeping. All would then be peace and tranquility at the public meeting. It worked well.

There was never any open hostility expressed by anyone, and the township was well run, with a competent secretary in place, a retired CPA volunteering to audit the records, and a good, practically self-directed labor force.

With my background and professional experience, coupled with the experience of the other two supervisors, we were able to smoothly handle all of the township's affairs easily.

One day, an invoice came in the morning's mail, from a citizen living in one of the small communities in the township. It was for $650 or so, as the fee for a plumber having brought a camera to view his sewer that was malfunctioning.

An accompanying letter claimed that since his sewer was connected to a larger sewer in the town, it was the township's obligation to clear it, the camera cost included.

So, I wrote him a response:

Dear Sir:

In view of the fact there are no public sewers anywhere in Bell Township, we can only assume yours is a wildcat, an illegally installed system.

We will be happy to inform the Department of Environmental Protection of your problem so you can obtain advice on how to proceed.

We never heard from him again.

We received one of those infamous correspondences one day: Intent to File Suit, by a citizen in another small town in the township.

This was that the citizen filing the suit, had several years before, requested the township to remove a storm water barrier along the front of his house, it being unsightly and difficult to mow around, assuring the township he would cope with any consequences of having removed the barrier. Over the past few years, the township fire department had been called in to pump out his basement, proving it was a mistake to have removed the storm water barrier.

This time, it was a severe storm with very heavy rain, and as a result, a lot of storm water found its way into his basement, triggering the threat of the lawsuit.

Daddy always told me, "Son, never get into a pissing contest with a skunk."

So, I called our local sewage enforcement officer, and requested he inspect the area of the leach bed serving his house. Well, no surprise, the big green spot is there, as expected.

Informing him, he must have concluded he would be better served paying a contractor to repair his sewage disposal system than a lawyer for a hopeless lawsuit.

A notice came from the state to the effect that a widespread infrastructure study was mandated by some future date. That being familiar territory for me, I said I would take care of it, well in advance of the required date.

I had never invoiced, as a courtesy, the township, for professional level services as a supervisor, and did not invoice for the several days' time in performing the township's mandated survey, so I was quite surprised when I received an invoice for the two township laborers who had helped me with the obligated survey.

So, I called, asking that, since the labor became my liability for their obligation, should I invoice for my time, at my considerably higher hourly rate? That ended it.

Sometime in my third year, a former acquaintance, Russ ___, initiated an ethical action investigation against me, in a totally untrue claim, proven in a long, vicious, PA State Investigation, that ultimately exonerated me completely.

That was the proverbial last straw. I resigned, short of my term limit.

So many good people, one __?__

225 Shear Pin

On a contracted job, repairing a serious washout of a township road, I was doing a final grading of the rebuilt out slope, a severely steep 40+ degrees, at or about the limit of a one-yard excavator to climb, backwards.

Reaching the road upon completion, I turned, went down the level road a short distance, then began reshaping a ditch to allow storm water to flow away from the jobsite.

On my first move backwards, I heard this loud snap. Stopping, I get down and look at the left track, sagged down, a sheared track pin.

Breathing a huge sigh of relief, I called my mechanic.

Why that pin didn't shear climbing up out of that steep grade, minutes ago, is something I will never understand, instead it waited till I was safe and sound, up on a level roadway, with minimal stress on the track, there.

Had that pin sheared on that upslope, I shudder when I think of the grief in getting that 25-ton machine up out of that bottom, in those conditions.

There is a God, he just proved it.

Someone, something, didn't allow that pin to shear on that steep grade.

Andy, Pat, Family

My brother, Andy, first born, favored son thereby automatically, in the Ukrainian social hierarchy, was just a little spoiled by Father, and learned a few less desirable traits, the rest of us kids only being interested observers.

Traits became habits, habits became problematical at times, including mixing with less than desirable people.

But finally, a sweet young thing, working for the same corporation, in the same building, caught his eye and not that much later became his wife, Pat.

Andy growing up as a bonafede country boy, doing his best to disguise it, thought he would try the big city life, the good life where someone else fixes the ruts and potholes, picks the rocks in the driveway.

So, husband and city girl wife, take up residence in a part of a big town that, historically, was one of the least dangerous, leaving beautiful Bell Township to fend for itself.

However, after a rather abbreviated period of city life, he, they, becoming weary of the nonstop sound of gunfire and sirens, decided the sound of coyotes howling and hoot owls hooting was far more desirable, far less endangering, and of course, he was enabled to return to one of his true first loves, filling ruts and fixing holes in the driveway to watch the snow pile up deeper, eventually calling his dear brother to plow the road open, again.

It appeared that mowing grass was exceptionally hazardous, calling for all out preparation for, and acquisition of protective gear capable of repelling the real or imaginative hordes of relentlessly attacking hornets, yellow jackets and sweat bees.

Just his appearance, fully prepped, could frighten little children and puppies, but it didn't seem to faze any of the bees. The onset of winter being the only real deterrent, they being naturally unable to function under a certain temperature, giving him a break till spring.

Generally speaking, Andy's family was blessed with reasonably good health, irrespective of his accusations of the senior members' penchant to search out, then arrange to travel to acquire new, recently publicized diseases, their preference being the ones in darkest Africa.

Growing up, I and the four sisters faithfully attended church, Andy not so much, preferring to run his trapline on Sunday mornings, reaping the rewards of his attendance immediately in the sale of fur, rather than hope for eventual rewards in a far-off Heaven.

CNX

I believe it was autumn, 2006, when the lead man of a new, innovative project harvesting the methane gas out of the multiple coal seams located below the previously mined Pittsburgh seam, called me to discuss a project, since it was centered around my area of operations.

He had been allotted fifty plus millions of dollars to drill at least 600 wells, and we discussed my being a contractor for the installation of them all.

My group agreed this could be a good thing, long-term, providing good jobs for at least ten people.

They, being part of a well-known, highly respected corporation in mining, captured my trust, and I went substantially into debt, acquiring the trucks and other equipment necessary for achieving the projects' goals.

Knowing the area and the people from years of surveying activity here, I had not only valuable knowledge of the property locations, but a trust that allowed me to honestly convince reluctant landowners to cooperate with the placement of the wells, that it would be beneficial, in great part, to them.

I was given free run to make minor changes and tradeoffs, which greatly expedited the smooth continuation of the installs.

Things went well deep into the expansion, physically, on the ground, but the storm clouds were already gathering on the horizon.

Communication was not an issue; finances were increasingly an issue.

Payment for substantial services and material provided was being held back for various flimsy reasons, or no reason at all. A go-between had been set up as a buffer between the responsible office and me.

Finally, when unpaid invoices reached the stop services level, a meeting was called, not only with me, but apparently with other unpaid contractors and suppliers.

The usual well-rehearsed spokesman was present from the responsible party, at the meeting, and presented their case for non-payment of contracted services.

It was very simple.

They wanted an agreement for a discount on the amounts due, of at least 15 percent.

In anticipation of this, I had quietly invited every field employee of theirs to attend the meeting, along with every local official, and they all came.

I then explained to their spokesman I was very aware of their tactics, told him to pass on to them that I did not build a profit into my services, since I worked by an hourly rate from hour meters, and mileage from odometers.

I then told him I knew he would be embarrassed if he went back empty handed, so I offered a five percent reduction on all invoices overdue.

I was thanked, a very hollow thanks, indeed, and excused.

They never took the five percent and did pay the invoiced total.

That ended our relationship, but not the lingering sour taste and smell.

I was also left with a huge debt I had incurred for the promised project.

How can supposedly big people be so small?

Gas Line at Karp

I had done the mapping and deed work for a friend who owned a big farm, giving his grandson a 10-acre tract for a home site, a mobile home placed there for a soon to be wife.

Having equipment nearby, I was asked if I would install a driveway across a deep gulley for the home, so I moved a 25-ton excavator to the site.

I prepared the base, purchased enough large diameter pipe to span the gulley, and moved to complete the excavation to set the home upon.

It was extremely wet and muddy around the home, but I had years of experience to call upon, and proceeded to navigate the steep, muddy slope to get past the haphazardly parked mobile home.

What I didn't know was there was a live 2-inch gas line laying in the grass and weeds, not visible, just a few feet from the trailer running parallel to the driveway, and up past the trailer. The owner of the gas line had not responded to the One Call notification. When I was crossing over the gas line, the soft earth gave way under my tracks, causing me to start sliding, slowly, down the slope toward the deep gulley, on top of the pipe toward where it was hanging in the open air, spanning the gulley.

It flashed in my head that if I reached that point, I and the excavator would smash the line, and I'd be on it with gas spewing out over everything, possibly causing a runaway engine sucking the gas, or a fire engulfing me. In the few seconds I had while sliding toward the gulley, I swung the bucket around to the downhill side, jammed it into the ground, hard, then quickly pushed and steered hard right, throwing the machine sharply away from the gas line, saving us both, then moving back onto the driveway.

The rest of the days' events are easy to tell. I parked the excavator and waited for a dry day to finish. Several days later, I was finished, the driveway done, ready for traffic to the trailer, when my friend stopped in and told me the good news. They no longer needed the home site. The wedding was off. The girl had taken all the money and run off with another man, the night before.

And I kissed 10 grand goodbye, and a week of my, and machine's time.

Letter to Joan

This story is a copy of a letter I wrote to my friend in California, after a brief stay in a local hospital.

Dear Joan:

I don't remember if I ever told you about one other idiosyncrasy I have, originated who knows where and why.

Being a compassionate fool, I make up four servings of commercial dog food, table scraps, and a can of Y2K goods Dolly had accumulated, daily, rain, shine, sleet, or snow, I take these to a plot of woods for my "Woodland Friends".

My motivation is in the knowing some little empty belly is filled, even if it's just briefly. My hope is that someday, somewhere, somehow, a world of no hunger, no pain, no fear, no killing will reign forever.

You are quite perceptive. A year or so ago, I was completing two major projects, very difficult projects. In running multiple businesses over all those years, stress was never a major issue, but in anticipation of ending the professional involvement in mining and surveying, it became overwhelming.

As a result, I spent several days in the hospital with near stroke symptoms.

That awakened me, and I was able to complete those, vowing never to return.

I haven't and won't, and I'm just fine, generally.

I'll call you soon, Love, Chuck

Excavator Lawsuit

Having encountered strata too hard to break out with conventional equipment, I rented a large excavator with a hammer, to address the problem rock, not being permitted to blast at that location.

Immediately after it was delivered, it broke down, needing some serious repairs. It being assumed the owner would normally be the one to repair it, I, after informing them of the breakdown, simply left it parked, waiting for their action.

None happened, and time passed.

Then I was invoiced for a month's rent, unpaid, since the machine never worked.

Then I was sued for $12,000, the monthly rent. Their lawyer claimed since the machine was in my possession, I owed them the rent, there being nothing to the contrary in the rental agreement.

So, I hired a newly ordained young lawyer to defend me. I may as well have hired the pizza delivery guy. Now what?

So, I went to work, assembled all the pertinent facts, aligned them in such order as to be able to present them reasonably correctly in a hearing before a judge.

I gave a long list of questions to my so-called attorney as my defense.

I may as well have not, since he remained mute for the most part, I having to do all the defending. Fine choice I had made.

My first move was to mount a tape recorder on the corner of the judge's desk.

When the opposition objected, I said I had a poor memory, and the judge ruled in my favor, leave it there. They were visibly shaken. I don't know why.

It just so happened the judge's name ended in 'sky', the same as mine, and he jokingly commented that he should be on my side. I agreed.

He was a good, common-sense judge.

He was visibly affected when I stated I had not been informed of the 3 day period where I could reject the whole deal initially.

What lawyer would even file so ridiculous a case where I was obligated to repair a nonfunctioning machine delivered to me as a rental?

The good judge didn't need much time to rule: the case was dismissed, with prejudice.

I don't know if their lawyer was young and stupid, like mine, or old and senile, and should retire to some beach, in some southern state, with a good wife to look after him and live happily ever after.

Joan – Early On

March 10, 2007

Hello Joan:

Yes, it was a pleasant surprise to receive a card and note, way back when, and yes, you do owe me a letter.

However, since I am in a bit of a lull, I thought I would respond, regardless.

I, too, continue to work in various business ventures, and have no intention of ever voluntarily stopping. I can respect anyone's choice to actually withdraw from the workplace, but the prospect of being unproductive sends a chill through me.

In sitting here on a Saturday morning with the interminable paperwork temporarily at bay, I find a reflective mood that rolls back through time with stops and starts as segments of life present themselves.

In not having cataloged any of these in any retrievable form other than our thoughts, they have become hazy and distant. The passing of a half century and then some, doesn't help.

In this vein, I cannot recall when you first arrived on the Bell Township scene. I don't remember you in the early (1-6) years, which could be simply my failing.

I do recall the Helena Inn, but not when it first opened. I also remember your mom and dad as being very friendly.

I believe we rode the same bus to and from school for some time, but at some point I started to drive my '37 Chevy pickup, so that, too, is hazy.

Did you pursue your ballerina interests after graduation, and did this play a part in your future vocation(s)?

In view of the fact it was such a major change point in life, the memory of June, 1952 still causes me to experience a bittersweet feeling, while it persists.

Even though one must recognize the fact that not many of the people we separated from were truly our friends, our comfort zone disappeared, and a great loneliness suddenly became apparent.

Other interests in life soon dispelled much of this, but somewhere deep within, there still lurks a hunger for some level of rekindling.

The 50-year reunion helped to accomplish this, and the occasional contact, like this, satisfies this need.

As I noted earlier, life has been extremely interesting, and rewarding, and presuming the interest will continue, I hope we can exchange thoughts and experiences for some foreseeable future.

I will end this now, with the assurance that I will forgive you for your extended delay in response.

I trust this finds you well, with a cheerful outlook on the future.

Best regards,

My In-laws

A wise friend used to say every once in a while, when in-laws were the topic in a conversation, "Hey Jack, remember, when you marry the girl, you also marry her family, too, like it or not."

Usually, the future association is predictable, both on the positive and negative. I was very confident mine would be positive, after just a short time. In my personal experience, I have only high praise for every one of my in-laws. They are the finest of the fine, and always have been.

Over the sixty years of unbroken affiliation, there has never been a single unpleasant exchange with any one or any group, not only in the direct family, but also in any extension of either family. A record that continues, a remarkable truth.

My father-in-law, Paul, was a fine man, leading a fine family. Naturally shy and introverted, he dreamed of striking it rich in the world of invention, but never made it.

He often waited up till Dolly and I would return home from a date, and with a little beer, would expound his social and political philosophies late into the night, falling asleep, I doing my best not to.

He built a nice, conventional trailer as a pet project, giving it to me when he no longer had any use for it when he became gravely ill 59 years ago, and it is still intact and in use here.

Mother-in-law, l can never say enough good things about her, serving me and our growing family with countless great dinners, trustworthy babysitting sessions and uplifting social exchange.

Experiencing considerable economic distress throughout the years due to unemployment and family needs, she never complained, but offered out personal services, always generating adequate income to carry on.

Dolly and I had begun a savings account in the local bank for our long-range future, and I was more than happy to have released it to her at a time of serious need.

She paid it back a hundred times over, through the years.

She enjoyed humor, and one day when a family gathering was held at my daughter's house, I induced her to make a smart, friendly, of course, remark about me, easily heard by most everyone.

So, I addressed her remark with (loudly):

"Hey, mother-in-law, do you want to know what I really think of you?"

Things suddenly went very quiet, a bit tense when she just looked at me, not saying anything.

So, I blurted out, "Well, I just think you are the - (pause) - best possible mother-in-law in the whole world."

The crowd erupted, then even more so when she jumped up, ran over to me and kissed me, a never before event.

Sadly, her wonderful husband, Paul, had passed away a few years earlier, and she had struggled with raising her family, doing a great job.

Happily, while working at a local restaurant, a road construction job was underway locally, and certain employees would come to that place for lunch. As time passed, and as it often happens, one of the highway specialists asked if she would go out with him.

She did, and the rest is history, a truly positive history. He was also a fine man, gentle, socially proper, old school, as per our standards, intelligent and hard working.

Our boys loved him. He took them fishing, hiking, just visiting. They would occasionally stay with them, and he would spin tall tales to them. I thought the world of him, too. He invested in a group of old oil wells, stripper wells, that provided the revenue for her retirement. Sadly, he passing away at just 61 years.

She, unfortunately, contracted Alzheimer's a few years later, but lived until age 86.

Older brother-in-law, Paul, Jr., was always congenial, ever active in sandlot sports. He was quite proficient in baseball and softball, where I fell short, but I was an advanced level pool player and golfer, and he refused to challenge me in either of those. He was an accomplished journeyman in the tool and die industry, rising to executive level management in a major corporation.

Brother-in-law no. 2, Ralph, was a born financier, having his own paper delivery route by age 10, diligently handling his income, showing tendencies early on towards being a banker.

When Ted, or his younger sister, Carolyn, needed money for some dire, urgent need, they would swallow their pride and come, on bended knee, according to them, to him and request the desired amount.

I do not know what unholy interest rate he charged them, as neither side ever divulged that. I do not know what other terms and conditions he placed on the loans, but they were stringent enough to illicit comment to this day, accusing him of being an understudy to Mr. Scrooge himself.

And, as fate apparently dictated, he became a bank manager, soon rising to executive levels.

Upon his retirement from banking, he must have pondered, "How can I continue to torture innocent people now?"

So, he became a preacher.

In concern for his flock, and his wonderful wife, Mary, I cautioned him, urged him, be a bible-based preacher, not one of those "do as I say, not do as I do" messenger.

In truth, few individuals one may ever meet will exceed Ralph, and his terrific wife, Mary, in overall personable excellence, and it's delightful to be around them.

I'm not sure which direction he's going; I don't have the courage to attend a service. The world would be well served with more people just like them.

And then, there's my dear sister-in-law, Carolyn, and her great husband, Frank.

She was just seven, if I recall accurately, when I first met her. She was oh, so cute, unafraid. We became instant friends. At times I would visit Dolly at her house, Carolyn was always nearby, welcome wholeheartedly, being intelligent and curious, asking questions and making comments that were surprisingly adult in understanding.

She was probably ten when I was inducted into the US Army, and we would exchange letters, much appreciated by me, her letters always ending with: Love, Carolyn. P.S. I did not write my best.

I would always write back, assuring her she was ultra safe now, the Army being in good hands now--mine. I would always end with: If you didn't write your best, why not?

She never answered that.

It has always been tucked away somewhere in the deep recess of my mind that she would occasionally reiterate her hope that I would marry her, instead of Dolly.

The sheer audacity of that expressed, has always held a special level of endearment to me, which I'm sure will linger forever.

My only comment regarding that, is that I am grateful she came to her senses as she aged, and married a guy with so many more positive attributes.

For whatever reason, as the years have gone by, there has been a somewhat melancholy separation, but the lasting love of early times will never die. I wish her, and Frank, the very best, always.

Missy - 1

With a variety of ongoing, and developing businesses, I maintained three offices routinely. I would work out of whichever one my presence was necessary, or simply by my choice.

Additional help was needed in the mining office, so my daughter, Cindy, hired a fellow college student suitable for our line of work, she fitting in nicely. A bit of a naive city girl, unaccustomed to some of our country ways, we, always looking for the humor in everything, helping to maintain our sanity.

Several months after her hiring, now settled into her own office, she goes to Cindy with an empty stapler, asking if a refill is available.

So, Cindy reloaded it for her, and away she went, back to her work, but had to make a pickup, first.

Since that office also served my son's transmission shop, just a few steps away, Missy would pick up the work he needed daily, so she went and collected it, returning a short time later.

While she was gone, Cindy quickly went over to Missy's office and emptied the stapler, returning it to its former place.

Missy filed the transmission shop's work, and returned to her original project, soon needing to staple something, discovering her stapler is empty of any staples.

Not yet developed as a deep thinker, she went to Cindy's office, requesting a refill of staples.

Cindy casually refilled the stapler again, Missy going back to work in her own office.

Then, Cindy asked her to run an errand over into town, less than a mile away for her, and she left.

While she was away, Cindy again emptied her stapler, carefully resetting it in its former place.

Missy returned from the errand and began working again, soon needing to staple something, and again finding her stapler empty.

Still no outcry, no painful accusations. Unsmiling, unflinching, very straight face, Cindy again refilled the stapler with those same recycled staples, handing it to her, expressionless.

I, watching the show, remained removed, distant.

By then it was lunch time, and Missy went out to buy a sandwich at the Subway, barely a mile out of town.

Again, while she's gone, Cindy removed the staples out of Missy's stapler. Lunch over, Missy returns to her desk, bound and determined to get something done, knowing she needs to staple something.

This time, the lights go on, brightly, and she squeals out loud, "Hey, what the hell's going on here? Have I gone crazy, or am I going to have to kill somebody?"

We just couldn't prevent, or stop laughing, to this day.

Missy - 2

Our mining headquarters were located just out of Saltsburg, but with the Conemaugh River in between us and town, and the Loyalhanna Creek, a major stream, so wild animals are not uncommon nearby.

The spillway of the Loyalhanna Dam being upstream about 2 miles, is a favorite spot for bald eagles, who would travel downstream in search of fish, to its intersection with the Conemaugh River, forming the Kiskiminetas River, and would often stop along the way, close to our office, fully in view.

Missy, becoming ever more comfortable with us and her surroundings, even spotted our resident bobcat once, who occasionally shows up here.

She began taking short walks outside, stand at the bank of the big creek, watching a family of beavers, who apparently abandoned their adopted area of the Kiski River and moved into the Loyalhanna Creek running past our office.

I never saw it, but their lodge must have been upstream, as they would cut edible pieces of trees, taking the pieces upstream.

Within a relatively short time they had eaten their way up out of sight, no longer active in our area.

But, Missy still went out when it was fit.

One day, after lunch, she started to go out, and as she opened the door, and stepped out onto the porch, she met a black bear coming up the ramp to visit the bird feeder and its sunflower seeds.

Equally surprised, she turned quickly back into the office, the bear went for a swim in the big creek, leaving without so much as a goodbye.

From that day on, she stopped, looked, and listened before making a dash for her car.

Missy – 3

Missy, fresh out of the city, must have spent too much time watching big city newscasts, where they don't know the difference between a bulldozer and any other machine.

She, trained by them, called everything a bulldozer, possibly stopping short at self-propelled riding lawn mowers.

I had my CAT skid steer upgrading the office parking lot this one day, and as they are made, it is very difficult, bordering impossible, to see what's directly behind you. Backup horns on them are there not only to aggravate anyone within a mile, but to warn idiots walking into their work area that they could be run over by it, moving backwards.

Here comes Missy to work, parking outside the work area, but must cross over it to get to the office.

Thinking about who knows what, if anything, she blindly zeroes in on the office ramp, and goes, totally ignoring the beep, beep, beep of the skid steer bearing down upon her, the operator not thinking there's someone dumb enough to challenge him for space.

At the last split second, something told him to physically turn around and look, rear view mirrors on skid steers only show you a limited version of what's behind you, behind him, and lo and behold, Missy's about to get run over, become part of the parking lot surface.

He stops, breathing a sigh of relief, she casually carries on, oblivious.

I am omitting the next few exchanges. They were not civil, not pretty.

So, wondering how we can either cure, or educate her, we decide to take her on a tour.

Cindy instructs her to dress properly, and the next day she takes Missy to both of our mines and the stone quarry.

At each site, she is taken to each machine, full identification is made.

This is a front-end loader, not a bulldozer. This is an excavator, not a bulldozer, and so on, with entrance up into each one, then working each machine with her in it.

Finally, she is introduced to a CAT D9H. This is a real bulldozer, Missy, see the tracks and blade in front. Hear the roar, feel the vibration. Get it, this is a bulldozer.

And then, the skid steer, completely different in every way.

She crawled into it, agreed, no you can't see backward very well, lucky to see forward.

She went home much enlightened that day, vowing to respect backup horns in the future.

However the appearance, we have believed, and always will believe, her presence over the 11 years with us was of greater benefit to us than our presence was to her.

We will love her always.

Clint

I bought a building just inside Saltsburg, along PA Route 286, initially to provide space for an automobile repair facility, as Jim and Steve were pretty good mechanics in their early years.

After a few years of less than rewarding general repair, Jim turned it into a transmission specialty repair service: Steve returned to the mining operations. There being only 10 feet from the travel way of the road, made for extremely dangerous moments getting vehicles into, and out of the building.

There being no other transmission repair shops in the area, the business was soon thriving. As the traffic expanded, so did the problems. Limited parking space was major, but the fast, six cars a minute flow of vehicles past the garage was the worst.

Six vehicles a minute zipping by, in a 25-mph speed zone, all going 45 to 50 mph, us hand pushing vehicles in and out across that speedway, kept our guardian angels on high alert, and duty, and a decision had to be made.

A house and a little land, across the river became available when an acquaintance passed on.

So, Jim bought it, nice double wide, and a small repair garage already on it. The original house was too far gone, so I demolished it with an excavator.

There was talk of a hidden vault containing cash, squirreled away by the previous spendthrift hoarder.

There wasn't one, I dug everywhere.

And we built the current repair garage much bigger, more user friendly, even for me, not much of a mechanic.

Even though the highway running past was equally busy as the original side, 6 cars a minute, it was a hundred or more feet away, not close to any activity.

And Jim went to work, hiring Clint out of our mining division, a promising young mechanic, to tear down and prepare vehicles for drive train and rebuild.

Understanding we're all different, Clint was a top-notch worker, but he had this penchant to be a clock watcher. The later in the workday, the more frequently the clock on the wall was checked.

At precisely 5 o'clock, Clint was out of there, day over. Clint had multiple areas he covered, so the clock was not always in ready view, so one day, after the start of the work day, Jim quietly moved the minute hand back about 15 to 20 minutes, when Clint wasn't near.

A couple hours later, he moved it back another 15 or 20 minutes.

When Clint went out to get a hoagie for lunch, Jim again moved it back 15 or 20 minutes. This was repeated at least two more times before day's end, which happened to be a Friday.

Well, Monday morning, here comes a somewhat irate Clint, angrily demanding to know if Jim had played with the clock on Friday, since he didn't get home till well after 6 o'clock, closer to 6:30 on Friday, and missed out on a date because of it.

Jim didn't lie, he simply stretched out his arm, exposing his wristwatch and said, "Buddy, there's the clock that I go by."

Clint never found out about the trick, and probably never will unless he hears or reads it in this telling.

Clint left us for big time corporate employment a short time later.

We remain good friends with him and his great family.

Waitress at Tina's

I stopped for lunch at a little restaurant and ordered a fish sandwich.

The bill came to $10.50.

I left a $5.00 tip at the table for the waitress, then got up to leave.

The same waitress accepted payment at the register, I giving her $11.00, a ten and a one-dollar bill.

She extended the 50 cents change, and I said, "No, the change is yours, I'll take a toothpick."

The look she flashed, involuntarily, was priceless, oh, for a body camera.

I would have liked to see the look on her face when she found the real tip on the table.

Anyhow, waitresses are just great, we love them all.

Charlie's in Heaven

On the exterior of my house, I have a small, metal sign that says, Heaven.

It's been there for years and is the official name of this home site.

On those days when I'm inclined to answer my ever-ringing house phone, the inevitable telemarketer will respond to my hello with, "Hello, is Charlie there?"

I will say, "Oh, I must tell you, Charlie's in Heaven now."

She/he will usually come back with, "Oh, I'm so sorry, I'll remove his name from our call list."

Mission accomplished, with truth, nothing but the truth.

Butler Backfill

Several years ago, I agreed to backfill and restore a small strip mine for a friend who had opened the job but was unable to sell the coal he had produced.

He piled it up, and the job was idled.

After 90 days, regulatory agencies get really nervous, and begin urging operators to either start mining, or close up and restore what was affected.

Or else.

There was an open pit and other holes that had to be addressed.

And there was that pile of unsaleable coal, representing considerable financial help in offsetting the costs incurred, if sold.

Time passed, we moved dirt, we filled all the holes, spread the topsoil, everything was done.

Except for the pile of coal.

The enclosed copy of a letter I sent picks up that part of this story.

If all business was conducted similar to that, what a wonderful world it would be.

Read on:

K M P Associates, Inc.

1094 Lantz Road
Avonmore, PA 15618-1241
(724) 639-8323
Fax (724) 639-9753

Todd Lacross, Plant Manager
Scrubgrass Generating Company, L.P.
2151 Lisbon Road
Kennerdell, Pa. 16374

Dear Todd:

In this rough and tumble world we find ourselves a part of, there are only few and rare occasions where the people involved demonstrate a level of competance and efficiency far above what can be considered the norm.

This was our recent experience in a transaction regarding a small amount of waste fuel that was presenting a severe negative consequence (with D.E.P.) for us at a reclamation site nearby.

The response to my call to the Scrubgrass Generating Company was totally professional, from the young lady that first answered, then to Jack Egley who immediately responded in courteously listening to our problem, who acquired samples, and shortly thereafter called to set up an Agreement which was concluded quickly.

Jack contacted Mike Lauer, who met me at the site, thereafter setting up the hauling.

Mike, and his drivers, were timely, courteous, and patient, and couldn't have been better in providing the service.

After having met with both Jack and Mike, I informed Jack I had a dilemma to contend with: I couldn't decide which of them was nicer to deal with.

This was not a real big deal for Scrubgrass, but it was the Proverbial "Drink in the Desert" to us.

Thanks much, how fortunate to have such great people!

Charlie Kravetsky, Consultant

Jim's House - Gas

Routinely attending church early, I would have Sunday morning available afterwards to make my usual run around our mining and quarrying operations, able to evaluate and plan future actions uninterrupted, or engaged.

One morning, having concluded my tour, I elected, for no definable reason, to return home the long way around, but just a few miles more than usual taking me through the town of Avonmore, where son Jim lived with his wife Debra, and I decided to stop and visit them.

Stopping and parking outside, then going into the kitchen through the front door, I noticed the strong smell of natural gas.

Questioning them about its presence and duration, they said it had been present for several days, but not to any degree to cause alarm.

Not agreeing, I said, "You better open the door and some windows", as I felt sure they had both adapted to the smell, not realizing it was escalating in severity.

I asked if there had been any recent activity with the gas lines by either himself or the utility company.

He said the only thing he had done, was to install a cover over a floor drain, in a single car garage located at basement level, accessible from ground level, and adjacent to the house basement.

The smell of gas over the first few weeks had caused him to do that in trying to diminish any flow through the drain into the basement if it was actually carrying the gas in.

They had not noticed any real positive change from installing the cover, and dismissed the issue, accepting the lingering smell of gas.

Viewing the cover, I said, "Let's remove it and see if anything happens."

Did it ever!

As I pried the cover off, pressure from within the drain popped it off, and a gush of gas flowed through, inundating the garage, which, fortunately had a closed door between it and the house basement, preventing the gas from flooding into it.

The cover off, we quickly plugged the 4-inch drain, stopping the inflow and evacuated the house of gas.

Contacting the gas company servicing the house, it was learned there is an 8-inch main line within a few feet of the house, in the paved street.

The pipe, being 80+ years old, had developed a leak sometime prior to this incident and had not been properly repaired at that time.

Being a high-pressure line, a new leak had opened, continuously flooding the surrounding fill with gas, which was migrating up into the borough storm drain system, which was connected into the floor drain in the garage.

Divine intervention?

Compliance Water Tech

One fateful day the phone rang, and a voice I recognized said, "Charlie, there's someone I think you should meet."

So, we met, in a small restaurant in West Kittanning.

It was with a guy named Dick ___. Dick had this dream, he would conquer the ever-elusive world of acid mine drainage restoration to compliance standards with his innovative genius, or so he said.

His sales pitch was so good, and my ignorance and gullibility so great, that I agreed to give him financial support. It was a given, based on some college girl's financial study, and projected plan, I would soon, very soon, be challenging Warren Buffet himself, in annual income.

He was a bottomless pit; he tried this, he tried that, nothing worked. We built a treatment facility in a box truck, guaranteed to work, his great plan.

Stupidly, I didn't realize until it was way too late that his whole dream was nothing more than a homemade reverse osmosis system, readily available as a commercial product.

Why no one was killed in the trials using his design, we'll never know.

I firmly believe it was the guardian angels that kept the pipes from exploding under the severely high pressures he sent into them in his attempt to extract undesirable metals from the water.

After a series of unpleasant exchanges, I abandoned him, and a considerable investment, and went home, so to speak.

In a final series of failures on his own, he apparently was overwhelmed, and was never heard from again.

Do you believe in Karma? I do. I have proof.

Rudy

I will never be certain as to why only one of my four sisters married but cannot help but wonder if the negativity they experienced in their formative years, particularly on chaotic weekends, coupled with the backwoods isolation and poverty, so influenced them as to reject the possibility of a similar life for them.

Of the four sisters, just one dared to venture into the world's biggest, best or among the worst arenas in life, dependent on an infinite list of variables and how they are met and addressed.

In sister Mary's case, her life in the care and comfort of her life partner, Rudy, who unselfishly provided what was most likely in the positive sector, generally, a happy 56 years together, raising a beautiful family.

I enclose the memoir I wrote for Rudy, a fine man, and a great brother-in-law for all those years.

In Memory of
— Rudolph C. Jaconetta —

January 7, 1932 – March 19, 2022

Some sixty+ years ago, a former Bell Township country girl, then living in the metropolitan area of Pittsburgh began frequenting the men's suits section of the Horne's Department Store in downtown Pittsburgh. One has to wonder why.

Was it to buy a suit? Unlikely, girls did not wear suits to work in those days. As a gift to her father, or brother? Hardly.

Could it have been that good looking guy working there that she spotted on one of her earlier shopping trips there?

As it happened, Rudy was introduced into our lives by Mary, our sister, and they became husband and wife a short time thereafter.

One by one, three beautiful children arrived, filling the house they had purchased, completing the family circle.

Time passed, Rudy persevered, aching feet, legs and back notwithstanding, from having to stand all day long greeting and serving customers at Horne's, year in and year out, rarely complaining.

He provided firm, but fair leadership in the household, helping to guide the children in becoming intelligent, respectful, productive members of society.

Was there ever a more likeable, gentler, respectable individual? Even mother-in-law, Mary K., openly stated her absolute admiration for Rudy, dismissing old country adversarial attitudes between their original nations of origin.

Throughout the years, decades, there was never a single negative spoken of Rudy, and to this day none is known.

We will forever regard it a privilege to have shared so many years of this planet with this gentle soul.

May God bless and keep Rudy forever in his fold, and from the bottom of our hearts we say, "Rudy, thank you, very, very much."

With much love,
Chuck, Cindy, John, Steve, Jim, and families

Taking Care of Dolly

Returning home one autumn day in 2014, expecting to find things normal as usual, supper being prepared, everything pretty much under control.

Pulling up to the garage and exiting my truck, I heard a faint call for help.

Moving towards the call, I find my dear wife Dolly, lying on the ground, shoulder against my concrete German shepherd, in obvious distress.

Trimming a rosebush, she had lost her balance, falling backwards against the canine figurine, fracturing her shoulder, seriously.

Having gone through the usual medical process in such cases, she was discharged from the hospital with her arm immobilized in a tight sling.

Now it gets serious, for me.

Suddenly, I'm chief of everything: cook, bottle washer, nurse, maid, everything.

Unhesitatingly, I assume total care of her, the words agreed to some years earlier, in sickness and in health, till death us do part, reside within me as an irrevocable promise, so I, unfailingly, execute any and every need: food, attire, bath, and so on, day in and day out.

Endless medical care, exercise, rehabilitation, consultation, acupuncture, trip after trip, all to no avail.

The arm, held too tightly in the sling for too long, deteriorated to the point of being useless, totally immobilized.

Finally, in an interview with a psychiatrist, she was properly diagnosed with advanced Parkinson's disease, apparently the root cause of the whole issue, including several damaging falls.

Then, against my instruction to her to not attempt to walk unassisted, she rose up out of a chair, took a step forward, then falling, striking the floor very hard, unable to rise even with help.

Determined to have sustained a major brain hemorrhage, she entered into palliative care, leaving us just seven days later.

Her very last words were, "My name is "Dolores...May... Kravetsky."

There is no doubt, she is now safely in God's hands.

Help!

When Jim bought the P___ property, there was already a repair facility on it, used for years by the former owner, Bill P____, who was, to say the least, an unusual individual with some idiosyncrasies that bordered on the occult. There was talk that he, though long gone, still hung around.

The addition we put on enclosed the original garage, utilizing its space.

When No. 3 son, Jim, was in Vale Tech learning auto mechanics, he had a reference manual covering many of the usual repairs in a variety of the most common vehicles of that time, forty plus years ago.

It was one of those big thick ones with 5 or 6 hundred pages of fine print, hard to find what you needed, even though help was in there, somewhere.

Anyhow, Jim was baffled by a problem with a Jeep Wagoneer, unable to conquer it after many hours of trying. So, at the end of the day, he set the manual on his work bench, stating, "Bill, I need some help with that Jeep."

The next morning, when Jim went into the garage to resume working, he looks at the repair manual he had left on the bench, noticing that it was open, as if someone had been reading it.

Really curious now, since he knew he had closed it completely the day before, he picked it up and saw what vehicle was featured on the open pages.

Yes, it was the Jeep Wagoneer section, explaining in precise detail how to repair the problem Jim was stymied by.

Joan – Letter and General Mining, Inc.

Having so many life stories to tell, I question if I will have enough time left to be able to tell them all, one at a time as planned, weekly. So, I am introducing another source of these stories, in letters in their original form, written over the past years and ongoing, to a former classmate in the Bell Township High School, located in the little village of Salina, Pennsylvania, where we attended until our graduation as class of '52.

She will be identified by first name only, and by her personality and character, having been one of the most popular and most prominent members of the class, involved in numerous activities, occasionally performing as a ballerina dancer on stage, a cheerleader, involved in class plays, sports and so on, throughout the years.

She was, is, a beautiful, intelligent, personable sweetheart then and now, and has a long list of noteworthy achievements in life, for example, having been the one who not only instituted the Mental Health Treatment Division of both Latrobe Hospital in Latrobe, Pennsylvania and in the Westmoreland Hospital in Greensburg, Pennsylvania, but personally assumed the responsibility of the fundraising of the millions of dollars required. We will never know how many and whose arms she twisted to accomplish this, and we will never know how many lives have benefitted from her action, long since done.

She has lived in the state of California for many years, now in retirement from a life of public service, in the company of her adorable cat, Baby Girl, and is still not sure who rescued whom.

The first of these letters, in near original form, is included as part of this episode, and mixes a business story with a human-interest story:

Dear Joan,

Being widely known as a professional land surveyor and an associated mining engineer, I would then let it be known of available permitted areas to my many clients, and then sell them the permit, so no mining activity was ever conducted by General Mining, Inc.

One fine day the local constable shows up at my door, and lo and behold, "You have been served." By whom? And for what?

Well, a lawyer group out of San Diego, California, are representing a client who had worked around asbestos at some point in his life. The suit was because the client was concerned that at some later time in his life, he may contract mesothelioma from his exposure to asbestos.

So, these evil lawyers searched nationwide for any mining company by name, found General Mining, Inc. responsible and liable for the potential future illness, even though they had never mined asbestos-related minerals, or anything else.

I, at first laughed at this, but my lawyer did not. It cost me $2,000 to shake them.

Then, what do you know! A year later, they are back, same pack of hyenas.

This time, it was lawsuit by the same client's son, who was four years old, whose fear was that someday he might contract mesothelioma from his father's exposure to asbestos.

Another two grand down the chute.

End of story.

Dolly - 80th Tribute

Today's session is not a story, but a copy of a testimonial held at the Route 66 Grille, in late November, 2016.

The following is the presentation I wrote to honor, at a commemorative dinner, my wonderful wife, Dolores, for her 80th birthday, and the four dynamic children she gave me and the world.

Also, as a personal tribute to some of the truly good people circulating in my life, who mean so much to me, and in that light:

Good evening, I am so privileged to have you here, thank you.

Looking around me, viewing the great group gathered here, I'd like to take the opportunity to express how unbelievably fortunate I have been, and AM, to have the world's best daughter, Cindy, who will unselfishly do anything in her power to contribute to the family well-being. I could go on and on.

To have the world's best three sons: John and his wonderful, ever tolerant wife, Tammy, who is simply a great daughter-in-law. Years and years of good relations. John's main problem is there are only 24 hours in a day. Running an ambulance service can have its moments, and then some.

Steve, regardless of what he may be asked to do, can be trusted to follow the dictates of words as written in an old gospel song. These words are, in part: 'what to do to be successful, do your duty, never fail, keep your hand upon the throttle, and your eye upon the rail'. He never quits, never gives up; the kind of guy you want on your side.

Jim and Debra, his extraordinary wife, who was, and remains so, one of the true blessings granted our family by an all-knowing, all-loving God, over a decade ago. She's a perfect fit, and not only because she's a registered nurse.

Jim, unquestionably the best transmission guy around. I admit he did not acquire his mechanical skills from me. He's also very good at mowing 30 acres of grass.

And Patricia; terrific sister-in-law. Kind, loving, warm, good heart. Pretty much a half century of being around her. Always positive, great relationship. She's our dinner angel. Prepares two great dinners for us every week, delivers and serves them, all because that's the way she is. Will only accept 'thank you'. We ask God to watch over her and bless her always.

Bob and Linda Eder; met Bob about 40 years ago when he came to tend a sick bulldozer for me. What a day it was, 10 below zero. He came, he saw, he conquered--10 miserably cold hours later. We always asked for him from then on, when we needed a mechanic. He was as good as it gets, regardless of the problem. Smart, too. Linda, do you have any idea how much your cards and letters are appreciated? By the way, I still wonder if Eder should have two Ds?

Dan and Justine Shondelmyer; what I know about Dan, other than the fact that I have known him for a long time, it is that he is one super guy.

Justine said so. Thanks for being here.

Justine is without question the best, the very best caregiver, companion, friend or whatever you call it, to Miz Dolly, as she is addressed. I have, in interviews with UPMC and others, embarrassed them by openly telling them their therapy, care, and rehab services don't even come close to Justine. We are grateful, indeed.

Charlie Fox: Pat's best friend, is another welcome addition to our group.

Always friendly, always positive, ever willing to help. Great guy.

Bill Rupert; a really good son-in-law for many, many years. Willing to jump in, and take over, just about anything I asked him to help me with.

Good truck driver, good mechanic, good attitude always. Thank you, Bill.

By the way, why do they call you Wilbur?

And, of course, Dolly.

We met some 63 years ago at the Midnight Eve movie at the DeLisi Theater in Avonmore, and married five years later, much to her father's relief.

We did our share of squabbling in those five years but have had peace and tranquility ever since. In the ensuing 58 years, she has been the perfect example of what a good wife and mother should be, according to Christian principles, and I have said it many times, the perfect candidate for sainthood.

Always gentle, loving, kind. Dinner waiting regardless of the late hour.

A firm hand with the kids, never shirking any responsibility for guidance or reprimand. Never complaining, working late into the night on many occasions to accomplish the task at hand.

Always willing to do double duty, working at the hospital, weekends, and contributing to the family cause.

And now, in our waning years, in medically difficult times, she is still the same kind and loving person she has always been.

I could go on and on for hours about her positive virtues, but will conclude by simply stating, thank you for a wonderful lifetime with you, MY BEAUTIFUL DOLORES.

Your ever-loving husband, Charles.

I would also like to include in this, the super people at the Route 66 Grille.

It's not possible to get better food, service, or accommodation that is routinely provided here, thanks to the firm, but fair, leadership of Mike, occasionally a bit crabby, the friendly, often humorous greeters, the prompt drink delivery, I only have to threaten legal action once, to have it done right, great servers, some with good memories, some not as good, proven good cooks, no known fatalities within the past six months, acceptably quick service and efficient, courteous cleanup crew.

Special thanks to Jess and Danielle for the smooth operation of tonight's dinner, and an extra special thanks to Jess for the beautiful cake she made in honor of Dolly and her nursing career.

A final word on the young people we know, and have known, at the Grille.

What we have experienced is uplifting because these are the future of this great country, and we are confident the future is in good hands.

Thank you all for coming tonight to celebrate Dolly. We are truly blessed.

Note: Dolly died peacefully on December 20, 2016, a short time after the commemorative dinner.

78 Dolly, In Memory Of Today, I'm putting forth the memoir I wrote for Dolly, my everlasting love, after passing into God's all embracing hands.

384

In Memory Of Dolores May Kravetsky

November 25, 1936 ~ December 20, 2016

My Beautiful Dolores:

As an old man sitting here on a wintry December morning pondering the future, I find a reflective mood that rolls back through time with stops and starts as various events of life have presented themselves.

In not having catalogued any of these in any retrievable form other than my memories, they have become somewhat hazy and distant, but bear with me. The passing of half a century and then some doesn't help.

In view of the fact that high school graduation in June of 1952 was such a major change point in my life, the memory of it still causes me to experience a bittersweet feeling when it re-emerges, realizing that one must recognize the fact that not many of the people we separated from were truly our friends, our comfort zone disappeared, and a great loneliness suddenly became apparent, and:

Sixty three years ago, I was very much alone. A recent graduate from high school, no ongoing school or childhood friendships, male or female, and a somewhat lackluster start in a career in agriculture.

A rudderless seventeen year old, drifting along life's turbulent, uncaring seas, with no real idea what the future might hold.

Then, on New Year's Eve, nineteen hundred fifty three, by what surely was a Divine Intervention, my life suddenly and permanently changed.

As was common in those days, the local movie theater offered a show that ushered in the new year, and I decided to attend, as did many of the local teenagers.

Inside and seated, I noticed there was, just a few seats away, a beautiful, breathtaking vision: was it the answer to this forlorn country boy's inaudible prayers?

It was! Her name was Dolly Culp. After introduction, we soon became close.

Our first years saw ups and downs, temporary separations by breakups, nursing school and two years in the military, much of which was in Korea.

The daily letters from her were memorable beyond belief. The twelve place set of real china from Tokyo that cost $35.00 (that are still intact) will be passed on to future generations.

The pride she felt in having been Valedictorian of her nursing class at Allegheny Valley Hospital.

The pain she felt when she was told she was too old to be hired (at age 54) when she applied for work at Allegheny Valley Hospital after a long hiatus to take care of home and family.

The joy she felt when Citizen's General Hospital hired her the very next day. She sincerely loved working at Citizen's over the next five years before retiring from nursing.

And, after five years, we embarked on a truly wonderful journey called Life.

January 25, 1958 was quite a day. Six inches of fresh snowfall, and a beautiful wedding, with great attendance by all of our relatives and neighbors.

A generous contribution by my wonderful sisters allowed us to spend a week in Washington, D.C. A really great experience we often ruminated on.

Then, back home and to reality. I was unemployed, and she had accepted a job nursing at Allegheny Valley Hospital, earning ten dollars ($10.00) a day.

We had moved into a basement apartment in Tarentum, with a small kitchen and a bed next to the furnace. Bathroom was way upstairs on the third floor.

I was recalled to work in a coal mine, and we moved back to Avonmore, then to Bell Township to my original home with my parents. Dolly took over the cooking (much to my Mother's delight) and my Mother took over babysitting full time (much to Dolly's delight.)

Dolly gave us four beautiful children, all during a time when I was building her a house. We moved in on Christmas Eve in 1962 and live there to this day.

Our house was livable, but quite basic. No kitchen cabinets, no sink, no doors, no finished floors. Windows that let in not only the light, but also much of the winter's cold. No siding or brick and a hayfield for a lawn.

It took thirteen years of relentless effort to finally arrive at the point where the house was completed. To this day, it is still "our new house", which she dearly loved and diligently cared for.

In the ensuing fifty nine years there were many good times, and also many hard times. I prefer to dismiss the hard times as much as possible. The good far outweighed the bad. She endured with me without ever complaining or disapproving. She accepted the same pain I may have been experiencing.
She was always gentle, loving and kind. She would work throughout the day, then prepare countless great meals for us all. As the kids were growing, dinner was always kept as a group. Turns to speak were rotated around the table, giving each the time to tell their story of the day.

She made all of our children's friends welcome in our home, at all times.

She was a firm, but fair disciplinarian with the kids. Only on rare occasions was there a need for any follow up.

She was always the doctor of the house. Patching up and bandaging up endless cuts and bruises, caring for the sick, and determining when a child could so...go to school.

And there was grass. Endless grass. She mowed, and she mowed. Trimmed and trimmed. Picked up hundreds of limbs, raked millions of leaves, and so on. She never wavered.

And there was the garden, and the flower beds, bushes and bulbs. The African Violets in my office have suddenly burst into bloom.

She planted two flowering cherries, and two peach trees. Sadly, the cherries both died, and one of the peaches. To this day, the surviving peach still gives us dozens of really, really good peaches.

Then there were dogs. Always had to have a dog. The first was Holly, a Collie, who died of old age. Then came Chingo (meaning friend in Korean), another Collie. He and Jim were inseparable. An inscription in the concrete floor of our shed is "Chingo, August 14, 1975." When he grew old (10+) he simply left in the night.

Our first German Shepherd, Lobo, was huge. 130 pounds of beautiful dog. His role around the kids was that of "peacemaker." A perfect babysitter. He stayed with the kids when they were outside, and would place himself in between any two that might be squabbling. If they started to fight, he would knock one of them down and growl.

Next was Bori, the second German Shepherd. He was so nice, so gentle, so attached to humans it was unreal. A framed picture of him is on the wall at the Fotorecord Company print shop in Greensburg, in honor of their attachment to him from my many trips there.

Then came Yuri, the third German Shepherd. I include within this package the complete Memoir written for Yuri, along with a copy of the Rainbow Bridge. The reason for this is explained later. Be careful reading the Rainbow Bridge part.

An now, there is Ivanhoe. Here's what happened: Dolly was very emotionally attached to Yuri, who slept at and on her feet when she watched TV. Then he would escort her to bed, and sleep at the foot of her side. When he died prematurely, she was very seriously affected, and went into severe depression to the extent that her well being was in jeopardy.

In observing this, I determined it was time to get another puppy, which she resisted. I insisted, and I began searching. A puppy was listed available in the local paper, and after a visit, Dolly had an eight week old puppy in her lap, heading home. Her spirits brightened noticeably on the way.

We named him Ivanhoe. Ivanhoe is a real sweetie, my boyhood dream come true. He is one hundred twenty five pounds of pure joy. Dolly and Ivanhoe were one of a kind. She a flawless companion, as is he.

Almost immediately after his arrival she came out of her depression and lived happily with us from then on.

Until the awful sickness came. Ever so slowly she began to withdraw, became tired more quickly, required more sleep. Asked for help more in yard and garden, kitchen and other. Some minor falling started to occur in the yard, where terrain was uneven.

Then, a series of falls exacerbated the damage being done by strokes and progressive Parkinson's Disease, causing the inability to continue to function in a normal manner.

Dolly bravely persevered, tolerating unknown pain and suffering, yet always ready to greet anyone with a smile.

And then, on December 20, 2016, at 8:20 am, a most kind and loving soul left our world, someone whose kindness, generosity and selflessness defies ready description.

She had enjoyed her final years tending to her husband, children, house, dog and garden(s), and, apparently, it was decreed that her work was done.

Perhaps a greater need elsewhere had arisen, and she was called to it.

Her first, and last love, was service to people, friend or stranger, without asking of or expectation of thanks.

Her selfless generosity within and outside of the Family was an ongoing, lifelong practice. Specific occasions are much too numerous to list.

For the privilege of sharing a lifetime with this gentle soul, and her generous ways, we are eternally grateful. The joy she brought whenever and wherever she was is too voluminous to detail, but it was just great.

We will never forget the kindnesses extended to her by you all.

To you, Relative and Friends, who have contributed so much throughout the years, and in those final hours, we say THANK YOU from the bottom of our hears.

It has been, and continues to be, a genuine pleasure to have you share this journey through life with us.

We wish for you all the very best that can be in your future, as we close this Chapter in Life.

With Kindest Regards,

Charles
Cynthia & William
John & Tammy
Steve
James & Debra

Valerie

Dolly, my dear wife, was in hospice care, waiting out her final hours on this fair earth, no visible interaction except possibly a nod or blink in response to some verbalization.

When I am there, that's all there is to it, I am just there, alone with my thoughts and memories.

No one visits, there's only the promise of a one-way communication, imaginary at best, awkward otherwise.

But she did get one visitor.

Unexpected, yes, surprised, no.

She brought gifts, snacks, all thoughtful, considered, as is her discipline through the years. Known to us both over 46 years as one of our finest friends, impeccable in character, presentation and action, her visit simply, unobtrusively demonstrating that.

At the time, I was unable to express my reaction, but now, years later, I can.

Valerie, you unselfishly provided to me that greatest gift of all gifts in a difficult and trying time and place, YOUR PRESENCE, and I say sincerely:

Thank you, Valerie, from the bottom of my heart.

May God always watch over, and keep you close, for all time.

The Fire

It was an ordinary late winter day, calm, cold, cloudy, down at my shop and storage area. I had taken several cardboard boxes filled with trash and paper to burn in the usual spot, the fenced-in burn area located some 25+ feet away the nearest corner of my big machine shed.

This was the case as it had been for over 20 years, with never an issue, and that day the amount was about the usual volume. I set the boxes of trash on fire and went to the old shed to work on my ongoing water treatment development.

About two hours later, I heard a loud, strange sounding "pop" that caused me to get up and go out for a look, horrified at what I saw.

Black smoke and extended flames were belching out of my big shed, the fire well underway, accelerated by the combustibles in the equipment housed in there.

I immediately called 911, reporting the ongoing event. Help soon came, but a wood structure housing combustible-filled equipment was quickly consumed by the intense heat, and a total loss of extensive agricultural equipment soon became apparent.

Yes, the building and the equipment was insured, but your education as to just how inadequately you are covered begins the moment the insurance assessment agent arrives. Up to that point, you only think you are protected from serious, heavy loss.

Final thought: you can never be careful enough with open flames. Even though I believed it was not possible, it did happen.

Addendum: I have had an intense fear of fire from childhood to this day. The fear had to have been instilled way back when, as a child, I witnessed the near disastrous fire climbing up the kitchen wall, doused by Mother's quick actions.

Returning home from school one winter day as a second grader, I believe, and in the early dark of a December evening observing a huge, ominous red glow in the eastern sky was extremely fear provoking. The next day I learned a large barn filled with cows had been destroyed by that awful conflagration.

There was a close call with disaster when my brother set the living room curtain on fire with the open flame carbide light, when going coon hunting one night.

We would have lost a shed and granary if we had not had water in a lily pond with which to douse out the fire I had inadvertently set, placing a forge too near the shed and activating it.

My tandem truck set itself on fire, thankfully saved by the chance presence of son, James, and having fire extinguishers available.

Then the still frightening memory of the chimney fire in the house, here, saved by the quick action of my former son-in-law, Calvin. And the unforgettable Super Bowl Sunday fire of the big house in Slickville, and of course, the awful, still puzzling machine shed destruction.

Vandals have taken their toll in various times and places too. A D8K bulldozer was burned, and a job trailer and equipment in it destroyed.

I am ever grateful that no person, including me, was ever injured in any of these unfortunate events.

Guardian angels apparently stand guard at fires, too. Thank God.

Letter to Stella
January 24, 2012

Dear Stell,

We may have been considered poor, but we didn't know it, and were happy anyway.

The process of visiting the cows, horse, chickens, barn, granary and spring; every January 6th, Christmas Eve, and repeating the Lord's Prayer at each stop.

The Christmas Eve dinner of boiled potatoes, prunes and halupkies.

How cold and snowy it usually was.

Mom's birthday being prayed over.

The excused absence from school.

The introduction to St. Matthew's Church and the nuns who took us to Hlywiak's basement for Catechism.

The chocolate milk we shared when I was in Second Grade and you were in Third.

The shows, stage performances and what-not that required a dime to attend.

Being in the group that didn't attend.

The pain of exclusion really wasn't that bad, and soon forgotten.

The deep snows of February slowly giving way to sheets of ice that made the trip to the bus a real adventure.

Trudging up over the hill through the deep snow to catch the bus.

Shoveling a path up over the hill that immediately blew shut.

The softening of the air as Spring gradually replaced Winter.

Watching the Hepatica and Johnny Jump-Ups compete with the grass for space.

Shedding the winter coat.

The new leaves bursting out all at once.

The awful moment when it was announced that we were at war with Germany, whatever that meant.

Then Pearl Harbor.

The air-raid drills in school.

Pulling the window blinds down when an airplane went over.

Monday mornings when war bonds and stamps were being sold.

When you had a dime to participate.

The excitement of Valentine's Day, and the box to put the cards into.

Not being among the rich who had one for everyone.

Not getting one from everyone.

The unforgettable sweet smell of the Crabapple blossoms in the woods along our path.

I say that is what Heaven smells like.

Daffodils and Dogwoods we'll never forget.

Singing 'Carry Me Back to Old Virginny' as we tromped along on the way to the bus on a beautiful sunny morning.

Having a complete family that, with its faults, was still a true blessing.

The anticipation of the final tests prior to the end of the school year.

Taking the tests and getting the results.

Reflecting on unevolved romances.

The birthday that coincided so closely to the end of the school year.

The last day of school, Grade _____.

My Health

In everyone's life, health is, of course, a major issue. We all have our positive, and negative experiences, differing in level or severity in either one. There is that school of thought that claims we experience what we most predominately think, in both health, and life, but it's going to take someone far smarter than I to prove or disprove that.

I have wondered for years now, knowing the truly humble circumstances I was born, and raised in, provided for as best they could, the environment of lack, routinely going to bed hungry, dependent primarily on milk, eggs, and potatoes for daily sustenance.

I, growing up into adulthood, contracted just the most common childhood diseases, never more than in routine pass through, rarely missing school.

Colds and flu came and went, never missing work days, always there.

A one-week break for a tonsillectomy was the only extended work stop, and a two-day break after my keratotomy. There was no break for either of two cardiac stent installations.

A stop at a hospital for a simple bladder infection gave them liberty to proclaim I had Covid. I strongly insisted I did not, and after two days of Covid prescribed torture, I escaped, going home, and haven't been back since.

Summing up a lifetime, a long lifetime, I will simply state how grateful I am to whatever power has allowed it to be so, that I, in 87+ years, have been so fortunate that:

I have never awakened with anything seriously sore or even partially disabled.

I thank God every day for that, every morning for a new day, and every day for His presence in my life.

In Memory of Ann

Anna, second sister, also followed Mother genetically, gentle, quiet, hardworking, focused on whatever purpose she embarked on to a fault.

She, being as best I know, the only student to ever have had straight A's on her report card, throughout her entire school attendance 1 - 12.

Subjects like gym, where she was not athletic, she would request other studies in order to make up for any short fall, always fulfilling the request, getting her A.

As class valedictorian, I'm told her farewell address was unforgettable.

Lamentably, her only hope for educational advancement was in the form of a scholarship from colleges, there being no funds available from home.

The only school that offered such scholastic achievement any help was Geneva College, who extended $50 - yes, $50 a year scholarship, effectively ending any hope of higher education for her.

She too, then migrated to Pittsburgh, working in various clerical, and then managerial positions until her passing at age 80.

A kind and gentle soul, may God always bless and keep her happy in His wondrous presence.

I include a copy of the memoir I wrote for her.

In Memory of Anna "Ann" Kravetsky
June 14, 1930 - January 13, 2010

And Then There Were Three

Three Forty Five, A.M., Jnuary 13, 2010, a kind and loving soul left our world, someone whose generosity and selflessness defies ready description.

A Skip Through Time would:

Define her as one who freely shared whatever she had, however little, with her three sisters and two brothers, throughout the early years.

Show a young girl that scoured the countryside for berries and fruits, willingly taking the risk in climbing trees, enduring the heat and briars, then converting these over an old coal fired kitchen stove into treats for us all. The pies, jellies and jams remain memorable to this day.

Recall a one of a kind girl, who relentlessly applied herself in her studies to achieve a straight A Report Card in every subject throughout the entire twelve years of Grade and High School, and being the Valedictorian of the Class.

How, after graduation, she sought employment and gave her earnings to improve our home, providing much comfort for Parents and Siblings.

Accept the arrival of Neices and Nephews to give cause for even greater outpouring of generosity, year after year after year. This will never be forgotten.

Demonstrate her willingness to share the load, whatever it may have been, which was legendary.

Identify her willingness to share with those in need, including those whose link was out of a remote and distant past, on another continent.

Confirm her unwavering giving of herself to Family and Faith, which was wholly apparent, for which we, Family, will be forever grateful, and trust her Faith has rewarded her with eternal joy and peace in the company of other Angels.

To you, Relatives and Friends, who contributed so much throughout the years and in these final hours, we say Thank You, from the bottom of our hearts.

It has been, and continues to be, a genuine pleasure to have you share this journey through life with us.

We wish for you all the very best that can be in the future, as we close this Chapter in Life.

With Kindest Regards,

Charles, Mary and Stella Kravetsky

Spider and Toad

While cleaning up one day after lunch, I saw a spider in my sink, and, being an admitted compassionate fool, I decided to spare him or her from the usual fate, so I trapped it in a napkin, carefully carried it outside, setting it on the front porch where it could escape into the yard.

As it happened, my resident toad was sitting on the porch where it was waiting for his lunch to come by.

And it did.

So much for the spider's reprieve.

Who Owns It

I've always had an introspective reflection regarding the native people here, the American Indian, who already occupied this wonderful land when the early Europeans landed.

The history recording the interaction of these is well documented, so there is no need for me to print my views here.

As a professional land surveyor, I have been party to many hundreds of land title documents, legal proof of ownership of a certain described tract.

Sometimes, I wonder, silently, do I legally own the prescribed land I am occupying, and you, yours?

Yes, I have sheets of paper recorded as prescribed by law, that I am the rightful owner, and so do you.

But I still question, what if I am not the rightful owner, then who is? When I die, title will pass to my heirs, and when they die, title will pass to their heirs, and so on.

Does this same process apply to someone out of the long ago? Could it be the American Indian?

I rest my case.

I have read: the Indian gives thanks not only to God, but to the animal he is about to consume to sustain his life, for giving up its being so he may continue being.

An Indian proverb tells: There are two wolves within each of us, a good, positive one, and a bad, negative one, and they constantly fight for control of us.

Which one wins the fight, daily?

The one that we feed.

Deb's Birthday – Letter

I am opening today's session with a background review of the text I sent for my dear daughter-in-law's birthday, so the text makes more sense.

18+ or minus years ago, both Jim and Deb were single and seeking companionship, both 40 or so.

Jim, and a fellow mechanic, a bit of an unsavory character, agreed to a double date arranged by the other guy.

The great moment came, and Jim met all three--the mechanic, and the two girls, whom he had never met before.

I knew the girl targeted for Jim, an equally unsavory type, but not the other girl, Debra.

At the introduction, perhaps it was divine intervention; they all suddenly agreed to switch dates. The rest is in my recent text to Debra (she is just great).

May, 2021

One morning my son, Jim, called me and said today is Deb's, now his wife, birthday, and would I be sure to call her sometime during the day.

I did not call, but texted to her phone:

Once upon a time, God noticed there was a shortage of angels in the little town of Avonmore.

And so, he chose a family that was worthy, loving, and would open their arms to such a divine gift in total appreciation.

Their only stipulations were that she must be really, really pleasant, beautiful, intelligent, and willing to become a part of their life.

So, God thought, what should I do?

Perhaps arrange a meeting of strangers for a double date, then watch what happens.

The rest is history over the last 18 years.

The response I received:

Dear father-in-law, you just made my day.

My Vision

As successive school years elapsed, I do not recall having much of a visual issue, until the fifth grade, when an ever-increasing amount of information, both for study, and testing, was placed onto the room's blackboard.

During group discussion of the material on it, I was constantly puzzled how other kids could respond, even recite, certain passages on the blackboard, easily reading the statements, or questions set there.

Generally speaking, the material on the blackboard was a total mystery to me.

It did not seem to affect my grades since most of the tests were printed out, and close reading for me was not an issue, and I scored well.

It didn't dawn on me that I was never assigned an outfielder position when playing baseball, or that I couldn't locate the North Star.

Sometime in my sixth grade, the powers that be instituted a program where a qualified nurse was brought into the school, and gave every student a medical exam, such as she was authorized to give, including a visual test.

The results were not communicated to me or my parents at all, and the school year ended.

What did happen though, strange as it may be:

That following summer, at a school board meeting, the examining nurse had been invited for a review of the program.

After the meeting, the usual chit chat session was going on between the nurse and one of the board members, Hazel, who was my next door neighbor, a trusted friend.

There being no confidentiality rules and regulations of any meaningful degree then, somehow it became known I had never been informed how I had scored on my test and especially on the eye exam.

Apparently, Hazel had informed someone at the school to that effect, and shortly thereafter, a letter from the school arrived at my home, with my exam results, emphasizing extreme deficiencies in both eyes, and that an optometrist should be contacted for a professional exam.

So, the appointment was made, and results were an anomaly, a shocking surprise: 20-400, nearly blind for my right eye, 20-100 for my left eye, functional.

Glasses were ordered and fitted.

What a revelation!

Now I understood why I couldn't read a blackboard, see a baseball in the air in the outfield, find the North Star or the Little Dipper in the night sky, or read road signs at any distance, just for starters.

The vision issues had been addressed quite successfully and satisfactorily, but some negative aspects were inherent with the glasses themselves.

The frames available at that time, 1947, were far less structurally sound, prone to breakage at the slightest bump, allowing the equally substandard prescription glass to smash, at will.

Replacing a broken pair was a costly time-consuming pain.

Among the negatives was the undeniable fact the frame's structure detracted from one's natural appearance, significantly.

How do I know?

It was nearing graduation, when in a private setting, for some unknown reason I was without my glasses, and I was conversing with a girl I had made numerous unsuccessful overtures to, over the past three years, when she said bluntly, "Chuck, without your glasses, the girls would all go crazy over you, they would go woo, woo, woo!"

She, a very nice girl, remained with a really fine guy, for life.

I, glasses, and all, found and married a far more beautiful girl, and lived with her, happily ever after.

In Memory of Stella

Stella was number five, I was number six child, a close relationship that continued for life, and as she counted down her days over the last three years, living as a welcome guest in my home here in Bell Township after an absence in Pittsburgh of 67 years.

As children growing up, Stella and I did those things that we boys normally do: hike, climb trees, pick berries, clean up around the barns and sheds.

She never did learn to ride my bike, though, or drive the tractor, but she rode on the tractor many hours with me plowing, harrowing or whatever other farm-related chores were.

We made hay, stacked grain bundles off the binder, and picked corn.

There was a huge void left when she left for employment in Pittsburgh, not to return for 67 years.

Her memoir, included with this telling, better outlining her final time here with me.

Stella

January, 2010: After reading my memoir of Ann Kravetsky, Stella said to someone in our presence, "I wonder what he'll write about me."

Wonder no more.

Stella was the fifth of six children born and raised in what then was referred to as the backwoods, now more colorfully described as a delightful rural retreat.

A small farm with a small house, absent the amenities we now demand, and take for granted.

She was part of the column trailing up over the hill, through the woods, through or around the neighbor's freshly planted fields, through an old orchard down to the "big road" (Rt. 380) to the bus stop.

Stella, sisters Catherine, Anna, and Mary, along with brother Charles, were usually on time but brother Andrew would typically be late, and often times would hide behind a tree, or corn shock, causing him to "miss the bus".

School was not his greatest interest.

There were good times and bad times. There were beautiful warm spring or autumn mornings when we sang "Carry Me Back to Old Virginny", and others as we traipsed along.

There were rainstorms without raincoats, snowstorms accumulating deep snow which at times was shoveled off the path by brothers and Father, (to no avail in windy areas).

There were bitterly cold days, tolerated as best she could, with her less than adequate outer wear. There were mornings when the spring thaw came when there was ice covering everything, making walking very dangerous.

She helped Mom prepare and plant her Olympic-sized gardens, and helped care for them throughout the summer and harvesting in the fall.

She picked wild raspberries and blackberries, then helped (mostly) Anna turn them into delicious jams and jellies.

Not being much of a climber, she stayed out of the cherry and apple trees.

The plum trees were too sharp limbed, so we waited for them to fall on their own.

And, as it will, time marched along, and Stella left beautiful Bell Township, and landed in the asphalt jungle locally known as Pittsburgh, actually, Bellevue, nearby.

Centered in Bellevue, she experienced several reasonably rewarding occupations in Pittsburgh throughout her employment years, then remaining there with sister Anna until her passing, then alone until an untimely hospital visit created the need for a change of location where necessary and limited care could be provided.

LOOKOUT, Bell Township! Sixty-six years later--Stella's back.

We all welcomed her to come and stay here as long as she's able, or necessary, no strings attached.

She did insist though, this was no free ride. It was agreed she would share in the costs of operating and maintaining a household, fairly.

There was never an issue.

To be certain, there were rules and regulations, so to speak. Adjustments had to be made, and duties to be shared. We did our best to ignore or tolerate her idiosyncrasies, and she quickly accepted ours. She learned being teased was part of life here. She readily accepted washing dishes and their handling, laundry and "clean up your own mess", etc.

She "adopted" a family of chipmunks that lived under the front porch, bought lots of peanuts and fed them every day they weren't hibernating.

A bird house was hung in the apple tree just outside the living room window, and she watched a family of eastern bluebirds do their thing over two consecutive years.

She watched deer who would often come for the apples that fell from that tree, giving her a full view.

She never did learn to like "Hannity". Maybe it was because he came on at 9:00 pm, and the television was automatically switched to him, from whatever other program was on. Rules are rules.

Jeanine Pirro also fell into that category.

She had an iPad, but like many of us, never conquered it.

She really did like Lisa, her longtime caregiver. She says Lisa knows and understands her and her ? ways and wouldn't be happy without her.

She learned that dogs were a fixture here. Ivanhoe was pleasant, but not overly attentive, and was not well, over much of her stay here.

Then, on December 18, 2018, guess who arrived?

It was THOR, God of thunder and lightning! Thor, who loves everyone, immediately set out to win her love and admiration, too. Of course, his method, which we all observed, was to first prove his gentleness, and in the process relieves her of the problem of uneaten dinner(s).

When he was unsuccessful from her right side, he would switch to the left side, often resting his head on the edge of the table, while staring at her with his soulful big golden eyes, ears erect for the slightest hint of success.

It took a while, but we thought he finally won her over, deftly catching tidbits she discreetly tossed over her shoulder toward him.

When re-entering the house after an absence, he always galloped down the hall to visit her, or into the living room to poke his nose at her.

He obviously misses her, as do we. Rarely was she not upbeat and cheerful, listening to my recitation of my life and business history at lunch.

Always asking intelligent questions or making intelligent comments.

She was openly supportive of my ongoing dreams and schemes.

Her presence was uplifting from day one.

Thank you, Stella, from the bottom of my heart for almost three great years.

If there is a Rainbow Bridge for people, I feel sure she'll be waiting there for us all.

I leave her in God's loving care, Godspeed.

—Chas

After she read this, the response from her was such that I will cherish it forever.

Think and Grow Rich

Having much more free time, I've embarked into one of my old loves, the study and development of Self.

Back in the early 60's, my brother and would stay up late, and just exchange thoughts, some goofy, but some perceptive. Why, Why, Why, was much in the conversation, Why do some rise into high places, acquire wealth to whatever level, attract the best people, remain in good health, etc.

We discovered that many who achieved some or many of these traits were learned in the great Literature of the past. What is it that one must do to join the ranks of the successful.?

In August of 1964, I set out to find out. I had joined the ranks of the mining professionals, by default, and was earning somewhat respectable payment for my time, but the question rose in me, "If I'm worth   as an employee, I must be worth more." So, as previously stated, I set out to find out.

It was a blistering hot summer day of 1964, I went to the Greengate Mall in Greensburg, PA. (It's gone now, Walmart moved in), and into their bookstore, where I bought a copy of Napoleon Hill's book, 'Think, and Grow Rich.'

Was this the secret.? I memorized it over the days that followed. Other, more modern books somehow surfaced, and I absorbed them all. I bought tapes of success studies, a pillow speaker for all night presentation to my subconscious and wrote out my wishes thousands of times. Relentless pursuit of my dreams of health, wealth, and so on.

Things began to change positively; ideas came and went. (failures) obstacles rose up, legal battles, nasty people, but more good people than bad showed up. More good Ideas came, and success endured.

Life became a roller coaster, rich, then poor in varying levels. Human Nature is such that we tend to let up when doing well, which inevitably invites trouble. Then, we buckle down and repeat the process, climbing up out of the stress - what stress; just keep going, push on.

With great success, often there comes great stupidity. You become vulnerable to the dangers, toils and snares that await the uninformed, the unwary. Dozens of examples, I'll not go into them here.

Am I preaching to the Choir? You may already know of these facets of life.

Maybe in the next one, be smarter. You 'II learn you are never smart enough.

Going back to future interests that do not necessarily involve hard, physical work, I've set intentions of upgrading physical spiritual, emotional and intellectual abilities, carefully integrating these into my psyche gradually.

Will I succeed, we'll see. I made the original goals within ten years. More on this as time goes on, but briefly, one of the aspects of my future studies and research involves the entering into the fourth and fifth dimension, which I know very little about.

As I understand, we are currently in the third dimension, vibrationally speaking.

I have had a number of forays into the higher dimension, related at various times in other stories in this last roundup.

Huh

It's not really a word; it's more of a grunt, a reaction.

How many times in life have you carefully related a story, an event that may be major or significant, or just plain talk, insignificant to someone you know or barely know, and you're not really asking for a specific answer in response? What is the typical response you get?

Huh.

It can be a grunt, non-committal, the lower the frequency, the less committal, the less interest.

The higher the frequency, and the higher the volume shows the level of interest, the reaction.

Now, let's reverse the event.

Someone carefully tells you a story, etc.

What is the typical response they get from you?

Huh.

The rest is the same, isn't it?

Huh.

Box of Staples

Working in my office, I ran out of staples, so texted my daughter, in her office:

Me: Cindy, I just ran out of staples, do you have any?

She: Yes, I have a full box you can have.

Me: OK, how many are in It.?

She: 5,000

Me: That should do it, I'm 87.

Cindy——Volunteer Firemen

Going past the Avonmore Fire Department Station on day, when Cindy was about six.

She was silent for a bit, then asked.

Do Volunteer Firemen get paid? We never let her forget it.

Reminiscing with Joan

September 1, 2014

Dear Joan:

I was and remain gratified and uplifted by the content of your letter.

Gratified by the reconnect, uplifted by the monumental display of strength that you show in the face of ongoing adversity.

There is no need to apologize for the delay, as time is such a fleeting thing. Are we sure there even is such a thing as time?

Speaking of time, I clearly recall in our sophomore year, eighth period study hall in Charles Prusack's room, the many fun times we had conversing with each other.

I remember you were very outgoing and attractive, and you issued fair warning: "Do not fall for me, you will be hurt", even though no visible overtures had been extended.

We all knew where your heart's desire was directed, so there was no problem at all.

It is somewhat pleasant to project back in time and place, and momentarily relive some of the truly stress-free fun times again.

We just couldn't know how fortunate we really were.

June, 1952 was a real wakeup call for many of us. The world was already in motion, and our sudden availability did not impress it.

My stated quest to be a "Gentleman Farmer" didn't work out quite as planned (or dreamed), so other avenues had to be explored.

A stint at ALCOA in New Kensington gave me a bit of comeuppance.

Working there, I had developed aspirations in becoming a carpenter, and when the apprenticeship test was offered, I took it. Even though I had a perfect score, was told very bluntly: Forget it, if your Father doesn't work here, you won't even be considered. Discrimination.

I then opted to join the Military, and wound up in Korea, at the DMZ looking at the Chinese Army.

The fourteen months there was a paid vacation as far as I was concerned.

Many interesting people, a different culture, and lessons in self-sufficiency.

There were ten of us living in a Quonset hut, setting our own work schedule in providing Communication Services for the Sixth ROK Army.

We traveled ten miles one way daily to eat, shower, etc., but we were all young and full of vigor.

The war was over, so there was little danger.

Interestingly, I met two former classmates going to Korea when I was processing out. (John Mainc and Frank Mengor)

Frank, as you may know, was killed in a bar he operated in Ohio a few years later.

Isn't it fun to get old? We are now the leading edge of the part of society that is dying off.

Do I fear it? Not at all. I'm becoming ever more curious as to what is next.

I am a firm believer that we never actually die, but go on forever in some form involving life.

I have studied the self in many aspects, and there is that school of thought that claims we choose our life experience for the sake of that experience. Who knows? I worked for five years with a great guy who would sometimes respond to a philosophic question with: "Who knows what the turtle knows, but the turtle?"

Ten years I spent underground in coal mines as a Surveyor/Engineer have given me much material to draw from.

I've experienced fires, roof collapse, explosions, runaway machinery, runaway mine cars, toxic smoke – among many others.

That's just one facet of life. I don't know if there are enough years left to tell it all.

When we were at the fiftieth reunion you appeared to be in good condition. Did the health issues begin after that? What caused the bad prescription drug? Did you consider malpractice litigation, if justified? Apparently you are not bitter about it, and you deserve the highest respect for that.

I hope to hear from you when you can, but do not allow this to provide or create additional stress. I will understand.

I still work a full day every day with our coal mine, stone quarry, and water treatment business I am in the process of developing.

In any case I certainly wish you well always and sincerely pray your life will be filled with as much joy as possible.

With kindest regards,
Chuck

Letter to Joan -
Life Misc. & Thor

6-29-20 Dear Joan:

As a very young person, I dreamed of going to California, Hollywood to be exact, in hope of meeting my then - Dream Actress, Elizabeth Taylor, and becoming a part of that world.

The old adage, be careful what you wish for, was not yet known to me.

At this late stage of life, I am about reduced to pretty much one final best friend. He is my beautiful black and tan German Shepherd. I enclose the story of his arrival in my life. He is With me 24 and 7, providing flawless companionship. entertainment and fulfillment.

I recall having mentioned to you some time ago that I have had an extremely interesting life and should write a book. As an entrepreneur I've experienced numerous ventures in varied professions and businesses, some successful and others dismal failures.

I entered politics, became a Township Supervisor. Thankless aggravation.

I wonder how many survivors there remain out of the Class of '52. Do you realize how long ago that was?

I am beginning to recognize a subtle, ongoing deterioration mentally and physically, and I'm hoping the challenges still ahead will forestall such indefinitely.

I am, of course, extremely fortunate in having 4 good kids, all living close by, 2 in Avonmore and 2 in Saltsburg, both just 4 miles distant.

I have ended my involvement in the Coal Mining and Quarrying businesses, and disposed of all of the equipment.

Catch me up with your life whenever you can. Ending this for now, and I hope you remain well and as happy as need be; wish the best for you always.

Much love,
Chuck

Guinness Record

I 'm not sure what, if any, value there is, except bragging rights, of being listed in the Guinness Book of Records, but
I believe I have an experience that should qualify me, us, to the
book.

The stage, as set for that experience is as follows:

Daughter-in-Law, Glenda, is in the final stages of childbirth,
the Ambulance Service, owned by me, and my family, has been
summoned. It is being attended by me, a Paramedic, by her
Mother-in-Law, Dolly, a Registered Nurse; also, by my oldest
Son, John, a Paramedic, and by my Daughter, an Emergency
Medical Technician - enroute to a local hospital, where delivery
of a healthy male grandchild is achieved.

Where- oh-where in the wide world will you ever duplicate
this:

1. The patient is part of the family.
2. The ambulance service is owned by the same family.
3. The attending Registered Nurse is the Mother-In-Law.
4. Attending paramedic is the Father-in-Law.
5. The second attending paramedic is a Son and the C.E.O.
of the service.
6. The attending E.M.T. is the Sister-in-Law.

Is it worth the aggravation to apply for listing in the Guinness Book of Records?

I seriously doubt it and haven't yet.

Wilbur

Who is Wilbur? Well, he's actually my current Son-In-Law, William. His having been the late comer for the name in our Company, it caused confusion when a CB call came over the air for Bill, so to end that, he was dubbed Wilbur, and it pretty much stuck.

Anyhow, he joined K.M.P. Associates in the late nineties at the Ehenger Strip as a rock truck operator first, then other equipment as time went on. Understandably, he was a bit green at it, but quickly picked up on how to make the proper moves and work safely.

As we expanded operations and added over-the-road trucks to the fleet he was sent to Truck Driving School, where he became a proficient operator of all of our trucks, including lowboy movement.

A stone spreader on our single axle was extremely valuable in keeping roads open and safe, and he never failed to be there on an icy day ahead of the coal haulers, making their travelways comfortable and passable.

He also became a favorite by the Public in general, who requested him to be the one to spread the stone on their driveways, always doing an exemplary job for them.

When we donated stone to the Avonmore Cemetery, he always spread it without any damage to the low-hanging branches in there.

He was like the Locomotive Engineer in that old Mountain Railroad song "Life is Like a Mountain Railroad Man, do your duty, never fail. Keep your hand upon the throttle, and your eye upon the rail."

He's in semi-retirement now, keeping things operational here, and locally at Busy Beaver.

Charlie's Grave

This tale is probably not one of a kind, but I'm sure it's uncommon.

I believe I am one of a rare few, if any, individuals who has, as a professional land surveyor, selected the spot, designed, surveyed, marked, and mapped their own grave site.

I am quite grateful it is still waiting to be occupied.

I Was Just Thinking – Why, God

Sometimes when I see awful things going on in the world, I'm confused, I say to myself; why, God?

But the words to an old song appear, and say to me; you're just a man, not meant for you to understand.

Writing Your Life Story

It's a lot of fun writing my life story.

I can enjoy the positive and humorous, and easily dismiss negative and painful experiences as I recall and relive them.

Try it, you'll see.

Feeding Kids-Joan letter

Today's story is a copy of a letter I wrote to my friend Joan.

March 4, 2021

Dear Joan,

I notice it takes five days for a letter to cross the country, so most likely this will not reach you prior to the eighth, the day of your surgery.

I gave up on computers for letters long ago, when it was a constant battle to keep the format normal, and for the time being, I'm back to printing, since my electric typewriter abandoned me.

Am very concerned about your aortic valve issue; my background as a medic, and as holder of three stents, does give considerable comfort in knowing the success rate is well into the 90's for your pending procedure.

Through the years of study of who and what we actually are, I delved into remote healing to a limited extent. This is a topic I rarely discuss, for obvious reasons. However, I have occasionally practiced such, with some success, and with no fanfare, as I am totally aware I am merely asking God for a favor for someone.

Further, it's well known that as a group of two or more people, requests are far more powerful.

I am beyond happy to join all others who may be asking for divine intervention in a safe surgery and speedy recovery thereafter for you.

I doubt this will reach you pre-surgery; but be assured; the prayers are in place already.

I'll end this with a bit of humor, I think.

Back in the good old days when I was less busy, Dolly worked weekends, and I babysat four kids.

Well, as all interviewees on television start with, dinner was my responsibility. My cooking skills being graded dangerously close to zero did not inspire much enthusiasm from them for my offerings.

Being somewhat of a disciplinarian, I would not allow filling up with junk, so it was eat it, learn to like it, beat it, injected with some humor, of course.

So, I contrived a plan. I began extending dinnertime gradually from normal 6 o'clock to 6:15, to 6:30, then to 7:30, a big jump, to 8:30 then to 9:00 o'clock, ever so gradually.

That instituted a philosophy and belief in how much better anything tastes, depending on how hungry you are!

That ended the complaints, and to this day we still joke about how effective that philosophy was then, and now.

And also, how much they still like eating Dinty Moore's stew.

God bless, you will be fine. Much love, Chuck.

Finding Mr. Right - Emma

Having been seated in our favorite restaurant one Saturday evening, awaiting the usual request for drinks choice by a fairly recent hire of several weeks, who, after delivery of our drinks, engaged daughter Cindy in some small talk.

She, quite attractive, very young, a recent nurse graduate, was asked if she was married. She said no that she was still looking for Mr. right, but so far was unsuccessful in finding him.

So, the following week, we again are at the same restaurant, and in a break of activity, I called her over to our table and said, are you still looking for Mr. Right? She said yes.

So, l, still being somewhat youthful in both physical and appearance attributes, said; here I am! I am beautiful, rich, single, personable, live alone in a beautiful house on 180 acres, and have a beautiful German Shepherd, who is with me seven and 24; and I'm only 87.

What's not to like?

Walking away, she shot back, I'll think about it, maybe we can work something out. Don't get too far away.

Oh, reality.

1.5 Million Miles

My claim to fame pales when comparing it people who make a living on the road. Truckers, Salesmen, people involved in far-flung construction projects, and so on. For a home-bound hustler, though, 1.5 million is a lot of miles, and the time in a vehicle in reaching that.

In adding up the mileage have driven in the various vehicles I've owned, I'm certain I'm at or even just above 1.5 million.

Mind, this is just an ordinary hustler trying different occupations, nearly always working at several of them at the same time, looking for more and better.

If were to assign a mileage equivalent to the thousands of hours I have been inside everything from small to big farm tractors, small to big bulldozers, front end loaders, track loaders, numerous excavators and backhoes and various trucks, I could well be into multiple millions of miles under my butt.

That pretty much winds up the high-level accumulation, as currently I 'm no longer traveling much at all.

Looking back, sometimes I wonder how I could have spent so much time riding in a vehicle, and still have time to work.

It's really very simple: there are 24 hours in a day.

My Wind Sock

About 30 years ago my Wife, Dolly, bought a pair of peach trees, planting them in full view of my office, and I watched them grow, flower, and produce peaches, and oh how they did produce.

One died some years ago, but the other lived on, making up for the departed one. And how it produced, year in, year out, total abundance.

Two years ago, it produced so many, that when they matured, about ready to eat, a vicious storm tore it apart, leaving it in pieces on the ground.

The deer had a picnic. I had to cut it off, leaving a stump, in hope a new tree would sprout out of it, and in memory of Dolly. No new tree came out of it, and most likely that it never will.

In order to see it when mowing, I put a tall hanging basket holder post beside the stump, then hung a two-feet long piece of surveyor's ribbon onto the top of the arc in the pole.

Now, when I am working, or in the present case writing my life story, or needing to rest my ageing eyes, I turn and look out my window toward the distant woods but see the windsock-like ribbon first.

The action of that ribbon, a small version of a windsock, absolutely fascinates me. Since I admit to being a little, or more, goofy, there's no need to make that accusation.

My little windsock sends me a continuous message as to wind movement outside, and I transmute that into Mind movement, as in everyone's life.

It can be hanging perfectly vertical, calm, unmoving, like those rare times in life. Then, it can suddenly lean out, away, in a bit of turbulence, picking up speed, now fluttering in a stronger breeze, now its halfway up from vertical, waving, not fluttering as the wind, an unseen force moves steadily along, beneficial in many aspects, not damaging to anything.

Gradually, or suddenly, the sock is straight out, perpendicular to calm, vibrating more so, to fluttering or waving, resisting to being torn from its mooring, riding out the storm.

Then, once again, a gradual or rapid return to gentle waving or fluttering, even return to calm, for the moment.

Within each of us, is there a parallel to this?

Skydiving

My good friend, Hugh, sustained painful, serious injuries in a fall from a ladder recently, but I credit him for maintaining a sense of humor.

When I heard about it I texted him:

Me: Hi Huie, Chuck

He texted back: Hi, Chuck

Me: Huie, I understand your first lesson in skydiving did not go well, it seems they forgot to strap on the parachute.

Season's End

Today, October 25, 2022, I'm resting my eyes from writing, leaning back in my office chair, looking out at my windsock, momentarily hanging straight down, vertical, then, as the wind just breathes, it dances, hula-style, twirling in all directions, then back down, now still.

It's an absolutely perfect late October day, blue skies, maple, and oak leaves still in fantastic color, lifting my spirits in their pure glory.

Having filled my bird Feeder, the competition is fierce, but peaceful.

The group of six big Blue Jays dominates the scene, but the black capped Chickadees, Sparrows, and Wrens flit in and out, getting their share.

It will be empty soon, then it will need to be recharged.

The Hummingbirds are long gone, the remaining nectar untouched.

One of my little girls, a bumblebee, comes flying, not realizing it's a hopeless cause, the flowers are all gone, there's no nectar to carry home.

According to Nature's rules, soon the Queen will go into hibernation, and all the workers. but the few tending her will die off.

I wait for Spring, and your return.

In the meantime, I welcome Winter, and get back to work.

Employee of the Month

At our favorite restaurant recently, one of the manager's kids, a fine, fine young man, our waiter, and upon our seating, he proudly announced he had been named the Employee Of the Month, and showed us the award, an 8 ½ by 11 placard, picturing all 15 employees, him, smiling in the center.

After the exposure of this monumental achievement, and after the cheering subsided, I said:

May I ask a few questions?

He said sure, what are they?

My answer:

Will you promise to at least act as if we are as good as you are?

Will we be required to genuflect and kiss your ring whenever we meet?

Will we be required to speak in hushed tones in your presence?

Young Waitress

In joking with one of my regular waitresses, I told her if she wanted to have some real fun, I would take her out, adding, I'm only 89, and I can still cut the mustard.

Her reply:

I 'm sorry to say, you already expired, you're well past your best if used by date.

It was her loss, I think, a free dinner and dancing.

Give Away

To whom much is given, much will be required, Luke 12:48.

Somewhere, somehow, without my being aware of this must have been a part of my DNA, both the desire and the willingness to give, be it my time, my knowledge, my belongings, or my services.

This began at a very early time, when a neighbor lady gave me an orange, which I dearly desired to eat, but didn't, saving it for my Mother, who then shared it with me.

Helping neighboring farmers with seasonal work, for no pay.

Even though I thoroughly enjoyed it, two years in the Military was a giving of my life, willingly.

Then, in joining the ranks of the business community, along with the Professional Services sector, my never-ending efforts in searching out suitable ventures that could provide jobs for people.

In my professional endeavors, I never charged clients unfairly, did not charge for travel mileage or travel time.

I never charged for telephone or on-site consultation, for copies of past services.

I never took anyone through the Court System for unpaid invoices for my services, and there are many.

Many times, the appearance was that I was losing, but, somehow, I kept winning, gaining.

I had acquired an active Church by default, gave it to the congregation for one dollar.

I gave several acres of land to another Church for an extension of their cemetery, giving them ownership of already occupied grave sites.

I routinely contribute to worthy causes, food banks, animal shelters, etc.

The few loans I have ever made to needy people, I have forgiven.

What have I received in return........EVERYTHING!

A great Family, great surroundings, great health, and a great German Shepherd, THOR.

Story Recall Affect

In this process of recording my experiences as memory retrieves them, there are those that have greatly affected my psyche at the present time, stirring up long hidden emotions, both positive and negative, both uplifting and depressing.

One focuses on Life and Love, Puppy Love to be exact.

That storied sweet mystery of Life, that emanates only from the soul, cannot be manufactured or self-created, and lives or dies according to actions and emotions not necessarily outlined in any predictable form.

A thirteen-year old's glimpse into that hallowed kingdom, and subsequent failure to follow up over a now apparent extended period of time, unknowingly allowing potential to fall untouched into the dustbin of History, until time finalizes the whole entanglement with the passing of the principals involved, one or both.

Another focuses on Life, and Death, that most feared, and most inevitable event.

In the telling of the story where I was coaxed into traveling into that part of the Jamison Mine where a Continuous Miner was mining directly toward a very live gas well, being just a few feet, and a very few minutes from a certain fiery explosion and instantaneous death; when I arrived there and stopped him from mining further.

The ramifications of this are horrendous. We all would have perished, in there, in moments.

What, or who caused me to agree to go in there with him, that day, I do not know.

No one, but I, and whomever might read or hear this story will ever know the truth of that fateful day, told here for the first time anywhere.

And, certainly, dreamy, happy times can also be drawn out of storage and revisited.

Become still, listen intently, and you can see and hear those dearest to you at will, dwelling as long as you wish on any past event.

Having the freedom to selectively recall the past, you also have the freedom to select, direct and project the future, here, and on into eternity, as you choose.

Only you will ever know how the story ends.

God Speed.

Missy Birthday

Once upon a time, God noticed there was a shortage of Angels In Irwin.

And, He thought, there's a really great guy there whose life would brighten greatly if I put one there, with him.

So, he did. His name is Patrick, hers is Missy.

Happy Birthday Missy.

Stella

Stella was the sister closest to me, both in age and in daily association.

She is mentioned elsewhere briefly, but in view of the close friend— ship we shared; I'm opting to include a much more inclusive review of her best accomplished in the form of copies of not only past events in memory, but also, in the memoir wrote and read at her funeral mass.

It is my hope you will commiserate with me in my wanting to permanently commemorate her.

Not a Lawyer

In the business world, you quickly learn to hate, detest, those certified letters, and equally, or worse, the appearance of the Star Car, containing that typically friendly, short-term visitor, a Constable, handing you the good news that you have been sued. sending your life once again into turmoil, bringing back again into your life - lawyers.

There have been Occasions where I have been accused of having missed my calling; that I should have been a lawyer, legitimately, since I have been openly accused of indulging in the practice surreptitiously, out of the shadows, or worse.

There have even been times attempts by some unnamed to reach agreement to practice only in our duly licensed professions, i.e., you do the Surveying, Engineering, etc., and I do the Lawyering.

I, choosing to neither deny nor admit venturing into the legal arena; nor to limit my rendering of opinion in any subject, not necessarily bearing any weight legally by inference or intent.

I am not a lawyer, have never been or pretended to be a lawyer, don't want (God forbid) to be a lawyer, even though there have been times I acted as one, but only in private.

God Bless them, most of them.

On second thought , some of them.

I Wanna Go Home

The Saturday following my negative experience with the normally disgruntled waiter- unappreciative of my light hearted approach to life in general, and my telephoned request to the owner / manager, that it would most likely be beneficial to the restaurant's future if I was not ever again be subjected to the less than cheerful acceptance of such temporary subjective servitude as is normally required in the servicing of me, and mine during a visit, brief though the assignment may be.

What, a total of just minutes to order, transfer to the kitchen, and later deliver and distribute, return at least once to assure we were all visibly alert, vital, and still In the process of consuming such fare as had been delivered earlier, and if said servant gave the slightest damn, to whatever degree had progress been made, and what additional element may be provided to continue such action, if anything.

I do not recall threatening more than twice to take legal action if he didn't immediately upgrade the wait.

Even my promise of a more than generous two-dollar tip didn't appear to have made or caused any adjustment in his attitude, except maybe to backslide some.

So, let's bring a little sunshine into these storm clouds, and learn what reaction and action was taken out of my less than disguised threat, regarding this troubled soul, and future service personnel for me.

A week later, seated in our usual spot, the semi-private alcove, anxiously waiting for our Martyr of the Week to appear.

And, as it happened, not one, not two, not three, but four downright personable sweet young things, all familiar and comfortable with my, at times, less that disarming approach to those lucky, or unlucky enough to have been assigned to the unknown demands forthcoming over the next sixty minutes or so.

I'm assuming that Brandy, Danielle, Jess and Kaitlin secretly drew straws to determine whose fate it would be to service me, us, and of course by unhesitant Manager Mike's confirmation, he deploys Jess, ever conforming, to perform the task, she aware of my own expressed philosophy that nothing lasts forever, and that, this too shall pass. She presents with, in the most aspects, the correct attributes, and also by appearances, the correct National affiliation, along with its tendencies to be a bit challenging.

As a Ukrainian, having plenty of experience to that over a lifetime, I was / am more than ready to countermand such at any time. She was all I could expect or hope for.

Establishing expectations and other boundaries early on, she went on over the next several years providing well above average service, with only a few complaints or legal threats from me, before running off and getting married, unceremoniously abandoning me forever.

I sometimes wonder if her patience and tolerance levels weren't exceeded, in part, by my story of the week, now deemed to be included in my future book, potentially boring many of this planet's occupants besides her in the future.

I do, without hesitation, credit and congratulate her regarding her choice of a soul mate in Scott, unquestionably a fine long-term partner.

Hold tightly to him, Jess. He's a winner.

I / we are quite content with Mike's choice of successors for us, but understanding that Brandy, Danielle, and Kaitlin, all having better things to do, are only rarely impressed to that duty, along with not only a sweet, mature thing, she absolutely beautiful in every way, and one who closely resembles my dear, departed oldest sister Kay – and is also named Kay.

I / we, always look forward to having any of these serve us, all a delightful change of scenery, never having to hear me sing – I wanna go home, I wanna go home, oh how I wanna go home.

And so, all's well that ends well, but I must ad lib one more.

That one, I, a bit grudgingly include is none other than the youthful image of ever-vigilant Mike, the Manager; being Christian – this one with considerably more charm and public impression, his already having achieved an Employee of the Month Award at such an early age, incites a bit of jealousy in me, as I have yet to have ever received such lofty recognition in almost a hundred years.

Could being self-employed have something to do with this?

Potatoes Today

We harvested our potatoes. The garden is at rest, waiting for Spring.

A perfect day, cool, a slight breeze nearly constant, Jim, Steve and me looking at 3000 square feet of rows, three-feet-apart.

Why did we plant so many potatoes?

So many dire warnings, food shortage imminent, prepare, prepare, prepare, cry all the news medias.

Food shortage, I was born and raised in a food shortage.

Potatoes, I love potatoes. In great part, that is why I'm here. I survived on potatoes, during that time of the year when the cows produce no, or minimal milk, and the chickens produce no, or minimal eggs, I survived on the potatoes that were stored in the dugout under the house.

Growing up, mashed potatoes were the usual evening meal, mashed with milk when it became available.

Who doesn't love French Fries, potato chips?

Anyhow, we're ready for a very hard, very long day, the four-wheel drive John Deere runs down the row, pushing most of the potatoes out where they are visible, reachable.

And the real fun begins, three guys with no bend down and reach exposure in years, are facing hours and hours of exactly that, very hard after about 5 tries. After a few more, the back needs a short break, then the legs, and knees.

We are gaining, but very slowly, time moving on, energy level still high, but a long way to go.

Lunch, a break, recharge the battery.

Another burst of energy, and the bigger of two sections are done, ready to begin the smaller one, still a formidable 1000 square feet, and it's pushing two o'clock, energy level diminishing quite a bit.

Line up the tractor, and go down the first row, watching for the out flow of beautiful, multiple red, this time, potatoes, of every dimension.

But, shock, shock, shock. There are no potatoes at all, from the first pass. Did he miss the row's location? No.

He moves over a little and tries again. Still no potatoes, maybe a handful.

So, he moves to the second row. Same result, maybe another handful from the whole row.

He moves to the third, then the fourth, and finally, to the last row.

Total yield from the second part of the garden: maybe a half bushel, a near total failure.

Maybe, maybe something else.

As I was first starting to be working in Section One, early on, something flashed in my skull.

It was an image of me lying on the ground, the others hovering about, waiting for an ambulance to arrive. I, being a Paramedic, am self-diagnosing that I have just experienced a cardiac failure, the future dim.

In particular, me with an unfinished writing of my life story, Thor without his buddy, potatoes unharvested.

My own Doctrine on the apparition?

I firmly believe the absence of potatoes in the Second section was a divine intervention, eliminating the demand to stressfully engage in the completion of the excavation before weather conditions changed to the negative, losing the last opportunity to harvest the potato crop.

We then wrapped up the entire operation, calmly accepting the void created by the absence of potatoes, really with no other choice.

The entire exercise ended happily as day peacefully blended into night. I, tired, but assuredly unimpaired, retreated to prepare our – me and Thor's – dinner.

Thank You, God, for Everything

Alone

I came here alone; I will leave here alone. Certainty, I received care adequate for survival, but cannot recall any holding of, or touching other than necessary for my physical movement.

Apparently, this developed a lifelong reluctance to engage in or display any desire to physically interact with any and all descendants, children, grandchildren, or great grandchildren.

I have said I'm an 'unusual' Grandfather, and I acknowledge it.

I won't fault my Brother or Sisters for my developed loneliness preferences, as age and gender interests were such as to readily exclude me for obvious reasons.

I am totally aware I could be completely incorrect in the following statement(s) and offer the same only as a possibility in one individual's development, mine.

After an extended, in-depth self-search for an answer, I have concluded that somehow, for some unknown reason, I was born to be a leader.

At this advanced stage of my very long life, I will reiterate, once again, a statement I have uttered many times, especially in those numerous trying, often emotionally desperate times: I'm the leader, even if, when I look behind me, there's no one following along.

Multiple meanings can be taken out of that statement, but I'll not offer any.

Evidence of early leadership could, and I emphasize could, be seen in the lack or absence of friends in my early grades, except for the apparent subconscious attraction of the teachers, in making me their pet.

There was a less visible continuance of this throughout high school, and an even less visible follow-up in the final school years when I was somewhat the leader of the Vocational Ag group, the bad boys who kept things stirred up.

And, of course, there was my wonderful subservient wife of over six decades. As we progressed into our children's adulthood, each followed me until more powerful psychological forces beckoned, understandably, or the comfort of participation retained them within the established group, for a time.

Upon dissolution of all group activities where I was involved, I once again was free to return to my original status.

Alone, and unfollowed, there's no one behind me now, I'm alone.

I now have the time to ponder, alone.

What does it mean to be alone?

You're not really alone until you feel alone, excluded from engaging in activities going on in your presence, by choice or by circumstance.

As a former active Paramedic, I saw firsthand all too often what it can mean to be alone, really alone.

Just go into any long-term care nursing facility and view the once valued, once respected, once productive remnants of humanity, now reduced to objects marking time, until their rendezvous with eternity.

Or, as a guest at a child's birthday party, a misfit teetotaler at a teen beer keg party.

I was never invited to either – ever.

Or one can view being alone as a new adventure, new freedom from Society's demands.

Long ago, I preferred to be alone, established what I referred to as the "over ___ exemption" from all parties.

No 1-year-old, 2-year-old or other parties, and so on.

For me, it's good to have a German Shepherd who really doesn't care or ask for much.

I came here alone.

I will leave here alone.

Only God knows what, then.

Ryan

I was trimming weeds along the Township Road bordering some of my property, when a pickup screeched to a stop beside me.

In it was a young man, who got out, courteously stretched his hand,

introducing himself, said he was looking for work, and could he take over what was doing.

Owning over a mile of road frontage, was only too glad to be relieved of that rough job.

He came, did that and other odd jobs around my 180 acres, always doing a good, efficient job.

Over the next couple of years, I got to know him better, gaining a certain respect and liking of him.

He was 25 years old, had had a hard start in Iife, his Mother had passed when he was very young, and he had been raised by various family members, all reluctantly, a Grandmother ultimately keeping him into adulthood.

Irregardless, mixing with a bad group, he got into trouble, and served a couple of years in prison.

He swore he had learned his lesson, a hard lesson, and wanted to make a better life for himself.

I, seeing a young man eager to work hard, willing to get out of bed early, and work late, decided to help him in his chosen vocation, lawn care and landscaping. I saw he had no real mower, except a small hand controlled one.

So, compassionate fool that I am, I bought a very expensive, top of the line commercial mower, and after securing him a major client, rented it to him, rent free for the first year.

Now he was earning 200 dollars for less than a days' work, able to pursue other clientele.

A friendly client gave him a good place to live, free, and he was doing quite well. Life was leveling out a bit.

Then, tragically, the friendly client died unexpectedly, very young, leaving Ryan at the mercy of heirs, who quickly notified him he must leave, would not consider renting to him any longer.

At this point I lost contact with him, but what happened, as I was told, he was very depressed, despondent, having lost one of his few friends. Never mind being put back out onto the street, now homeless. He went back to selling drugs.

It was only a matter of time, smashing up a friend's pickup while high, he was arrested.

He also had sold my mower to another drug dealer, whereabouts of it unknown. He is now serving 2 to 6 years in state prison and we are no longer friends.

So sad, he had potential.

Apollo, Train Crossing

Late as usual, for some perceived ultra-important meeting with a prospective client, I was traveling North on Rt. 66, almost to the railroad crossing just West of Apollo, PA; a big wide crossing, when red flashing lights warned of an oncoming train, also traveling North, so I stopped, with no one ahead of me at the tracks.

I was first out of the hole, as they say, when the train passed. So, I wait for it to go by, growing a bit more impatient than is sensible.

It was a long, slow train, but finally, the caboose is beside me, and I'm ready to go, starting to drift along with it, clearing the crossing.

I got about halfway into the crossing when I hear this Godawful train horn, and I'm looking straight at a fast-approaching train heading South, on the other track, straight at me.

Other people waiting at the crossing are also blaring their horns at me, not wanting to be prime witnesses to gross stupidity, impatience, and the unhappy consequences thereafter.

I slammed on the brakes, stopping a not so comfortable 10 or 12 feet from a certain introduction to my Creator.

Now backing up, then waiting. Ready for a fresh start.

After that train passed, some wise guy parked his pickup, went to the center of the crossing, pretending he was a traffic cop, held up his hand stopping all other traffic wanting to cross, then waved me through, safely.

I waved a thank you kindly, went across just a bit wiser.

Saltsburg Canal

I don't remember the date, but it was somewhere in the 1980's when the work on the restoration of the Saltsburg Canal was started. I recall the conversation, but not who it was with, regarding the demolition of the Lockkeeper's Dwelling, and also the clearing of stumps and rough railroad grade left after removal of the ballast and cinders from the tracks. Long ago.

I then moved a 25-ton excavator in, and proceeded to take down the dwelling, a frame structure located very close to the canal itself. I remember pushing the material into the canal void, where others must have burned it.

There were dozens of huge stumps that I dug out, then buried in a deep trench I made alongside the old railroad fill. I then rough graded the area, which was fine graded by Bob Treece, if I remember correctly, at a later time.

I have been Saltsburg's Surveyor ever since I received my License in 1967.

To date, some 55 years.

My most significant involvement has been in the layout of the Canal as it currently exists.

Few are aware of the thousands upon thousands of calculations and field shots required to accurately reproduce the original physical installation and appearance of the canal, along with a facsimile of the moving stream that carried the canal boats along.

The blending in of the streets and natural features into the centerpiece compliments the entire installation nicely.

The installing workers and the supervisors did a marvelous and commendable job, already time proven.

The year 2022 celebrated the 31st Anniversary. I am often in Saltsburg, and I admit, I always feel a certain pride when I pass by the Canal reproduction, the elegance of it, and in the part I played, even though I'm the only one who knows it.

Getting Along

I know I have mentioned this several times in the telling of these stories, but I hope to sum it up this time for good.

Dolly and I were married for 59 years, and never once had an argument, much less a fight. Yet, few have ever asked, how did you do it.? Something of an accomplishment in any circumstance.

There is no esoteric secret to the reason or method at all. It is simply combining early on, great respect for each other, proper praise when necessary, and putting it all together in your own way, perhaps as I, we, did throughout the years, then decades; in one sentence that to me, said it all.

Daily, daily, when appropriate, I would simply reiterate to her:

Your Happiness is what matters most of all.

And I meant it. For all 59 years.

You take it from there.

Thor - Guardian Angel

As you age, death and taxes are not the only inevitable certainty in life, as we are now joined by prescription meds.

Recently, needing a dose of chemical assistance, I went to our local Pharmacy here in Saltsburg to fill this need.

Thor, my German Shepherd, was with me, as usual, and I had parked along a very busy street in full view of the pharmacy, half a block away. It was warm out, and stupidly, I left the driver's side window down.

Intensely loyal to be with me; after watching me go into the building, he climbed out of the vehicle, out onto the busy street, and proceeded to the door where I had disappeared into, dodging traffic the whole way, I was told.

As it happened, an unknown motorist, seeing this activity, quickly parked in a laundromat lot, jumped out and risking his own well-being in heavy traffic, was able to corral him, grab his collar, and was holding him, safe and secure on the sidewalk outside the pharmacy when I emerged.

He graciously, even led him to my vehicle, depositing him into it, safe and sound.

He will never know how truly grateful I am, and will always be, for his action.

Do dogs have Guardian Angels?

YES!

Hair Cut

I stopped at my local, friendly Barber P. J.'s one day for my somewhat sporadically spaced haircut.

It having been a bit longer than usual between cuts, I had done a little barbering, just to beat back the shade and let in the sun, so to speak, and made do with it till now, sitting in the Barber chair.

He started whacking, quiet for a short time, then, knowing each other quite well, he said, Chuck, you're a man of many talents, but take my word for it, Barbering isn't one of them. Could you stick with one of the others, instead, in the future?

I agreed.

Goodbye, My Friend

I met this wonderful man, Dick W., many years ago when I was a coal mine laborer with a future progression of unknown potential beyond an increase in hourly wages and a future pension.

Five years working with him gave me knowledge and experience far above and beyond that of a coal mine laborer.

Thanks, in great part to him, I am well on my way to an ongoing future of high promise, secure and already rewarding beyond my wildest dreams.

In his guidance, I found patience, wisdom, and direction for a bright future. I want to publicly thank him from the bottom of my heart. Thank you all for listening.

Dick retired when the mine he was working for closed during a mines' strike.

I, very busy, totally occupied long hours every day, rarely took time to visit with Dick. He, now living in town with his wife, Irene, happened to meet my daughter and told her that Dick would like to have me visit him, reasonably soon, at his house.

So, the next day, I stopped in and had a memorable half-hour visit with him, reminiscing about the past history we shared and so on, a very nice moment in time.

I bade him goodbye; He died a few days later.

He was 82. God Bless and keep him forever, a truly fine man.

In Memory of Mary
August 25, 1931 — January 10, 2024

Mary, early on, was accepted as the leader of the pack. She was the thinker, the one who thought out the day's activities for the four sisters, and assigned the duties involved to each.

"Pip" was a favorite game, sort of an original "House", which featured a family going about their daily affairs. The Sunday newspaper provided the characters, and makeshift cardboard was crudely shaped into a house.

Being a boy, and much younger, my role in the games was minimal at best, told to "beat it" most of the time. No great loss.

As it happened, we had the same bus driver throughout all the years, and we being something less than social, clashed with Mary's equally challenging personality when she preferred to walk, not run to "meet" the bus those times she was a little tardy, and he had to wait a short time for her.

It actually reached the point where one morning she was within a few feet of the waiting bus, walking but not running, when he closed the door and drove away, abandoning her by the roadside.

She wrote a report on the incident and turned it into the office as a part of her excuse for being absent.

The end result for him did not go well, and he was severely reprimanded for his action.

Mary did not change her approach in the future but it never happened again.

Interaction with teachers was a sensitive arena, and grades given by certain teachers escalated into one on one confrontations at times, when Mary would challenge grades that, in her belief, were less than she expected, and would back up her argument with references and other proof. Oftentimes the grade would be changed up, which did not endear her much to the teacher who had to make the change.

Please understand, it was Mary's all out intention to follow the footsteps of sister Anna, who had been the prior year's Valedictorian.

Mary was born with limited vision, and, as a child struggled greatly with school work and its demands for endless close up study and blackboard reading.

Regardless, with superhuman effort and a never give up attitude she still maintained a 4.0 grade average, and was the Valedictorian of the Class of 1949.

Mary and one teacher in particular, became considerably less than socializing friends, and was the target of her Brother Charlie's library watering event several years later, described in his book in detail.

Being somewhat aggressive and confrontational, Mary accepted the role of Editor In Chief of the school newspaper, known as the Bell-Echo.

Interviewing anyone and everyone as she sought out newsworthy articles, including Coach Hamilton, she soon became known as a hard sell, pulling no punches on sports games when losses were obviously the result of poor coaching, poor play, or poor decisions in general.

Headstrong, egotistical coaches, both male and female, would defend their negative results by calling her into their office and chastising her for her embarrassing editorials.

Just Plain Charlie volunteered to be a reporter, assigned to cover all sports events.

His tenure lasted just one term (six weeks) as Editor In Chief Mary didn't think much about Reporter Charlie's selection of topics, nor the elaborately extended description of such topics, labeling his work as totally boring, ad infinitum, ad nauseam, printing just the score.

Charlie's reaction was in lamenting the discouragement of a possible career in journalism for him.

Mary had a kind side too. As kids growing up with few amenities, certain foods not on any list to have in the pantry, she would often enlist in innovative ways what was available with the hand-picked fruits or berries, creating truly delectable dishes or desserts. These were served as a family gathering in play form, a memorable event I will forever harbor.

Somewhere, she thought learning to ride a bike was not difficult, just get it to a point where gravity would take you back down to the house, get on and away you go.

So, one evening she must have thought, I'm going to learn to ride a bike. Taking mine up our driveway for a short distance, getting on and away she went, picking up speed at an alarming rate.

Being unaware there is a steering mechanism to guide your direction, and a braking mechanism to help control your rate of descent, she, out of control, slammed directly into a big post, the corner of a garden fence alongside the driveway.

Unhurt, she hid the bike in the nearby barn, saying nothing to anyone, including me, unaware of any activity regarding my bike.

Including the fact the forks of the bike were now facing in an East-West direction, not the factory prescribed North-South direction.

Mary was watchful regarding money. You could always depend on her having some money.

One day, our class announced there was a bus taking kids to a skating party at a rink not far away.

I, just plain broke Charlie, seeing the opportunity to score points with a cute classmate, asking her to "go with me" to the skate. She readily accepted my invitation with a yes. The problem was that I didn't have the money for the bus fee, or the rink fee, and the hour to go was fast approaching.

My hope that either Father or Mother would give me the funds was quickly dashed, they being destitute.

Neither my brother nor senior sister could help, my sinking ship now in desperate straits.

There was a God! Mary learned of my dilemma and said: "Chas (as I was called then), I have enough for you to be able to save the day, and fulfill your foolish commitment." All's well that ends well, although no progress was made romantically.

Mary was very generous in many ways, returning home (original) fairly often, always bringing practical gifts for Mother and the house.

Combining with sisters Ann and Kay, a radio and television landed there, modern kitchen appliances, and an electric blanket for me, among many others.

Then, life turned for her. A wonderful husband became a reality, and then, life's most precious and welcome of all, children: Sue, Patty and Jim. All great additions then, and through the years, ongoing.

- Epilogue -

Post graduation, that late spring day in June of 1949, a decision was made: Pittsburgh, here I come, ready or not.

She went, she conquered, she lived a long and happy life, joining the Angels at 92.

May she Rest In Peace.

Safe Passage

In concluding this Life dissertation, I'd like to borrow a portion of a beautiful Gospel Song that says: Through many dangers, toils and snares I have already come, and at this late date I am meandering back nearly nine decades mentally revisiting those many challenges in my quest for respectable prosperity.

I harbor a feeling of absolute and utmost gratitude for the unseen power that both guided and protected me, along with those who accompanied me in that perilous, at times, journey involving our Mining, Quarrying, Construction, and various Business Services.

In the three-quarters of a Century that I was a part of, along with those individuals with varying time and presence durations, all collectively numbering up to a hundred people in multiple job categories, some classified as hazardous.

Thankfully, we had no lost time accidents of any type.

Of particular note was our Mining group of typically eight to ten people who mined coal and stone over a forty-year span.

Mere words cannot possibly, properly convey the true appreciation for the constant, unfailing life preservation actions of our ever-present Heaven-sent Guardian Angels in so many instances.

Summing up, humbly, and without fanfare, may I simply say - -

Thank You very much, Dear God.

Stay Home Wis Us

It was sometime in the early 1960's - I was working full time as a laborer in the Seanor Coal Company's coal mine, was very busy in the masonry and various home repair services to the public in my so-called "spare time", and was helping to raise and entertain four children ages one through five, so life was chaotic, to say the least.

Dolly was employed full time as a Registered Nurse at the Allegheny Valley Hospital, while our mothers took care of the kids.

I had taken up golf, playing with my good friend Leo, which provided a much-needed break from the hectic pace I was operating in, which Dolly was in complete agreement with, even though her life was equally, or more, demanding.

It was a fine summer Sunday morning, and I was packing my clubs and shoes into the trunk of my car, waiting for my friend Leo to join me, when Cindy came out of the house, obviously dressed and ready, hoping to have someone, me, to play with her in the sand box.

Watching what I was doing, she asked me what I was going to do, and I replied that I was going golfing with my friend.

I cannot recall if ever in my life I have experienced a more heart-wrenching response anywhere – that was in her reaction – one that still tears at my heart when it resurfaces.

Fighting back the tears, she dropped the sand bucket and toy shovel she was carrying, slowly turned away from me and started back toward the house, and wistfully uttered, "why don't you stay home wis us?"

Having been committed to the golfing, I had to follow through, but it was far less than an enjoyable outing.

That was eighty years ago, but I still clearly see that scene as if it had occurred yesterday, whenever it revisits me.

Even though I believe I have made up for it through the years, it haunts me still, the pain is always waiting in there somewhere, but thankfully, has dimmed considerably with the passage of all these years.

Epilogue

The last roundup has been made; the curtains drawn.

The characters through all these years all real, none imagined, have either vanished into the boundless storehouses of consciousness, or continue in their assigned roles, in fulfilling their promised obligations or continue into their life stories, yet to be written.

In recognizing we, each, are in fact, a part of God, Life itself is God, should we not be grateful for our allotted time space here, even looking forward to whatever Is next on our agenda?

I, believing there is much, much more yet to be a part of, hereby sign off, Unable to truly express with mere words my most profound appreciation of all those who have, for whatever reason, either traveled with me in this marvelous journey, or have granted to me, an unknown, the absolute honor of experiencing with me so many of my life experiences in your reading of them.

Thank you, may God bless and keep you in His closest circle.

—Charlie, Just plain Charlie.

WA